Data Science
Unlocking Insights for
Transforming Data into Knowledge

Data Science: Unlocking Insights for Transforming Data into Knowledge

By Theophilus Edet

Theophilus Edet

 theoedet@yahoo.com

 facebook.com/theoedet

 twitter.com/TheophilusEdet

 Instagram.com/edettheophilus

Table of Contents

Preface

The Power of Data in the Modern Era

In today's world, data drives decisions, shapes innovations, and influences nearly every facet of life. From personalized healthcare to financial forecasting and global logistics, data science has become the linchpin of transformation. This book, *Data Science: Unlocking Insights for Transforming Data into Knowledge*, serves as a comprehensive guide to mastering this essential discipline. Its goal is to equip readers with the tools and understanding needed to convert raw data into actionable insights that drive meaningful change.

Bridging the Knowledge Gap

Despite the ubiquity of data and the rapid development of tools for analysis, there remains a critical gap in understanding how to extract, process, and communicate insights effectively. This book seeks to bridge that gap by providing a balanced blend of theoretical foundations and practical applications. Whether you are a student entering the field, a professional looking to expand your skillset, or an enthusiast eager to explore data science, this book offers a structured approach to learning and mastering the craft.

Data Science as Storytelling

At its essence, data science is the art of storytelling. Every dataset holds a unique narrative, waiting to be uncovered and told. These stories have the power to inform decisions, inspire innovation, and reveal truths that may otherwise remain hidden. This book emphasizes not just the technical processes but also the critical thinking and creativity required to uncover these narratives. Readers will learn how to craft compelling data-driven stories that resonate with diverse audiences.

Practical and Hands-On Learning

A standout feature of this book is its emphasis on practical application. Each module is rich with real-world examples, case studies, and Python-based code snippets, allowing readers to see theories in action. From building predictive models to designing intuitive visualizations and constructing secure data systems. These practical tools enable readers to tackle complex challenges confidently and develop solutions that have real-world impact.

The Human Element of Data Science

Data science is not only about algorithms and analysis—it is also about communication and collaboration. A significant portion of this book is dedicated to teaching how to present findings effectively, design impactful visualizations, and engage with both technical and non-technical stakeholders. These soft skills are vital for bridging the gap between raw data and actionable insights, ensuring that analyses lead to informed decisions and meaningful outcomes.

Preparing for the Future of Data Science

As the field of data science evolves, it brings both opportunities and challenges. Emerging technology, ethical consideration, and the growing demand for scalable solutions require data scientists to remain adaptable and forward-thinking. This book prepares readers to thrive in this dynamic environment by fostering a mindset of continuous learning and innovation. It highlights best practices and principles that will remain relevant as the field progresses.

A Journey of Empowerment

Data Science: Unlocking Insights for Transforming Data into Knowledge is more than a textbook; it is a guide for anyone seeking to harness the transformative power of data. By the end of this book, readers will have not only technical proficiency but also a deep appreciation for the role of data science in shaping the world.

Welcome to this exciting journey. Together, let's unlock the insights hidden within data and make a meaningful impact.

Theophilus Edet

Data Science: Unlocking Insights for Transforming Data into Knowledge

The Era of Data-Driven Transformation

We are living in the age of data—a time when information flows from every interaction, transaction, and observation. Whether it is consumer behavior, scientific experiments, or social trends, data holds the potential to uncover patterns and insights that drive progress. In this context, data science has emerged as a critical field, offering tools and methodologies to transform raw data into actionable knowledge. *Data Science: Unlocking Insights for Transforming Data into Knowledge* aims to guide readers on a journey through this fascinating discipline, providing the skills and understanding necessary to navigate the data-driven world effectively.

What Is Data Science?

At its core, data science is an interdisciplinary field that combines statistics, computer science, and domain expertise to analyze and interpret data. It spans activities such as data collection, cleaning, exploration, analysis, and visualization. However, data science is more than just technical proficiency—it is about solving problems, telling stories, and delivering value. This book emphasizes the holistic nature of data science, encouraging readers to approach data with curiosity, creativity, and a focus on meaningful outcomes.

Purpose and Scope of This Book

The purpose of this book is twofold: to demystify data science for beginners and to deepen the expertise of seasoned practitioners. Its scope covers the entire lifecycle of a data project, from raw data acquisition to the presentation of polished insights. Along the way, it explores foundational concepts, advanced techniques, and practical applications across industries. By providing real-world examples, Python-based code snippets, and case studies, the book ensures that readers can apply their knowledge to real challenges.

The Structure of the Book

This book is divided into comprehensive modules, each focusing on a key aspect of data science. The progression is designed to build a strong foundation while gradually introducing advanced concepts. Some of the major themes include:

1. **Data Analysis and Preparation**: Understanding the importance of clean, well-structured data and the tools to achieve it.

2. **Machine Learning**: Exploring algorithms that enable predictive modeling and automated decision-making.

3. **Visualization and Communication**: Learning to present findings effectively using graphs, dashboards, and storytelling.

4. **Big Data and Cloud Computing**: Addressing the challenges of scale and leveraging modern infrastructure.

5. **Ethics and Governance**: Ensuring responsible data usage and compliance with regulations.

Each module provides a mix of theory, practical examples, and exercises to solidify understanding and develop a hands-on skillset.

The Importance of Data Storytelling

One of the unique aspects of this book is its focus on data storytelling. Data alone cannot drive change; it is the insights derived from data, combined with a compelling narrative, that influence decisions. This book teaches readers to structure data stories that resonate with diverse audiences, bridging the gap between complex analyses and actionable insights.

Who Is This Book For?

This book is designed for a wide audience, including:

- **Students**: Those pursuing data science or related fields who seek a comprehensive introduction to the subject.

- **Professionals**: Data analysts, engineers, and scientists looking to expand their skills and stay current with industry trends.

- **Enthusiasts**: Individuals curious about data science and eager to learn its principles and applications.

- **Decision-Makers**: Business leaders and managers seeking to understand how data science can drive organizational success.

By catering to varying levels of expertise, this book serves as both a primer and a reference for ongoing learning.

The Role of Python in Data Science

Throughout this book, Python is the primary programming language used for examples and exercises. Known for its simplicity and versatility, Python has become a favorite among data scientists worldwide. The book includes practical Python scripts to demonstrate data manipulation, machine learning, visualization, and more. Each example is designed to be accessible, ensuring that readers can follow along regardless of their coding experience.

The Challenges and Opportunities of Data Science

While data science offers immense opportunities, it also comes with challenges. The rapid growth of data, the complexity of algorithms, and the ethical implications of data usage require practitioners to remain vigilant and adaptable. This book addresses these challenges by emphasizing best practices, fostering critical thinking, and promoting ethical decision-making.

Preparing for the Future

Data science is a dynamic field, continuously evolving with advancements in technology and methodologies. This book equips readers with a foundation that will remain relevant while encouraging a mindset of continuous learning. Whether it is mastering new tools, exploring emerging techniques, or addressing unforeseen challenges, readers will be prepared to grow alongside the field.

A Journey of Discovery

Data Science: Unlocking Insights for Transforming Data into Knowledge is more than a textbook; it is an invitation to embark on a journey of discovery. By the end of this book, readers will not only have a thorough understanding of data science but also the confidence to apply their knowledge in meaningful ways.

The world of data awaits. Let this book be your guide as you unlock the insights hidden within and transform data into knowledge that drives progress.

Part 1:

Foundations of Data Science

What is Data Science?

Data science is an interdisciplinary field that combines techniques from statistics, computer science, and domain expertise to extract meaningful insights from complex data. It evolved from the foundational principles of statistics and computing into a dynamic discipline with applications across various industries. The term "data science" often overlaps with fields like machine learning and artificial intelligence (AI), but it extends beyond predictive modeling to include data exploration, cleaning, and the communication of findings. In the modern world, data science plays a crucial role across industries, as organizations increasingly rely on data to make informed decisions, optimize processes, and innovate.

The Data Science Lifecycle

The data science lifecycle represents the full process of turning raw data into actionable insights. It begins with data collection and preparation, where raw data is gathered from various sources and cleaned for analysis. In the exploration and analysis phase, patterns and relationships within the data are identified, often using visualizations or statistical methods. The next step involves model building and validation, where predictive models are created and tested for accuracy. The final phase is deployment and maintenance, which involves integrating the model into real-world applications and monitoring its performance to ensure its reliability over time.

Data and Its Ecosystem

Data science deals with multiple types of data, including structured, unstructured, and semi-structured data, each requiring different handling techniques. Structured data fits neatly into rows and columns, while unstructured data, such as text and images, does not. Semi-structured data, like XML or JSON, falls somewhere in between. Data sources range from APIs and databases to files and streams, each with different formats and storage requirements. Big data, characterized by high-volume, high-velocity, and high-variety, has reshaped the landscape of data science by introducing new challenges and opportunities for real-time data analysis.

Tools and Technologies

Data science relies on various programming languages and tools. Python and R are popular for their rich ecosystems of libraries and frameworks, while SQL remains essential for querying structured databases. Tools for data visualization, like Tableau and Power BI, help transform raw data into insightful graphics. Machine learning libraries, such as TensorFlow, PyTorch, and Scikit-learn, provide the foundation for building and deploying predictive models. Cloud platforms and distributed systems, such as AWS, Azure, and Hadoop, support large-scale data processing, enabling data scientists to work with big data and complex models.

Module 5: Mathematics for Data Science

Mathematics forms the backbone of data science. Linear algebra is crucial for understanding data transformations, especially in machine learning and deep learning. Probability and statistics underpin data analysis, helping to quantify uncertainty, model distributions, and test hypotheses. Calculus is essential for optimization, enabling data scientists to adjust model parameters and improve predictions. Graph theory and networks play a role in applications such as recommendation systems and network analysis, where relationships between entities are key.

Ethics and Fairness in Data Science

Ethics is a central concern in data science, particularly regarding the responsible collection and use of data. Ensuring fairness in algorithms is crucial to prevent bias and discrimination. Transparency and interpretability are vital for making sure models can be understood and trusted. Data privacy regulations like GDPR and HIPAA govern how personal data is handled, and data scientists must adhere to these standards to protect individuals' privacy while leveraging data for analysis and decision-making.

Case Studies in Data Science Foundations

Real-world case studies demonstrate the practical application of data science concepts. Success stories highlight how companies have used data-driven decision-making to gain competitive advantages or solve complex problems. Additionally, analyzing failures can offer valuable lessons on common mistakes, such as inadequate data quality or overfitting models. As the field evolves, understanding the future trends in data science, such as automation and AI integration, will be essential for staying ahead in this rapidly changing domain.

Module 1:

What is Data Science?

Data science has emerged as a field that blends mathematical theories, technological advancements, and domain-specific expertise to unlock valuable insights from complex data sets. This module introduces the essence of data science, tracing its evolution, key concepts, interdisciplinary nature, and its growing significance in industries worldwide. By the end of this module, learners will gain a foundational understanding of data science and its role in transforming raw data into actionable knowledge.

The Evolution of Data Science: From Statistics to AI

Data science has evolved over several decades, beginning with the basic principles of statistics. Early on, it focused on collecting and analyzing numerical data to make predictions. With the rise of technology, the field expanded to include machine learning algorithms, artificial intelligence (AI), and big data analytics. This shift enabled data scientists to process and analyze much larger datasets, using sophisticated methods to uncover patterns, trends, and insights that were previously unimaginable. Today, data science encompasses a variety of techniques, including deep learning and neural networks that are transforming industries and improving decision-making.

Key Concepts and Terminologies: Definitions and Jargon

To truly grasp data science, it's essential to familiarize oneself with its core terminology. Key concepts include data cleaning, which involves preparing raw data for analysis; machine learning, which enables systems to learn from data without explicit programming; and predictive modeling, used to forecast future outcomes. Other important terms include supervised learning, unsupervised learning, algorithms, features, and models. Understanding these concepts and their relationships provides a strong foundation for anyone entering the field. The language of data science can initially seem daunting, but mastering the jargon is critical for success in this ever-evolving discipline.

The Interdisciplinary Nature of Data Science: Intersection of Math, Tech, and Domain Expertise

One of the defining features of data science is its interdisciplinary nature. It combines mathematical theories, such as statistics and probability, with technological tools like programming languages and software frameworks. In addition, domain expertise is crucial for interpreting data in context and making informed decisions. A data scientist must be able to understand the nuances of a specific field, whether healthcare, finance, or marketing, and apply analytical techniques accordingly. This unique intersection allows data scientists to create models and solutions that are not only mathematically sound but also relevant to real-world problems.

Importance in the Modern World: Why Every Industry Needs Data Science

In today's data-driven world, data science is crucial across every sector. From healthcare to finance, retail to education, organizations are increasingly relying on data science to make informed decisions, improve processes, and gain a competitive edge. For example, companies use data science to optimize supply chains, predict customer behavior, and detect fraud. Healthcare providers utilize data science to improve patient care, analyze treatment efficacy, and predict disease outbreaks. As data becomes more abundant and complex, the demand for skilled data scientists continues to grow, making it an essential field for the modern economy.

The Evolution of Data Science: From Statistics to AI

Data science has evolved significantly over the last few decades, growing from traditional statistical analysis to the cutting-edge field it is today, encompassing artificial intelligence (AI) and machine learning (ML). Understanding this evolution is crucial to appreciating the full scope of data science and its impact across various industries.

From Statistics to Data Science

In its early days, data science was largely synonymous with statistics. Statisticians used mathematical methods to analyze data and infer patterns, relying on methods like regression analysis, hypothesis testing, and probability theory. The goal was to understand data and extract meaningful insights using a rigid, predefined set of rules.

However, as the volume of data exploded with the advent of digital technology, traditional statistical techniques were no longer sufficient to handle the scale, complexity, and diversity of data. This is where data science, as we know it today, began to emerge. Data science combines statistics with computer science, offering new tools and techniques to analyze vast amounts of data efficiently.

Incorporating Technology and Automation

With the rise of computers and more sophisticated software, data science expanded to include areas like data mining, machine learning, and artificial intelligence. These technologies made it possible to process larger datasets and uncover patterns in ways that were previously unimaginable. Algorithms and automation became critical, as they allowed for data analysis on a scale that human statisticians simply couldn't manage.

The Role of Machine Learning and AI

Machine learning and AI have been integral to the evolution of data science. Unlike traditional statistical models that required predefined rules, machine learning algorithms allow computers to learn from data and improve over time. AI and ML models can identify hidden patterns, classify data, and even make predictions without being explicitly programmed to do so.

For example, consider the following Python code to build a simple machine learning model using the popular scikit-learn library. The code shows a basic classification task using the Iris dataset:

```python
# Import necessary libraries
import pandas as pd
from sklearn.model_selection import train_test_split
from sklearn.ensemble import RandomForestClassifier
from sklearn.metrics import accuracy_score

# Load the Iris dataset
from sklearn.datasets import load_iris
data = load_iris()
df = pd.DataFrame(data.data, columns=data.feature_names)
df['target'] = data.target

# Split the data into training and test sets
X = df.drop('target', axis=1)
y = df['target']
X_train, X_test, y_train, y_test = train_test_split(X, y, test_size=0.3,
            random_state=42)

# Build and train the model
model = RandomForestClassifier(n_estimators=100, random_state=42)
model.fit(X_train, y_train)

# Make predictions and evaluate the model
y_pred = model.predict(X_test)
accuracy = accuracy_score(y_test, y_pred)

print(f'Accuracy of the model: {accuracy:.2f}')
```

In this code, the RandomForestClassifier algorithm is used to classify flowers into different species based on their measurements. This illustrates the power of machine learning in data science—using data to train a model and make predictions automatically, without needing explicit rules for classification.

Data Science Today

Today, data science incorporates vast domains including natural language processing (NLP), computer vision, and deep learning. These advanced techniques are revolutionizing industries such as healthcare, finance, retail, and transportation. Data scientists now use large-scale datasets and AI tools to solve complex, real-world problems, continuing the evolution from simple statistical methods to comprehensive, automated systems.

Key Concepts and Terminologies: Definitions and Jargon

Understanding key concepts and terminologies is foundational to grasping data science. The field's interdisciplinary nature involves terms from statistics, computer science, and domain expertise, making it essential to demystify its jargon for newcomers. This section provides clear definitions of crucial concepts that form the backbone of data science.

Data, Information, and Knowledge

Data is the raw, unprocessed input—facts, figures, or observations. For instance, a CSV file containing customer purchases is data. Information arises when data is processed, organized, or structured, providing context and meaning. Knowledge, the highest level, emerges from synthesizing information to draw actionable insights. A simple Python example demonstrates converting raw data into information:

```python
# Example: Summarizing customer purchase data
import pandas as pd

# Sample data
data = {'Customer': ['Alice', 'Bob', 'Alice'],
        'Purchase': [50, 20, 30]}
df = pd.DataFrame(data)

# Calculate total purchase by customer
summary = df.groupby('Customer')['Purchase'].sum()
print(summary)
```

Here, raw data is processed into a summary showing total purchases per customer, transitioning from data to information.

Key Data Science Concepts

1. **Algorithms**: Step-by-step procedures for solving problems, like sorting or classifying data. Machine learning models are built using algorithms such as linear regression, decision trees, or neural networks.

2. **Big Data**: Extremely large datasets that cannot be processed using traditional methods. Tools like Hadoop and Spark are used to manage big data.

3. **Features and Labels**: Features are input variables used in a model, while labels are the output. For example, in predicting housing prices, features might include square footage and location, and the label would be the price.

4. **Training and Testing**: Data is split into training and testing sets for model evaluation. The training set helps the model learn, while the testing set assesses its accuracy.

Key Terminologies

1. **ETL (Extract, Transform, Load)**: The process of extracting data from sources, transforming it into a usable format, and loading it into storage or analysis tools.

2. **Data Cleaning**: The process of removing errors, inconsistencies, or missing values to prepare data for analysis.

3. **Data Pipeline**: A series of steps that automate data movement and transformation. Pipelines are essential for scaling data workflows.

4. **Hyperparameters**: Configurations external to a model that control its training process, such as the number of trees in a random forest.

Bridging Jargon to Understanding

Mastering jargon is crucial for communicating in data science. Words like "dimensionality reduction" (reducing variables) or "overfitting" (model too tailored to training data) may seem complex initially but become second nature with practice. For example, consider the term "overfitting," which occurs when a model performs well on training data but poorly on new data. Avoiding overfitting is a fundamental goal in model building.

Python example to detect overfitting:

```
# Example: Training and testing a model
from sklearn.linear_model import LinearRegression
from sklearn.metrics import mean_squared_error

# Generate sample data
X_train, y_train = [[1], [2], [3]], [1, 2, 3]
X_test, y_test = [[4], [5]], [4, 5]

# Train the model
model = LinearRegression().fit(X_train, y_train)

# Evaluate on training and test sets
train_error = mean_squared_error(y_train, model.predict(X_train))
test_error = mean_squared_error(y_test, model.predict(X_test))

print(f"Train Error: {train_error}, Test Error: {test_error}")
```

In this example, discrepancies between training and test errors can indicate overfitting.

By understanding these foundational concepts and terminologies, learners can navigate data science more effectively, bridging theory to practical applications.

The Interdisciplinary Nature of Data Science: Intersection of Math, Tech, and Domain Expertise

Data science thrives at the intersection of three core disciplines: mathematics, technology, and domain expertise. Each discipline contributes unique tools and methods essential for deriving meaningful insights from data. This section explores how these fields integrate to create a robust framework for solving complex problems in diverse industries.

Mathematics: The Analytical Foundation

Mathematics underpins the analytical processes in data science, particularly through statistics and linear algebra. Statistics enables data scientists to understand patterns, distributions, and relationships within datasets. Techniques such as hypothesis testing, regression analysis, and probability modeling allow for making informed predictions. Linear algebra is equally vital, forming the basis of machine learning algorithms. For example, matrix operations power recommendation systems or deep learning.
In Python, basic statistical operations can be performed as follows:

```
# Example: Calculating basic statistics
import numpy as np

data = [2, 4, 6, 8, 10]
mean = np.mean(data)
std_dev = np.std(data)
print(f"Mean: {mean}, Standard Deviation: {std_dev}")
```

Here, mathematics transforms raw data into actionable metrics, forming a critical pillar of data science.

Technology: The Computational Enabler

Technology enables the practical implementation of mathematical models on vast datasets. It involves programming languages like Python or R, frameworks such as TensorFlow and Scikit-learn, and infrastructure for data storage and processing. Tools like Hadoop and Spark handle big data, while cloud platforms like AWS or Google Cloud offer scalable computing power.
A simple Python example demonstrates using technology for a basic machine learning task:

```
# Example: Simple linear regression
from sklearn.linear_model import LinearRegression

X, y = [[1], [2], [3]], [2, 4, 6]
model = LinearRegression().fit(X, y)
prediction = model.predict([[4]])
print(f"Prediction for input 4: {prediction[0]}")
```

Here, technology bridges mathematical models with real-world data, ensuring scalability and efficiency.

Domain Expertise: Contextualizing Data

Domain expertise contextualizes raw data, ensuring insights are relevant and actionable. For example, in healthcare, understanding medical terminology and patient care workflows enables data scientists to develop better diagnostic tools. In finance,

21

domain knowledge helps in creating fraud detection systems or investment strategies. Without domain expertise, data science risks generating insights that lack practical significance or misinterpret key patterns.

Collaboration between data scientists and domain experts is crucial. The latter ensures models are aligned with industry-specific challenges, while the former brings analytical rigor.

The Synergy of Disciplines

Data science succeeds when mathematics, technology, and domain expertise work in harmony. Consider predictive maintenance in manufacturing: mathematical algorithms identify patterns in sensor data, technology enables real-time monitoring, and domain knowledge ensures insights are applied to reduce downtime. This synergy allows data science to tackle multifaceted problems, making it indispensable across industries.

In essence, the interdisciplinary nature of data science ensures that insights are accurate, scalable, and actionable, driving innovation and value creation.

Importance in the Modern World: Why Every industry Needs Data Science

Data science has emerged as a cornerstone of decision-making and innovation in the modern world. Its ability to transform raw data into actionable insights has made it indispensable across industries, from healthcare to retail, finance to education. This section explores why data science is crucial for businesses, governments, and society as a whole.

Driving Innovation and Competitive Advantage

In today's data-driven economy, organizations leverage data science to innovate and gain a competitive edge. Companies like Amazon and Netflix use predictive analytics to enhance customer experiences through personalized recommendations. In the automotive industry, data science drives the development of autonomous vehicles by analyzing sensor data in real-time. Businesses that integrate data science into their strategies outperform competitors by predicting trends, optimizing operations, and enhancing product development.

For example, using data science, a retailer can predict customer behavior:

```
# Predicting sales using linear regression
from sklearn.linear_model import LinearRegression

# Example data: number of ads and corresponding sales
ads = [[1], [2], [3], [4], [5]]  # Number of ads
sales = [100, 200, 300, 400, 500]  # Sales in dollars

model = LinearRegression().fit(ads, sales)
```

```
prediction = model.predict([[6]])  # Predict sales for 6 ads
print(f"Predicted sales for 6 ads: ${prediction[0]:.2f}")
```

Here, data science ensures efficient resource allocation, improving decision-making and boosting profits.

Enabling Data-Driven Decision-Making

Data science empowers decision-makers with evidence-based insights, minimizing reliance on intuition. Governments use data analytics to address public health challenges, allocate resources, and predict economic trends. Similarly, businesses employ analytics to identify market opportunities, optimize supply chains, and monitor performance metrics. Tools like dashboards and visualization platforms facilitate real-time monitoring, enabling leaders to respond swiftly to changing circumstances.

For instance, in finance, real-time fraud detection algorithms identify suspicious transactions, protecting institutions and customers. Data-driven decision-making fosters transparency and accountability, essential for long-term success.

Transforming Industries and Society

From revolutionizing patient care in healthcare to enhancing sustainability in agriculture, data science is transforming industries and benefiting society. In healthcare, machine learning models predict disease outbreaks, optimize treatment plans, and analyze genomic data for personalized medicine. In agriculture, predictive analytics improve crop yields by analyzing weather patterns, soil conditions, and irrigation needs.

A Python example illustrating the application of data science in healthcare:

```
# Predicting patient risk using logistic regression
from sklearn.linear_model import LogisticRegression

# Example data: patient features (e.g., age, BMI) and risk (1: high, 0: low)
X = [[25, 22], [45, 30], [50, 28], [60, 35]]  # Age, BMI
y = [0, 1, 1, 1]  # Risk level

model = LogisticRegression().fit(X, y)
risk_prediction = model.predict([[40, 27]])  # Predict risk for a new
            patient
print(f"Predicted risk level: {risk_prediction[0]}")
```

Such applications demonstrate how data science addresses global challenges, improving quality of life and fostering sustainable development.

Preparing for the Future

As industries generate increasing amounts of data, the role of data science will only expand. Emerging technologies like artificial intelligence, Internet of Things (IoT), and quantum computing will amplify its impact. Data science equips organizations to navigate complexities, seize opportunities, and anticipate future disruptions. For individuals, mastering data science opens doors to high-demand careers in a rapidly evolving landscape.

By leveraging the power of data science, organizations and societies are better prepared to adapt and thrive in a data-rich world. Its transformative potential ensures it remains a driving force in shaping the future.

Module 2:

The Data Science Lifecycle

The data science lifecycle is a structured process that guides data scientists through each stage of transforming raw data into actionable insights. This module outlines the essential phases of the lifecycle, from data collection and preparation to deployment and maintenance. Understanding this process is key for any aspiring data scientist aiming to turn data into valuable predictions and decisions.

Data Collection and Preparation: Gathering Raw Data and Preprocessing It

The first step in the data science lifecycle is data collection. This phase involves gathering raw data from various sources such as databases, APIs, and sensors. Once collected, the data must be preprocessed to ensure its quality. This includes cleaning the data by handling missing values, removing duplicates, and standardizing formats. Preprocessing also involves transforming the data into a suitable format for analysis, such as scaling numerical values or encoding categorical variables. Proper data preparation is crucial, as the quality of the data directly impacts the success of the entire analysis.

Data Exploration and Analysis: Identifying Patterns and Generating Insights

Once the data is cleaned and ready, the next phase is data exploration and analysis. This involves using statistical techniques and visualization tools to uncover patterns, trends, and relationships within the data. Descriptive statistics, such as means, medians, and standard deviations, are calculated to summarize the data. Data scientists also visualize the data using charts and graphs to identify any hidden insights. Exploratory data analysis (EDA) helps inform decisions about which features to focus on, the types of models to apply, and the hypotheses to test. This phase is crucial for understanding the data before building predictive models.

Model Building and Validation: Creating and Evaluating Predictive Models

The model building phase focuses on creating predictive models using machine learning algorithms. Data scientists select the most appropriate model based on the type of data and the problem at hand. For example, classification algorithms may be used for categorical outcomes, while regression models are suited for continuous predictions. Once the model is built, it must be validated using techniques such as cross-validation and performance metrics like accuracy, precision, and recall. This stage is essential to ensure that the model generalizes well to new, unseen data and performs reliably in real-world scenarios.

Deployment and Maintenance: Operationalizing Models and Ensuring Reliability

After validation, the final stage is model deployment and maintenance. Deployment involves integrating the model into the production environment, where it can make real-time predictions or inform business decisions. Data scientists must ensure that the model is scalable, efficient, and able to handle new data inputs. Ongoing maintenance is necessary to monitor the model's performance and make updates as needed. As new data becomes available, the model may need retraining to adapt to changes in patterns or behaviors. Ensuring the reliability and accuracy of deployed models is crucial for their long-term success and utility.

Data Collection and Preparation: Gathering Raw Data and Preprocessing It

The foundation of any data science project lies in the process of data collection and preparation. This stage ensures the availability of high-quality, relevant data for analysis and modeling. It involves gathering raw data from diverse sources, cleaning it to remove inconsistencies, and transforming it into a structured format suitable for further analysis. Proper data preparation not only enhances model accuracy but also prevents pitfalls caused by errors in the data pipeline.

Gathering Raw Data

Data collection involves acquiring data from multiple sources, such as APIs, databases, sensors, or web scraping. The choice of data source depends on the problem being solved and the availability of relevant datasets. For example, e-commerce platforms might collect data from transaction records, user interactions, and external market trends.

Here's a simple Python script demonstrating data collection from an API:

```python
import requests
import pandas as pd

# Collecting weather data from an API
api_url = "https://api.open-meteo.com/v1/forecast"
params = {"latitude": 40.7128, "longitude": -74.0060, "hourly":
        "temperature_2m"}
response = requests.get(api_url, params=params)

if response.status_code == 200:
    data = response.json()
    df = pd.DataFrame(data["hourly"]["temperature_2m"],
        columns=["Temperature"])
    print(df.head())
else:
    print("Failed to fetch data")
```

This script retrieves weather data, which can be used in predictive modeling for agricultural or retail applications.

Cleaning Raw Data

Raw data often contains missing values, duplicates, or inconsistencies that must be addressed to ensure reliability. Data cleaning processes include handling missing data (e.g., through imputation or deletion), correcting data entry errors, and removing irrelevant or duplicate records.

Python offers tools like pandas for data cleaning. For example:

```
import pandas as pd

# Sample dataset with missing values
data = {"Age": [25, None, 30, 22], "Salary": [50000, 60000, None, 40000]}
df = pd.DataFrame(data)

# Handling missing values
df["Age"].fillna(df["Age"].mean(), inplace=True)
df["Salary"].fillna(df["Salary"].median(), inplace=True)
print(df)
```

This code replaces missing values with mean or median values, preparing the data for analysis.

Structuring and Transforming Data

After cleaning, the data must be transformed into a usable format. This step includes normalization, encoding categorical variables, and feature extraction. These processes enhance the consistency and scalability of the data for machine learning algorithms.

For example, encoding categorical data can be performed using one-hot encoding:

```
from sklearn.preprocessing import OneHotEncoder
import pandas as pd

# Sample categorical data
data = {"City": ["New York", "London", "Paris"]}
df = pd.DataFrame(data)

# Encoding categorical data
encoder = OneHotEncoder()
encoded_data = encoder.fit_transform(df[["City"]]).toarray()
print(encoded_data)
```

This transforms the "City" column into a numerical format suitable for analysis.

Importance of Data Preparation

Data preparation ensures the integrity and reliability of subsequent analyses and models. Without proper preprocessing, even the most advanced algorithms may yield inaccurate or biased results. By investing time in this stage, data scientists lay the groundwork for meaningful insights and robust predictions, highlighting the critical role of data preparation in the lifecycle.

Data Exploration and Analysis: Identifying Patterns and Generating Insights

Once data is collected and prepared, the next step in the data science lifecycle is exploration and analysis. This phase involves delving into the dataset to understand its structure, identify trends, and uncover hidden patterns. Through visualization and statistical methods, data exploration provides critical insights that guide decision-making and model development.

Understanding Data Characteristics

Before diving into advanced analytics, it's essential to understand the dataset's basic properties. Key statistics, such as means, medians, standard deviations, and distributions, reveal trends and potential outliers. Descriptive statistics form the foundation for deeper exploration and help in assessing data quality.

For example, using Python's pandas library, basic data exploration can be done as follows:

```
import pandas as pd

# Sample dataset
data = {"Age": [25, 30, 35, 40, 29], "Salary": [50000, 60000, 70000, 80000,
        55000]}
df = pd.DataFrame(data)

# Summary statistics
print(df.describe())
```

This script provides insights into central tendencies, variability, and range, helping data scientists prepare for more sophisticated analysis.

Visualizing Data for Patterns

Data visualization is a powerful tool for identifying patterns, trends, and anomalies in a dataset. Charts like histograms, scatterplots, and heatmaps highlight relationships and correlations that may not be evident from raw data alone.

Here's an example of a scatterplot to visualize the relationship between age and salary:

```
import matplotlib.pyplot as plt

# Scatterplot
plt.scatter(df["Age"], df["Salary"])
plt.title("Age vs. Salary")
plt.xlabel("Age")
plt.ylabel("Salary")
plt.show()
```

Such visualizations help uncover key patterns, such as whether age positively correlates with salary.

Using Statistical Methods for Insights

Statistical techniques like correlation analysis, hypothesis testing, and clustering help refine insights. For instance, Pearson correlation can measure the strength of the relationship between two variables.

Using Python's scipy library, correlation analysis can be performed:

```
from scipy.stats import pearsonr

# Correlation coefficient
correlation, p_value = pearsonr(df["Age"], df["Salary"])
print(f"Correlation: {correlation}, P-Value: {p_value}")
```

This identifies whether age and salary are statistically correlated, offering direction for further investigation.

Exploratory Data Analysis (EDA) for Decision-Making

Exploratory Data Analysis (EDA) combines statistical and visual methods to guide hypotheses and inform model selection. During EDA, patterns like seasonal trends or clusters may emerge, allowing data scientists to refine their questions or hypotheses.

For example, heatmaps can reveal relationships in multidimensional datasets:

```
import seaborn as sns

# Heatmap
sns.heatmap(df.corr(), annot=True, cmap="coolwarm")
plt.title("Correlation Heatmap")
plt.show()
```

EDA bridges raw data and actionable insights, ensuring models are built on a solid foundation of understanding.

The Value of Exploration

Data exploration and analysis are critical to understanding the narrative hidden in data. This phase not only identifies relationships and anomalies but also equips data scientists with a roadmap for model development. Without this step, key insights may remain undiscovered, limiting the potential of the data.

Model Building and Validation: Creating and Evaluating Predictive Models

The core of data science lies in transforming insights into actionable predictions, achieved through model building and validation. This stage involves selecting algorithms, training models, and assessing their performance to ensure they generalize well to unseen data. A systematic approach ensures reliable predictions that drive decision-making.

Selecting the Right Algorithm

Choosing the appropriate algorithm is crucial for effective model building. The choice depends on the problem type—classification, regression, or clustering. For instance, decision trees are excellent for classification tasks, while linear regression is ideal for predicting continuous variables.

In Python, the scikit-learn library offers robust tools for implementing various algorithms:

```
from sklearn.linear_model import LinearRegression

# Sample dataset
X = [[25], [30], [35], [40], [29]]  # Age
y = [50000, 60000, 70000, 80000, 55000]  # Salary

# Train the model
model = LinearRegression()
model.fit(X, y)
print(f"Intercept: {model.intercept_}, Coefficient: {model.coef_}")
```

This code trains a linear regression model to predict salary based on age.

Training Models with Optimal Parameters

Model training involves feeding the algorithm with data to adjust its parameters. Techniques like cross-validation ensure the model is not overfitted to the training data. Overfitting occurs when the model performs well on training data but poorly on unseen data.

Using Python's scikit-learn for cross-validation:

```
from sklearn.model_selection import cross_val_score

# Cross-validation
scores = cross_val_score(model, X, y, cv=3)
print(f"Cross-Validation Scores: {scores}")
```

This ensures the model's robustness by testing it on different subsets of data.

Evaluating Model Performance

Model evaluation metrics provide insights into a model's accuracy, precision, and generalizability. Common metrics include mean squared error (MSE) for regression tasks and accuracy or F1-score for classification tasks.

Here's an example of evaluating a regression model:

```
from sklearn.metrics import mean_squared_error

# Predictions
predictions = model.predict(X)
```

```
# Mean Squared Error
mse = mean_squared_error(y, predictions)
print(f"Mean Squared Error: {mse}")
```

This evaluates how closely the model's predictions align with actual data, guiding further refinements.

Iterative Model Tuning

Building predictive models is an iterative process. Techniques like hyperparameter tuning and feature engineering refine model performance. Tools such as grid search automate the selection of optimal parameters:

```
from sklearn.model_selection import GridSearchCV

# Grid search for parameter tuning
parameters = {'fit_intercept': [True, False]}
grid_search = GridSearchCV(LinearRegression(), parameters, cv=3)
grid_search.fit(X, y)
print(f"Best Parameters: {grid_search.best_params_}")
```

This ensures the model achieves the best performance within the constraints of the data.

Bridging Insight and Prediction

Model building and validation form the backbone of data science by converting raw data into actionable predictions. By rigorously selecting algorithms, validating performance, and iterating improvements, data scientists create models that deliver reliable, impactful results. A strong foundation here is essential for success in deployment and maintenance.

Deployment and Maintenance: Operationalizing Models and Ensuring Reliability

Deploying a machine learning model into a real-world environment marks the transition from theoretical analysis to practical application. This stage involves integrating models into production systems, ensuring they operate reliably over time, and adapting to changing conditions. Effective deployment and maintenance are crucial for sustained success and value delivery.

Operationalizing Models in Production

Model deployment translates a trained algorithm into a system that delivers real-time or batch predictions. This requires integrating the model into existing workflows and making it accessible to end-users via APIs or applications. Tools like Flask or FastAPI in Python simplify model deployment.

```
from flask import Flask, request, jsonify
```

```
import pickle

# Load trained model
model = pickle.load(open('model.pkl', 'rb'))

# Set up Flask app
app = Flask(__name__)

@app.route('/predict', methods=['POST'])
def predict():
    data = request.get_json()
    prediction = model.predict([data['features']])
    return jsonify({'prediction': prediction.tolist()})

if __name__ == '__main__':
    app.run()
```

This code demonstrates how to deploy a model using Flask, enabling real-time predictions via an HTTP endpoint.

Monitoring Model Performance

Once deployed, models must be monitored to ensure consistent performance. Data drift, where the input data distribution changes over time, can degrade model accuracy. Tools like Evidently AI or built-in logging frameworks help track metrics such as prediction accuracy, latency, and user interactions.

```
import logging

# Logging predictions
logging.basicConfig(filename='model.log', level=logging.INFO)
logging.info('Model deployed successfully')
```

Regular monitoring identifies issues early, minimizing the risk of degraded performance.

Ensuring Scalability and Reliability

Scalability ensures the model can handle increasing workloads efficiently, while reliability guarantees consistent service availability. Techniques such as containerization with Docker and orchestration with Kubernetes provide robust solutions for scaling model deployments.

```
# Dockerfile example
FROM python:3.9
COPY model.pkl /app/
WORKDIR /app
RUN pip install flask
CMD ["python", "app.py"]
```

This Dockerfile encapsulates the model and its dependencies, enabling easy scaling and deployment across diverse environments.

Maintaining and Updating Models

Models must adapt to evolving conditions, requiring periodic retraining and updates. Automated pipelines using tools like MLflow or Airflow streamline this process. Retraining involves integrating new data, ensuring the model remains accurate and relevant.

```
# Example of automated retraining
from sklearn.model_selection import train_test_split
from sklearn.linear_model import LinearRegression

# New data for retraining
X_train, X_test, y_train, y_test = train_test_split(X_new, y_new,
        test_size=0.2)
model.fit(X_train, y_train)
pickle.dump(model, open('updated_model.pkl', 'wb'))
```

Retraining ensures the deployed model continues to deliver value as data evolves.

Sustaining Value Through Reliability

Deployment and maintenance are vital stages in the data science lifecycle. They ensure that the model transitions smoothly from development to real-world applications and continues to deliver accurate, reliable results. A well-deployed and maintained model becomes a long-term asset, driving decision-making and innovation.

Module 3:

Data and Its Ecosystem

Data science involves working with a variety of data types and sources. Understanding the types of data, data storage solutions, and the role of big data is essential for processing and analyzing information effectively. This module explores the ecosystem of data, focusing on its types, sources, storage, and the impact of big data.

Types of Data: Structured, Unstructured, and Semi-Structured Data

Data can be classified into three main types: structured, unstructured, and semi-structured. Structured data is highly organized, often found in relational databases, and follows a fixed schema. Unstructured data, such as text, images, and videos, lacks a predefined format, making it challenging to process. Semi-structured data, like JSON and XML files, contains some organization but is more flexible than structured data. Each data type requires different techniques for processing and analysis, and understanding these differences is crucial for selecting the right tools and methods in data science projects.

Data Sources and Formats: APIs, Databases, Files, and Streams

Data can come from various sources, including APIs, databases, files, and data streams. APIs (Application Programming Interfaces) provide real-time data from external systems, allowing for integration with other platforms. Databases, both relational and NoSQL, store large amounts of structured and unstructured data. Files, such as CSV, JSON, and XML, are common ways to share and store data. Data streams offer continuous data, often used in real-time analytics, from sources like social media or IoT devices. Understanding these formats and sources is crucial for data scientists to gather and work with data efficiently.

Data Storage Solutions: Relational Databases, NoSQL, and Cloud Storage

Choosing the right storage solution is vital for managing data. Relational databases are best suited for structured data, where data is stored in tables with predefined relationships. NoSQL databases, like MongoDB and Cassandra, offer flexible storage options for unstructured and semi-structured data. These databases can scale horizontally, handling large volumes of data across multiple servers. Cloud storage, such as Amazon S3 and Google Cloud Storage, provides scalable and cost-effective storage solutions. Cloud platforms also offer various data processing tools, making them essential for modern data science workflows, especially when dealing with big data.

The Role of Big Data: The Shift Towards High-Volume, High-Velocity, and High-Variety Data

Big data refers to datasets that are too large, fast, or complex for traditional data processing tools to handle. It is often characterized by the three V's: volume, velocity, and variety. Volume refers to the massive amount of data being generated every day. Velocity involves the speed at which this data is created, processed, and analyzed. Variety highlights the different types and sources of data, including structured, unstructured, and semi-structured data. Big data technologies, such as Hadoop and Spark, are designed to handle these challenges, enabling data scientists to extract insights from vast and diverse datasets.

Types of Data: Structured, Unstructured, and Semi-Structured Data

Data forms the backbone of data science, enabling insights and decision-making. Understanding its types—structured, unstructured, and semi-structured—is essential for managing and processing it effectively. Each type offers unique characteristics and challenges, influencing how data is stored, processed, and analyzed in diverse applications.

Structured Data: Organized and Relational

Structured data is neatly organized into rows and columns, often stored in relational databases. It adheres to a predefined schema, making it easy to query using SQL. Examples include sales records, customer information, and financial transactions.

```
import pandas as pd

# Example: Reading structured data
data = pd.read_csv('sales_data.csv')
print(data.head())
```

This Python snippet loads structured data from a CSV file into a Pandas DataFrame for analysis. Structured data's well-defined format enables efficient storage, retrieval, and manipulation, making it ideal for business intelligence and analytics.

Unstructured Data: Free-Form and Versatile

Unstructured data lacks a predefined schema, encompassing formats such as text, images, videos, and social media posts. It represents the majority of data generated today but requires specialized tools for processing, such as natural language processing (NLP) or image recognition algorithms.

```
# Example: Reading unstructured text data
with open('customer_reviews.txt', 'r') as file:
    reviews = file.readlines()
print(reviews[:5])
```

In this example, textual customer reviews are loaded for further processing. While unstructured data offers flexibility and richness, its lack of structure presents challenges in storage and analysis.

Semi-Structured Data: A Flexible Middle Ground

Semi-structured data combines elements of both structured and unstructured data, often stored in formats like JSON, XML, or YAML. Although it doesn't adhere to a rigid schema, it includes tags or markers to organize data hierarchically. Examples include API responses, log files, and sensor data.

```
import json

# Example: Parsing semi-structured data
with open('api_response.json', 'r') as file:
    api_data = json.load(file)
print(api_data['customer']['name'])
```

The Python code above demonstrates reading and parsing a JSON file. Semi-structured data's flexibility enables seamless integration between structured systems and unstructured data sources.

Significance of Understanding Data Types

Recognizing the distinctions between structured, unstructured, and semi-structured data is vital for designing appropriate storage and processing solutions. Structured data supports fast querying and analytics, unstructured data unlocks insights from diverse sources, and semi-structured data bridges these extremes with its adaptability. Together, these types form the foundation of the modern data ecosystem.

Understanding data types prepares data scientists to tackle challenges across various industries. With the growing volume and complexity of data, mastering the nuances of structured, unstructured, and semi-structured data ensures effective analysis, helping organizations derive meaningful insights.

Data Sources and Formats: APIs, Databases, Files, and Streams

Data scientists interact with a diverse array of data sources and formats, each suited for specific needs. APIs, databases, files, and streams are the main sources, offering different levels of accessibility and structure. Understanding these sources enables data scientists to efficiently acquire and manage data for analysis and modeling.

APIs: Facilitating Seamless Data Exchange

Application Programming Interfaces (APIs) enable the programmatic exchange of data between systems. They provide structured data responses in formats such as JSON or

XML, making APIs a popular choice for real-time data retrieval from web services, social media platforms, and public datasets.

```
import requests

# Example: Fetching data from an API
response = requests.get("https://api.example.com/data")
if response.status_code == 200:
    data = response.json()
    print(data)
```

This Python example demonstrates how to fetch and parse data from an API. APIs streamline integration and are vital for accessing up-to-date information. However, rate limits and authentication requirements often pose challenges.

Databases: Structured and Persistent Storage

Databases, both relational (SQL) and non-relational (NoSQL), are foundational data sources. Relational databases, like MySQL and PostgreSQL, store structured data in predefined schemas, while NoSQL databases, such as MongoDB and Cassandra, manage semi-structured or unstructured data.

```
import sqlite3

# Example: Querying a relational database
conn = sqlite3.connect('example.db')
cursor = conn.cursor()
cursor.execute("SELECT * FROM sales")
rows = cursor.fetchall()
print(rows)
conn.close()
```

Databases offer reliable, scalable, and secure data storage. SQL databases excel in transaction-based applications, while NoSQL systems are better suited for handling high-volume, unstructured data.

Files: Versatile and Widely Used

Files remain one of the simplest and most versatile data formats, encompassing CSV, Excel, JSON, XML, and text files. They are suitable for small-scale projects or when data sharing doesn't require complex systems.

```
import pandas as pd

# Example: Reading a CSV file
df = pd.read_csv("data.csv")
print(df.head())
```

This Python snippet demonstrates loading a CSV file into a DataFrame for analysis. File-based formats are easy to use and widely supported, though they lack the scalability and performance of databases for large datasets.

Streams: Real-Time Data in Motion

Data streams represent real-time, continuous flows of information from sources like IoT devices, social media feeds, and financial transactions. Tools like Apache Kafka and Apache Flink handle streaming data efficiently, enabling near-instantaneous processing.

```
# Example: Simulating a simple data stream
import time

stream_data = ["event1", "event2", "event3"]
for event in stream_data:
    print(f"Processing {event}")
    time.sleep(1)
```

Streaming data enables quick responses to events, crucial for applications like fraud detection and live analytics. However, it requires specialized tools and architectures to manage its velocity and volume.

By leveraging APIs, databases, files, and streams, data scientists can access and integrate a broad range of data sources. Mastering these diverse formats ensures effective data collection, enabling insights across various industries and applications.

Data Storage Solutions: Relational Databases, NoSQL, and Cloud Storage

Data storage solutions form the backbone of any data-driven initiative, offering platforms to store, retrieve, and manage data effectively. This section delves into the three primary storage paradigms: relational databases, NoSQL databases, and cloud storage. Each approach has distinct advantages and use cases that align with specific data science needs.

Relational Databases: Organized and Structured Storage

Relational databases (RDBMS), such as MySQL, PostgreSQL, and Oracle, use tables with predefined schemas to organize structured data. SQL serves as the standard language for querying and manipulating these databases, making RDBMS ideal for applications requiring consistent and reliable transactions.

```
import sqlite3

# Example: Creating and querying a relational database
conn = sqlite3.connect('example.db')
cursor = conn.cursor()
cursor.execute('''CREATE TABLE IF NOT EXISTS users (id INTEGER, name
        TEXT)''')
cursor.execute('''INSERT INTO users (id, name) VALUES (1, 'Alice')''')
conn.commit()

# Query the data
cursor.execute("SELECT * FROM users")
rows = cursor.fetchall()
print(rows)
conn.close()
```

38

RDBMS excels in maintaining data integrity and handling relationships between data entities. However, they may struggle with scalability and flexibility when dealing with unstructured or semi-structured data.

NoSQL Databases: Flexible and Scalable

NoSQL databases, such as MongoDB, Cassandra, and DynamoDB, cater to unstructured or semi-structured data. These databases adopt diverse storage models, including key-value pairs, documents, and wide-column stores, making them suitable for big data and real-time applications.

```python
from pymongo import MongoClient

# Example: Working with a NoSQL database (MongoDB)
client = MongoClient('mongodb://localhost:27017/')
db = client['example_db']
collection = db['users']
collection.insert_one({'id': 1, 'name': 'Alice'})

# Query the data
user = collection.find_one({'id': 1})
print(user)
```

NoSQL systems scale horizontally, accommodating massive data volumes across distributed infrastructures. Their flexibility allows storage without rigid schemas, enabling rapid development for dynamic data needs.

Cloud Storage: Scalability and Accessibility

Cloud storage solutions like Amazon S3, Google Cloud Storage, and Microsoft Azure Blob Storage offer unparalleled scalability and accessibility. These platforms allow businesses to store and retrieve data from anywhere, with the added benefits of durability, redundancy, and security.

```python
import boto3

# Example: Uploading a file to AWS S3
s3 = boto3.client('s3')
s3.upload_file('local_file.txt', 'my_bucket', 'uploaded_file.txt')
print("File uploaded successfully!")
```

Cloud storage is particularly advantageous for data science projects, offering pay-as-you-go pricing and support for advanced features like lifecycle management and integration with big data tools. Despite these benefits, concerns around data privacy and dependence on third-party services must be managed.

Choosing the Right Storage Solution

Selecting the best data storage solution depends on the nature of the data, project requirements, and scale. Relational databases shine in structured and transactional contexts, NoSQL systems handle scalability and flexibility for semi-structured data, and cloud storage provides a cost-effective, scalable infrastructure for diverse applications.

The Role of Big Data: The Shift towards High-Volume, High-Velocity, and High-Variety Data

Big data is a term used to describe data sets that are too large or complex for traditional data-processing tools to handle effectively. The rise of big data has transformed industries and data science, enabling organizations to extract insights from vast amounts of diverse data. In this section, we'll explore the three key characteristics of big data: volume, velocity, and variety.

Volume: Managing Massive Data Sets

The volume of data refers to the sheer amount of data being generated. Modern data systems must be able to manage and store petabytes or even exabytes of data across various platforms and infrastructures. This explosion of data comes from sensors, social media, transactional logs, and more.

Handling such vast volumes requires specialized storage systems and distributed computing frameworks like Hadoop and Spark. These tools break data into smaller chunks, process them in parallel across multiple machines, and combine the results. Big data solutions are designed for scalability to accommodate growing data needs.

```
# Example: Reading large files in chunks with pandas
import pandas as pd

# Read a large CSV file in chunks
chunk_size = 10000  # Adjust based on the system's memory
for chunk in pd.read_csv('large_file.csv', chunksize=chunk_size):
    # Process each chunk
    print(chunk.head())
```

Without the proper infrastructure, processing large data sets can be impractical or inefficient. However, big data technologies like Hadoop have made it feasible to store and analyze massive datasets efficiently.

Velocity: The Speed of Data Generation

Velocity refers to the speed at which data is generated and processed. In many modern applications, data is produced in real-time, making it necessary to process and analyze it quickly. This is especially important in applications like fraud detection, social media analytics, and live recommendation systems, where immediate insights are crucial.

To manage the velocity of data, stream processing tools like Apache Kafka, Apache Flink, and Spark Streaming are used. These tools allow data scientists to process data continuously as it arrives, ensuring timely analysis and action.

```
# Example: Real-time data processing using Kafka (basic setup)
```

```python
from kafka import KafkaConsumer

consumer = KafkaConsumer('real-time-topic',
        bootstrap_servers=['localhost:9092'])
for message in consumer:
    print(f"Received message: {message.value.decode()}")
```

Real-time data processing is an essential component of the big data ecosystem, enabling organizations to respond swiftly to changing conditions and make data-driven decisions in real-time.

Variety: Dealing with Different Data Formats

Variety refers to the diverse formats of data generated today. Big data can come in many forms, including structured, semi-structured, and unstructured data. Structured data is typically stored in tables, while semi-structured data includes XML or JSON files, and unstructured data includes text, images, and videos.

Big data systems must be capable of handling these various data types efficiently. NoSQL databases, for example, provide flexibility in storing semi-structured and unstructured data, while Hadoop's ecosystem can process large-scale, heterogeneous data.

The Impact of Big Data on Data Science

Big data has reshaped data science, offering new opportunities for discovery, personalization, and optimization. With the ability to process high volumes of fast-moving, diverse data, data scientists can gain deeper insights and make more informed decisions. The combination of big data technologies, such as Hadoop, Spark, and real-time analytics tools, empowers organizations to tackle complex challenges across industries.

Module 4:

Tools and Technologies

Data science relies heavily on a variety of tools and technologies to process, analyze, and visualize data. The right tools can streamline the workflow and enhance the insights derived from data. This module explores the programming languages, data visualization tools, machine learning libraries, and cloud platforms commonly used in data science projects.

Programming Languages for Data Science: Python, R, SQL, and Others

Programming languages are fundamental in data science. Python is widely used due to its simplicity and rich ecosystem of libraries like NumPy, Pandas, and Matplotlib. R is another popular choice, particularly for statistical analysis and data visualization. SQL remains essential for querying relational databases and managing structured data. Other languages like Java and Julia are also used, but Python and R dominate the field. Choosing the right language often depends on the nature of the data, the complexity of the analysis, and the specific requirements of the project.

Data Visualization Tools: Tableau, Power BI, and Open-Source Alternatives

Data visualization is crucial for presenting complex data insights in an accessible and engaging way. Tableau and Power BI are widely used commercial tools, known for their powerful features and user-friendly interfaces. These platforms allow users to create interactive dashboards and visualizations with minimal coding. Open-source alternatives, such as Matplotlib, Seaborn, and Plotly in Python, offer flexibility for customized visualizations. These tools help data scientists communicate their findings effectively, making it easier for decision-makers to understand and act upon the data.

Machine Learning Libraries and Frameworks: TensorFlow, PyTorch, Scikit-Learn

Machine learning libraries and frameworks are essential for building and deploying models. TensorFlow and PyTorch are two leading frameworks for deep learning, supporting advanced neural networks and large-scale model training. Scikit-learn, on the other hand, is a go-to library for traditional machine learning algorithms, such as classification, regression, and clustering. These libraries simplify the development of machine learning models, offering pre-built functions and tools for model evaluation, tuning, and deployment. The choice of library or framework depends on the complexity and type of machine learning task at hand.

Cloud Platforms and Distributed Systems: AWS, Azure, GCP, and Hadoop Ecosystems

Cloud platforms and distributed systems are integral for managing large-scale data science projects. AWS (Amazon Web Services), Azure, and Google Cloud Platform (GCP) offer comprehensive cloud solutions for data storage, processing, and machine learning. These platforms provide scalable resources that are essential for handling big data and complex computations. The Hadoop ecosystem, including tools like HDFS and Spark, is widely used for distributed data processing. Cloud platforms and distributed systems help data scientists scale their projects, manage large datasets efficiently, and deploy models in production environments.

Programming Languages for Data Science: Python, R, SQL, and Others

In data science, programming languages are essential tools for manipulating, analyzing, and visualizing data. The choice of programming language often depends on the task at hand, the complexity of the problem, and the ecosystem surrounding the language. In this section, we will explore the most commonly used programming languages for data science: Python, R, SQL, and others.

Python: The Versatile Powerhouse

Python is the most widely used language in data science due to its simplicity, versatility, and extensive ecosystem. It supports various data manipulation libraries, machine learning frameworks, and data visualization tools. Libraries such as Pandas, NumPy, and Matplotlib make Python an excellent choice for data preprocessing, analysis, and visualization.

Python's ease of learning and vast community support makes it ideal for both beginners and professionals. It also integrates well with other languages and platforms, including Hadoop, Spark, and cloud services, making it scalable for large datasets. Python's flexibility also extends to machine learning with libraries like Scikit-learn and deep learning frameworks like TensorFlow and PyTorch.

```python
# Example: Data manipulation and analysis with pandas
import pandas as pd

# Load a dataset
data = pd.read_csv('dataset.csv')

# Basic data exploration
print(data.head())
print(data.describe())
```

Python's versatility makes it suitable for a wide range of tasks, from basic data cleaning to complex machine learning algorithms, making it the go-to choice for many data scientists.

R: A Statistical Powerhouse

R is another popular language for data science, particularly in the statistical analysis and research domains. It was designed with statistics in mind and excels at performing statistical tests, generating reports, and creating advanced visualizations. R has a rich ecosystem of packages tailored for data manipulation, statistical modeling, and visualization, such as ggplot2, dplyr, and tidyr.

R is also commonly used in academic research and data analysis environments where statistical rigor is crucial. It is well-suited for exploratory data analysis (EDA) and handling complex datasets that require advanced statistical techniques.

```
# Example: Basic data analysis in R
data <- read.csv("dataset.csv")

# Summarize the dataset
summary(data)

# Plot data using ggplot2
library(ggplot2)
ggplot(data, aes(x=variable)) + geom_histogram()
```

Despite being specialized for statistical analysis, R can be integrated with other programming languages like Python and SQL, allowing for a more flexible approach to data science tasks.

SQL: Querying Relational Databases

SQL (Structured Query Language) is essential for managing and manipulating relational databases. It is the standard language for querying databases and is integral to most data science workflows, especially for data extraction and storage. SQL allows data scientists to efficiently retrieve, insert, update, and delete data from relational databases.

Many organizations store their data in SQL databases such as MySQL, PostgreSQL, or Microsoft SQL Server, making SQL a vital skill for any data scientist. Using SQL, data scientists can filter, aggregate, and join data across multiple tables, which is crucial for data preprocessing before analysis.

```
-- Example: Basic SQL query to retrieve data
SELECT column1, column2 FROM dataset WHERE column1 > 100;
```

SQL remains the backbone of data management, ensuring smooth data extraction, cleaning, and preparation processes that form the foundation for data analysis.

Other Programming Languages: Java, Scala, and Julia

Besides Python, R, and SQL, other languages like Java, Scala, and Julia are also used in data science, especially in big data and performance-critical applications. Java is commonly used for distributed computing in environments like Apache Hadoop and Spark. Scala, with its functional programming features, is frequently used with Spark to build scalable data processing pipelines. Julia is gaining traction due to its high-performance capabilities for scientific computing and data analysis.

The right programming language for a data science project depends on the specific needs of the task at hand. Python is the most versatile and widely used language, R is powerful for statistical analysis, and SQL is essential for managing and querying relational databases. Understanding the strengths of each language allows data scientists to choose the best tool for each stage of their workflow.

Data Visualization Tools: Tableau, Power BI, and Open-Source Alternatives

Data visualization is a critical part of data science that helps turn complex data into clear, actionable insights. It involves using charts, graphs, and other visual representations to understand trends, relationships, and patterns in data. In this section, we'll examine some of the most popular data visualization tools: Tableau, Power BI, and open-source alternatives.

Tableau: A Leader in Data Visualization

Tableau is a widely-used commercial data visualization tool that allows users to create interactive and shareable dashboards. It is known for its user-friendly interface, which allows even non-technical users to generate complex visualizations. Tableau can connect to a variety of data sources, from spreadsheets to databases and cloud services, enabling data analysts to quickly explore and visualize data.

Tableau offers advanced visualization options such as heatmaps, scatter plots, and geospatial maps, making it suitable for a wide range of industries. It's also ideal for creating dashboards that can be shared with stakeholders in real-time.

```
# Tableau works with Python via TabPy (Tableau Python Integration) to allow
        advanced analytics
# Example: Using Python in Tableau for a predictive model output
import tabpy
from tabpy.tabpy_tools.client import Client

client = Client('http://localhost:9004')
client.deploy('my_model', model, 'Model to predict sales')
```

Tableau's ability to quickly generate visually appealing and insightful visualizations makes it a favorite tool for business intelligence professionals.

Power BI: Microsoft's Visualization Solution

Power BI is Microsoft's suite of data visualization tools that allows users to create interactive reports and dashboards. Like Tableau, Power BI connects to multiple data sources, including databases, Excel files, and cloud platforms. Power BI is especially popular among businesses that are already using Microsoft products, as it integrates seamlessly with services like Excel, Azure, and SharePoint.

Power BI's drag-and-drop interface is intuitive, making it easy for users to create complex reports without needing coding expertise. The tool also features AI-powered visualizations and custom visual extensions, offering high flexibility for data analysts.

```
# Power BI integrates with Python for advanced analytics and machine
          learning models
# Example: Using Python for a Power BI dashboard
import pandas as pd
from sklearn.linear_model import LinearRegression

data = pd.read_csv('sales_data.csv')
model = LinearRegression().fit(data[['months']], data['sales'])
predictions = model.predict(data[['months']])

# Power BI would then visualize this data for reporting
```

Power BI is especially favored in enterprise environments for its affordability, integration with Microsoft products, and ease of use.

Open-Source Alternatives: Matplotlib, Seaborn, and Plotly

For those who prefer open-source tools, there are several powerful libraries for data visualization, especially in Python. Libraries such as Matplotlib, Seaborn, and Plotly provide flexibility and control over visualizations.

- **Matplotlib** is the most widely-used Python library for creating static, animated, and interactive plots. It offers a wide range of customization options, making it highly versatile for various types of charts.

- **Seaborn** builds on Matplotlib and simplifies the creation of more complex visualizations. It is particularly useful for statistical visualizations, like heatmaps and regression plots.

- **Plotly** is an open-source visualization tool for creating interactive, web-based visualizations. Plotly integrates well with Python and offers a range of advanced chart types like 3D charts, geographic maps, and more.

```
# Example: Plotting a scatter plot with Seaborn
import seaborn as sns
import matplotlib.pyplot as plt

data = sns.load_dataset('iris')
sns.scatterplot(x='sepal_length', y='sepal_width', data=data)
plt.show()
```

These open-source libraries provide data scientists with the flexibility to create customized visualizations for different audiences, from technical reports to business presentations.

Choosing the Right Tool

The choice of data visualization tool largely depends on the project requirements, the skill level of the users, and the available resources. Tableau and Power BI are excellent for business users who need powerful, easy-to-use tools with drag-and-drop functionality. However, open-source alternatives like Matplotlib, Seaborn, and Plotly provide greater customization and control, especially when programming is involved.

Machine Learning Libraries and Frameworks: TensorFlow, PyTorch, Scikit-Learn

Machine learning is at the heart of data science, enabling systems to learn from data and make predictions or decisions. This section explores three essential machine learning libraries and frameworks: TensorFlow, PyTorch, and Scikit-Learn. These tools are foundational for building, training, and deploying machine learning models in real-world data science applications.

TensorFlow: Google's Deep Learning Framework

TensorFlow is an open-source framework developed by Google for building and deploying machine learning models, especially deep learning models. It supports both CPU and GPU computation, making it highly efficient for large-scale tasks. TensorFlow is particularly popular for tasks like image recognition, natural language processing, and time series forecasting due to its robustness and scalability.

The flexibility of TensorFlow lies in its ability to support low-level programming for custom models, as well as high-level APIs for easier model development. With its extensive ecosystem, TensorFlow includes TensorFlow Lite (for mobile devices) and TensorFlow.js (for running models in JavaScript environments).

```
import tensorflow as tf
from tensorflow.keras.models import Sequential
from tensorflow.keras.layers import Dense

# Example: Simple neural network in TensorFlow
model = Sequential([
    Dense(64, activation='relu', input_shape=(32,)),
    Dense(64, activation='relu'),
    Dense(10, activation='softmax')
])

model.compile(optimizer='adam', loss='sparse_categorical_crossentropy',
          metrics=['accuracy'])
```

TensorFlow's integration with cloud platforms such as Google Cloud and its tools for production-grade deployment make it a top choice for deep learning practitioners.

PyTorch: Flexibility and Speed for Deep Learning

PyTorch is an open-source machine learning library developed by Facebook, known for its flexibility, dynamic computation graphs, and ease of use. It is particularly favored by researchers and developers due to its simple, Pythonic interface and seamless debugging. PyTorch's dynamic computational graph allows for changes during runtime, making it easier to experiment with models.

PyTorch is commonly used for computer vision, natural language processing, and reinforcement learning tasks. It has strong support for GPUs and provides powerful utilities for efficient deep learning model training. PyTorch also features the TorchServe model deployment framework, simplifying model deployment.

```python
import torch
import torch.nn as nn
import torch.optim as optim

# Example: Defining a simple neural network in PyTorch
class SimpleNN(nn.Module):
    def __init__(self):
        super(SimpleNN, self).__init__()
        self.layer1 = nn.Linear(32, 64)
        self.layer2 = nn.Linear(64, 10)

    def forward(self, x):
        x = torch.relu(self.layer1(x))
        x = self.layer2(x)
        return x

model = SimpleNN()
optimizer = optim.Adam(model.parameters(), lr=0.001)
```

PyTorch's research-focused design and intuitive interface have made it one of the most widely used deep learning libraries in academia and industry.

Scikit-Learn: A Versatile Library for Classical Machine Learning

Scikit-Learn is one of the most popular machine learning libraries in Python. It provides simple and efficient tools for data mining and data analysis, and is built on top of other scientific libraries like NumPy, SciPy, and matplotlib. Scikit-Learn is ideal for classical machine learning tasks, such as classification, regression, clustering, and dimensionality reduction.

The library includes a wide range of models like decision trees, random forests, support vector machines, and k-nearest neighbors, as well as tools for model evaluation, hyperparameter tuning, and data preprocessing. It is perfect for users who want a robust, easy-to-use tool for machine learning tasks without diving into deep learning.

```python
from sklearn.datasets import load_iris
from sklearn.model_selection import train_test_split
from sklearn.ensemble import RandomForestClassifier
from sklearn.metrics import accuracy_score

# Example: Random Forest classifier using Scikit-Learn
data = load_iris()
```

```
X_train, X_test, y_train, y_test = train_test_split(data.data, data.target,
        test_size=0.3)

model = RandomForestClassifier(n_estimators=100)
model.fit(X_train, y_train)
predictions = model.predict(X_test)

print("Accuracy:", accuracy_score(y_test, predictions))
```

Scikit-Learn's simplicity and broad functionality make it an excellent choice for anyone working with classical machine learning models.

Choosing the Right Tool

The choice between TensorFlow, PyTorch, and Scikit-Learn depends largely on the task at hand. TensorFlow and PyTorch are best suited for deep learning, with TensorFlow providing a more production-oriented ecosystem, while PyTorch excels in flexibility and ease of experimentation. Scikit-Learn, on the other hand, remains the go-to library for classical machine learning tasks due to its simplicity and broad support.

Cloud Platforms and Distributed Systems: AWS, Azure, GCP, and Hadoop Ecosystems

The rapid growth of data science has driven the adoption of cloud platforms and distributed systems. These technologies offer powerful solutions for data storage, processing, and analysis at scale. This section explores the key cloud platforms and distributed systems that are essential for modern data science workflows, including AWS, Azure, Google Cloud Platform (GCP), and Hadoop ecosystems.

Cloud Platforms Overview: AWS, Azure, and GCP

Cloud computing platforms such as Amazon Web Services (AWS), Microsoft Azure, and Google Cloud Platform (GCP) provide a comprehensive range of tools and services for data science, machine learning, and data storage. These platforms support data scientists by offering scalable infrastructure, analytics services, and specialized tools for building, training, and deploying machine learning models.

AWS, for example, provides a broad array of tools like Amazon S3 for data storage, EC2 for computing, and SageMaker for model building. Azure offers services like Azure Blob Storage, Azure Machine Learning, and Databricks. GCP provides tools like BigQuery for data analysis, AI Platform for machine learning, and Google Cloud Storage.

Each platform has its strengths, with AWS known for its broad adoption and extensive services, Azure excelling in hybrid cloud solutions, and GCP being strong in data analytics and machine learning tools.

```
# Example: Loading data from AWS S3 using Python's boto3 library
import boto3

s3 = boto3.client('s3')
s3.download_file('bucket-name', 'file-name', 'local-file')
```

These platforms also allow for seamless integration with data science tools and offer powerful computing resources, such as GPUs and TPUs, for training large models, making them essential for handling big data in real-time.

Hadoop Ecosystem: Big Data Processing Framework

Hadoop is an open-source framework that enables the distributed processing of large datasets across clusters of computers. It is particularly well-suited for big data applications where storage and computation need to be scaled horizontally. The Hadoop ecosystem includes a number of key components such as HDFS (Hadoop Distributed File System), MapReduce, and Apache Hive.

HDFS allows for the distributed storage of data across many machines, while MapReduce provides a programming model for processing large datasets in parallel. Hive, a data warehouse system built on top of Hadoop, simplifies querying and analyzing large datasets. These technologies are fundamental for data scientists who need to work with high-volume, high-variety data.

```
# Example: Basic use of Hadoop's PySpark for distributed data processing
from pyspark import SparkContext

sc = SparkContext("local", "example")
data = sc.textFile("hdfs://path-to-data")
word_count = data.flatMap(lambda line: line.split()).map(lambda word: (word,
            1)).reduceByKey(lambda x, y: x + y)
word_count.collect()
```

Hadoop's ecosystem provides a robust foundation for building scalable data pipelines and performing complex data processing tasks across distributed systems.

Distributed Systems and Data Science

Distributed systems allow data scientists to scale their computations efficiently across multiple machines. These systems are critical for handling large datasets and performing computationally expensive tasks such as training machine learning models or running big data analytics.

Frameworks like Hadoop and Apache Spark provide the infrastructure for distributing computations, ensuring that data is processed in parallel across multiple nodes. This enables the processing of large datasets that would otherwise be too time-consuming or resource-intensive for a single machine.

Apache Spark, in particular, has become a favorite tool among data scientists due to its speed and ease of use. It can handle both batch and stream processing, making it versatile for a wide range of data science applications.

```
# Example: Running a simple transformation with Apache Spark
from pyspark.sql import SparkSession

spark = SparkSession.builder.appName("example").getOrCreate()
df = spark.read.csv("data.csv", header=True)
df.show()
```

The ability to process vast amounts of data efficiently is essential for modern data science, particularly when dealing with real-time analytics, machine learning model training, and data exploration.

Cloud and Distributed Systems in Data Science

Cloud platforms and distributed systems provide the infrastructure and tools necessary for tackling the challenges of modern data science. AWS, Azure, GCP, and Hadoop ecosystems offer scalable, cost-effective, and flexible solutions that empower data scientists to work with large datasets, run complex models, and leverage the power of parallel computing. These platforms are indispensable in today's data-driven world.

Module 5:

Mathematics for Data Science

Mathematics is the backbone of data science, providing the foundation for modeling, analyzing, and optimizing data-driven solutions. This module covers the essential mathematical concepts required in data science, including linear algebra, probability and statistics, calculus for optimization, and graph theory. These topics are critical for building robust models and making data-driven decisions.

Linear Algebra Essentials: Matrices, Vectors, and Transformations

Linear algebra is fundamental to many data science techniques, especially in machine learning and deep learning. Matrices and vectors represent data in a structured form, facilitating operations such as multiplication, addition, and inversion. These operations are essential in algorithms like principal component analysis (PCA) and linear regression. Transformations, such as rotating or scaling data, rely on matrix multiplication to manipulate data in higher-dimensional spaces. Mastery of linear algebra enables data scientists to work with large datasets, optimize models, and perform complex computations efficiently.

Probability and Statistics Foundations: Probability Distributions and Hypothesis Testing

Probability and statistics form the core of data analysis. Probability distributions describe how data points are likely to occur within a dataset, with common examples like normal and binomial distributions. Hypothesis testing is used to determine whether a given assumption about data is statistically valid. This involves testing a null hypothesis against an alternative hypothesis using methods such as t-tests and chi-square tests. Understanding these concepts allows data scientists to draw meaningful conclusions from data, quantify uncertainty, and make informed decisions based on statistical evidence.

Calculus for Optimization: Derivatives, Gradients, and Optimization Techniques

Calculus plays a critical role in optimizing data science models. Derivatives represent the rate of change in functions, which is crucial for understanding how model parameters affect outcomes. Gradients, the vector of partial derivatives, are used in gradient descent to find the optimal parameters for machine learning models. Optimization techniques like gradient descent help minimize error functions in tasks like regression and classification. By adjusting model parameters based on these calculations, data scientists can improve model performance and accuracy, making calculus an essential tool in the development of predictive models.

Graph Theory and Networks: Applications in Network Analysis and Recommendation Systems

Graph theory is key to understanding complex relationships in data. In network analysis, graphs are used to represent interconnected entities, such as social media connections or transportation systems. Data scientists use graph algorithms to identify clusters, shortest paths, and influence patterns. Recommendation systems, commonly used in platforms like Netflix and Amazon, rely on graph theory to predict user preferences based on historical interactions. By analyzing these networks, data scientists can uncover hidden patterns, optimize connections, and enhance user experiences, making graph theory essential in solving real-world problems.

Linear Algebra Essentials: Matrices, Vectors, and Transformations

Linear algebra is foundational to data science, serving as the backbone for numerous algorithms in machine learning, statistics, and optimization. It provides the tools for understanding and manipulating data in higher dimensions and forms the mathematical basis for techniques such as Principal Component Analysis (PCA), singular value decomposition (SVD), and support vector machines (SVM). In this section, we will explore the essential concepts of matrices, vectors, and transformations that are key to solving data science problems.

Vectors and Their Properties

A vector is an ordered list of numbers that can represent a point in space or a direction. Vectors are crucial for representing data in multi-dimensional space, such as the features of a dataset. In machine learning, a vector might represent a single data point, where each dimension corresponds to a feature.

In Python, vectors can be easily represented using the numpy library, which provides efficient operations for vector manipulation.

```python
import numpy as np

# Create a vector with 3 elements
vector = np.array([2, 3, 5])

# Perform basic operations on vectors
magnitude = np.linalg.norm(vector)
normalized_vector = vector / magnitude

print("Vector:", vector)
print("Magnitude:", magnitude)
print("Normalized Vector:", normalized_vector)
```

A vector's properties, such as its magnitude and direction, are central to various machine learning algorithms that rely on geometric interpretations.

Matrices: Structure and Operations

A matrix is a two-dimensional array of numbers arranged in rows and columns. In data science, matrices are used to represent datasets, where rows represent data points and columns represent features. Operations like matrix multiplication, addition, and inversion are essential for solving systems of linear equations, transforming data, and training models.

Matrix multiplication, for example, is used extensively in linear regression, where a matrix of features is multiplied by the model's weights to make predictions.

```python
# Create two matrices
A = np.array([[1, 2], [3, 4]])
B = np.array([[5, 6], [7, 8]])

# Multiply matrices
result = np.dot(A, B)
print("Matrix A:\n", A)
print("Matrix B:\n", B)
print("Matrix A * B:\n", result)
```

Matrix operations like these are fundamental to understanding how data is transformed and manipulated in machine learning models.

Linear Transformations and Applications

A linear transformation is a function that maps a vector to another vector, typically through matrix multiplication. It is used in various applications, such as data normalization, scaling, and dimensionality reduction. In machine learning, linear transformations help adjust the features of a dataset to make them more suitable for modeling.

For example, a linear transformation can be used to rotate or scale data points in feature space, which is crucial in techniques like PCA and SVM.

```python
# Define a transformation matrix
transformation_matrix = np.array([[2, 0], [0, 2]])

# Apply the transformation to a vector
transformed_vector = np.dot(transformation_matrix, vector[:2])  # Use only
          the first two elements
print("Transformed Vector:", transformed_vector)
```

By applying transformations, we can change the representation of the data to improve the effectiveness of machine learning models.

Applications in Data Science

Linear algebra's applications in data science are vast. It forms the foundation of algorithms for regression, classification, clustering, and dimensionality reduction. For instance, in PCA, linear algebra is used to compute the covariance matrix, find its

54

eigenvectors, and reduce the dataset's dimensionality by projecting it onto a lower-dimensional subspace.

Similarly, in deep learning, neural networks rely heavily on matrix multiplication to compute forward passes and backpropagate errors during training.

Understanding the basics of linear algebra equips data scientists with the tools to interpret and manipulate data effectively, paving the way for more advanced techniques in machine learning and optimization.

Probability and Statistics Foundations: Probability Distributions and Hypothesis Testing

Probability and statistics are the core disciplines that help data scientists make sense of uncertainty and variability in data. These fields provide the foundation for analyzing datasets, testing hypotheses, and making predictions. In this section, we will explore key concepts such as probability distributions, hypothesis testing, and their applications in data science.

Probability Distributions: Understanding Uncertainty

Probability distributions describe how the values of a random variable are distributed. They are essential for modeling the uncertainty inherent in real-world data. Some commonly used probability distributions include the Normal distribution, Binomial distribution, and Poisson distribution. Each distribution has its unique properties and applications.

For example, the Normal distribution, which is symmetrical and bell-shaped, is widely used to model continuous data like heights, test scores, or stock prices. In Python, we can use libraries like scipy and numpy to visualize and analyze these distributions.

```python
import numpy as np
import matplotlib.pyplot as plt
from scipy.stats import norm

# Generate data from a Normal distribution
data = np.random.normal(loc=0, scale=1, size=1000)

# Plot the distribution
plt.hist(data, bins=30, density=True, alpha=0.6, color='g')
xmin, xmax = plt.xlim()
x = np.linspace(xmin, xmax, 100)
p = norm.pdf(x, 0, 1)
plt.plot(x, p, 'k', linewidth=2)
plt.title('Normal Distribution')
plt.show()
```

This example generates and visualizes data following a Normal distribution, helping to understand the concept of continuous random variables and their distributions.

Hypothesis Testing: Drawing Conclusions from Data

55

Hypothesis testing is a statistical method used to make inferences or draw conclusions about a population based on sample data. In hypothesis testing, a null hypothesis (H0) is tested against an alternative hypothesis (H1), typically using a test statistic such as the t-test or chi-square test.

The process involves calculating the p-value, which indicates the probability of observing the data given that the null hypothesis is true. If the p-value is smaller than a predefined significance level (usually 0.05), we reject the null hypothesis.

```
from scipy.stats import ttest_1samp

# Sample data (e.g., heights of a group of people)
sample_data = np.array([175, 160, 185, 170, 180])

# Perform a one-sample t-test (testing if the mean height is 170)
t_stat, p_value = ttest_1samp(sample_data, 170)

print("T-statistic:", t_stat)
print("P-value:", p_value)
```

In this example, we use the t-test to compare the sample mean against a known value (170). The result helps determine whether there is significant evidence to support or reject the null hypothesis.

Understanding Statistical Significance

Statistical significance helps determine whether the results of an experiment or analysis are likely to be genuine or if they might have occurred by chance. It is crucial to evaluate statistical significance to avoid drawing incorrect conclusions from data. The p-value plays a central role in this process.

For example, a p-value below 0.05 suggests that the result is statistically significant, meaning there is strong evidence against the null hypothesis. Conversely, a p-value greater than 0.05 implies that the null hypothesis cannot be rejected at the 95% confidence level.

Applications in Data Science: Decision Making and Predictions

Probability and statistics provide data scientists with the tools to make informed decisions based on data. In predictive modeling, for instance, probabilistic models such as Naive Bayes or Bayesian networks rely heavily on probability distributions to make predictions. Similarly, hypothesis testing allows data scientists to evaluate the effectiveness of different features or algorithms before deploying a model.

In real-world applications like A/B testing, statistical methods are used to test whether changes in a system lead to significant improvements, guiding decision-making in business and technology.

Calculus for Optimization: Derivatives, Gradients, and Optimization Techniques

Calculus plays a crucial role in data science, particularly in the areas of optimization, machine learning, and model training. Optimization is the process of finding the best parameters for a model, which typically involves minimizing or maximizing a function. Derivatives, gradients, and optimization techniques are at the heart of this process. In this section, we will explore how calculus is used to optimize functions and improve model performance.

Derivatives: Understanding Rate of Change

The derivative of a function measures the rate of change of a function with respect to its variables. In the context of data science, derivatives help us understand how changes in model parameters affect the model's performance. For instance, in machine learning, we use derivatives to determine how the loss function changes with respect to the parameters, guiding the optimization process.

For example, the derivative of the function $f(x)=x^2$ with respect to x is $f'(x)=2x$. This tells us how the output of the function changes as we change x.

```
import sympy as sp

x = sp.symbols('x')
f = x**2
derivative_f = sp.diff(f, x)
print("Derivative of x^2:", derivative_f)
```

This Python code uses the sympy library to calculate the derivative of the function x^2, helping us understand how the function behaves and how to optimize it.

Gradients: Multivariable Optimization

When dealing with multivariable functions, we use gradients to determine the direction in which the function increases most rapidly. The gradient is a vector that contains the partial derivatives of the function with respect to each variable. In machine learning, the gradient is used in gradient descent algorithms to iteratively update model parameters in the direction that minimizes the loss function.

Consider a function $f(x,y)=x^2+y^2$. The gradient of this function is the vector $\nabla f=(2x,2y)$, indicating the direction of steepest ascent.

```
f = x**2 + y**2
gradient_f = [sp.diff(f, var) for var in (x, y)]
print("Gradient of x^2 + y^2:", gradient_f)
```

In this example, the gradient of x^2+y^2 is calculated, which will guide the optimization algorithm in improving model parameters during training.

Optimization Techniques: Gradient Descent

Gradient descent is an optimization algorithm used to minimize a function by iteratively moving towards the minimum. In machine learning, it is used to minimize the loss function. The basic idea is to update the parameters in the direction opposite to the gradient to reduce the value of the loss function.

The update rule in gradient descent is given by:

$$\theta = \theta - \eta \cdot \nabla J(\theta)$$

Where η is the learning rate, θ are the model parameters, and $J(\theta)$ is the loss function.

```
import numpy as np

# Example of gradient descent with a simple quadratic function
def gradient_descent(learning_rate, iterations):
    theta = 10  # Initial guess
    for _ in range(iterations):
        gradient = 2 * theta  # Derivative of theta^2
        theta = theta - learning_rate * gradient  # Update rule
    return theta

# Run gradient descent
final_theta = gradient_descent(learning_rate=0.1, iterations=100)
print("Final theta after gradient descent:", final_theta)
```

This code demonstrates a simple gradient descent implementation, where the function θ^2 is minimized. The result shows the parameter θ converging to the optimal value.

Applications in Machine Learning: Improving Model Accuracy

Calculus-based optimization techniques are integral to machine learning algorithms, especially in deep learning and neural networks. In these models, optimization algorithms like stochastic gradient descent (SGD) are used to train complex models by minimizing the loss function over a large dataset. The ability to efficiently find the optimal parameters is key to the success of many machine learning applications, such as image recognition and natural language processing.

In real-world scenarios, optimization ensures that models achieve high accuracy by fine-tuning parameters and reducing errors through techniques like backpropagation in neural networks.

Graph Theory and Networks: Applications in Network Analysis and Recommendation Systems

Graph theory is a branch of mathematics that studies the relationships between objects represented as vertices (nodes) connected by edges (links). It is a powerful tool used extensively in data science, especially for network analysis and recommendation systems. This section explores how graph theory and network analysis techniques are applied to solve complex real-world problems.

Graph Theory: Understanding the Basics

At its core, graph theory provides a framework to model relationships between entities. In a graph, nodes represent the entities, and edges represent the relationships between them. A graph can be directed (edges have a direction) or undirected (edges do not have a direction). Graphs can be used to model a wide variety of systems, from social networks to transportation systems.

For example, in a social network, people can be represented as nodes, and their friendships as edges. This allows for analyzing how people are connected, detecting communities, or finding influential users.

```python
import networkx as nx

# Create a simple graph using NetworkX
G = nx.Graph()
G.add_edges_from([(1, 2), (2, 3), (3, 4)])

# Visualize the graph
nx.draw(G, with_labels=True)
```

In the above Python code, we use networkx to create a simple graph representing relationships between four nodes. The visualization helps to understand how nodes are connected, forming a basic network.

Network Analysis: Identifying Important Nodes

Network analysis focuses on studying the structure and properties of graphs. It helps identify important nodes (also known as central nodes), understand connectivity, and discover communities within the network. Key metrics like degree centrality, betweenness centrality, and closeness centrality help quantify the importance of nodes in a network.

For instance, degree centrality measures how connected a node is by counting the number of edges connected to it. A node with a high degree centrality is likely to be more influential in the network.

```python
# Calculate degree centrality of the nodes
degree_centrality = nx.degree_centrality(G)
print("Degree Centrality of nodes:", degree_centrality)
```

This code calculates the degree centrality of each node in the graph, which can help identify the most connected nodes.

Recommendation Systems: Leveraging Graphs for Personalized Recommendations

Graph theory plays a central role in recommendation systems, which provide personalized suggestions to users. These systems often rely on collaborative filtering, where recommendations are based on the interactions or preferences of similar users. A popular approach is to model the recommendation process as a bipartite graph, where users and items are represented as nodes, and edges represent interactions (e.g., user-item ratings).

For example, in movie recommendation systems like Netflix, the graph can represent users and movies, with edges indicating ratings given by users to movies. By finding similarities between users or movies using graph-based techniques, the system can recommend movies that similar users have enjoyed.

```
# Example of collaborative filtering using a simple graph
# Let's assume users (U) and movies (M) are represented as bipartite graph
B = nx.Graph()
B.add_edges_from([(1, 'Movie1'), (2, 'Movie2'), (1, 'Movie3'), (3,
        'Movie2')])

# Find neighbors of a user (node 1)
user_neighbors = list(B.neighbors(1))
print("User 1's movie recommendations:", user_neighbors)
```

This code creates a bipartite graph where users and movies are nodes, and interactions (ratings or views) are edges. By finding the neighbors of a user, we can generate recommendations based on the movies they are connected to.

Applications in Real-World Networks

Graph theory and network analysis are applied in various domains, such as social networks, communication networks, and biological networks. In social networks, graph algorithms help identify communities, detect influential users, and analyze the spread of information or diseases. In communication networks, graph algorithms optimize the routing of data. In recommendation systems, graph-based algorithms provide personalized suggestions based on user behavior, driving engagement and improving user experiences.

Module 6:

Ethics and Fairness in Data Science

Ethics and fairness are critical considerations in data science, ensuring that data-driven solutions are responsible, transparent, and equitable. This module explores the ethical challenges in data science, focusing on responsible data usage, addressing biases in algorithms, ensuring model transparency, and complying with data privacy regulations. Understanding these principles is essential for building trust and accountability in data-driven decisions.

Ethical Data Usage: Responsible Sourcing and Processing

Ethical data usage involves sourcing and processing data in a responsible manner. This includes obtaining consent from individuals whose data is being used, ensuring data is accurate, and protecting against misuse. Data scientists must be mindful of the impact their analyses can have, particularly in areas like healthcare, finance, and hiring. Ethical considerations also involve avoiding data manipulation or cherry-picking, ensuring that data collection and usage adhere to industry standards and social norms. By practicing responsible data usage, data scientists can avoid harm and maintain the integrity of their work.

Addressing Bias and Fairness: Mitigating Bias in Algorithms

Bias in data and algorithms is a significant concern in data science. Data scientists must be vigilant about identifying and addressing biases that may arise from skewed data or biased training processes. This includes ensuring that datasets are representative and diverse, particularly when developing models for decision-making in sensitive areas like lending, hiring, and law enforcement. Techniques such as fairness constraints and adversarial debiasing can help mitigate bias. Ensuring fairness in algorithms requires ongoing evaluation, as biases may emerge over time as data or societal norms change. Tackling bias is crucial for building fair and equitable systems.

Transparency and Interpretability: Ensuring Explainability in Models

Transparency and interpretability are vital for building trust in data science models. Complex machine learning algorithms, especially deep learning models, are often seen as "black boxes," making it difficult to understand how they make decisions. Ensuring model transparency involves developing interpretable models or using techniques to explain the inner workings of black-box models. This includes methods like feature importance scores, decision trees, or LIME (Local Interpretable Model-Agnostic Explanations). Ensuring explainability helps stakeholders understand and trust the model's decisions, which is especially important in high-stakes domains such as healthcare, criminal justice, and finance.

Data Privacy Regulations: GDPR, HIPAA, and Other Standards

Data privacy regulations are essential to protect individuals' personal data and ensure compliance with legal frameworks. The General Data Protection Regulation (GDPR) in the European Union and the Health Insurance Portability and Accountability Act (HIPAA) in the U.S. are key regulations that govern how personal data must be handled. These regulations require organizations to obtain explicit consent from individuals, ensure data security, and provide transparency regarding how data is used. Data scientists must be aware of these regulations and ensure that their work adheres to privacy standards, safeguarding individuals' rights while leveraging data for analysis.

Ethical Data Usage: Responsible Sourcing and Processing

Ethical data usage is crucial in ensuring that data science practices align with moral standards, legal requirements, and social expectations. This section focuses on responsible sourcing, processing, and handling of data, ensuring that the rights and privacy of individuals are respected throughout the data science lifecycle.

Responsible Data Sourcing: Obtaining Data Legally and Ethically

The first step in ethical data usage is sourcing data responsibly. This includes obtaining data from legal, reputable, and ethical sources, ensuring that proper consent has been obtained when necessary. It is vital to ensure that data is not acquired through illegal, exploitative, or deceptive practices, such as scraping personal information without consent or using data obtained through unfair means.

For instance, when collecting data from social media platforms, scraping data from users' profiles without their consent would be an unethical practice. A responsible approach includes ensuring that users are informed about the data being collected and that they have given their consent explicitly.

```python
import requests

# Example of ethical data sourcing via an API
url = 'https://api.example.com/data'
response = requests.get(url, headers={'Authorization': 'Bearer token'})

if response.status_code == 200:
    data = response.json()
    print("Data retrieved successfully:", data)
else:
    print("Failed to retrieve data")
```

In this example, data is retrieved through an authorized API call with a valid authentication token. This ensures that the data is collected legally and ethically by respecting access permissions and privacy.

Data Processing: Ensuring Ethical Handling

Once data is sourced, it must be processed ethically. Data cleaning, transformation, and analysis should be performed in ways that respect the rights of individuals and avoid harm. Ethical processing also includes anonymizing sensitive information, ensuring that personal identifiers are removed or obfuscated before analysis or sharing.

For example, when working with sensitive data such as medical records, removing personally identifiable information (PII) ensures that individual privacy is protected. Ethical processing practices also involve ensuring that data is not misused, such as using personal data in a way that could harm individuals or groups.

```
import pandas as pd

# Example of anonymizing data by removing PII
df = pd.read_csv('data.csv')
df = df.drop(columns=['Name', 'Email'])  # Removing personal identifiers
print(df.head())
```

In this code, personal identifiers (e.g., "Name" and "Email") are removed from the dataset before analysis to ensure that privacy is maintained.

Minimizing Harm: Mitigating Risks of Data Misuse

It is essential to minimize the risk of harm when handling data. This includes avoiding using data for purposes that could lead to discrimination, invasion of privacy, or exploitation. For example, using biased data in predictive modeling may perpetuate discrimination, leading to unfair outcomes for specific groups.

To mitigate harm, data scientists must identify potential risks and take proactive steps to ensure that their models and analyses do not reinforce negative stereotypes or inequalities. This can include auditing data for fairness, implementing safeguards, and ensuring diverse representation in training datasets.

Creating an Ethical Data Culture

Creating an ethical data culture within an organization is vital to ensure that data practices align with core values. This involves educating data science teams on ethical considerations, providing guidelines for responsible data usage, and promoting transparency in how data is collected, processed, and used. Ethical leadership within an organization can help ensure that data science initiatives prioritize fairness and respect for privacy.

By fostering a culture of ethics in data science, organizations can build trust with the public and create long-term value that benefits individuals, businesses, and society as a whole.

Addressing Bias and Fairness: Mitigating Bias in Algorithms

Addressing bias and fairness in data science is a critical concern to ensure that algorithms and models operate without discriminatory effects on individuals or groups. This section explores the importance of identifying, addressing, and mitigating bias in data, algorithms, and decision-making processes to ensure fairness and equity in data science practices.

Understanding Bias in Data Science: The Role of Data and Algorithms

Bias in data science can arise at multiple stages of the data pipeline— from data collection and preprocessing to model development and deployment. Bias can emerge from unrepresentative datasets, historical prejudices encoded in data, or skewed algorithmic predictions. Understanding the sources of bias is the first step in mitigating its effects.

For instance, a facial recognition system trained on a dataset predominantly composed of lighter-skinned individuals may have lower accuracy for people with darker skin tones. In this case, the model's performance would be biased against people of color, leading to unfair outcomes. Recognizing such biases is essential to designing inclusive models.

Identifying Bias in Datasets: Fairness Audits and Bias Detection

To ensure fairness, it is essential to identify biases present in the data before model training begins. Conducting fairness audits and using techniques like disparity analysis can help detect unequal distributions in the data. Common biases include sampling bias, label bias, and measurement bias.

For example, a dataset used to predict creditworthiness might over-represent certain demographic groups, leading to a model that discriminates against underrepresented groups. Identifying such biases requires careful examination of data distributions and outcomes across various subgroups.

```
import pandas as pd

# Example of detecting bias in a dataset using group analysis
df = pd.read_csv('credit_data.csv')
bias_check = df.groupby('Gender').mean()['Credit_Score']
print(bias_check)
```

In this code, the average credit scores are analyzed across different gender groups to identify any disparities that might suggest bias in the dataset.

Mitigating Bias in Algorithms: Techniques and Strategies

Once bias is identified, the next step is to mitigate it. Several techniques can help reduce bias in algorithms, such as re-sampling the dataset to ensure diverse representation, using fairness constraints during model training, and applying post-processing techniques to adjust model outcomes.

For example, if a predictive model disproportionately favors one demographic group, applying fairness constraints (such as equalized odds or demographic parity) during model training can ensure that outcomes are more balanced across groups. These techniques encourage fairness by explicitly including fairness considerations in the optimization process.

```
from sklearn.metrics import confusion_matrix

# Example of calculating fairness by checking equalized odds
y_true = [1, 0, 1, 1, 0, 1, 0, 0]
y_pred = [1, 0, 0, 1, 0, 1, 0, 0]

cm = confusion_matrix(y_true, y_pred)
print(cm)
```

In this code, a confusion matrix is used to analyze the predicted outcomes for different classes, helping to detect potential biases in model predictions.

The Importance of Fairness in Real-World Applications

Ensuring fairness in real-world applications of data science is vital to prevent discriminatory practices that can harm marginalized communities. For example, biased algorithms used in hiring, healthcare, or criminal justice systems can perpetuate societal inequalities. Ensuring fairness helps promote equal opportunities for all individuals, regardless of their demographic background.

Incorporating fairness into algorithmic decision-making promotes trust, transparency, and accountability. By focusing on fairness, data scientists can create models that positively impact society and ensure that AI-driven decisions are just and equitable.

Transparency and Interpretability: Ensuring Explainability in Models

Transparency and interpretability in data science are crucial for building trust in machine learning models and ensuring their ethical use. In this section, we explore the importance of making models explainable, the techniques used to achieve interpretability, and the role these practices play in responsible data science.

The Need for Transparent Models in Data Science

Transparency in machine learning refers to the clarity with which the workings of a model can be understood by humans. As algorithms are increasingly used in critical decision-making processes, such as in healthcare or criminal justice, ensuring that these models are transparent is vital for fostering trust among stakeholders.

For example, if a medical diagnosis model makes an incorrect prediction, the ability to understand why it reached that conclusion can be crucial for addressing the error. Transparent models allow users to evaluate and verify the reasoning behind predictions, making it easier to detect potential biases and inaccuracies.

Interpretable Models vs. Black-Box Models: Trade-offs

There are two primary types of models in terms of interpretability: interpretable models and black-box models. Interpretable models, such as decision trees or linear regression, offer clear insights into how decisions are made, with straightforward rules or coefficients that can be understood. However, these models might not always capture complex relationships in the data.

On the other hand, black-box models, such as deep neural networks, often deliver better performance but at the cost of interpretability. The challenge is balancing the accuracy of sophisticated models with the need for human understanding. One approach to achieving this balance is using post-hoc interpretability techniques.

Post-Hoc Interpretability: Techniques and Tools

Post-hoc interpretability involves applying tools and techniques to explain predictions made by complex models after they have been trained. Common methods for enhancing the interpretability of black-box models include:

- **LIME (Local Interpretable Model-agnostic Explanations)**: This technique explains the prediction of any model by approximating it with a simpler, interpretable model around the prediction instance.

- **SHAP (Shapley Additive Explanations)**: SHAP values provide a way to explain the contribution of each feature to the final prediction by distributing the prediction's value fairly among the features.

  Example using SHAP:

  ```
  import shap
  import xgboost as xgb

  # Train an example model
  model = xgb.XGBClassifier()
  model.fit(X_train, y_train)

  # Apply SHAP for model interpretation
  explainer = shap.TreeExplainer(model)
  shap_values = explainer.shap_values(X_test)

  # Plot SHAP values
  shap.summary_plot(shap_values, X_test)
  ```

This code demonstrates how to use SHAP to visualize the impact of features on predictions made by an XGBoost model.

The Role of Explainability in Ethical AI

Explainability plays a crucial role in ensuring that AI systems are used responsibly. Transparent and interpretable models help data scientists, stakeholders, and end-users understand the rationale behind decisions. In sectors like healthcare or finance, where decisions can have life-changing consequences, it's essential to ensure that the decision-making process is both understandable and justifiable.

Moreover, regulatory bodies are increasingly emphasizing explainability, with laws like the GDPR requiring that automated decisions be explainable to individuals. By adhering to these principles, data scientists can promote fairness, accountability, and transparency in AI systems.

Data Privacy Regulations: GDPR, HIPAA, and Other Standards

Data privacy is one of the most pressing concerns in modern data science, particularly as the volume and scope of personal data used for analysis continue to grow. This section explores key data privacy regulations, including GDPR and HIPAA, and the standards and principles guiding data privacy in data science.

General Data Protection Regulation (GDPR): Key Principles

The General Data Protection Regulation (GDPR), enacted by the European Union in 2018, is one of the most comprehensive data protection laws globally. Its goal is to ensure that organizations handle personal data in a transparent, secure, and responsible manner. GDPR introduces several key principles:

- **Data Minimization**: Collect only the data necessary for the specific purpose.

- **Consent**: Obtain explicit consent from individuals for processing their data.

- **Data Subject Rights**: Allow individuals to access, correct, and delete their data.

- **Accountability**: Ensure organizations can demonstrate compliance with data protection laws.

GDPR imposes strict penalties for non-compliance, including fines of up to 4% of global annual revenue, which has made it a critical consideration for businesses handling European Union residents' data.

Health Insurance Portability and Accountability Act (HIPAA)

HIPAA, enacted in the United States, governs the protection of health information, specifically for healthcare providers, insurers, and their business associates. HIPAA applies to protected health information (PHI) and lays down regulations for its collection, use, and sharing. Key components of HIPAA include:

- **Privacy Rule**: Protects individuals' health information from unauthorized access or disclosure.

- **Security Rule**: Establishes standards for securing PHI, particularly for electronic records.

- **Breach Notification Rule**: Requires covered entities to notify individuals if their PHI is compromised.

For data scientists, HIPAA requires ensuring the security of sensitive health data during analysis and processing, which includes encryption, secure storage, and anonymization techniques.

Other Standards and Regulations

Besides GDPR and HIPAA, several other privacy laws and standards influence data science practices. These include:

- **California Consumer Privacy Act (CCPA)**: A regulation in California that grants consumers rights over their personal data, including the right to access, delete, and opt out of data sales.

- **Children's Online Privacy Protection Act (COPPA)**: A U.S. law that regulates the collection of personal information from children under 13 years old.

- **Payment Card Industry Data Security Standard (PCI DSS)**: A global standard for organizations that handle credit card information, aiming to secure sensitive payment data.

These regulations collectively set the framework for privacy-conscious data handling practices across industries.

Ensuring Compliance and Best Practices in Data Science

Data scientists must ensure that their practices align with these regulations. This includes implementing robust data anonymization and encryption methods, especially when dealing with sensitive data, such as health records or financial transactions. It's also essential to understand the rights of data subjects and incorporate mechanisms for users to opt out or withdraw consent when necessary.

Additionally, organizations should regularly audit their data practices and stay informed about changing legal landscapes to ensure ongoing compliance. By adhering to these regulations, data scientists not only protect individuals' privacy but also build trust with stakeholders.

Module 7:

Case Studies in Data Science Foundations

Case studies are powerful tools for understanding how data science can be applied across various industries. This module highlights real-world applications, success stories, lessons from failures, and key takeaways to prepare data scientists for future trends. By studying these cases, learners gain practical insights into the challenges and opportunities in data science.

Real-World Applications Overview: Insights from Diverse Fields

Data science is transforming industries ranging from healthcare and finance to entertainment and transportation. In healthcare, predictive models assist with patient diagnosis and treatment planning. Financial institutions use data science for fraud detection and risk management. In entertainment, recommendation algorithms shape user experiences, while transportation companies optimize routes and improve safety. Each of these applications highlights the potential of data science to solve complex problems and improve outcomes, demonstrating the versatility of the discipline.

Success Stories in Data-Driven Decision Making: Examples from Top Organizations

Several organizations have harnessed data science to drive innovation and achieve success. For example, Netflix uses data science to recommend personalized content, improving user engagement. Amazon leverages predictive analytics to optimize inventory and delivery processes. In healthcare, companies like IBM Watson are using machine learning to aid in cancer diagnosis. These success stories demonstrate how data-driven decision-making leads to increased efficiency, reduced costs, and improved customer satisfaction, reinforcing the power of data science in driving business and societal impact.

Lessons from Failures: Avoidable Mistakes and their Outcomes

Not all data science projects succeed. Failures, though valuable, often highlight common pitfalls that can be avoided. For instance, an overreliance on biased data can lead to inaccurate predictions and unfair outcomes, as seen in biased hiring algorithms. Lack of model transparency or interpretability has led to mistrust and regulatory scrutiny. Poor data quality and insufficient preprocessing can result in unreliable insights. By analyzing these failures, data scientists can learn the importance of thorough data cleaning, ethical considerations, and ongoing model evaluation to mitigate risks and improve project outcomes.

Key Takeaways and Future Directions: Preparing for Future Trends

The field of data science is constantly evolving, and staying ahead of trends is crucial for long-term success. Emerging technologies such as artificial intelligence, quantum computing, and advanced automation are poised to revolutionize data science. As more industries adopt data-driven approaches, the demand for skilled data scientists will grow. Preparing for future trends involves mastering new tools and methodologies, understanding ethical implications, and staying informed about regulatory changes. The future of data science promises exciting opportunities for innovation and problem-solving, making it an essential field for both professionals and organizations.

Real-World Applications Overview: Insights from Diverse Fields

Data science has transformed a wide array of industries by enabling data-driven decision-making and uncovering patterns that were previously difficult to detect. This section explores how data science has been applied in various fields, demonstrating its far-reaching impact and versatility.

Healthcare: Revolutionizing Patient Care

In healthcare, data science has significantly improved diagnostics, patient care, and operational efficiency. Machine learning algorithms are used to predict patient outcomes, such as the likelihood of developing chronic conditions or complications. For example, predictive models have been developed to forecast the risk of heart attacks or strokes based on patient data such as age, medical history, and lifestyle factors.

A notable application is in medical imaging, where deep learning models help radiologists detect anomalies in X-rays or MRIs. These models can identify early signs of diseases like cancer, improving the chances of early intervention and better patient outcomes. In addition, healthcare systems are utilizing data science to optimize hospital resource management, such as predicting patient inflows and adjusting staffing levels accordingly.

Finance: Enhancing Fraud Detection and Risk Management

The finance sector has adopted data science techniques to detect fraud, optimize trading strategies, and assess credit risk. Fraud detection algorithms analyze transaction patterns in real time, identifying suspicious activities that deviate from typical behavior. For instance, machine learning models flag unusual transactions based on features such as transaction amount, location, and frequency. These models improve the accuracy of fraud detection systems and reduce false positives.

Moreover, banks and financial institutions leverage predictive analytics to assess the creditworthiness of individuals and businesses. By analyzing historical data on loan repayments, income, and other financial variables, these models provide more accurate credit risk assessments, leading to better lending decisions and minimizing defaults.

Retail: Personalized Recommendations and Inventory Management

Retailers have significantly benefited from data science by enhancing customer experience and improving operational efficiency. Personalized recommendation systems, often powered by collaborative filtering and content-based filtering techniques, analyze customer behavior and preferences to suggest products. Companies like Amazon and Netflix use these systems to drive sales and engagement by offering tailored suggestions to users.

In addition to personalization, data science plays a crucial role in inventory management. By analyzing historical sales data, weather patterns, and seasonal trends, retailers optimize stock levels to meet customer demand without overstocking or running out of products. Predictive models also help identify which products are likely to become popular, enabling proactive stocking strategies.

Transportation and Logistics: Optimizing Routes and Reducing Costs

In transportation and logistics, data science is used to optimize routes, reduce fuel consumption, and improve delivery times. Companies like UPS and FedEx use predictive analytics to determine the most efficient delivery routes based on real-time traffic data and historical patterns. Machine learning models can predict traffic congestion, weather disruptions, and other factors that might affect delivery schedules.

Moreover, data science helps reduce operational costs by optimizing vehicle maintenance schedules. By analyzing sensor data from vehicles, companies can predict when a vehicle is likely to require maintenance or repairs, minimizing downtime and ensuring the efficient operation of their fleet.

Success Stories in Data-Driven Decision Making: Examples from Top Organizations

Many top organizations have successfully adopted data science to drive strategic decision-making, enhance operational efficiency, and gain a competitive edge. In this section, we examine a few success stories that demonstrate how data science has been applied effectively in various sectors.

Netflix: Personalized Recommendations and Content Optimization

Netflix is a prime example of a company that has effectively leveraged data science to improve user experience and increase customer retention. By using data on user preferences, viewing history, and interactions, Netflix's recommendation system suggests movies and shows tailored to individual tastes. This personalization is powered by algorithms such as collaborative filtering, content-based filtering, and matrix factorization.

Additionally, Netflix uses data science to guide content production decisions. By analyzing user data, Netflix identifies popular genres, shows, and movie types, helping the company decide which types of original content to produce. The success of shows like "Stranger Things" and "The Crown" is partly due to Netflix's ability to predict what will resonate with its audience based on data-driven insights.

Amazon: Efficient Supply Chain and Dynamic Pricing

Amazon has used data science extensively to enhance its e-commerce platform, optimize its supply chain, and personalize customer interactions. One of Amazon's most successful implementations is its dynamic pricing model, which adjusts prices for products in real-time based on factors such as demand, competition, and inventory levels. This enables Amazon to maximize profits while ensuring competitive pricing for customers.

In its supply chain, Amazon employs predictive analytics to forecast demand and optimize inventory management. By using historical sales data and external factors like weather and holidays, Amazon can predict when to restock items, which reduces stockouts and excess inventory. Additionally, Amazon's vast fulfillment network relies on machine learning to optimize delivery routes and reduce shipping times, providing a faster and more efficient service.

Target: Predicting Consumer Behavior

Target, a major retailer, is known for its ability to predict customer behavior using data science techniques. One famous example is Target's predictive analytics model, which can identify when customers are likely to be pregnant based on their shopping patterns. By analyzing purchase data, such as the frequency of certain product combinations (e.g., vitamins, unscented lotion), Target can send targeted marketing materials to customers, increasing the likelihood of a sale.

This data-driven approach has not only improved Target's marketing strategies but has also helped the company better understand consumer behavior, leading to more personalized promotions and increased customer loyalty.

Spotify: Data-Driven Music Recommendations and Playlist Creation

Spotify's use of data science is central to its success as a leading music streaming service. The company uses machine learning models to analyze listening patterns and create personalized playlists for users, such as "Discover Weekly" and "Release Radar." By studying the musical preferences and behaviors of users, Spotify provides song recommendations tailored to each individual's taste.

Spotify also uses data science to curate playlist content, leveraging user feedback, likes, and listening history to ensure that the playlists remain relevant and engaging. This approach has helped Spotify build a loyal user base, increase engagement, and attract new subscribers.

Lessons from Failures: Avoidable Mistakes and their Outcomes

While many organizations have successfully implemented data science strategies, several have faced challenges that resulted in costly mistakes. These failures provide valuable lessons for future data science projects and highlight the importance of avoiding common pitfalls.

Target's Pregnancy Prediction Controversy

One of the most well-known failures in data science is Target's attempt to predict customer pregnancies, which backfired and resulted in a public relations crisis. Target's predictive model used purchasing patterns to identify pregnant customers and send them targeted ads for baby products. While the model was accurate, its implementation caused ethical concerns when a teenage girl's father discovered she had received such advertisements, even before she had told her parents about her pregnancy.

The key lesson here is the importance of privacy and ethical considerations in data science projects. While predictive models can be powerful, companies must ensure that they respect customer privacy and understand the potential consequences of their data-driven decisions. Furthermore, organizations must be cautious when making assumptions about sensitive personal information, as it can lead to reputational damage and loss of customer trust.

Amazon's Controversial Recruitment Algorithm

Amazon's AI-based recruitment tool, designed to automate the hiring process, faced significant challenges due to biases in its algorithms. The tool was trained on resumes submitted to Amazon over a 10-year period, a dataset that predominantly consisted of male applicants. As a result, the algorithm learned to favor male candidates and penalize resumes that included words associated with women, such as "women's" or "female."

This failure highlights the importance of addressing bias in machine learning models. When training models, it is essential to ensure that the data used is representative and free of any biases that could lead to discrimination. In Amazon's case, the failure to account for gender bias in the training data ultimately led to the abandonment of the tool. Companies must actively monitor and test their algorithms for fairness and inclusion to avoid perpetuating systemic biases.

Uber's Self-Driving Car Incident

In 2018, Uber's autonomous vehicle, operating under the company's self-driving program, was involved in a fatal accident. The vehicle, which was using machine learning algorithms to detect obstacles, failed to recognize a pedestrian crossing the road. Despite the car's sensors detecting the pedestrian, the algorithm did not react in time to prevent the collision, resulting in a tragic death.

The Uber case demonstrates the importance of ensuring that machine learning models are thoroughly tested and validated, particularly in safety-critical applications. In this instance, the lack of robust real-time testing and validation led to the loss of human life. It is essential for data science teams working on such high-risk applications to conduct rigorous testing and validation to ensure safety and reliability.

Theranos: Misleading Data for Health Tech Innovation

Theranos, a health tech company that claimed to revolutionize blood testing, faced a massive downfall after it was revealed that the data behind its claims was misleading. The company used faulty technology to produce inaccurate test results, and its leadership misled investors, doctors, and patients about the capabilities of its devices.

This case underscores the importance of transparency and accuracy in data science. Manipulating data or presenting results that are not supported by reliable evidence can have severe consequences, particularly in fields like healthcare. Ethical responsibility and scientific integrity are fundamental when working with data that impacts people's lives.

Key Takeaways and Future Directions: Preparing for Future Trends

As data science continues to evolve, understanding key takeaways from past experiences and recognizing future trends is crucial for success. This section highlights lessons learned, outlines emerging trends, and offers guidance for those preparing for the next wave of advancements in the field.

Embrace Continuous Learning and Adaptation

One of the most significant takeaways from the case studies in data science is the importance of continuous learning. The field is rapidly evolving, with new algorithms, tools, and techniques emerging regularly. To stay competitive, data scientists must remain open to learning and adapting to new developments. This includes upskilling in areas like machine learning, deep learning, and data engineering, as well as keeping up with the latest advancements in data privacy, security, and ethics.

Organizations must create a culture of continuous learning to empower their data science teams. This could involve regular training, attending conferences, participating in webinars, and encouraging collaboration between teams to share knowledge. Those who do not adapt risk falling behind in an increasingly competitive landscape.

Addressing Ethical Considerations from the Start

The importance of ethics in data science cannot be overstated. As demonstrated in the failures of Amazon's hiring tool and Target's pregnancy prediction model, a lack of attention to ethical considerations can lead to negative outcomes. Moving forward, data scientists must prioritize ethics, transparency, and fairness when developing algorithms and using data. This can be achieved by establishing clear guidelines, conducting bias audits, and involving ethicists in the design and implementation of data-driven systems.

Companies should integrate ethical frameworks into their data science workflows to ensure responsible practices. Proactively addressing ethical issues early on prevents costly setbacks and helps maintain public trust.

Leveraging Emerging Technologies for Innovation

The future of data science is heavily influenced by emerging technologies such as quantum computing, artificial intelligence, and blockchain. Quantum computing, in particular, holds promise for solving complex problems in areas like cryptography, optimization, and simulation. Data scientists who familiarize themselves with these technologies and explore how they can integrate them into their workflows will be better prepared for future advancements.

Artificial intelligence continues to make strides in automation and efficiency, and its applications will only expand. From automated machine learning (AutoML) to natural language processing (NLP), data scientists must be ready to embrace and experiment with these innovations to drive more sophisticated insights and solutions.

Blockchain, with its emphasis on decentralized and secure data management, is also poised to disrupt data science practices. Understanding how blockchain can be used to ensure data integrity, privacy, and transparency will be crucial for those involved in data-driven projects.

Collaboration Across Disciplines

Finally, the future of data science will increasingly involve interdisciplinary collaboration. Data scientists must work alongside domain experts, engineers, business analysts, and ethicists to deliver impactful solutions. The combination of technical expertise and domain knowledge is essential for understanding complex problems and providing actionable insights.

Future data science teams will need to be highly collaborative, leveraging diverse perspectives and skill sets. By fostering a culture of collaboration, organizations can ensure that their data science initiatives are well-rounded, effective, and aligned with business objectives.

Part 2:

Data Science Programming Languages

Overview of Programming Languages for Data Science
Selecting the right programming language for data science is essential for achieving optimal performance. This module covers the criteria for choosing a language, such as versatility, community support, and tools. We explore the strengths and weaknesses of popular languages like Python, R, and Julia, with a focus on their roles in data manipulation, statistical analysis, and high-performance computing. Additionally, we discuss emerging languages like Rust and Go, which are gaining traction for their efficiency and potential in data science. Finally, we explore how different languages can be combined to leverage their unique strengths in multilingual projects.

Python for Data Science
Python is a dominant language in data science due to its simplicity and powerful ecosystem. This module introduces Python's key libraries such as Pandas for data manipulation, Matplotlib and Seaborn for data visualization, and Scikit-learn for machine learning. We focus on data cleaning, visualization techniques, and building machine learning models using these libraries. By the end, learners will be able to efficiently use Python to perform a variety of data science tasks, from dataset preparation to model building.

R for Statistical Computing
R is renowned for its statistical analysis and data visualization capabilities. This module dives into R's key features, including libraries like dplyr and tidyr for data manipulation and ggplot2 for creating visualizations. We also explore advanced statistical techniques, such as regression analysis and Bayesian modeling. R's unique focus on statistical computing makes it an excellent tool for academics and statisticians looking to perform complex data analysis.

SQL and NoSQL for Data Science
SQL remains essential for querying structured data, and this module covers its role in data science. We explore advanced SQL techniques, including aggregate functions, window functions, and Common Table Expressions (CTEs). The module also introduces NoSQL databases like MongoDB and Cassandra, highlighting their use cases in handling unstructured data. Furthermore, we explore querying big data through tools like Presto and Google BigQuery, which enable data scientists to process large datasets efficiently.

Scala and Spark for Big Data Analytics
Scala, with its functional programming paradigm, is an excellent language for big data analytics. This module introduces Scala's role in data science, particularly through its integration with Apache Spark. Learners will explore the core components of Spark, its distributed processing capabilities, and how Spark's MLlib library supports building scalable machine learning models. The module emphasizes how Scala and Spark enable efficient big data analytics and ETL (Extract, Transform, Load) pipelines.

Julia for High-Performance Data Science
Julia is gaining popularity for high-performance data science tasks, particularly in numerical and scientific computing. This module covers the key features of Julia, including its ability to handle large datasets with ease and perform computations faster than Python or R. We explore Julia's data science libraries such as DataFrames and Flux.jl for machine learning. Learners will also compare Julia's performance with other languages and understand when to use it for performance-critical applications.

Comparing Programming Languages
In this module, we compare Python, R, Julia, and other programming languages to help learners make informed

decisions based on project needs. We discuss the trade-offs in performance, usability, and available tools. Additionally, we explore how to integrate multiple languages in a single project, using tools like PySpark and reticulate, which allow for smooth transitions between languages. Industry examples illustrate how to select the right language for specific data science tasks.

Module 8:

Overview of Programming Languages for Data Science

In data science, programming languages play a crucial role in developing and deploying models, analyzing data, and creating visualizations. This module explores the criteria for selecting programming languages, compares popular ones like Python, R, and Julia, and examines emerging languages such as Rust and Go. Understanding these languages is essential for effective data science work.

Criteria for Choosing a Programming Language: Versatility, Community, and Tools

When selecting a programming language for data science, versatility, community support, and available tools are key factors. A versatile language can handle a wide range of tasks, from data cleaning to machine learning. Strong community support ensures access to resources like tutorials, forums, and libraries. Furthermore, the availability of specialized libraries and tools—such as TensorFlow for deep learning or Pandas for data manipulation—greatly enhances productivity. Choosing a language with a rich ecosystem of tools and an active community can significantly streamline the development process and accelerate learning.

Strengths and Weaknesses of Popular Languages: Python, R, Julia, and More

Python is the most popular language in data science due to its simplicity, readability, and extensive libraries like Pandas and Scikit-learn. Its vast community provides continuous support and development. R is preferred for statistical analysis and data visualization, offering powerful libraries like ggplot2 and dplyr. Julia, while newer, excels in high-performance computing, making it ideal for large-scale numerical analysis. However, Python's slower execution speed compared to Julia may limit its use in performance-critical tasks. Each language has its strengths and weaknesses, and the choice depends on the project's specific requirements.

Interoperability and Multilingual Support: Combining Languages Effectively

In real-world data science projects, using multiple languages can enhance efficiency. Interoperability allows data scientists to combine the strengths of different languages. For instance, Python's versatility can be paired with R's statistical capabilities, or Julia's performance can be combined with Python's extensive libraries. Tools like Jupyter notebooks, which support multiple languages, facilitate seamless integration. Additionally, using APIs and packages like rpy2 and pyjulia helps bridge the gap between languages, enabling data scientists to leverage the best features of each language in a single project, ensuring optimal performance and flexibility.

Emerging Languages in Data Science: Rust, Go, and other Up-and-Comers

As data science continues to evolve, new programming languages are gaining attention for their performance and efficiency. Rust, known for its memory safety and speed, is emerging as a potential alternative to Python for performance-critical applications. Go, with its simplicity and concurrency features, is increasingly used for large-scale data processing and system design. These languages offer compelling advantages in specific contexts, particularly in high-performance computing and real-time data applications. As data science faces growing demands for efficiency and scalability, these emerging languages are likely to play a larger role in shaping the future of the field.

Criteria for Choosing a Programming Language: Versatility, Community, and Tools

Selecting the right programming language is a fundamental step in data science. The choice impacts everything from project efficiency to the available ecosystem of libraries, tools, and frameworks. In this section, we will explore key criteria for choosing a programming language in data science, focusing on versatility, community support, and the availability of tools.

Versatility: Flexibility across Domains

One of the primary factors when choosing a programming language for data science is its versatility. A good language should be capable of handling various tasks in the data science pipeline, including data manipulation, visualization, statistical analysis, and machine learning. It should be adaptable to different domains and industries, whether it's healthcare, finance, or marketing.

For example, Python is renowned for its versatility. It can be used for web development, automation, and machine learning applications, making it a preferred choice across multiple domains. This versatility is particularly important for data scientists who often work on end-to-end workflows, needing to manipulate data, build models, and deploy solutions. Python's ability to interface with different systems and perform various tasks in one environment streamlines workflows and increases productivity.

Community Support: Access to Knowledge and Collaboration

A robust and active community is essential when choosing a programming language. Community support enables data scientists to access resources such as tutorials, forums, and open-source projects, which can significantly accelerate learning and troubleshooting. In addition, having a strong community fosters the growth of a language through continuous updates, bug fixes, and new features.

Python, for example, has one of the largest and most active data science communities, which makes it a reliable language for solving problems. The Python Package Index (PyPI) contains thousands of libraries and tools tailored to data science, making it easy to implement a solution for almost any problem. Similarly, R has a well-established community, particularly in academic and statistical research, offering numerous specialized packages for statistical analysis and data visualization.

Tools and Libraries: Building Efficient Workflows

The availability of powerful tools and libraries is another critical factor when choosing a programming language. For data scientists, this includes libraries for data manipulation, statistical analysis, visualization, machine learning, and deep learning. The broader the selection of libraries, the more tools data scientists have at their disposal to solve complex problems without reinventing the wheel.

Python stands out for its rich ecosystem of libraries like Pandas for data manipulation, Matplotlib and Seaborn for data visualization, and TensorFlow, Keras, and Scikit-learn for machine learning and deep learning. R is similarly known for its extensive statistical and data visualization libraries, such as ggplot2 and dplyr. In contrast, Julia, while growing in popularity, still lags behind Python and R in terms of available libraries but is gaining attention in the high-performance computing space.

Choosing the Right Tool for the Task

Ultimately, the ideal programming language depends on the specific needs of the data science project. A versatile language with an active community and rich toolsets will help data scientists work efficiently, collaborate with others, and stay current with evolving trends in the field. The right language empowers data scientists to focus on solving problems rather than wrestling with technical limitations.

Strengths and Weaknesses of Popular Languages: Python, R, Julia, and More

Choosing a programming language in data science often comes down to the specific needs of a project, the strengths and weaknesses of available languages, and the expertise of the data science team. In this section, we'll examine the strengths and weaknesses of some of the most popular programming languages for data science: Python, R, Julia, and a few others.

Python: Strengths and Versatility

Python is the most widely used language in data science, favored for its versatility, ease of learning, and powerful ecosystem of libraries. Its strengths lie in its wide applicability across many domains, from data manipulation with Pandas to machine learning with Scikit-learn, TensorFlow, and PyTorch. Python's syntax is easy to understand, making it an excellent choice for both beginners and experienced data scientists.

However, Python does have some weaknesses. Despite its versatility, it can be slower than some other languages like C++ or Java, especially for computationally intensive tasks. Python's performance can be a bottleneck in large-scale data processing tasks, although this can be mitigated through optimization techniques or by leveraging Python bindings to more efficient languages.

R: Statistical Power with a Steep Learning Curve

R is a language specifically designed for statistical analysis, making it the preferred tool for statisticians and academics. It has a rich ecosystem of libraries tailored to complex statistical models, hypothesis testing, and visualizations (e.g., ggplot2, dplyr). R also excels in generating high-quality plots and graphs, which makes it popular in research and academia.

However, R has some drawbacks. Its syntax can be more difficult to learn compared to Python, and while it is highly specialized for statistics, it is less versatile for other tasks such as web development or general-purpose programming. Additionally, R's performance can be limited when working with large datasets, especially compared to Python or Julia.

Julia: Speed and Performance for Scientific Computing

Julia is a relatively new language in the data science space, designed with performance in mind. It offers the speed of low-level languages like C and Fortran, making it an excellent choice for computationally intensive applications such as numerical simulations, machine learning, and data analysis. Julia's just-in-time (JIT) compilation allows it to execute code at near-C speeds, offering significant performance advantages over Python and R in certain tasks.

Despite its speed, Julia is still growing in terms of community support and libraries. While it has made great strides in scientific computing, it lacks the extensive ecosystem of Python and R. This can make it harder to find pre-existing solutions for common data science tasks, and it may require more effort to implement certain workflows.

Other Languages: SQL, Java, and Scala

SQL remains the primary language for querying databases and is indispensable for data extraction and transformation in most data workflows. Its strength lies in its simplicity and efficiency for working with structured data. However, it is limited in terms of data manipulation and analytics capabilities compared to languages like Python or R.

Java and Scala, often used in big data systems like Hadoop and Spark, are powerful in distributed computing but are not as user-friendly or specialized for data analysis as Python and R. Java's verbosity and Scala's steep learning curve can deter data scientists who prioritize ease of use and rapid development.

Interoperability and Multilingual Support: Combining Languages Effectively

In data science, no single language can do it all. Often, data scientists and engineers need to combine multiple languages to take advantage of their individual strengths. This section will explore how different languages can work together in a data science workflow, improving both performance and productivity. By leveraging interoperability and multilingual support, you can optimize your data science projects to meet specific needs.

Combining Python and R for Specialized Tasks

Python and R are two of the most widely used languages in data science, and they often complement each other well. Python, with its versatility and extensive machine learning libraries, is used for general-purpose programming and building scalable solutions. Meanwhile, R's strength lies in statistical analysis and complex data visualization.

One common practice is to use Python for data wrangling, machine learning model building, and deploying applications, while relying on R for sophisticated statistical analysis and creating publication-ready plots. To facilitate interoperability, tools like rpy2 allow Python users to access R functionalities directly from Python scripts. This seamless integration can save time and effort by avoiding the need to manually switch between languages.

Using Python and SQL for Data Extraction

SQL is the go-to language for querying databases and extracting large volumes of data. In many data science workflows, SQL is used in combination with Python to handle data extraction and manipulation. Python's Pandas library is well-suited for handling data once it's retrieved from a database, and tools like SQLAlchemy allow for easy interaction with relational databases.

For example, one can write SQL queries in Python using libraries like sqlite3 or pandas' .read_sql() function to load data from a database into a Pandas DataFrame.

84

Afterward, Python can be used to clean, transform, and analyze the data, leveraging its broad ecosystem of machine learning libraries. This combination gives you the power of SQL for data extraction, along with Python's flexibility for data manipulation and analysis.

Integrating Python with Big Data Technologies

For big data projects, languages like Java and Scala are often used to work with distributed systems, particularly in the Hadoop ecosystem and with tools like Apache Spark. However, Python can be integrated into these workflows using libraries like PySpark. PySpark allows Python users to write Spark applications and perform large-scale data processing directly within their familiar Python environment.

This ability to combine the simplicity of Python with the performance of distributed systems makes it a powerful tool in big data contexts. Moreover, Python's machine learning libraries, such as Scikit-learn and TensorFlow, can be integrated with these big data systems for predictive modeling, while using Spark for handling massive datasets.

Using Julia with Python for Performance Boosts

While Python is versatile, its speed may not always be sufficient for computationally demanding tasks. Julia, known for its high performance, can be integrated with Python to take advantage of Julia's speed while still utilizing Python's broader ecosystem.

Python's PyJulia package allows seamless communication between Python and Julia, enabling data scientists to call Julia functions from Python code. This interoperability can be particularly useful when working with machine learning models or simulations that require significant computational power. By combining Python's flexibility and Julia's performance, you can create highly efficient and scalable data science applications.

Emerging Languages in Data Science: Rust, Go, and other Up-and-Comers

As data science continues to evolve, new programming languages are emerging that promise to address the shortcomings of existing languages. Rust, Go, and other up-and-coming languages are increasingly gaining attention for their performance, concurrency, and memory management capabilities. In this section, we'll explore these emerging languages and their potential in the world of data science.

Rust: Performance and Memory Safety

Rust is gaining popularity for its emphasis on memory safety and performance. It is particularly well-suited for systems programming, where control over memory allocation and low-level optimization is crucial. Unlike languages like C or C++, Rust's unique ownership system ensures memory safety without the need for a garbage collector, making it a great choice for performance-critical applications.

In data science, Rust can be used for building high-performance computing systems, data pipelines, and machine learning libraries. Its growing ecosystem, with libraries like ndarray for numerical computing, makes it an increasingly attractive alternative to Python in scenarios where performance is critical. By leveraging Rust's low-level control and high-speed execution, data scientists can build tools and algorithms that can handle large datasets more efficiently than Python.

Go: Concurrency and Scalability

Go (or Golang) is another emerging language that is becoming popular in data science, especially for distributed systems and parallel processing. Go was designed by Google to address the limitations of concurrency in traditional languages. Its simple syntax and built-in support for goroutines make it ideal for building scalable systems and managing concurrent tasks.

In data science, Go is increasingly being used in developing data pipelines, back-end services, and APIs for real-time data processing. For tasks that involve handling multiple simultaneous connections, Go's concurrency model can significantly reduce overhead and improve performance. Although Go is not yet as widely adopted in data science as Python, its performance and ease of use make it a promising candidate for large-scale data applications.

Other Emerging Languages: Kotlin and Swift

Other emerging languages like Kotlin and Swift are also starting to make their mark in the data science space. Kotlin, originally developed for Android development, has gained attention for its modern syntax and compatibility with Java. Its potential in data science lies in its ability to interact with Java-based tools and frameworks, offering a more concise and expressive alternative to Java for building data-centric applications.

Swift, traditionally associated with iOS and macOS development, has gained traction as a potential language for data science. Apple's Swift for TensorFlow project has demonstrated the language's ability to handle machine learning tasks, making it an exciting prospect for data scientists working in Apple's ecosystem. While Swift is still in its early stages for data science, its emphasis on performance and safety could make it a strong contender in the future.

Embracing a Multilingual Future

While Python continues to dominate the data science landscape, emerging languages like Rust, Go, Kotlin, and Swift are carving out their own niches. These languages offer unique advantages in terms of performance, concurrency, and memory management, which can be leveraged for specific use cases in data science. As the data science ecosystem grows, it's likely that these languages will become more integrated into workflows, offering new possibilities for building scalable, efficient, and performant data systems.

Module 9:

Python for Data Science

Python has become the go-to language for data science due to its versatility, readability, and a powerful ecosystem of libraries. This module provides an overview of Python's strengths, focusing on its libraries for data manipulation, visualization, and machine learning. Mastering Python's tools is essential for any data scientist aiming to tackle complex datasets and build impactful models.

Python Ecosystem and Libraries: An Overview of Python's Strengths

Python's ecosystem is vast, with libraries that address nearly every aspect of data science. Libraries like NumPy provide efficient numerical operations, while Pandas excels in data manipulation and cleaning. Matplotlib and Seaborn make data visualization accessible, and Scikit-learn simplifies machine learning. Python's simple syntax and powerful libraries make it a versatile tool for both beginners and experts in data science. The active community behind Python ensures continuous development of resources and tools, further cementing its status as the preferred language for data analysis and machine learning.

Data Manipulation with Pandas: Cleaning and Preparing Datasets

Pandas is a cornerstone of data manipulation in Python. It allows data scientists to handle structured data with ease, offering features like DataFrames for storing tabular data. With Pandas, cleaning and preparing datasets—such as handling missing values, filtering data, and transforming columns—becomes straightforward. The library also supports merging and reshaping datasets, crucial for integrating different data sources. Its integration with other libraries like NumPy ensures seamless handling of large datasets, making it an indispensable tool for preprocessing data before analysis or modeling.

Data Visualization with Matplotlib and Seaborn: Creating Clear Visuals

Visualization is a key part of data science, and Python offers powerful libraries like Matplotlib and Seaborn for creating insightful plots. Matplotlib provides a flexible framework for creating a wide range of visualizations, including line plots, bar charts, and histograms. Seaborn builds on Matplotlib, offering a high-level interface that simplifies the creation of beautiful, informative visuals with minimal code. Data scientists use these libraries to uncover trends, detect outliers, and communicate findings effectively. By using clear, well-designed visuals, Python enables data scientists to present data insights in an easily digestible format.

Machine Learning with Scikit-learn: From Simple Models to Pipelines

Scikit-learn is the go-to library for machine learning in Python, offering tools for everything from simple regression models to complex classification algorithms. It provides implementations of many machine learning techniques, including decision trees, support vector machines, and k-means clustering. Scikit-learn's pipeline feature simplifies the process of applying multiple machine learning steps, from data preprocessing to model evaluation. By automating tasks like feature scaling and model selection, Scikit-learn allows data scientists to build, evaluate, and deploy machine learning models efficiently, making it a fundamental library for predictive analytics.

Python Ecosystem and Libraries: An Overview of Python's Strengths

Python has emerged as the leading programming language in the field of data science due to its simplicity, versatility, and extensive ecosystem of libraries and tools. This section provides an overview of Python's strengths, emphasizing the libraries that make it a powerful tool for data manipulation, analysis, visualization, and machine learning.

Ease of Use and Readability

One of the key reasons Python is favored by data scientists is its ease of use and readability. Its syntax is clean and simple, which allows data scientists to focus more on solving problems and less on debugging complex code. This is especially important in data science, where complex data transformations and analyses must be performed efficiently and accurately. Python's readability makes it an accessible choice for both beginners and experienced professionals, enabling collaborative work across teams with diverse skill sets.

Rich Ecosystem of Libraries

Python's ecosystem is perhaps the most important factor that drives its popularity in data science. The language offers a wide array of libraries for nearly every aspect of data science, ranging from data manipulation and analysis to machine learning and visualization.

- **Pandas**: For data manipulation and analysis, pandas is indispensable. It provides powerful data structures, like DataFrames and Series, which allow for easy manipulation of structured data.

- **NumPy**: For numerical computing, NumPy is a core library in the ecosystem. It allows for high-performance matrix operations and is integrated with many other libraries.

- **Matplotlib and Seaborn**: These libraries are designed for data visualization. Matplotlib offers basic plotting capabilities, while Seaborn builds on it with enhanced statistical graphics.

- **SciPy**: This library builds on NumPy and provides additional functionality for scientific computing, such as optimization, integration, and signal processing.

- **Scikit-learn**: This is a key library for machine learning, offering a wide range of tools for building and evaluating models, from simple regression to advanced clustering.

This diverse ecosystem means that Python can handle nearly every aspect of a data science project, from gathering and cleaning data to building complex models.

Integration with Other Tools

Python's ability to integrate with other programming languages and tools further strengthens its position in data science. For example, Python can interact with databases through libraries like SQLAlchemy, allowing for efficient data retrieval and storage. It also integrates well with big data tools like Apache Spark and Hadoop, making it an ideal choice for large-scale data processing. Python's compatibility with cloud services (AWS, Google Cloud, Azure) allows data scientists to leverage scalable computing resources for their analyses.

Additionally, Python can be embedded within web applications, making it an excellent choice for building data-driven applications that need real-time insights or predictions.

Active Community and Support

Another factor contributing to Python's strength in data science is its large and active community. Python's open-source nature means that it is constantly being improved and updated. There are numerous forums, online courses, and tutorials available, which makes it easy for beginners to start learning and for experienced developers to troubleshoot issues. The community also provides support through conferences, meetups, and webinars, ensuring that Python continues to evolve in line with the latest data science trends and technologies.

Python's Dominance in Data Science

Python's combination of simplicity, powerful libraries, integration capabilities, and community support has made it the go-to language for data science. Whether you are cleaning data, building models, or visualizing insights, Python's rich ecosystem provides the necessary tools to streamline the workflow and facilitate successful data-driven decision-making. Its continued growth and adaptability promise to keep it at the forefront of the data science landscape for the foreseeable future.

Data Manipulation with Pandas: Cleaning and Preparing Datasets

Data manipulation is a crucial aspect of data science, and pandas is the go-to library for this task in Python. With its powerful DataFrame structure and various built-in functions, pandas simplifies the cleaning, transformation, and preparation of data for analysis. This section explores how to use pandas for data manipulation, focusing on tasks such as handling missing values, filtering data, and transforming datasets.

Introduction to Pandas and DataFrames

At the heart of pandas lies the DataFrame — a two-dimensional, size-mutable, and potentially heterogeneous tabular data structure. It allows data to be stored in rows and columns, similar to a spreadsheet or SQL table, making it intuitive to work with. Pandas also provides a Series object, which represents one-dimensional labeled data, perfect for handling single columns or variables.

To get started with pandas, first install the library (if not already installed):

```
pip install pandas
```

Loading and Inspecting Data

The first step in any data analysis workflow is loading the data into a pandas DataFrame. This can be done with various functions depending on the data source, such as read_csv(), read_excel(), or read_sql(). Once the data is loaded, it's essential to inspect its structure to understand what needs cleaning or transformation.

```
import pandas as pd

# Load data
df = pd.read_csv('data.csv')

# Inspect the first few rows of the data
print(df.head())
```

Handling Missing Data

Real-world datasets often have missing or incomplete entries. Pandas offers several ways to deal with missing data, such as using dropna() to remove missing values or fillna() to replace them with specific values or statistical measures.

```
# Drop rows with missing values
df_cleaned = df.dropna()

# Replace missing values with the column mean
df['column_name'] = df['column_name'].fillna(df['column_name'].mean())
```

Filtering and Selecting Data

Once the data is clean, filtering and selecting relevant data is the next step. Pandas makes this task easy with powerful indexing and boolean selection. You can filter rows based on conditions, such as selecting all rows where a specific column value meets a threshold.

```
# Select rows where column 'age' is greater than 30
df_filtered = df[df['age'] > 30]
```

Pandas also supports advanced operations like grouping, aggregating, and applying functions across columns.

```
# Group data by 'gender' and calculate the mean of 'age'
df_grouped = df.groupby('gender')['age'].mean()
```

Data Transformation and Feature Engineering

Data transformation involves reshaping the data to fit the analysis or modeling needs. With pandas, you can easily manipulate data through operations like adding new columns, merging datasets, and performing mathematical transformations.

```
# Create a new column based on existing data
df['age_squared'] = df['age'] ** 2

# Merge two DataFrames
df_merged = pd.merge(df1, df2, on='id')
```

Feature engineering often involves creating new variables that help the model better understand the underlying patterns in the data. Pandas simplifies this process, whether it's extracting features from dates, scaling numerical values, or encoding categorical variables.

Efficient Data Preparation with Pandas

Pandas is an indispensable tool for data scientists, providing a flexible and powerful set of tools for data manipulation. With pandas, cleaning, transforming, and preparing data for analysis becomes a streamlined process. Its intuitive syntax and comprehensive functionality ensure that data scientists can spend more time analyzing insights and less time cleaning their data.

Data Visualization with Matplotlib and Seaborn: Creating Clear Visuals

Data visualization is a key component of data analysis, helping to convey insights in a clear and impactful way. In Python, matplotlib and seaborn are two of the most popular libraries for creating a wide range of static, animated, and interactive visualizations. This section focuses on how to use these libraries to create effective and informative data visualizations.

Introduction to Matplotlib

Matplotlib is one of the oldest and most widely used data visualization libraries in Python. It provides a wide variety of tools for creating static, interactive, and animated plots. The library is highly customizable, enabling users to create complex visualizations for a variety of data types.

To start using matplotlib, install it using:

```
pip install matplotlib
```

The core component of matplotlib is the pyplot module, which provides functions for creating plots and controlling the layout and appearance of visualizations.

```
import matplotlib.pyplot as plt

# Basic line plot
x = [1, 2, 3, 4, 5]
y = [1, 4, 9, 16, 25]

plt.plot(x, y)
plt.xlabel('X-axis')
plt.ylabel('Y-axis')
plt.title('Basic Line Plot')
plt.show()
```

Creating Visualizations with Seaborn

Seaborn is built on top of matplotlib and provides a high-level interface for drawing attractive and informative statistical graphics. It simplifies the creation of complex visualizations, such as heatmaps, pair plots, and violin plots, with just a few lines of code.

Install seaborn via pip:

```
pip install seaborn
```

One of the most common uses of seaborn is to create distribution and relationship plots that provide a deeper understanding of the data.

```
import seaborn as sns

# Load example dataset
data = sns.load_dataset('iris')

# Create a pairplot to show relationships between variables
sns.pairplot(data, hue='species')
plt.show()
```

This creates a set of scatter plots and histograms to visualize the relationships between the features in the dataset, colored by the species.

Customizing Visuals: Adding Titles, Labels, and Legends

Effective visualizations are not just about the data but also how it is presented. matplotlib and seaborn allow users to customize various aspects of the plot, including titles, axis labels, and legends, to make the plot more informative and visually appealing.

```
# Create a bar plot in Seaborn
sns.barplot(x='species', y='sepal_length', data=data)

# Customizing the plot
plt.title('Sepal Length by Species')
plt.xlabel('Species')
plt.ylabel('Sepal Length')
plt.show()
```

Advanced Visualizations with Matplotlib and Seaborn

For more advanced visualizations, matplotlib offers fine-grained control over the elements of the plot. Customizing the axes, colors, markers, and more can help highlight important features of the data.

```
# Creating a heatmap with Seaborn
correlation_matrix = data.corr()
sns.heatmap(correlation_matrix, annot=True, cmap='coolwarm')
plt.title('Correlation Heatmap')
plt.show()
```

The heatmap visualizes the relationships between numerical variables in the dataset and shows their correlation coefficients. Such visualizations help identify patterns and correlations at a glance.

Clear and Informative Visualizations

Both matplotlib and seaborn are essential tools in a data scientist's toolbox. While matplotlib provides the foundation for creating basic plots and customizing their appearance, seaborn simplifies the creation of more complex statistical visualizations. Together, these libraries enable effective communication of data insights through clear and meaningful graphics.

Machine Learning with Scikit-learn: From Simple Models to Pipelines

Scikit-learn is one of the most widely used libraries for machine learning in Python. It provides simple and efficient tools for data mining and data analysis, built on top of other powerful Python libraries like NumPy, SciPy, and matplotlib. In this section, we will explore how to use scikit-learn to build machine learning models, evaluate their performance, and create pipelines for reproducible workflows.

Introduction to Scikit-learn

Scikit-learn is a comprehensive library for machine learning, offering a wide range of algorithms for classification, regression, clustering, dimensionality reduction, and model selection. It supports a consistent API that allows users to build, evaluate, and deploy models seamlessly. To get started, install scikit-learn using:

```
pip install scikit-learn
```

Scikit-learn's core components are the datasets, models, and metrics modules. Let's begin by building a simple classification model using the famous Iris dataset.

```python
from sklearn.datasets import load_iris
from sklearn.model_selection import train_test_split
from sklearn.ensemble import RandomForestClassifier
from sklearn.metrics import accuracy_score

# Load dataset
iris = load_iris()
X = iris.data
y = iris.target

# Split dataset into training and testing sets
X_train, X_test, y_train, y_test = train_test_split(X, y, test_size=0.3,
        random_state=42)

# Create a Random Forest model
model = RandomForestClassifier()

# Train the model
model.fit(X_train, y_train)

# Make predictions
y_pred = model.predict(X_test)

# Evaluate model accuracy
accuracy = accuracy_score(y_test, y_pred)
print(f'Accuracy: {accuracy:.2f}')
```

Building and Tuning Machine Learning Models

Scikit-learn provides a wide range of algorithms for building machine learning models. These algorithms can be tuned using hyperparameters to improve model performance. For instance, when working with a decision tree classifier, you can adjust the depth of the tree to prevent overfitting:

```python
from sklearn.tree import DecisionTreeClassifier

# Create a Decision Tree model with max_depth
dt_model = DecisionTreeClassifier(max_depth=3)

# Train and evaluate the model
dt_model.fit(X_train, y_train)
y_pred_dt = dt_model.predict(X_test)
accuracy_dt = accuracy_score(y_test, y_pred_dt)
print(f'Decision Tree Accuracy: {accuracy_dt:.2f}')
```

Hyperparameter tuning is essential to optimize model performance. Scikit-learn provides tools such as GridSearchCV for performing exhaustive search over a specified parameter grid.

Model Validation and Evaluation

After building a model, it is crucial to evaluate its performance using metrics such as accuracy, precision, recall, and F1-score. Scikit-learn offers a set of tools for this purpose:

```
from sklearn.metrics import classification_report

# Print classification report
print(classification_report(y_test, y_pred))
```

This report provides a detailed view of how well the model is performing across different classes. Scikit-learn also supports cross-validation, which allows for a more reliable assessment of model performance by splitting the data into multiple training and testing sets.

```
from sklearn.model_selection import cross_val_score

# Perform cross-validation
cross_val_scores = cross_val_score(model, X, y, cv=5)
print(f'Cross-validation scores: {cross_val_scores}')
print(f'Mean cross-validation score: {cross_val_scores.mean():.2f}')
```

Creating Machine Learning Pipelines

Scikit-learn's pipeline module enables users to streamline the workflow by chaining together preprocessing steps and model training into a single object. This allows for easier experimentation and ensures reproducibility:

```
from sklearn.pipeline import Pipeline
from sklearn.preprocessing import StandardScaler

# Create a pipeline with data scaling and a classifier
pipeline = Pipeline([
    ('scaler', StandardScaler()),
    ('classifier', RandomForestClassifier())
])

# Train and evaluate the pipeline
pipeline.fit(X_train, y_train)
y_pred_pipeline = pipeline.predict(X_test)
accuracy_pipeline = accuracy_score(y_test, y_pred_pipeline)
print(f'Pipeline Accuracy: {accuracy_pipeline:.2f}')
```

The pipeline helps ensure that preprocessing steps such as scaling are applied consistently to both the training and testing data. It also simplifies the process of testing multiple models and preprocessing techniques.

Scikit-learn is an invaluable tool for machine learning in Python, providing easy-to-use functions for building, evaluating, and optimizing models. The ability to create pipelines for end-to-end machine learning workflows ensures reproducibility and efficiency, making it an essential library for data science practitioners.

Module 10:

R for Statistical Computing

R is a powerful language specifically designed for statistical computing and data visualization. This module delves into R's key features for data science, exploring its capabilities in data manipulation, visualization, and statistical modeling. By mastering R, data scientists can perform in-depth analysis and create insightful visualizations to inform decisions.

Key Features of R for Data Science: Visualization and Statistics-Focused

R is widely recognized for its statistical and visualization capabilities. Unlike general-purpose programming languages, R is tailored for data analysis, offering a comprehensive suite of statistical tools. It excels at hypothesis testing, statistical modeling, and creating visually appealing graphics. The R ecosystem includes numerous packages that streamline data manipulation, statistical analysis, and plotting, making it a go-to language for data scientists working with complex datasets. R's focus on statistics allows data professionals to perform advanced analyses with ease, making it indispensable for statisticians and researchers.

Data Manipulation with dplyr and tidyr: Reshaping and Analyzing Data

Data manipulation in R is facilitated by powerful packages like dplyr and tidyr. dplyr simplifies tasks like filtering, summarizing, and arranging data, allowing data scientists to efficiently transform datasets. tidyr complements dplyr by focusing on reshaping data, helping analysts "tidy" data for easier analysis. These packages enable data scientists to clean, organize, and explore data quickly, ensuring a smooth workflow from raw data to meaningful insights. Together, dplyr and tidyr provide a flexible and intuitive approach to data manipulation, making them essential tools in the R ecosystem.

Visualization with ggplot2: Creating Elegant and Complex Plots

ggplot2 is one of the most powerful data visualization libraries in R. It enables users to create elegant, complex plots using a layered grammar of graphics. ggplot2 supports a wide range of visualizations, from bar charts to scatter plots and heatmaps, allowing data scientists to effectively communicate insights. Its flexibility and customization options make it suitable for a variety of datasets, from simple exploratory analysis to detailed, publication-quality visuals. By mastering ggplot2, data scientists can visually represent data relationships, trends, and distributions, enhancing the clarity of their findings and making data more accessible.

Statistical Models and Beyond: Advanced Regression and Bayesian Modeling

R is renowned for its advanced statistical modeling capabilities. It offers a wide range of regression techniques, including linear, logistic, and generalized linear models. For more complex analyses, R supports Bayesian modeling through packages like rstan and brms, which enable probabilistic modeling and inference. These tools allow data scientists to model uncertainty and make predictions based on prior knowledge. R's robust statistical framework empowers users to perform sophisticated analyses, including time series forecasting and machine learning algorithms. By leveraging R for statistical models, data scientists can tackle complex problems and derive actionable insights.

Key Features of R for Data Science: Visualization and Statistics-Focused

R is a powerful programming language specifically designed for statistical computing and data analysis. Its widespread use in academia and research has made it a go-to tool for statisticians, data scientists, and analysts. This section will explore the key features of R, focusing on its strengths in visualization and statistical analysis.

R's Strength in Statistics

R was built from the ground up with statistics in mind, and its extensive set of statistical functions makes it an excellent choice for data analysis. R's capabilities span from basic descriptive statistics to more advanced techniques, such as hypothesis testing, regression analysis, and time series forecasting. For example, performing linear regression in R can be done easily using the lm() function:

```
# Linear regression example in R
data(mtcars)
model <- lm(mpg ~ wt + hp, data = mtcars)
summary(model)
```

This simple line of code fits a linear model to predict miles per gallon (mpg) based on weight (wt) and horsepower (hp). The output gives us coefficients, R-squared, p-values, and more, enabling in-depth analysis of relationships between variables.

Data Manipulation with R

R's data manipulation capabilities are largely enhanced by the dplyr and tidyr packages, both of which provide intuitive functions for reshaping and summarizing data. dplyr allows users to filter, select, and summarize data efficiently using verbs like filter(), select(), and summarize():

```
library(dplyr)

# Using dplyr to filter and summarize data
mtcars %>%
  filter(mpg > 20) %>%
  summarize(mean_hp = mean(hp))
```

The above code filters rows where mpg is greater than 20 and calculates the mean horsepower (hp) for these rows. tidyr, on the other hand, focuses on reshaping data, making it easy to convert between wide and long formats using functions like gather() and spread().

Visualization with ggplot2

One of R's most powerful features is its ability to create elegant and insightful visualizations using the ggplot2 package. ggplot2 is based on the Grammar of Graphics, which provides a systematic approach to creating visual representations of data. Here's an example of creating a scatter plot with ggplot2:

```
library(ggplot2)

# Scatter plot using ggplot2
ggplot(mtcars, aes(x = wt, y = mpg)) +
    geom_point() +
    theme_minimal() +
    labs(title = "Scatter Plot of Weight vs. MPG",
        x = "Weight (1000 lbs)",
        y = "Miles per Gallon")
```

This code generates a scatter plot of the mtcars dataset, displaying the relationship between weight and miles per gallon. ggplot2 provides a flexible and consistent approach to creating complex plots, from basic visualizations like histograms and bar charts to more sophisticated plots such as heatmaps and faceted grids.

R for Statistical Modeling

Beyond basic statistics, R excels in more advanced statistical modeling. For example, R provides powerful tools for fitting complex models, including multiple linear regression, logistic regression, and even Bayesian models. A logistic regression model in R can be created using the glm() function, which allows users to model binary outcomes:

```
# Logistic regression example in R
data(iris)
model <- glm(Species ~ Sepal.Length + Sepal.Width, data = iris, family =
        binomial)
summary(model)
```

In this example, a logistic regression model is built to predict the species of the iris flowers based on their sepal length and width. R's flexibility with statistical models enables data scientists to quickly implement and evaluate various modeling approaches.

R's specialized capabilities in statistical analysis and visualization make it a key tool for data scientists working with large datasets and complex statistical tasks. Its powerful ecosystem, from data manipulation with dplyr and tidyr to advanced statistical modeling, ensures that R remains a central part of the data science toolkit. By mastering R, data scientists can leverage its full potential for data exploration, visualization, and modeling.

Data Manipulation with dplyr and tidyr: Reshaping and Analyzing Data

Data manipulation is an essential skill for data scientists, as it enables them to clean, reshape, and analyze datasets before applying any advanced analysis or modeling techniques. R, with its powerful packages dplyr and tidyr, offers efficient tools for performing a wide range of data manipulation tasks. In this section, we will explore how to use these packages to transform raw data into meaningful insights.

Overview of dplyr for Data Manipulation

The dplyr package is one of the most popular tools for data manipulation in R. It provides a set of easy-to-use functions that allow users to manipulate data frames with minimal effort. The core functions of dplyr are designed around a set of verbs, each representing a specific type of operation. Some of the most commonly used functions include:

- filter(): Select rows based on certain conditions.

- select(): Choose specific columns.

- mutate(): Create new variables or modify existing ones.

- summarize(): Apply summary statistics to the data.

- arrange(): Order the data by one or more variables.

Here's an example of using dplyr to filter and summarize data:

```
library(dplyr)

# Example data from the mtcars dataset
data(mtcars)

# Filter cars with mpg > 20 and summarize the average horsepower
result <- mtcars %>%
  filter(mpg > 20) %>%
  summarize(mean_hp = mean(hp))

print(result)
```

In this code, we use filter() to select rows where miles per gallon (mpg) is greater than 20, and then summarize() calculates the average horsepower (hp) for those rows. This highlights how easily dplyr can help manipulate data for specific insights.

Using tidyr for Data Reshaping

100

While dplyr is excellent for manipulation and summarization, the tidyr package is designed specifically for reshaping data. Sometimes, raw data might be in an inconvenient format, such as wide format (multiple columns representing different variables) that needs to be transformed into a long format (one column representing all values of a variable). tidyr provides functions to easily handle these transformations, such as:

- gather(): Converts wide data to long format.

- spread(): Converts long data to wide format.

- separate(): Splits a single column into multiple columns.

- unite(): Combines multiple columns into one.

Here's an example of how to use gather() and spread() to reshape data:

```
library(tidyr)

# Example data with sales data in wide format
sales_data <- data.frame(
  year = c(2020, 2021, 2022),
  product_A = c(100, 120, 130),
  product_B = c(80, 110, 140)
)

# Convert from wide to long format
long_data <- gather(sales_data, key = "product", value = "sales", -year)

print(long_data)

# Convert back to wide format
wide_data <- spread(long_data, key = "product", value = "sales")

print(wide_data)
```

The gather() function transforms the dataset from a wide format, where each product has its own column, to a long format where all product sales are stacked in a single column. The spread() function can reverse this transformation.

Handling Missing Data

A common challenge in data manipulation is dealing with missing values. dplyr and tidyr provide straightforward ways to address missing data. For example, mutate() can be used to replace missing values with the mean or median of the column:

```
# Replace missing values with the column mean
mtcars[is.na(mtcars)] <- mean(mtcars$mpg, na.rm = TRUE)
```

Alternatively, you can use tidyr's fill() function to propagate values forward or backward in a dataset:

```
# Fill missing values with the previous value in the column
```

```
data_with_na <- data.frame(a = c(1, NA, 3, NA, 5))
filled_data <- fill(data_with_na, a)
```

These techniques allow for efficient handling of missing data, ensuring that the dataset remains usable for analysis.

Data manipulation is a fundamental skill in data science, and R's dplyr and tidyr packages make it easy to clean, reshape, and analyze data. By mastering these packages, data scientists can prepare their datasets for analysis and visualization, enabling them to extract valuable insights. Whether it's filtering data, summarizing statistics, or reshaping tables, these packages provide the flexibility needed to tackle a wide range of data manipulation tasks.

Visualization with ggplot2: Creating Elegant and Complex Plots

Effective data visualization is a crucial part of data science, as it allows for the clear communication of complex insights. R's ggplot2 package is one of the most powerful and flexible tools for creating elegant, complex plots. It is based on the "Grammar of Graphics" philosophy, which provides a systematic approach to building visualizations by layering components. This section explores how to use ggplot2 to create meaningful and visually appealing plots.

Overview of ggplot2

ggplot2 is a highly versatile package for creating a wide variety of static, interactive, and complex visualizations. Unlike traditional plotting systems, ggplot2 builds plots layer by layer, allowing users to specify different elements of the plot, such as data, aesthetics, geometry, and statistics. The core syntax in ggplot2 involves specifying a dataset and mapping variables to aesthetics (such as position, color, and size) and then adding layers that define the type of plot, such as points, lines, or bars.

The basic syntax for ggplot2 is as follows:

```
ggplot(data, aes(x = variable_x, y = variable_y)) +
  geom_type()
```

Where:

- data is the dataset to be used.

- aes() maps variables to plot aesthetics (e.g., x, y, color).

- geom_type() defines the type of plot (e.g., geom_point() for scatter plots, geom_line() for line plots).

Creating Basic Plots with ggplot2

The simplicity of ggplot2 allows users to create basic plots quickly. For example, a scatter plot of mpg (miles per gallon) versus hp (horsepower) from the mtcars dataset can be created using the following code:

```
library(ggplot2)

# Basic scatter plot
ggplot(mtcars, aes(x = hp, y = mpg)) +
  geom_point()
```

In this example, ggplot() initializes the plot, and geom_point() adds a scatter plot layer. The aes() function maps the hp variable to the x-axis and the mpg variable to the y-axis. This produces a simple visualization of the relationship between horsepower and miles per gallon.

Customizing Visualizations

One of the strengths of ggplot2 is the ease with which visualizations can be customized. You can change colors, shapes, sizes, and labels, allowing for a more informative and visually appealing plot. For instance, to add color to the points based on the number of cylinders (cyl) in the mtcars dataset, you can modify the code as follows:

```
ggplot(mtcars, aes(x = hp, y = mpg, color = factor(cyl))) +
  geom_point() +
  labs(color = "Number of Cylinders") +
  theme_minimal()
```

This code adds a color scale to the scatter plot, with different colors representing different numbers of cylinders in the cars. The labs() function is used to add a legend title, and theme_minimal() changes the plot's background to a clean, minimalistic style.

Complex Plots: Facets and Geometric Layers

For more complex visualizations, ggplot2 allows users to add multiple layers to a plot and create facets (subplots) for comparing data across different categories. For example, to create a series of scatter plots of mpg versus hp, separated by the number of cylinders (cyl), you can use the facet_wrap() function:

```
ggplot(mtcars, aes(x = hp, y = mpg, color = factor(cyl))) +
  geom_point() +
  facet_wrap(~ cyl) +
  theme_minimal()
```

This code generates a scatter plot for each value of cyl, allowing you to compare the relationship between horsepower and miles per gallon for cars with different cylinder counts. The facet_wrap() function automatically creates a grid of plots based on the cyl variable.

Advanced Plotting Techniques

ggplot2 also supports more advanced visualizations, such as heatmaps, violin plots, and density plots, by adding specific geometric layers. For example, to create a violin plot showing the distribution of mpg for different values of cyl, you can use the geom_violin() function:

```
ggplot(mtcars, aes(x = factor(cyl), y = mpg)) +
  geom_violin() +
  labs(x = "Number of Cylinders", y = "Miles per Gallon") +
  theme_minimal()
```

This plot provides a visual summary of the distribution of miles per gallon for cars with different cylinder counts, helping to identify patterns and outliers.

The ggplot2 package is an essential tool in R for creating beautiful, informative, and complex visualizations. By leveraging its powerful syntax and flexibility, data scientists can build a wide range of plots to communicate insights effectively. Whether creating simple scatter plots or advanced faceted plots, ggplot2 provides the tools necessary to explore and present data visually.

Statistical Models and Beyond: Advanced Regression and Bayesian Modeling

R is well-known for its statistical computing capabilities, making it an ideal tool for building and analyzing statistical models. This section explores advanced regression techniques and the basics of Bayesian modeling, both of which are vital for performing complex data analysis and making informed predictions.

Advanced Regression Techniques

In addition to basic linear regression, R supports a variety of advanced regression models, including logistic regression, polynomial regression, and regularized regression models like Lasso and Ridge regression. These techniques allow data scientists to model relationships between variables more flexibly, particularly when data exhibits non-linear patterns or the presence of multicollinearity.

For example, polynomial regression can be used when the relationship between the independent and dependent variables is non-linear. Here's how to perform polynomial regression in R:

```
# Polynomial regression example
model <- lm(mpg ~ poly(hp, 2), data = mtcars)
summary(model)
```

In this code, poly(hp, 2) adds a second-degree polynomial term for hp, allowing the model to fit a curve instead of a straight line. Polynomial regression is often used when there is evidence of curvature in the data.

104

Another important technique is regularized regression, which helps prevent overfitting by adding a penalty to the regression model. Here's an example of Ridge regression:

```
library(glmnet)

# Ridge regression example
ridge_model <- glmnet(x = as.matrix(mtcars[, -1]), y = mtcars$mpg, alpha =
        0)
summary(ridge_model)
```

In this example, glmnet() is used for Ridge regression, with alpha = 0 specifying that the penalty is purely L2 (Ridge). This model is useful for datasets where many predictor variables may be correlated or redundant.

Introduction to Bayesian Modeling

Bayesian modeling is a powerful statistical framework based on Bayes' Theorem, which updates the probability estimate for a hypothesis as more evidence becomes available. R has several packages for implementing Bayesian models, such as rstan, brms, and JAGS. These models are especially useful when dealing with uncertainty in the data or when prior knowledge about the data can inform the model.

To demonstrate basic Bayesian linear regression using the brms package, consider the following example:

```
library(brms)

# Bayesian linear regression model
bayesian_model <- brm(mpg ~ hp + wt, data = mtcars)
summary(bayesian_model)
```

Here, brm() fits a Bayesian linear regression model using the mpg as the dependent variable and hp and wt as predictors. The model estimates the posterior distribution of the coefficients, which represents the uncertainty about the true values of the model parameters.

MCMC Sampling and Model Evaluation

Bayesian models rely on Markov Chain Monte Carlo (MCMC) methods to sample from the posterior distribution of the model parameters. The brms package uses MCMC to draw samples from the posterior, and the results can be evaluated using diagnostic tools like trace plots and posterior predictive checks.

To visualize the MCMC samples in the brms package, you can use the following:

```
# Visualizing MCMC samples
plot(bayesian_model)
```

This code generates trace plots for the parameters, helping to assess the convergence of the MCMC chains. Convergence is crucial for ensuring the accuracy of the Bayesian model's estimates.

Model Checking and Interpretation

Once a Bayesian model is fitted, it is important to assess its fit and interpret its parameters. This is often done using posterior predictive checks, which compare the predicted values from the model to the observed data. The pp_check() function in brms can be used for this purpose:

```
# Posterior predictive check
pp_check(bayesian_model)
```

This generates diagnostic plots that show how well the model's predictions match the observed data. By visually inspecting these plots, one can assess whether the model is overfitting or underfitting.

Advanced regression techniques and Bayesian modeling are powerful tools in statistical analysis. R's flexibility in fitting and interpreting these models makes it an essential tool for data scientists. By using techniques like polynomial regression, Ridge regression, and Bayesian models, analysts can build more accurate and interpretable models to tackle complex datasets and make predictions with uncertainty.

Module 11:

SQL and NoSQL for Data Science

SQL and NoSQL databases play critical roles in data science, allowing data scientists to access, analyze, and manipulate both structured and unstructured data. This module provides an overview of SQL for structured data querying, advanced SQL techniques for deeper analysis, and introduces NoSQL databases and tools for handling big data. Mastery of both SQL and NoSQL is essential for working with diverse datasets in data science.

The Role of SQL in Data Science: Querying Structured Data Effectively

SQL (Structured Query Language) is a fundamental tool for data scientists working with relational databases. It enables efficient querying, filtering, and aggregation of structured data. SQL is ideal for accessing data stored in tables, where relationships between entities can be easily defined. With SQL, data scientists can extract insights from large datasets, join multiple tables, and perform aggregations, making it an indispensable skill for data analysis. Understanding SQL is essential for performing tasks like data extraction, transformation, and loading (ETL), laying the groundwork for further analysis in data science projects.

Advanced SQL for Analysis: Aggregates, Window Functions, and CTEs

Advanced SQL techniques allow data scientists to perform complex analyses on large datasets. Aggregates such as SUM, COUNT, and AVG help summarize data, while window functions (e.g., ROW_NUMBER, RANK, and LEAD) enable operations like running totals and moving averages. Common Table Expressions (CTEs) are useful for simplifying complex queries and improving readability. These advanced techniques allow for more nuanced insights, such as analyzing trends over time or comparing data across groups. Mastering these advanced SQL features enables data scientists to extract detailed insights and perform in-depth analysis on structured data.

Introduction to NoSQL Databases: MongoDB, Cassandra, and Use Cases

NoSQL databases, such as MongoDB and Cassandra, are designed to handle unstructured or semi-structured data. Unlike SQL databases, NoSQL systems allow for flexible schema design, making them suitable for applications where data structures may evolve over time. MongoDB, a document-oriented database, stores data in JSON-like format, making it easy to work with complex, nested data. Cassandra, a wide-column store, excels in handling large volumes of data across distributed systems. These NoSQL databases are particularly useful for data science applications that require scalability and high availability, such as real-time analytics, big data processing, and handling semi-structured data.

Querying Big Data with SQL Tools: Presto, Hive, and Google BigQuery

For querying large-scale datasets, specialized SQL tools like Presto, Hive, and Google BigQuery provide powerful solutions. Presto is a distributed SQL query engine that allows data scientists to query data across multiple data sources, including Hadoop and relational databases. Apache Hive is built on top of Hadoop, offering a SQL-like interface for querying big data in distributed environments. Google BigQuery, a fully managed cloud data warehouse, enables lightning-fast SQL queries on massive datasets. These tools enhance data scientists' ability to work with big data, providing scalable and efficient solutions for querying large volumes of data.

The Role of SQL in Data Science: Querying Structured Data Effectively

SQL (Structured Query Language) is one of the foundational tools for data scientists, particularly when working with relational databases that store structured data. This section explores the role of SQL in data science, focusing on how it facilitates effective querying, manipulation, and analysis of structured data.

Structured Data and SQL's Relevance

Structured data is organized into rows and columns within a table, often found in relational databases. SQL is the standard language for managing and querying this type of data, providing a powerful, efficient way to extract insights. In the data science workflow, SQL is used to retrieve specific data, aggregate information, and join multiple datasets for analysis.

The main components of SQL include SELECT, WHERE, JOIN, GROUP BY, and ORDER BY, each playing a vital role in querying and organizing data. For example, the SELECT statement allows data scientists to specify the columns they want to retrieve from a table, while the WHERE clause filters records based on conditions. SQL's flexibility allows for complex data manipulations, which are essential for preparing datasets for analysis.

Querying Data with Basic SQL Commands

In SQL, a simple query to extract data from a table would look like this:

```
SELECT column1, column2
FROM table_name
WHERE condition;
```

For example, if you have a table called employees and want to retrieve the name and salary of employees who earn more than $50,000, the SQL query would be:

```
SELECT name, salary
FROM employees
WHERE salary > 50000;
```

This query filters the employees table and returns only the records where the salary is greater than $50,000. SQL queries like this allow data scientists to easily retrieve specific subsets of data, making SQL indispensable for structured data analysis.

Handling Joins and Relationships

A key feature of relational databases is the ability to store data in multiple related tables. SQL provides JOIN operations to combine these tables. JOINs enable data scientists to merge information from different sources based on common columns. For example, a typical JOIN query may look like this:

```
SELECT employees.name, departments.department_name
FROM employees
JOIN departments
ON employees.department_id = departments.department_id;
```

This query retrieves employee names alongside their respective department names by joining the employees table with the departments table on the department_id. The JOIN operation is crucial in relational databases, enabling data scientists to work with data from multiple tables simultaneously.

Aggregating Data for Insights

SQL's ability to aggregate data is another reason why it is so valuable for data science. Aggregation functions like SUM, COUNT, AVG, and MAX allow data scientists to compute summary statistics directly within the database. For example, to calculate the average salary of employees in each department:

```
SELECT department_id, AVG(salary)
FROM employees
GROUP BY department_id;
```

This query calculates the average salary per department by grouping the employees table by department_id. SQL makes it easy to aggregate and analyze large datasets, which is crucial for data scientists when summarizing data and identifying patterns.

Subqueries and Nested Queries

Subqueries, or nested queries, allow for more complex operations where the result of one query is used as input for another. For instance, to find employees whose salary is above the average salary for their department:

```
SELECT name, salary, department_id
FROM employees
WHERE salary > (SELECT AVG(salary) FROM employees WHERE department_id =
          employees.department_id);
```

In this query, the subquery calculates the average salary within each department, and the outer query retrieves employees who earn more than that average. Subqueries provide flexibility in SQL, enabling the execution of complex data analyses within a single query.

SQL is a cornerstone tool for data scientists working with structured data. Its ability to query, filter, join, and aggregate data enables data scientists to efficiently extract and manipulate data for analysis. Understanding SQL is fundamental for anyone pursuing data science, as it provides the foundation for interacting with databases and preparing data for further analysis.

Advanced SQL for Analysis: Aggregates, Window Functions, and CTEs

In this section, we will explore some advanced SQL features that enable data scientists to perform deeper analysis on structured data. These include aggregate functions, window functions, and common table expressions (CTEs). These powerful tools allow data scientists to derive valuable insights from large datasets with greater efficiency and precision.

Aggregate Functions for Summarizing Data

SQL aggregate functions are used to perform calculations on multiple rows of data and return a single result. Some common aggregate functions include SUM(), AVG(), COUNT(), MIN(), and MAX(). These functions are frequently used in data science for summarizing data or performing group-based calculations.

For example, to calculate the total revenue and the average revenue per transaction in a sales dataset:

```
SELECT SUM(revenue) AS total_revenue, AVG(revenue) AS average_revenue
FROM sales;
```

This query computes the total and average revenue from the sales table. Aggregates like SUM and AVG are often used to create summary statistics, which are essential for making data-driven decisions in fields such as finance and business.

Using GROUP BY with Aggregates

The GROUP BY clause in SQL is often used in combination with aggregate functions to group data into subsets. This is useful for breaking down data into smaller, meaningful groups, such as calculating the total sales by product category.

```
SELECT category, SUM(revenue) AS total_revenue
FROM sales
GROUP BY category;
```

This query groups the sales table by the category column and calculates the total revenue for each product category. GROUP BY helps analyze data across various dimensions, making it an essential tool in exploratory data analysis and reporting.

Window Functions for Row-by-Row Calculations

Window functions, also known as analytic functions, allow data scientists to perform calculations across a set of rows related to the current row without collapsing the result into a single value. Unlike aggregate functions, window functions do not reduce the number of rows in the output.

For example, to calculate the running total of sales for each transaction in the sales table, you can use the SUM() window function:

```
SELECT transaction_id, revenue,
       SUM(revenue) OVER (ORDER BY transaction_date) AS running_total
FROM sales;
```

This query computes the cumulative sum of the revenue column, ordered by transaction_date, and displays the running total for each row. Window functions are particularly useful for time series analysis, ranking, and comparing values across partitions of data.

Common Table Expressions (CTEs) for Readability and Reusability

CTEs are temporary result sets defined within the execution scope of a SELECT, INSERT, UPDATE, or DELETE statement. They make queries more readable and reusable, especially when dealing with complex joins and subqueries.

For example, to find employees whose salary is above the average salary within their department, a CTE can be used to first calculate the average salary:

```
WITH DepartmentAvg AS (
    SELECT department_id, AVG(salary) AS avg_salary
    FROM employees
    GROUP BY department_id
)
SELECT e.name, e.salary, e.department_id
FROM employees e
JOIN DepartmentAvg da
ON e.department_id = da.department_id
WHERE e.salary > da.avg_salary;
```

This query defines a CTE (DepartmentAvg) that calculates the average salary by department and then uses it to filter employees whose salary exceeds the department's average. CTEs improve query organization and are particularly helpful for complex multi-step analyses.

Advanced SQL features such as aggregates, window functions, and CTEs are invaluable tools for data scientists. They allow for sophisticated data summarization, row-by-row calculations, and improved query structure. Mastery of these SQL techniques enhances a data scientist's ability to perform in-depth analyses on structured data and efficiently solve complex problems.

Introduction to NoSQL Databases: MongoDB, Cassandra, and Use Cases

NoSQL databases are designed to handle unstructured or semi-structured data, providing flexibility, scalability, and high performance for modern data-intensive applications. In this section, we will explore the characteristics of NoSQL databases, focusing on MongoDB, Cassandra, and their use cases.

Overview of NoSQL Databases

NoSQL (Not Only SQL) databases differ from traditional relational databases by offering a more flexible schema. They are well-suited for applications that need to handle large volumes of data, quick iterations, and high availability. Unlike SQL databases, NoSQL systems do not rely on fixed tables or columns, and they often scale horizontally across many machines.

NoSQL databases can be classified into four main types: document stores, key-value stores, column-family stores, and graph databases. MongoDB and Cassandra are two widely used NoSQL databases, each with distinct use cases and features.

MongoDB: Document-Oriented NoSQL Database

MongoDB is a document-oriented NoSQL database that stores data in JSON-like format (BSON). This allows it to store complex, nested data structures, which is useful for applications dealing with unstructured or semi-structured data, such as content management systems or IoT applications.

In MongoDB, each record is called a "document" and is represented as a BSON object. This structure allows for flexible schema design, where documents in a collection may have different fields.

For example, storing a user's information might look like this:

```
{
  "name": "John Doe",
  "email": "john.doe@example.com",
  "age": 30,
  "addresses": [
    { "type": "home", "street": "123 Main St", "city": "Springfield" },
    { "type": "work", "street": "456 Oak Rd", "city": "Greenville" }
  ]
}
```

MongoDB is particularly useful in applications where the data structure is dynamic and may evolve over time, such as social media platforms or e-commerce systems that track user preferences.

Cassandra: Column-Family Store for High Availability

Cassandra is a highly scalable, distributed NoSQL database that falls under the category of column-family stores. Unlike MongoDB, which organizes data as documents, Cassandra organizes data into rows and columns within a table, making it efficient for handling large volumes of data across many servers.

Cassandra is optimized for high availability and fault tolerance. It uses a masterless architecture, meaning there is no single point of failure, and data is replicated across multiple nodes in a cluster. This makes it an ideal choice for applications that require 24/7 availability, such as real-time analytics platforms, social media feeds, and recommendation systems.

Here is an example of a Cassandra table schema for storing user information:

```
CREATE TABLE users (
  user_id UUID PRIMARY KEY,
  name TEXT,
  email TEXT,
  age INT,
  last_login TIMESTAMP
);
```

Cassandra is particularly suited for applications that need to scale horizontally and handle large amounts of write-heavy workloads, such as IoT systems or global e-commerce websites.

Use Cases for NoSQL Databases

NoSQL databases excel in situations where traditional relational databases are not efficient. Some of the common use cases for NoSQL databases include:

- **Real-time Analytics**: NoSQL databases like Cassandra are ideal for real-time data analytics, where high throughput and low latency are crucial.

- **Big Data**: NoSQL systems are designed to scale horizontally, making them suitable for big data applications such as data lakes and distributed data storage.

- **Content Management**: MongoDB's flexible schema makes it a great choice for content management systems, where data types evolve frequently.

- **Social Media**: With its support for high write throughput, Cassandra is often used to store social media posts and interactions at scale.

NoSQL databases like MongoDB and Cassandra offer flexible and scalable alternatives to traditional relational databases. MongoDB's document-based structure is ideal for handling dynamic data, while Cassandra's high availability and horizontal scalability make it a perfect choice for big data applications. Understanding the use cases and strengths of these NoSQL systems is essential for data scientists working with large, unstructured datasets.

Querying Big Data with SQL Tools: Presto, Hive, and Google BigQuery

As data volumes increase exponentially, traditional SQL databases face limitations in terms of scalability and speed. Big data tools such as Presto, Hive, and Google BigQuery are designed to handle large-scale data processing efficiently. This section covers these tools and how they extend SQL capabilities to manage vast datasets.

Presto: Distributed SQL Query Engine

Presto is an open-source distributed SQL query engine optimized for querying large datasets across multiple data sources, including Hadoop, S3, and relational databases. Unlike traditional databases, Presto performs in-memory querying, which significantly speeds up processing. Presto allows you to execute SQL queries on data stored in various sources simultaneously, making it an excellent tool for data integration.

For example, you can query data from both a relational database and a data lake using a single query:

```
SELECT customer_id, total_spent
FROM hive.sales
JOIN mysql.customer_info
ON sales.customer_id = customer_info.customer_id
WHERE total_spent > 1000;
```

Presto's flexibility makes it suitable for enterprises that need to query disparate datasets from cloud storage, data warehouses, and other platforms. It is widely used for ad-hoc queries and interactive analytics in real-time.

Hive: Data Warehouse for Hadoop

Hive is a data warehouse system built on top of Hadoop, designed to manage large-scale data processing. It uses a SQL-like language called HiveQL, allowing users to run queries on data stored in Hadoop's distributed file system (HDFS). While Hive's performance is slower compared to traditional relational databases, it excels at batch processing and is ideal for complex queries on large data sets.

Hive provides an abstraction layer for Hadoop, allowing data scientists to query and analyze massive datasets without needing to learn the complexities of MapReduce. It supports data aggregation, filtering, and joining operations on large data sources, making it suitable for tasks like log analysis, ETL processes, and batch reporting.

A typical Hive query might look like this:

```
SELECT product_id, AVG(rating)
```

```
FROM reviews
WHERE date > '2023-01-01'
GROUP BY product_id;
```

Hive is particularly useful for historical data analysis and processing data stored in Hadoop, such as logs, event data, or large transactional datasets.

Google BigQuery: Managed Data Warehouse for Real-Time Analytics

Google BigQuery is a fully managed, serverless data warehouse that excels in handling real-time analytics on massive datasets. It allows users to run SQL queries on structured data stored in Google Cloud Storage or Google Drive. BigQuery leverages distributed computing and columnar storage, making it capable of processing petabytes of data in seconds.

BigQuery's integration with Google Cloud's ecosystem allows for seamless data ingestion from various sources, making it ideal for real-time business intelligence, machine learning, and large-scale data analytics. With its pay-per-query model, users only pay for the queries they run, offering significant cost savings for ad-hoc analysis.

A sample query in BigQuery might be:

```
SELECT user_id, COUNT(*) as total_orders
FROM `my_project.my_dataset.orders`
WHERE order_date > '2023-01-01'
GROUP BY user_id;
```

BigQuery is optimized for both batch and real-time analytics, with features such as partitioned tables, machine learning capabilities, and integration with data visualization tools like Looker and Data Studio.

Presto, Hive, and Google BigQuery are powerful tools for querying big data, each designed for specific use cases. Presto's distributed nature enables querying multiple data sources in real-time, Hive provides scalability for batch processing within the Hadoop ecosystem, and BigQuery offers serverless real-time analytics at massive scale. Understanding how to use these tools allows data scientists to process and analyze large datasets efficiently, regardless of their format or storage system.

Module 12:

Scala and Spark for Big Data Analytics

Scala and Apache Spark are powerful tools for big data analytics. This module explores the reasons for using Scala in data science, the core components of Apache Spark, how Spark's MLlib can be used for machine learning, and how to build scalable data pipelines with Spark. Mastery of these tools is essential for handling large-scale data projects.

Why Scala for Data Science?: Functional Programming and Scalability

Scala is a highly scalable language that combines the strengths of functional and object-oriented programming. Its concise syntax and functional programming capabilities make it well-suited for data science tasks that require efficient handling of large datasets. Scala's immutability and high-order functions support parallel and distributed computation, which is crucial for big data analytics. By leveraging Scala's interoperability with Java, data scientists can take advantage of existing Java libraries while benefiting from Scala's more succinct code. Its ability to process large datasets efficiently makes it an excellent choice for building scalable data applications.

Introduction to Apache Spark: Core Components and Workflows

Apache Spark is an open-source distributed computing system designed for big data processing. Its core components include the Spark Core, which handles task scheduling and resource management, and Spark SQL, which allows for querying structured data using SQL. The Spark Streaming component supports real-time data processing, while Spark MLlib and GraphX enable machine learning and graph processing, respectively. Spark's distributed nature allows it to process massive datasets in parallel across a cluster of machines, making it highly scalable and suitable for large-scale data analytics workflows. Understanding Spark's architecture and components is crucial for leveraging its full potential in big data projects.

Spark's MLlib for Machine Learning: Building Distributed ML Models

Spark's MLlib is a library specifically designed for machine learning on large datasets. It provides scalable algorithms for classification, regression, clustering, and collaborative filtering. MLlib allows data scientists to build and train machine learning models in parallel across a distributed system, significantly speeding up the model-building process. It includes support for feature extraction, transformation, and model evaluation. By using MLlib, data scientists can apply machine learning techniques to vast amounts of data without compromising performance. This makes Spark an invaluable tool for building distributed machine learning models that can handle big data efficiently.

Building Scalable Pipelines: Integrating ETL and ML in Spark

In addition to machine learning, Apache Spark is ideal for building scalable data pipelines. With Spark, data scientists can integrate ETL (Extract, Transform, Load) processes and machine learning workflows into a seamless pipeline. Data can be ingested, processed, and transformed in parallel across a cluster of machines, and models can be trained and evaluated within the same pipeline. Spark's ability to handle both batch and real-time data makes it versatile for various big data use cases. By combining ETL and machine learning in a unified Spark pipeline, data scientists can build end-to-end solutions for processing and analyzing large-scale datasets.

Why Scala for Data Science?: Functional Programming and Scalability

Scala is a powerful language that combines functional and object-oriented programming paradigms, making it a popular choice for data science and big data analytics. Its ability to handle both concurrent and distributed computing efficiently makes it particularly suitable for large-scale data processing tasks, often required in the realm of data science.

Functional Programming in Scala

One of the key features that make Scala attractive for data science is its support for functional programming (FP). FP focuses on immutability, higher-order functions, and treating computation as the evaluation of mathematical functions. These principles reduce side effects, making code more predictable and easier to test. In Scala, functions are first-class citizens, meaning they can be passed as arguments or returned as results from other functions. This makes Scala an excellent choice for writing concise and expressive data processing code.

For instance, when processing large datasets, you can leverage higher-order functions like map, reduce, and filter for transformations and aggregations, simplifying the process. Here's an example of using Scala for data transformation:

```
val data = List(1, 2, 3, 4, 5)
val squaredData = data.map(x => x * x)
println(squaredData)
```

This Scala code demonstrates how easy it is to apply functional transformations to datasets, allowing data scientists to work efficiently with complex data structures.

Scalability and Concurrency

Another significant advantage of Scala is its scalability. Scala's strong concurrency model, built around immutable data structures, allows it to perform well in multi-threaded and distributed environments. The language integrates seamlessly with the

Apache Spark framework, which is designed for processing large-scale data in parallel across clusters of machines. Spark's APIs are written in Scala, and using Scala to write Spark applications offers performance benefits over other languages.

For example, when dealing with massive datasets, Scala's ability to handle parallel computation makes it a suitable tool for running distributed algorithms efficiently. Here's an example of how Scala's parallel collections can speed up computations:

```
val largeDataSet = (1 to 1000000).toList
val sum = largeDataSet.par.sum
println(sum)
```

This code calculates the sum of a large dataset in parallel, leveraging Scala's parallel collections. For data scientists working with big data, this level of parallelism is essential for speeding up the processing of large datasets.

Interoperability with Java

Scala runs on the Java Virtual Machine (JVM), which makes it highly interoperable with Java-based technologies. This is particularly useful in the world of big data analytics, where many tools and libraries are written in Java. Spark, for example, is a Java-based framework, but its APIs are available in Scala, Python, and R. Scala's compatibility with Java allows data scientists to use the vast ecosystem of Java libraries and tools without worrying about compatibility issues.

By using Scala for big data analytics, you can leverage both the powerful Java ecosystem and Scala's own functional programming capabilities to build scalable and efficient solutions.

Scala's functional programming capabilities, scalability, and interoperability with Java make it an ideal language for data science, especially in the context of big data processing. When combined with frameworks like Apache Spark, Scala enables data scientists to handle massive datasets and perform complex computations efficiently. Its concise syntax and expressive features simplify the development of sophisticated data analysis and machine learning workflows, making Scala a preferred choice for data professionals working in distributed environments.

Introduction to Apache Spark: Core Components and Workflows

Apache Spark is one of the most widely used distributed data processing frameworks in the world of big data analytics. Built on top of Hadoop's MapReduce, Spark provides significant improvements in speed and ease of use, making it the preferred tool for data scientists and engineers working with large datasets. It is designed for fault-tolerant, scalable, and parallel computation across clusters, making it suitable for big data applications.

Core Components of Apache Spark

At its core, Apache Spark consists of several key components that work together to perform distributed data processing. These include the Spark Core, Spark SQL, Spark Streaming, MLlib, and GraphX.

- **Spark Core**: This is the foundational component of Spark. It handles task scheduling, memory management, fault tolerance, and interactions with storage systems. Spark Core is responsible for executing the basic operations that make up Spark applications.

- **Spark SQL**: Spark SQL provides an interface for querying structured data. It supports SQL queries, the DataFrame API, and the Dataset API. This component enables users to run SQL-based queries on large datasets and combine them with other Spark transformations.

- **Spark Streaming**: Spark Streaming allows for the processing of real-time data streams. It divides the incoming data stream into small batches, which are processed in parallel across the Spark cluster.

- **MLlib**: Spark's library for machine learning, MLlib, provides scalable algorithms for classification, regression, clustering, and collaborative filtering. It also includes tools for feature extraction, transformation, and model evaluation.

- **GraphX**: GraphX is Spark's API for graph processing, allowing for the computation of graph-based algorithms like PageRank and community detection.

Spark Workflows

A typical Spark workflow involves several stages, from data ingestion to data processing and model development. These stages allow data scientists to harness the full power of distributed computing for big data analytics.

1. **Data Ingestion**: Spark can read data from various sources such as HDFS, Amazon S3, Apache Cassandra, and databases. It supports multiple file formats like CSV, JSON, Parquet, and Avro.

2. **Data Transformation**: Once the data is loaded, Spark allows users to apply transformations such as filtering, aggregating, joining, and reshaping data using its powerful APIs. These transformations are lazy, meaning they are not executed until an action (e.g., count, collect) triggers them.

3. **Machine Learning**: After transforming the data, Spark MLlib can be used to build and evaluate machine learning models. It offers algorithms for tasks like classification, regression, clustering, and dimensionality reduction.

4. **Data Storage**: The processed data can be written back to various storage systems, including HDFS, databases, or other distributed file systems.

Here's an example of loading a dataset, performing transformations, and applying a machine learning algorithm using Spark in Scala:

```scala
import org.apache.spark.ml.classification.RandomForestClassifier
import org.apache.spark.ml.feature.VectorAssembler
import org.apache.spark.sql.SparkSession

val spark = SparkSession.builder.appName("SparkML").getOrCreate()

// Load data
val data = spark.read.option("header", "true").csv("path/to/data.csv")

// Feature engineering
val assembler = new VectorAssembler().setInputCols(Array("feature1",
        "feature2")).setOutputCol("features")
val transformedData = assembler.transform(data)

// Model training
val rf = new
        RandomForestClassifier().setLabelCol("label").setFeaturesCol("fea
        tures")
val model = rf.fit(transformedData)

// Make predictions
val predictions = model.transform(transformedData)
predictions.show()
```

This example shows the ease with which Spark allows you to perform data preprocessing and build machine learning models.

Fault Tolerance and Scalability

One of the key features of Apache Spark is its fault tolerance. Spark uses a concept called Resilient Distributed Datasets (RDDs), which are collections of objects that can be processed in parallel. RDDs ensure that data is automatically recovered in case of a failure, providing reliability even in distributed environments.

Additionally, Spark's ability to scale horizontally across multiple nodes allows it to handle massive datasets, making it a go-to tool for big data processing.

Apache Spark is a versatile and powerful framework that provides a unified approach to big data analytics. By combining data processing, machine learning, and graph processing into a single platform, Spark makes it easier to build end-to-end data science workflows. Its core components, fault tolerance, and scalability have made it an indispensable tool for data scientists working with big data.

Spark's MLlib for Machine Learning: Building Distributed ML Models

Apache Spark's MLlib is a scalable machine learning library built into the Spark framework. It provides a suite of machine learning algorithms and tools for data preparation, model evaluation, and performance tuning. Unlike traditional machine learning libraries, MLlib is designed to handle large-scale data by leveraging Spark's distributed computing capabilities. MLlib supports both supervised and unsupervised learning, enabling users to apply a wide range of algorithms to solve real-world problems efficiently.

Key Features of MLlib

MLlib is a comprehensive library that includes various algorithms, utilities, and tools for building machine learning models. Some of the key features of MLlib include:

1. **Classification and Regression**: MLlib provides algorithms for classification (e.g., logistic regression, decision trees) and regression (e.g., linear regression, support vector machines).

2. **Clustering**: MLlib includes clustering algorithms such as K-means and Gaussian Mixture Models, enabling unsupervised learning of data patterns.

3. **Collaborative Filtering**: Spark's MLlib offers collaborative filtering methods like alternating least squares (ALS) for building recommendation systems.

4. **Dimensionality Reduction**: Techniques such as Principal Component Analysis (PCA) help reduce the feature space while preserving the most critical information.

5. **Feature Engineering**: MLlib offers tools for transforming raw data into suitable formats for machine learning algorithms, including normalization, scaling, and encoding categorical features.

Building a Machine Learning Pipeline in Spark

In Spark, machine learning is done in a systematic pipeline approach. A typical ML pipeline consists of several stages, including data preprocessing, feature engineering, model training, and model evaluation. Spark makes it easier to work with data at scale by automating most of these steps and allowing for the creation of end-to-end workflows.

Here's an example of building a classification model using a machine learning pipeline in Spark with Python:

```
from pyspark.ml.feature import VectorAssembler
from pyspark.ml.classification import LogisticRegression
from pyspark.ml import Pipeline
from pyspark.sql import SparkSession

# Initialize Spark session
```

```
spark = SparkSession.builder.appName("SparkML").getOrCreate()

# Load the dataset
data = spark.read.csv("path/to/data.csv", header=True, inferSchema=True)

# Feature engineering
assembler = VectorAssembler(inputCols=["feature1", "feature2", "feature3"],
        outputCol="features")
transformed_data = assembler.transform(data)

# Split the data into training and testing sets
train_data, test_data = transformed_data.randomSplit([0.7, 0.3])

# Build the model
lr = LogisticRegression(labelCol="label", featuresCol="features")
pipeline = Pipeline(stages=[assembler, lr])

# Train the model
model = pipeline.fit(train_data)

# Make predictions
predictions = model.transform(test_data)
predictions.select("prediction", "label").show()
```

In this example, the VectorAssembler is used to combine features into a single vector, which is required for input into MLlib's algorithms. The model is trained using logistic regression, and predictions are made on the test data.

Model Evaluation

After training the model, it is important to evaluate its performance using various metrics such as accuracy, precision, recall, F1 score, and area under the ROC curve (AUC). Spark's MLlib provides built-in evaluation metrics for classification and regression tasks.

For example, in classification tasks, you can use the MulticlassClassificationEvaluator for evaluating the model's accuracy and other performance measures:

```
from pyspark.ml.evaluation import MulticlassClassificationEvaluator

# Evaluate the model
evaluator = MulticlassClassificationEvaluator(labelCol="label",
        predictionCol="prediction", metricName="accuracy")
accuracy = evaluator.evaluate(predictions)
print("Accuracy: ", accuracy)
```

Advantages of MLlib

1. **Scalability**: MLlib can handle massive datasets by utilizing the distributed computing capabilities of Spark, which allows for parallel execution of machine learning tasks.

2. **Ease of Use**: The unified API in Spark allows users to easily integrate machine learning with data processing, making it simpler to build, test, and deploy machine learning models.

3. **Performance**: MLlib's optimization techniques allow for faster model training and evaluation on large datasets.

Spark's MLlib offers powerful, scalable tools for building machine learning models on big data. By leveraging Spark's distributed architecture, users can process large volumes of data efficiently while still utilizing advanced machine learning algorithms. MLlib's ability to integrate seamlessly with the broader Spark ecosystem makes it a powerful choice for data scientists working with large-scale data analytics.

Building Scalable Pipelines: Integrating ETL and ML in Spark

One of the key strengths of Apache Spark is its ability to create end-to-end, scalable data processing pipelines. Building scalable pipelines involves integrating data ingestion, transformation, and machine learning (ML) workflows. These pipelines allow for efficient handling of large datasets, from raw data collection to actionable insights through predictive modeling. Spark's distributed processing and parallelism ensure that even complex data workflows can be executed at scale with minimal latency.

ETL in Spark

ETL (Extract, Transform, Load) is the process of extracting raw data from various sources, transforming it into a usable format, and loading it into storage systems. Spark makes it easier to perform ETL tasks using its powerful DataFrame and RDD (Resilient Distributed Dataset) APIs. Spark supports a wide range of data sources such as HDFS, S3, relational databases, and NoSQL systems, allowing users to extract data from almost any source.

Here is an example of how Spark can be used to load and transform data:

```python
from pyspark.sql import SparkSession

# Initialize Spark session
spark = SparkSession.builder.appName("ETL_Pipeline").getOrCreate()

# Load data from a CSV file
data = spark.read.csv("path/to/input_data.csv", header=True,
        inferSchema=True)

# Data transformation: filtering and creating a new column
transformed_data = data.filter(data["age"] > 30).withColumn("age_group",
        data["age"] / 10)

# Show transformed data
transformed_data.show()
```

This code reads data from a CSV file, filters it based on the age column, and adds a new column age_group by dividing the age by 10. The transformation steps can be more complex depending on the use case, such as handling missing values, joining multiple datasets, or applying aggregations.

123

Integrating Machine Learning into the Pipeline

Once data is transformed, it is ready for machine learning. Spark's MLlib allows us to seamlessly integrate machine learning steps into the ETL pipeline, enabling end-to-end automation. This includes data preparation, feature engineering, model building, and evaluation.

A pipeline can be constructed using Spark's Pipeline API, where each stage of the pipeline is represented by a transformer or estimator. For example, the following code creates a pipeline that preprocesses data and trains a classification model:

```python
from pyspark.ml.feature import VectorAssembler
from pyspark.ml.classification import RandomForestClassifier
from pyspark.ml import Pipeline

# Feature engineering
assembler = VectorAssembler(inputCols=["feature1", "feature2", "feature3"],
            outputCol="features")

# Random forest classifier
rf = RandomForestClassifier(labelCol="label", featuresCol="features")

# Create pipeline
pipeline = Pipeline(stages=[assembler, rf])

# Train model
model = pipeline.fit(transformed_data)

# Make predictions
predictions = model.transform(transformed_data)
predictions.select("prediction", "label").show()
```

This pipeline consists of two stages: transforming the features using VectorAssembler and training a Random Forest classifier. By chaining these steps together, the pipeline ensures that each stage is executed in sequence.

Optimizing and Scaling Pipelines

Spark is designed to handle large datasets efficiently, but optimizing the pipeline for scalability is essential, especially when dealing with high-volume data. Several techniques can be used to ensure scalability and performance:

1. **Partitioning**: Ensure that data is evenly distributed across Spark's worker nodes. This can be achieved through partitioning strategies like hash partitioning or range partitioning.

2. **Caching and Persistence**: For repeated operations, caching intermediate results can reduce computation time. For example, caching transformed data ensures that it is readily available for subsequent stages of the pipeline.

3. **Tuning Parameters**: Spark allows tuning the number of executors, memory settings, and other parameters to improve performance based on the workload.

Deploying Pipelines

Once the pipeline is built and optimized, the next step is deploying it for production use. Spark integrates with various deployment frameworks like Apache Mesos, Kubernetes, and cloud-based platforms like AWS, Azure, and Google Cloud, allowing users to scale the pipeline across clusters of machines for large-scale processing.

Building scalable pipelines in Spark involves seamlessly integrating ETL processes with machine learning workflows. The power of Spark lies in its ability to handle large datasets efficiently and provide a unified framework for both data transformation and model training. By combining these capabilities, Spark enables data scientists to automate complex workflows, improve data-driven decision-making, and deploy models at scale.

Module 13:

Julia for High-Performance Data Science

Julia is an emerging programming language known for its high performance and ease of use in data science. This module introduces Julia's strengths, its popular data science libraries, its capabilities for machine learning, and its speed optimization features. By the end, data scientists will understand how Julia can significantly enhance performance in large-scale data analysis and machine learning tasks.

Introduction to Julia: Strengths and Learning Curve

Julia is designed for high-performance numerical and scientific computing, combining the best of Python, R, and C. It's known for its speed, often matching or exceeding the performance of C and Fortran. Julia's syntax is easy to learn, making it accessible to data scientists familiar with other languages. However, its unique features, like Just-In-Time (JIT) compilation, can present a learning curve for those accustomed to traditional scripting languages. Despite this, Julia's flexibility and power make it an excellent choice for data scientists seeking to optimize performance in large-scale analytics and high-performance computing environments.

Julia's Data Science Libraries: DataFrames, Flux.jl, and Others

Julia offers robust libraries for data science tasks, enhancing its appeal for data scientists. The **DataFrames.jl** library, similar to pandas in Python, allows efficient manipulation of structured data. For machine learning, **Flux.jl** provides a flexible and easy-to-use framework for building models, making it ideal for those looking to apply deep learning techniques. Additionally, Julia boasts libraries for linear algebra, optimization, and statistics, which provide an extensive toolkit for various data science needs. These libraries empower data scientists to process, model, and analyze data effectively while leveraging Julia's speed.

Machine Learning with Julia: Practical ML Pipelines

Julia simplifies the creation of machine learning pipelines through its dedicated libraries like **Flux.jl** and **MLJ.jl**. These libraries support a wide range of machine learning algorithms, from classification and regression to clustering and deep learning. By using Julia's high-level abstractions, data scientists can easily define, train, and evaluate models. Moreover, Julia's multi-threaded nature allows for faster training times on large datasets, making it particularly beneficial in building scalable machine learning systems. By integrating Julia's performance with its machine learning libraries, data scientists can build sophisticated, real-time analytics solutions.

Speed Optimization with Julia: Performance Comparisons and Use Cases

One of Julia's key strengths is its performance. Compared to Python and R, Julia can run data-intensive computations significantly faster. Its JIT compilation allows for optimizations that make Julia well-suited for tasks like large-scale matrix computations, simulations, and machine learning model training. Julia also offers fine-tuned control over memory usage and parallel processing, making it ideal for high-performance computing tasks. In use cases such as financial modeling, image processing, and scientific simulations, Julia's speed provides a clear advantage, enabling data scientists to handle large datasets and complex algorithms with efficiency.

Introduction to Julia: Strengths and Learning Curve

Julia is a high-performance, dynamic programming language specifically designed for numerical and scientific computing. Over the years, it has gained considerable attention for its ability to combine the speed of compiled languages like C and Fortran with the ease of use typical of interpreted languages such as Python and R. Julia was designed with performance in mind, focusing on the needs of data science, machine learning, and big data analytics.

Strengths of Julia

One of the key strengths of Julia is its execution speed. It is built for high-performance numerical computing, which makes it suitable for tasks that require intensive computation, such as simulation, optimization, and large-scale data analysis. Unlike Python, which relies on third-party libraries like NumPy for efficient computations, Julia is designed to execute directly with native machine code, offering speeds that rival lower-level languages.

Moreover, Julia supports parallel and distributed computing natively, which means it can handle large datasets more efficiently. This is particularly beneficial for data science projects that require significant computational resources, enabling faster execution of tasks such as training machine learning models or performing simulations.

Julia's syntax is also designed to be user-friendly, similar to Python. The ease of learning and its powerful features, such as automatic differentiation and its ability to define new types, make Julia an attractive choice for data scientists who need both performance and flexibility in their work.

Learning Curve of Julia

While Julia offers a wealth of advantages in terms of performance, learning the language requires some initial effort. For those familiar with languages like Python or R, the transition to Julia is relatively smooth, especially considering its high-level syntax. However, some aspects, such as its multi-dispatch system for function overloading and its rich ecosystem of packages, might pose challenges for new users.

The concept of multiple dispatch, where the function being executed depends on the types of its arguments, is central to Julia's design. This concept is powerful but may require a deeper understanding for users coming from more traditional object-oriented programming backgrounds. For example, defining a function in Julia might involve writing multiple versions of the same function to handle different data types, which can be difficult for beginners to grasp at first.

Julia's Ecosystem

Julia's ecosystem has rapidly evolved, with libraries and packages emerging across multiple domains of data science, machine learning, and statistics. The DataFrames.jl library, for instance, is an equivalent of Pandas in Python and offers powerful data manipulation capabilities. Julia also provides Flux.jl for deep learning, which allows users to define and train neural networks in a highly flexible manner. Additionally, the Julia package ecosystem supports a range of other useful libraries for visualization, optimization, and statistical analysis.

A simple example of working with DataFrames.jl might look like this:

```julia
using DataFrames

# Creating a DataFrame
data = DataFrame(A = 1:5, B = 6:10)

# Viewing the DataFrame
println(data)

# Basic manipulation
data.A .+= 5   # Adding 5 to each element in column A
println(data)
```

This example demonstrates the ease of data manipulation in Julia, which mirrors many common data science workflows.

When to Use Julia

While Julia is ideal for performance-critical tasks in data science, its ecosystem, while growing rapidly, is still not as extensive as Python's. This means that for many tasks, Python may offer more mature libraries or greater community support. However, for applications where speed and performance are paramount—such as large-scale simulations or high-frequency trading—Julia stands out as a top choice.

In the context of data science, Julia is especially beneficial when dealing with computations that involve heavy numerical processing, large datasets, or real-time data processing. Julia's ability to perform computations natively, along with its growing ecosystem of specialized libraries, makes it a powerful addition to a data scientist's toolkit.

Julia's Data Science Libraries: DataFrames, Flux.jl, and Others

Julia's ecosystem is rich with libraries designed to tackle a wide array of data science tasks, from data manipulation and visualization to machine learning and statistical modeling. In this section, we will explore some of the key libraries that make Julia a powerful tool for data science, focusing on DataFrames.jl, Flux.jl, and other essential libraries.

DataFrames.jl for Data Manipulation

DataFrames.jl is one of the most widely used Julia packages for data manipulation. It serves as a core tool for handling and analyzing structured data, similar to Python's Pandas. The DataFrames.jl library provides a versatile framework for creating, modifying, and summarizing tabular data. It is designed for both small and large datasets, offering high performance without sacrificing usability.

The library allows users to perform common data operations, such as filtering, sorting, grouping, and aggregating. It is also capable of handling missing data, which is common in real-world datasets. For instance, to create a simple DataFrame and perform some basic operations, you can use the following code:

```
using DataFrames

# Create a DataFrame
df = DataFrame(A = [1, 2, 3, 4], B = [5, 6, 7, 8])

# Show the DataFrame
println(df)

# Filter rows where A > 2
filtered_df = df[df.A .> 2, :]
println(filtered_df)
```

In this example, the DataFrame is created from vectors, and a filter is applied to extract rows where the value of column A is greater than 2. DataFrames.jl allows for seamless handling of tabular data in a way that is intuitive and efficient.

Flux.jl for Machine Learning

For machine learning tasks, Flux.jl is Julia's go-to library. Flux.jl is a flexible and high-level framework for defining and training machine learning models, particularly deep learning models. It provides an intuitive interface to work with neural networks, making it easy to implement custom architectures, optimization strategies, and loss functions.

One of the standout features of Flux.jl is its ability to handle all stages of machine learning workflows, from data preprocessing and model building to training and evaluation. The library supports a variety of machine learning tasks, including supervised learning, unsupervised learning, and reinforcement learning.

Here's a simple example of using Flux.jl to define a neural network model:

```
using Flux

# Define a simple neural network
model = Chain(
    Dense(2, 5, relu),
    Dense(5, 1)
)

# Create some dummy data
X = rand(2, 100)  # 100 samples, 2 features
y = rand(1, 100)  # 100 labels

# Define a loss function
loss(x, y) = sum((model(x) .- y).^2)

# Train the model using stochastic gradient descent
opt = Descent(0.1)
for i in 1:1000
    Flux.train!(loss, params(model), [(X, y)], opt)
end

println("Model trained!")
```

In this code, a simple neural network is defined with two layers. The train! function is used to optimize the model using gradient descent. This simplicity and flexibility make Flux.jl highly attractive for data scientists and researchers.

Other Julia Libraries for Data Science

In addition to DataFrames.jl and Flux.jl, Julia has several other important libraries that enhance its functionality for data science tasks:

• **Plots.jl**: This is a powerful library for creating static, interactive, and animated visualizations. It can be used for creating simple plots or more complex visualizations like 3D plots.

• **StatsBase.jl**: A statistical library that provides essential tools for descriptive statistics, random number generation, and various statistical tests.

• **CSV.jl**: A fast library for reading and writing CSV files, which is essential for data science workflows involving CSV-based data.

Julia's growing ecosystem of data science libraries makes it a compelling language for data scientists. With tools like DataFrames.jl for data manipulation and Flux.jl for machine learning, Julia provides a high-performance environment for handling and analyzing large datasets, building machine learning models, and more. Its flexibility and speed offer a competitive advantage, particularly in fields requiring high-performance computations.

Machine Learning with Julia: Practical ML Pipelines

Machine learning (ML) in Julia is facilitated by its rich ecosystem of libraries that combine high performance with ease of use. This section will guide you through the process of building practical ML pipelines in Julia, using popular libraries such as Flux.jl and MLJ.jl. These libraries offer a simple yet powerful interface for defining models, evaluating their performance, and deploying them for real-world tasks.

MLJ.jl for Structured Machine Learning Pipelines

MLJ.jl is another important library in Julia for machine learning. Unlike Flux.jl, which is focused on deep learning, MLJ.jl is aimed at general machine learning tasks and offers an easy-to-use interface for building structured machine learning workflows. It supports a variety of models, including decision trees, support vector machines, and linear models.

A key feature of MLJ.jl is its consistent interface for different types of machine learning algorithms. This uniformity allows users to switch between models with minimal code changes. Additionally, MLJ.jl supports automatic hyperparameter tuning and model evaluation using cross-validation.

Here's a basic example of building a machine learning pipeline using MLJ.jl:

```julia
using MLJ
using RDatasets

# Load dataset
data = dataset("datasets", "iris")

# Define the features and target variable
X = select(data, Not(:Species))  # Features
y = data.Species  # Target variable

# Split the data into training and testing sets
train, test = partition(eachindex(y), 0.7)

# Choose a model
model = @load RandomForestClassifier

# Train the model
trained_model = fit!(model, X[train, :], y[train])

# Evaluate the model on the test set
y_pred = predict(trained_model, X[test, :])

# Evaluate accuracy
accuracy = sum(y_pred .== y[test]) / length(y[test])
println("Model accuracy: $accuracy")
```

In this example, we load the well-known Iris dataset and use the RandomForestClassifier from MLJ.jl to train and evaluate a model. The pipeline consists of loading the data, splitting it into training and test sets, training the model, and evaluating its accuracy.

Building a Practical Pipeline in Julia

A practical machine learning pipeline in Julia typically includes several key stages: data preprocessing, model selection, training, hyperparameter tuning, and evaluation. The code example above demonstrates how to build a simple pipeline, but real-world scenarios often require more complex preprocessing and model selection steps.

For instance, before training a model, it's common to preprocess the data by handling missing values, scaling features, and encoding categorical variables. Julia's DataFrames.jl and MLJ.jl libraries provide tools for preprocessing tasks such as feature scaling and encoding.

Another important aspect of a complete ML pipeline is hyperparameter tuning. Julia's ecosystem offers tools like Tuning.jl to automate hyperparameter searches, which can greatly improve model performance by selecting optimal parameters.

Integration of Julia with Other Tools

One of the key strengths of Julia for machine learning is its ability to integrate seamlessly with other tools and frameworks. For instance, you can combine Julia's ML libraries with Python libraries via PyCall.jl, or integrate with Spark for distributed machine learning via Spark.jl. This flexibility allows Julia to fit into existing data science workflows, enabling the use of Julia's high-performance capabilities alongside other established tools.

Additionally, Julia supports GPU acceleration, which is particularly useful for training deep learning models. Libraries like Flux.jl can leverage GPU support for faster training, making Julia ideal for both small-scale and large-scale machine learning tasks.

Machine learning in Julia is highly efficient due to its ecosystem of libraries that combine ease of use with high performance. Libraries like MLJ.jl and Flux.jl provide the necessary tools to build practical machine learning pipelines, while the language's speed and flexibility enable rapid model development and evaluation. By leveraging Julia's power, data scientists can handle complex tasks more efficiently and effectively, positioning Julia as a strong contender for machine learning workflows.

Speed Optimization with Julia: Performance Comparisons and Use Cases

One of Julia's key selling points is its remarkable speed, particularly for high-performance computing tasks. This section will explore how Julia achieves high performance through just-in-time (JIT) compilation and its ability to handle complex numerical computations. We'll also discuss when to use Julia for data science tasks and how it compares to other languages in terms of speed and scalability.

The Power of Just-in-Time Compilation

Julia is a compiled language, and one of its standout features is the use of Just-in-Time (JIT) compilation. When you run Julia code, it is compiled directly into machine code using LLVM (Low-Level Virtual Machine) during runtime. This allows Julia to perform computations with speeds comparable to C and Fortran, two languages traditionally known for their performance in numerical computing.

The speed of Julia comes from its ability to combine the ease of a high-level language with the performance of a low-level one. For example, you can write expressive, human-readable code while still achieving speeds close to those of languages that require more intricate coding practices, such as C++. Julia's JIT compilation ensures that performance is optimized dynamically based on the specific needs of the code being executed.

Performance Comparisons: Julia vs. Python and R

In terms of speed, Julia often outperforms Python and R, especially in tasks involving numerical optimization and large-scale computations. Python and R are interpreted languages, which means they are generally slower than compiled languages like Julia. While Python has extensive libraries for scientific computing (e.g., NumPy, SciPy), these are often implemented in lower-level languages like C, which still doesn't match the direct performance Julia offers through native compilation.

Let's compare the performance of a simple numerical task in Python and Julia to demonstrate the difference in speed. In this example, we will perform a matrix multiplication, a common operation in data science.

Python Example (using NumPy):

```
import numpy as np
import time

# Create two random matrices
A = np.random.rand(1000, 1000)
B = np.random.rand(1000, 1000)

# Start the timer
start_time = time.time()

# Perform matrix multiplication
C = np.dot(A, B)
```

```
# Print time taken
print("Python time:", time.time() - start_time)
```

Julia Example:

```
# Create two random matrices
A = rand(1000, 1000)
B = rand(1000, 1000)

# Start the timer
start_time = time()

# Perform matrix multiplication
C = A * B

# Print time taken
println("Julia time: ", time() - start_time)
```

In general, the Julia version will outperform the Python version in terms of execution speed, as Julia directly compiles to machine code, while Python relies on the slower interpreted approach.

Use Cases for Julia's Speed

Julia shines in areas that require heavy mathematical computations or large-scale data processing. This includes fields such as:

- **Scientific Computing**: Julia is widely used in fields such as physics, biology, and chemistry, where complex mathematical models and simulations are common.

- **Big Data Analytics**: Julia's ability to handle large volumes of data, particularly when integrated with parallel computing tools like SharedVector.jl or cluster computing systems, allows for efficient analysis of massive datasets.

- **Machine Learning and AI**: Julia's speed makes it particularly attractive for training deep learning models, which often require substantial computational resources.

For example, Julia is used in high-frequency trading, computational finance, and simulations of dynamic systems in engineering, where its speed and scalability are paramount.

Optimization Techniques in Julia

Julia provides several ways to optimize performance, even further, for data science tasks:

- **Type Declarations**: Specifying types for function arguments and variables can significantly speed up code execution by reducing type inference overhead.

- **Parallel and Distributed Computing**: Julia has built-in support for parallel computing and distributed computing, which allows data scientists to split computational tasks across multiple processors or even machines, further improving performance.

- **GPU Computing**: For tasks that can be parallelized, Julia supports GPU-based computing using packages like CUDA.jl to harness the power of graphics cards for even faster execution.

Julia's speed optimization capabilities, combined with its just-in-time compilation, make it an excellent choice for data science tasks that require heavy computational resources. Compared to Python and R, Julia outperforms in areas involving numerical computing and large-scale data processing. By utilizing Julia's performance features, data scientists can achieve higher productivity and faster results, particularly when working with complex machine learning models or scientific simulations.

Module 14:

Comparing Programming Languages

Choosing the right programming language is crucial for data science projects, as different languages excel in different aspects. This module compares Python, R, and other popular languages, providing insights into when to use each language based on the specific use case, performance trade-offs, integration in multilingual projects, and industry-specific applications.

When to Use Python, R, or Others?: Decision-Making Based on Use Case

Python and R are the two most widely used languages in data science, each suited for different tasks. Python's general-purpose nature makes it ideal for machine learning, web development, and automation, while R is optimized for statistical analysis and data visualization. Julia, on the other hand, shines in high-performance computing scenarios. The choice between these languages depends on the task—Python is better for scalable solutions, R is optimal for statistical analysis, and Julia excels in high-performance simulations. Understanding the strengths of each language is essential when deciding which one to use for specific projects.

Trade-offs in Performance and Usability: Memory, Speed, and Ease of Use

Each programming language has its trade-offs between performance and usability. Python is highly user-friendly with a rich ecosystem of libraries but may lag in execution speed for computation-heavy tasks. R is excellent for statistical computing but can struggle with larger datasets or complex workflows. Julia offers superior performance and speed, particularly in numerical tasks, but its learning curve can be steeper compared to Python or R. The decision on which language to use often depends on the balance required between speed, memory efficiency, and ease of use, as well as the complexity of the task at hand.

Multilingual Projects and Integration: Tools Like reticulate and pySpark

In many data science projects, different languages may be used in parallel to leverage their strengths. Tools like **reticulate** (for integrating Python with R) and **pySpark** (for using Python with Spark) allow seamless interaction between languages. This enables data scientists to combine the strengths of Python's extensive libraries, R's statistical prowess, and Spark's distributed computing capabilities. These tools allow for more efficient workflows and make it easier to integrate specialized language-specific features, leading to more flexible and scalable solutions. Integrating languages becomes essential in large projects requiring diverse functionality.

Choosing the Right Language for Specific Applications: Industry Examples

Different industries favor different programming languages depending on their unique needs. In finance and high-frequency trading, C++ and Julia dominate due to their performance in handling large datasets and executing complex computations at high speeds. In healthcare and pharmaceuticals, R's specialized statistical packages make it a go-to for clinical trials and research. Python is often favored in technology and machine learning applications for its ease of use and flexibility. Understanding the industry-specific requirements and the problem at hand helps data scientists make informed decisions about the most appropriate language for their project.

When to Use Python, R, or Others? Decision-Making Based on Use Case

Selecting the right programming language for a data science project is crucial for its success. Python, R, and other languages each have their unique strengths, and understanding when to use each one can lead to more efficient and scalable solutions. In this section, we'll discuss the decision-making process based on the specific use case of your project.

Python for Versatility and Scalability

Python is often the go-to language for general-purpose data science tasks due to its versatility, ease of use, and robust ecosystem of libraries. It is widely used for machine learning, data analysis, automation, and web development, making it an excellent choice for projects requiring integration across multiple domains. With libraries like pandas for data manipulation, matplotlib for visualization, and scikit-learn for machine learning, Python can handle virtually any data science challenge.

For example, Python is the best choice for building end-to-end machine learning pipelines. Its simplicity in integrating with different platforms, such as cloud services (AWS, GCP), and its strong support for deep learning with libraries like TensorFlow and PyTorch, make Python an ideal option for large-scale AI applications.

R for Statistical Analysis and Visualization

R excels in statistical analysis and complex data visualization. It has an extensive set of statistical packages, and its syntax is designed with statisticians in mind, making it the preferred language in academia and research. The ggplot2 package for visualization and dplyr for data manipulation are standout tools in the R ecosystem.

R is highly suitable for data exploration and visual storytelling, especially when detailed statistical modeling and exploratory analysis are required. For example, R would be ideal for a project that involves advanced statistical tests, like time-series analysis or survival analysis, where built-in statistical functions are optimized and well-supported.

Other Languages: Julia, Scala, and SQL

While Python and R dominate the field of data science, other languages like Julia, Scala, and SQL can also play important roles depending on the context. Julia, with its high-performance capabilities for numerical computation, is ideal for projects requiring intensive mathematical modeling or large-scale simulations. For tasks involving big data analytics, Scala and Apache Spark provide a scalable solution to handle distributed computing and parallel processing efficiently.

SQL is essential when working with large relational databases. It is indispensable for querying and manipulating structured data, making it vital for backend data extraction in any data science project. While Python and R can interact with databases, SQL is optimized for managing large datasets.

Decision-Making Based on Use Case

Choosing the right programming language for your data science project hinges on the specific requirements of the use case. For example, Python is preferred for machine learning model development and automation scripts, while R is more suitable for academic research and specialized statistical modeling. If performance is a key concern, Julia should be considered, especially for complex mathematical tasks. For large-scale data processing and big data projects, Scala paired with Spark is an excellent choice.

In practice, many data science teams use a combination of these languages. Python for machine learning, R for statistical analysis, and SQL for database management are often integrated in a single workflow. The decision is rarely one language versus another, but rather the best tool for each part of the project.

When selecting a programming language for a data science project, consider the specific requirements and goals of the project. Python's versatility, R's statistical capabilities, Julia's performance, and SQL's database management make them complementary tools in the data science toolkit. Choosing the right language for each aspect of the project ensures that the best solution is implemented efficiently.

Trade-offs in Performane and Usability: Memory, Speed, and Ease of Use

When choosing between programming languages for a data science project, one of the most important factors to consider is the trade-off between performance and usability. Languages such as Python, R, Julia, and others each offer different balances of memory efficiency, processing speed, and ease of use. This section explores these trade-offs and helps determine which language is most suitable for your specific needs.

Memory Efficiency: Managing Resources

Memory efficiency is crucial in data science, particularly when working with large datasets. Some programming languages handle memory better than others, allowing for faster and more efficient processing.

Python, for example, is known for being relatively memory-hungry compared to other languages. This is particularly noticeable when dealing with large datasets that exceed the available system memory. Libraries like pandas are efficient for smaller datasets, but they can consume significant memory when scaled up. Optimizing Python code to handle large datasets often requires extra effort, such as breaking datasets into smaller chunks, or using libraries like Dask to enable parallel processing.

In contrast, languages like Julia are designed with memory efficiency in mind, especially for high-performance numerical tasks. Julia allows for more control over memory allocation, and its Just-in-Time (JIT) compiler helps reduce memory overhead. For data scientists working with large-scale simulations or computations, Julia provides the advantage of better memory management and faster computation times.

R, although not as efficient as Julia in terms of memory, can be optimized through packages like data.table and ff, which are designed to handle larger datasets without overloading the memory.

Speed: Performance and Execution Time

Speed is another critical factor when selecting a programming language. Some tasks, such as machine learning model training or processing large datasets, demand high computational power, and certain languages are better suited to these requirements.

Python is an interpreted language, which means it generally runs slower than compiled languages. However, it offers robust support for optimization libraries like NumPy and Cython, which can speed up computations by offloading the heavy lifting to lower-level languages like C. For example, the NumPy library, by leveraging optimized C routines, can provide significant performance gains for numerical operations.

Julia shines in this aspect because it is designed for high-performance computing. Its JIT compiler allows it to execute code at speeds comparable to C and Fortran, making it particularly well-suited for computationally intensive tasks, such as matrix operations and numerical simulations. For large-scale data analysis, Julia's speed is a significant advantage.

R, while fast in statistical modeling, is often not as fast as Python or Julia for general-purpose tasks. Its speed can be improved through parallel computing techniques and by using specialized libraries like Rcpp, which integrates R with C++ for performance boosts.

Ease of Use: Learning Curve and Developer Productivity

Ease of use is another significant trade-off. For those new to programming, Python is widely regarded as one of the easiest languages to learn. Its simple syntax, readable code, and vast community support make it an excellent choice for both beginners and experienced developers. Python's versatility allows it to be used across a variety of fields, from data analysis to web development, making it the most popular language in data science.

R is also relatively easy to learn, especially for statisticians or researchers familiar with statistical analysis. Its syntax is more specialized and geared towards statistical modeling, which makes it a natural fit for data analysis tasks. However, it may not be as intuitive for those unfamiliar with statistical techniques.

Julia, while faster and more efficient, has a steeper learning curve. Its syntax is similar to that of Python, but the language is more focused on performance and mathematical modeling, which may require a higher level of expertise, especially in areas such as parallel programming and optimization.

Balancing the Trade-offs

Each language has its advantages and disadvantages when it comes to memory, speed, and ease of use. Python offers excellent usability and a rich ecosystem of libraries, making it the most versatile language for a broad range of data science tasks. R is particularly suited for specialized statistical analysis, while Julia excels in high-performance computing. When performance is a primary concern, Julia is the ideal choice, but Python can often bridge the gap through optimization techniques. Understanding these trade-offs and selecting the right language based on project requirements is key to successful data science outcomes.

Multilingual Projects and Integration: Tools Like reticulate and pySpark

In modern data science projects, it is not uncommon to work with multiple programming languages to leverage the strengths of each. Multilingual integration allows for a combination of tools and libraries across languages, increasing efficiency and expanding capabilities. This section explores how multilingual projects can be managed, with a focus on tools like reticulate and PySpark for seamless integration between Python, R, and other languages.

The Need for Multilingual Projects

In complex data science workflows, different languages often excel at different tasks. For example, Python is widely used for data manipulation, machine learning, and automation, whereas R shines in statistical analysis and visualization. Similarly, Scala and Julia offer better performance for high-scale computations and big data analytics. Instead of choosing one language, integrating them allows teams to use the best of each, boosting productivity and improving results.

However, managing a multilingual environment introduces challenges, such as interoperability, compatibility, and data exchange between languages. Thankfully, tools like reticulate (for R-Python integration) and PySpark (for Python-Scala integration) help to bridge the gap and facilitate seamless communication between languages.

Using reticulate for R-Python Integration

reticulate is an R package that provides a comprehensive interface between R and Python. It enables R users to call Python code directly from R scripts, access Python libraries, and exchange data between R and Python seamlessly. This integration allows users to take advantage of Python's powerful libraries like pandas, NumPy, and scikit-learn while still utilizing R for its strengths in statistical modeling and visualization.

For example, to use Python's pandas for data manipulation in an R environment, you can do the following:

```
# Load the reticulate package
library(reticulate)

# Use Python within R
pd <- import("pandas")

# Create a simple dataframe in Python
data <- pd$DataFrame(list(A=c(1, 2, 3), B=c(4, 5, 6)))

# Print the dataframe
print(data)
```

This allows data scientists to harness the best of both Python and R, combining Python's rich ecosystem with R's specialized statistical tools without leaving the R environment.

Using PySpark for Python-Scala Integration

Apache Spark is a distributed computing system designed for processing big data, and it is commonly used in data science for scalable machine learning and data analysis. PySpark is the Python API for Apache Spark, allowing Python users to interact with Spark's underlying distributed computing framework. Since Spark is primarily written in Scala, Python developers can access Spark's powerful features without needing to learn Scala.

PySpark integrates well with Python, enabling distributed data processing across clusters, which is especially beneficial for handling big data. Below is an example of using PySpark to create a Spark DataFrame and perform a simple operation:

```
from pyspark.sql import SparkSession

# Initialize Spark session
spark = SparkSession.builder.appName("Example").getOrCreate()

# Create a DataFrame
data = [("Alice", 1), ("Bob", 2), ("Charlie", 3)]
df = spark.createDataFrame(data, ["name", "value"])

# Show the DataFrame
df.show()
```

While PySpark allows Python users to interact with Spark, it also enables them to scale their analysis and models on large datasets across multiple nodes. Thus, PySpark is an essential tool for Python developers working in big data environments.

Integrating Multiple Languages in a Single Workflow

The ability to integrate languages like Python, R, and Scala is invaluable when working on large-scale data science projects that require high performance, scalability, and specialized analysis. By using tools like reticulate and PySpark, data scientists can create pipelines that leverage the strengths of each language, ensuring that each aspect of the project is handled in the most efficient and effective way possible.

For instance, a data pipeline might involve using R for data cleaning and visualization, Python for machine learning, and Scala (via PySpark) for large-scale data processing. This multilingual approach allows teams to avoid the limitations of any one language while benefiting from the combined power of all the languages in the workflow.

Choosing the Right Language for Specific Applications: Industry Examples

Choosing the right programming language for a data science project can significantly impact its success. The decision depends on various factors such as the type of data, the nature of the problem, available libraries, scalability requirements, and team expertise. In this section, we explore how different industries select programming languages based on their unique needs, providing examples across several domains.

Financial Sector: Python and R for Data Analysis and Quantitative Modeling

In the financial industry, data scientists work with complex datasets and need to conduct quantitative modeling, risk analysis, and forecasting. Python and R are commonly used due to their rich ecosystems and extensive libraries for statistical analysis, time series analysis, and machine learning.

Python's pandas library is a go-to tool for handling financial data, while R's extensive statistical packages, like quantmod and TTR, make it the preferred choice for econometric modeling. Additionally, Python's deep learning libraries such as TensorFlow and Keras are used in financial institutions for predictive modeling and algorithmic trading.

For instance, Python is often used for building automated trading strategies, where real-time data ingestion and rapid model updates are critical. Meanwhile, R is frequently used for time-series forecasting and in-depth statistical analysis to assess market risks.

Healthcare and Biotech: R for Statistical Analysis, Python for Machine Learning

In healthcare and biotech, the choice of language often depends on the specific application. R's strengths in statistical modeling and biostatistics make it a primary choice for analyzing clinical trial data, genetic data, and epidemiological studies. R has well-established libraries such as survival, lme4, and ggplot2 for performing statistical analyses and visualizing complex medical datasets.

On the other hand, Python is preferred for machine learning applications, especially for tasks like predictive analytics, image processing, and natural language processing. Python libraries like scikit-learn for traditional machine learning, TensorFlow for deep learning, and OpenCV for image analysis are widely used in healthcare for diagnosing diseases from medical images, such as in radiology.

For example, a company developing medical imaging software might use Python for developing convolutional neural networks (CNNs) to automatically detect diseases like cancer from X-rays or MRI scans, while R would be used for performing statistical analysis on clinical trial data.

E-commerce: Python and Scala for Big Data Processing

In e-commerce, handling large-scale customer data, transaction records, and website analytics is a critical task. Python is often used in customer analytics, recommendation systems, and sales forecasting. Python's machine learning libraries, such as scikit-learn for traditional models and TensorFlow or PyTorch for deep learning, are essential for building recommendation engines that suggest products to customers based on their browsing and purchase history.

For big data processing, companies may rely on Scala, especially in combination with Apache Spark. Scala's performance with Spark makes it ideal for processing and analyzing large datasets, such as customer behavior logs and real-time sales transactions. Spark's ability to perform distributed computing allows e-commerce platforms to handle vast amounts of transactional data efficiently.

For example, a recommendation system used by an e-commerce company may be built with Python, leveraging deep learning to predict customer preferences, while the backend data processing and batch jobs might be managed with Scala and Spark for scalability.

Telecommunications: Python and SQL for Data Management and Customer Insights

In telecommunications, managing large volumes of customer data, network performance data, and call records is essential. Python is widely used for data cleaning, analysis, and modeling, as it provides powerful libraries for data manipulation (pandas), machine learning (scikit-learn), and data visualization (matplotlib).

SQL, on the other hand, is the preferred language for querying and managing relational databases. In telecommunications, SQL is crucial for extracting and aggregating data from customer relationship management (CRM) systems, billing databases, and network monitoring systems.

For example, telecommunications companies often use Python to analyze customer churn and predict future trends using machine learning models, while SQL is used for querying large transactional datasets and preparing the data for analysis.

Choosing the right programming language for a data science project is essential for achieving the best results. Industries such as finance, healthcare, e-commerce, and telecommunications rely on specific programming languages to meet their unique needs. Python and R dominate the data science landscape due to their versatility and rich ecosystems. However, other languages like Scala and SQL are also indispensable in certain use cases, such as big data processing and database management.

Part 3:

Data Manipulation and Analysis

Data Wrangling

Data wrangling, or data cleaning, is an essential skill for data scientists. This module covers the core techniques for transforming raw data into a usable format. Key topics include identifying and handling missing values, dealing with outliers, and using imputation strategies to ensure dataset completeness. Learners will also explore feature engineering techniques, which involve creating new variables from existing ones to improve model performance. Additionally, we examine the automation of data wrangling processes through tools and programming techniques to make this critical step more efficient.

Exploratory Data Analysis (EDA)

Exploratory Data Analysis (EDA) is a key step in understanding datasets and uncovering underlying patterns. This module focuses on visualizing distributions and relationships in data through histograms, scatter plots, and box plots. Learners will also explore methods to identify trends, anomalies, and patterns in data, using both visual and statistical techniques. The module emphasizes the importance of summarizing data with statistical methods, such as measures of central tendency and variability. Tools like Python's Seaborn and R's ggplot2 will be discussed for performing EDA effectively.

Data Visualization Principles

Effective data visualization is crucial for conveying complex insights clearly and persuasively. This module delves into the principles of designing effective visuals, focusing on clarity, accuracy, and aesthetics. Topics include choosing the right type of chart or graph to represent data, from bar charts to heatmaps and line graphs. The module also explores interactive dashboards that allow users to engage with the data dynamically, as well as the role of storytelling in data visualization. Learners will gain insights into how to present data in a compelling narrative format that informs decision-making.

Statistical Data Analysis

Statistical data analysis is a foundation of data science, allowing practitioners to make informed decisions from data. This module covers descriptive statistics, including measures like mean, median, mode, variance, and standard deviation, to summarize data effectively. We then move into inferential statistics, focusing on hypothesis testing and confidence intervals. Key techniques such as correlation and regression analysis are explored, helping learners understand relationships between variables and how to model these relationships. These techniques are critical for drawing conclusions and making predictions based on data.

Handling Big Data

Handling big data requires specialized techniques and tools to process massive datasets efficiently. This module introduces the basics of distributed computing, explaining how data can be processed across multiple machines. We discuss two major big data frameworks: Apache Hadoop and Apache Spark, covering their architectures and use cases. The module also explores the differences between batch processing and stream processing, providing insights into when each approach is appropriate. Additionally, we discuss how to optimize data pipelines to ensure scalability and speed when working with large datasets.

Dimensionality Reduction

In high-dimensional datasets, reducing the number of features can improve model performance and interpretation. This module covers techniques like Principal Component Analysis (PCA), t-SNE, and UMAP, which help reduce dimensions while preserving important patterns in the data. Feature selection methods are also explored, allowing learners to identify and retain the most relevant variables. We examine the impact of dimensionality reduction on model performance, highlighting its role in improving computational efficiency and avoiding overfitting.

Applied Data Analysis Case Studies

This module focuses on real-world applications of data analysis across different industries, offering case studies that showcase the application of data manipulation and analysis techniques. Learners will explore cross-domain insights, learning how methods from one field can inform solutions in another. The module also features interactive solutions, providing hands-on experience with applied data analysis. Discussions around the limitations and opportunities of data analysis in various sectors will deepen learners' understanding of the complexities involved in real-world data science work.

Module 15:

Data Wrangling

Data wrangling is a crucial step in the data science workflow, as raw data is often messy, incomplete, and inconsistent. This module covers the key aspects of data wrangling, including cleaning and transforming data, handling missing and outlier data, feature engineering, and automating the data wrangling process to streamline workflows and improve data quality for analysis.

Cleaning and Transforming Data

The first step in data wrangling involves cleaning the data to ensure its accuracy and consistency. This includes removing duplicates, correcting errors, and standardizing formats. Transforming the data follows, which may involve aggregating, normalizing, or reshaping the data to fit the required structure for analysis. Effective cleaning and transformation ensure that the dataset is ready for further exploration and modeling.

Handling Missing and Outlier Data

Missing data and outliers are common challenges in real-world datasets. Handling missing data requires strategies like imputation or deletion, depending on the context and the importance of the missing values. Outliers can distort analyses, so identifying and treating them—either by removal or transformation—helps ensure more reliable results. Proper treatment of missing and outlier data is essential for maintaining data integrity.

Feature Engineering Techniques

Feature engineering involves creating new variables or modifying existing ones to improve model performance. Techniques like encoding categorical variables, scaling numerical features, and creating interaction terms can significantly enhance predictive accuracy. It also includes domain-specific approaches to deriving features that capture important patterns or relationships in the data. Well-engineered features lead to better-performing models and more insightful analyses.

Automating Data Wrangling Processes

Automating data wrangling processes can greatly increase efficiency, especially when working with large datasets or frequent updates. Automation tools, such as scripting in Python or using specialized libraries, allow for the repetitive cleaning, transformation, and preparation tasks to be executed automatically. This reduces manual errors and saves time, allowing data scientists to focus on more complex aspects of the analysis and model building.

Cleaning and Transforming Data

Data wrangling, also known as data cleaning or preprocessing, is a critical step in the data science lifecycle. It involves transforming raw data into a format suitable for analysis, which includes cleaning up errors, handling missing values, and reshaping the data. In this section, we explore the importance of cleaning and transforming data, the methods used, and how to perform these tasks efficiently using Python.

The Importance of Cleaning and Transforming Data

Raw data is often messy, incomplete, or inconsistent, which makes it unsuitable for analysis. Before performing any analysis, it's crucial to clean and transform the data to ensure that it is accurate, consistent, and structured in a way that allows for meaningful insights. This process improves the quality of data and ensures that machine learning models or statistical analyses are based on reliable information.

Cleaning involves identifying and rectifying errors such as incorrect formatting, duplicates, or inconsistent values. Transformation, on the other hand, is about reshaping the data—whether it's aggregating, normalizing, or converting it into a more useful structure. A clean dataset leads to more accurate results and helps avoid misleading conclusions.

Handling Missing Data

One of the most common issues in data wrangling is handling missing data. Missing values can arise for various reasons, such as errors in data collection, system failures, or non-responses in surveys. Ignoring missing data can introduce bias, so it's important to handle it correctly.

There are several approaches to handling missing data:

- **Rows/Columns**: If the missing data is minimal and not critical, you can drop the rows or columns containing missing values.

- **Imputation**: For numerical data, imputation can be used to fill missing values with the mean, median, or mode. For categorical data, the missing values can be replaced with the most frequent category.

In Python, the pandas library provides several tools for dealing with missing data. Here's an example of how to handle missing values:

```
import pandas as pd
# Sample DataFrame with missing values
```

```
data = {'Name': ['Alice', 'Bob', None, 'David'],
        'Age': [25, None, 30, 22]}
df = pd.DataFrame(data)

# Filling missing values with the mean
df['Age'].fillna(df['Age'].mean(), inplace=True)

# Dropping rows with missing values
df.dropna(inplace=True)

print(df)
```

In this example, missing values in the 'Age' column are replaced with the mean, and any remaining rows with missing values are dropped.

Handling Outliers

Outliers are extreme values that deviate significantly from other observations in a dataset. While outliers might represent valid variations, they can often distort statistical analyses or machine learning models. Therefore, identifying and handling outliers is an essential step in data wrangling.

Several methods for detecting outliers include:

- **Visualization**: Tools like box plots or scatter plots can help visually identify outliers.

- **Statistical Methods**: The Z-score or Interquartile Range (IQR) can be used to mathematically detect outliers. A data point can be considered an outlier if it falls outside 1.5 times the IQR.

Here's an example using IQR to detect and remove outliers:

```
import numpy as np

# Sample data
data = [10, 12, 13, 10, 100, 11, 9, 9, 12, 10]

# Calculate IQR
Q1 = np.percentile(data, 25)
Q3 = np.percentile(data, 75)
IQR = Q3 - Q1

# Detect outliers
outliers = [x for x in data if x < (Q1 - 1.5 * IQR) or x > (Q3 + 1.5 * IQR)]

# Removing outliers
clean_data = [x for x in data if x >= (Q1 - 1.5 * IQR) and x <= (Q3 + 1.5 *
          IQR)]
print("Outliers:", outliers)
print("Cleaned Data:", clean_data)
```

This method identifies and removes outliers based on the IQR criterion, leaving a dataset free from extreme values.

Feature Transformation Techniques

Feature transformation involves modifying existing features to enhance the performance of machine learning models. Common techniques include:

- **Normalization**: Scaling numerical features to a range, typically 0 to 1, to ensure they are on the same scale.

- **Standardization**: Transforming features to have a mean of 0 and a standard deviation of 1, often required for algorithms like Support Vector Machines (SVM) or K-means.

Here's an example of feature scaling using Python's sklearn library:

```python
from sklearn.preprocessing import StandardScaler

# Sample data
data = [[1, 2], [3, 4], [5, 6], [7, 8]]

# Standardize features
scaler = StandardScaler()
scaled_data = scaler.fit_transform(data)

print(scaled_data)
```

This code standardizes the dataset, ensuring that each feature has a mean of 0 and a standard deviation of 1.

Data cleaning and transformation are fundamental steps in the data wrangling process. By addressing missing values, handling outliers, and transforming features, you ensure that the data is ready for meaningful analysis and machine learning. Python's rich libraries, like pandas, numpy, and sklearn, provide powerful tools for these tasks, making data wrangling both efficient and effective.

Handling Missing and Outlier Data

In data wrangling, one of the most common issues encountered is dealing with missing data and outliers. These issues can affect the accuracy and quality of your analyses, making it crucial to handle them properly. This section discusses strategies for handling missing values and outliers, along with Python code examples to illustrate the techniques.

Handling Missing Data

Missing data is a widespread challenge in real-world datasets. Whether due to non-responses in surveys, data corruption, or errors during data collection, missing values can lead to biased results or loss of information. There are several techniques to handle missing data:

1. **Removing Missing Data**: If the amount of missing data is minimal, one option is to simply remove the rows or columns containing missing values. However, this should be done carefully, as removing too much data can lead to biased or incomplete analysis.

2. **Imputation**: Instead of removing missing values, they can be replaced with estimates. Common techniques for imputation include:

   o Replacing with the **mean**, **median**, or **mode** of the column for numerical or categorical data.

   o Using more advanced methods such as **K-nearest neighbors (KNN)** or **multivariate imputation**.

The following Python code demonstrates how to handle missing data using imputation and removal using pandas:

```python
import pandas as pd

# Sample data with missing values
data = {'Name': ['Alice', 'Bob', None, 'David'],
        'Age': [25, None, 30, 22]}
df = pd.DataFrame(data)

# Impute missing values with mean for numerical columns
df['Age'].fillna(df['Age'].mean(), inplace=True)

# Drop rows with missing values
df.dropna(inplace=True)

print(df)
```

In this example, the missing Age value is replaced with the mean of the column, and any remaining rows with missing data are dropped.

Handling Outlier Data

Outliers are extreme values that differ significantly from other data points. While outliers can sometimes provide valuable insights, they often distort statistical models and analyses. It's important to detect and manage outliers to prevent them from skewing results.

Outlier detection methods include:

- **Visual Methods**: Boxplots or scatter plots are effective for visually identifying outliers.

- **Statistical Methods**: The **Interquartile Range (IQR)** and **Z-scores** are commonly used to define thresholds beyond which values are considered outliers.

Here's an example of using IQR to detect and remove outliers in a numerical dataset:

```python
import numpy as np

# Sample data
data = [10, 12, 13, 10, 100, 11, 9, 9, 12, 10]

# Calculate IQR
Q1 = np.percentile(data, 25)
Q3 = np.percentile(data, 75)
IQR = Q3 - Q1

# Detect outliers
outliers = [x for x in data if x < (Q1 - 1.5 * IQR) or x > (Q3 + 1.5 * IQR)]

# Remove outliers
clean_data = [x for x in data if x >= (Q1 - 1.5 * IQR) and x <= (Q3 + 1.5 *
        IQR)]
print("Outliers:", outliers)
print("Cleaned Data:", clean_data)
```

This code detects outliers based on the IQR method, which considers values outside 1.5 times the IQR as outliers and removes them from the dataset.

Imputation for Outliers

For outliers that cannot be removed without compromising the integrity of the dataset, another strategy is to replace them using imputation techniques. This can be done by replacing outliers with values based on statistical measures, such as the median or mean of the surrounding data.

For example, after identifying outliers using IQR, you could replace them with the median value of the data to maintain consistency:

```python
# Replace outliers with median value
median_value = np.median(data)
data_no_outliers = [x if (x >= (Q1 - 1.5 * IQR) and x <= (Q3 + 1.5 * IQR))
        else median_value for x in data]

print("Data with outliers replaced by median:", data_no_outliers)
```

This technique helps preserve the structure of the data while mitigating the effects of extreme values.

Handling missing data and outliers is a crucial step in the data wrangling process. While removing missing data can be effective, imputation techniques provide an alternative that preserves the dataset's size. Outliers, on the other hand, can be handled using statistical methods like IQR or Z-scores, or by replacing them with more representative values. With Python's robust libraries like pandas, numpy, and scipy, these tasks can be performed efficiently, ensuring that the data is ready for analysis and machine learning models.

Feature Engineering Techniques

Feature engineering is one of the most critical aspects of data preparation in the machine learning pipeline. It involves creating new features or modifying existing ones to improve the performance of machine learning algorithms. Properly engineered features can make the difference between a mediocre model and a highly accurate one. In this section, we will discuss several key techniques used in feature engineering, along with Python code examples.

Understanding Feature Engineering

Feature engineering is the process of transforming raw data into meaningful inputs for machine learning models. It involves selecting the right features, creating new ones, and transforming the data to help the algorithm make better predictions. The process includes various steps such as encoding categorical variables, scaling numerical features, and creating interaction terms.

Feature engineering is highly dependent on domain knowledge and creativity. A good feature engineer can often turn raw data into valuable insights that significantly improve model performance.

Techniques for Feature Engineering

1. **Handling Categorical Variables:**

Categorical variables (e.g., gender, country, etc.) need to be converted into numerical values for machine learning algorithms to process them. This is typically done through one-hot encoding or label encoding:

   o **One-hot encoding**: Converts categorical variables into a binary format, creating new columns for each category.

   o **Label encoding**: Assigns a unique integer to each category.

Python's pandas library provides easy-to-use functions for both encoding methods. Here's an example of one-hot encoding using pandas:

```
import pandas as pd

# Sample dataset with categorical data
data = {'Color': ['Red', 'Green', 'Blue', 'Green']}
df = pd.DataFrame(data)

# One-hot encode the 'Color' column
df_encoded = pd.get_dummies(df, columns=['Color'])

print(df_encoded)
```

This code converts the 'Color' column into three separate columns, one for each color, with binary values indicating the presence of each category.

2. Scaling Numerical Features:

Some machine learning algorithms are sensitive to the scale of numerical features. For example, algorithms like k-nearest neighbors (KNN) or support vector machines (SVM) perform better when features are on similar scales. Common scaling techniques include:

- **Standardization**: Scales the data to have a mean of 0 and a standard deviation of 1.

- **Normalization**: Rescales the data to fall between 0 and 1.

Here's an example of feature scaling using standardization with Python's scikit-learn:

```python
from sklearn.preprocessing import StandardScaler

# Sample dataset with numerical data
data = {'Height': [5.6, 6.0, 5.4, 5.9], 'Weight': [150, 160, 140, 155]}
df = pd.DataFrame(data)

# Standardize the features
scaler = StandardScaler()
df_scaled = pd.DataFrame(scaler.fit_transform(df), columns=df.columns)

print(df_scaled)
```

This code standardizes the 'Height' and 'Weight' columns so that they have a mean of 0 and a standard deviation of 1.

3. Creating Interaction Features:

Interaction features are combinations of two or more features that may have a significant impact on the model's prediction. For example, if you're working with data on income and age, creating a feature such as "income-to-age ratio" might help the model capture relationships between these two variables more effectively.

Here's how to create an interaction feature in Python:

```python
# Sample dataset with 'Income' and 'Age'
df = pd.DataFrame({'Income': [50000, 60000, 55000, 65000], 'Age': [25, 30, 35, 40]})

# Create an interaction feature: income to age ratio
df['Income_to_Age_Ratio'] = df['Income'] / df['Age']

print(df)
```

This code adds a new feature, Income_to_Age_Ratio, which is the ratio of income to age.

4. Handling Missing Data during Feature Engineering:

Missing data is a common challenge in feature engineering. One approach is to create a binary feature indicating whether a value is missing or not. This way, missing data is treated as a separate category, which can be useful for algorithms that can handle missing values. For example:

```
# Sample dataset with missing values
df = pd.DataFrame({'Age': [25, None, 30, None]})

# Create a binary feature indicating missing values
df['Age_is_missing'] = df['Age'].isnull().astype(int)

print(df)
```

This code creates a new column, Age_is_missing, that indicates whether the 'Age' value is missing (1 if missing, 0 if not).

Feature engineering is a crucial step in building successful machine learning models. Techniques such as handling categorical variables, scaling numerical features, and creating interaction terms can significantly improve model performance. The ability to effectively preprocess and engineer features is essential for data scientists to transform raw data into actionable insights. By combining domain knowledge with data manipulation tools in Python, data scientists can create robust features that enhance model accuracy and efficiency.

Automating Data Wrangling Processes

Automating data wrangling processes is essential for improving efficiency, ensuring consistency, and managing large datasets. Data wrangling involves cleaning, transforming, and reshaping data to make it suitable for analysis and machine learning. While data wrangling is typically a manual and time-consuming task, automation can streamline the process, reduce errors, and accelerate data preparation.

In this section, we will explore various techniques for automating data wrangling processes using Python and other tools, focusing on automation techniques for common tasks such as data cleaning, transformation, and feature engineering.

Automating Data Cleaning

Data cleaning is the first and most crucial step in the data wrangling process. It involves removing duplicates, handling missing values, correcting errors, and standardizing data formats. Automating these tasks is possible using Python libraries like pandas and numpy.

Removing Duplicates Automatically:

Duplicate records can distort analysis and should be identified and removed. Here's how to automate the process of removing duplicates in a dataset:

```
import pandas as pd

# Sample dataset with duplicates
data = {'ID': [1, 2, 2, 4], 'Name': ['Alice', 'Bob', 'Bob', 'David']}
df = pd.DataFrame(data)

# Removing duplicate rows
df_cleaned = df.drop_duplicates()

print(df_cleaned)
```

This code automatically identifies and removes duplicate rows based on all columns, leaving only unique records.

Handling Missing Values:

Missing values can be handled in different ways, such as by filling them with a default value, using interpolation, or removing the rows entirely. Here's how to automatically fill missing values:

```
# Sample dataset with missing values
data = {'Age': [25, None, 30, None], 'Income': [50000, 60000, 55000, 65000]}
df = pd.DataFrame(data)

# Fill missing 'Age' values with the mean
df['Age'] = df['Age'].fillna(df['Age'].mean())

print(df)
```

This code fills missing values in the 'Age' column with the mean of the existing values, which is a common approach to handling missing data.

Automating Data Transformation

Data transformation involves changing the format or structure of data to make it compatible with analytical models. Common transformations include normalizing data, encoding categorical variables, and feature scaling. Automating these tasks can save a lot of time, especially when working with large datasets.

Automatic Data Scaling:

Scaling numerical features ensures that they are all on a similar scale, which is important for machine learning algorithms like k-nearest neighbors (KNN) or support vector machines (SVM). Here's an automated approach to scale features using scikit-learn:

```
from sklearn.preprocessing import StandardScaler

# Sample dataset with numerical features
data = {'Height': [5.6, 6.0, 5.4, 5.9], 'Weight': [150, 160, 140, 155]}
df = pd.DataFrame(data)

# Standardize the features using StandardScaler
scaler = StandardScaler()
```

```
df_scaled = pd.DataFrame(scaler.fit_transform(df), columns=df.columns)

print(df_scaled)
```

This automatically standardizes the 'Height' and 'Weight' columns by scaling them to have a mean of 0 and a standard deviation of 1.

Encoding Categorical Variables:

Automating the encoding of categorical variables is necessary for machine learning models, which cannot work with non-numeric data. The pandas library provides simple methods to automatically encode categorical variables:

```
# Sample dataset with a categorical variable
data = {'Color': ['Red', 'Green', 'Blue', 'Green']}
df = pd.DataFrame(data)

# Automatically one-hot encode the 'Color' column
df_encoded = pd.get_dummies(df, columns=['Color'])

print(df_encoded)
```

This code automatically applies one-hot encoding to the 'Color' column, creating binary columns for each category.

Automating Feature Engineering

Feature engineering is a critical step in the data wrangling process, where raw data is transformed into meaningful features that improve model performance. Automating feature engineering techniques such as creating interaction features or generating polynomial features can save considerable time and effort.

Creating Interaction Features:

Interaction features capture the relationship between two or more variables, which can improve the model's predictive power. Here's how you can automate the creation of interaction features in Python:

```
# Sample dataset with two features
df = pd.DataFrame({'Income': [50000, 60000, 55000, 65000], 'Age': [25, 30,
        35, 40]})

# Automatically create interaction feature
df['Income_Age_Interaction'] = df['Income'] * df['Age']

print(df)
```

This code automatically creates a new column that is the product of 'Income' and 'Age', capturing the interaction between the two features.

Automating with Pipelines

One of the best practices for automating data wrangling processes is using pipelines. Pipelines allow you to chain together multiple steps, such as data cleaning, transformation, and feature engineering, into a seamless process. Libraries like scikit-learn and pandas make it easy to create pipelines for automating data wrangling tasks.

For instance, a simple pipeline can be created to preprocess data, handle missing values, and scale features automatically:

```python
from sklearn.pipeline import Pipeline
from sklearn.preprocessing import StandardScaler
from sklearn.impute import SimpleImputer
from sklearn.compose import ColumnTransformer

# Sample dataset with missing values
df = pd.DataFrame({'Age': [25, None, 30, None], 'Income': [50000, 60000,
          55000, 65000]})

# Create a pipeline for data processing
pipeline = Pipeline(steps=[
    ('imputer', SimpleImputer(strategy='mean')),  # Fill missing values with
          the mean
    ('scaler', StandardScaler())                  # Standardize the features
])

# Apply pipeline to the data
df_processed = pipeline.fit_transform(df)

print(df_processed)
```

This pipeline handles both missing data and feature scaling automatically, simplifying the data wrangling process.

Automating data wrangling processes is essential for saving time and ensuring the consistency of your data preparation pipeline. By leveraging libraries such as pandas, scikit-learn, and creating efficient workflows, you can streamline repetitive tasks such as data cleaning, transformation, and feature engineering. Automation not only improves efficiency but also enhances reproducibility, making it easier to handle large datasets and complex workflows.

Module 16:

Exploratory Data Analysis (EDA)

Exploratory Data Analysis (EDA) is a critical first step in understanding data before applying complex models. It involves visualizing data distributions, identifying patterns and trends, and applying statistical methods to gain insights. This module will explore techniques and tools that help uncover key features of the data, allowing data scientists to make informed decisions about the next steps in analysis.

Visualizing Distributions and Relationships

Visualizations are essential for exploring data. Histograms, box plots, and density plots help in understanding the distribution of individual variables. Scatter plots, pair plots, and correlation matrices are used to visualize relationships between variables. These visual tools provide a clear view of data trends, helping identify any underlying structures or outliers early in the analysis process.

Identifying Patterns and Trends

EDA aims to identify hidden patterns, trends, and anomalies that could influence the modeling process. Techniques like clustering, trend analysis, and decomposition help reveal periodicity, seasonality, and other recurring patterns. Understanding these patterns is crucial for informing model selection and feature engineering, making it easier to build models that reflect real-world processes.

Statistical Methods for EDA

Statistical methods play a vital role in EDA, helping to quantify relationships and assess the significance of patterns observed visually. Descriptive statistics such as mean, median, variance, and skewness provide insight into the data's central tendency and spread. Correlation tests and hypothesis testing help confirm relationships, guiding further analysis or model development.

Tools for EDA

Several tools and libraries are designed to streamline EDA. Python libraries like Pandas, Matplotlib, Seaborn, and Plotly are popular for data manipulation and visualization. R also provides robust tools such as ggplot2 and dplyr for exploratory analysis. These tools help data scientists perform comprehensive data exploration efficiently, saving time and uncovering valuable insights quickly.

Visualizing Distributions and Relationships

Exploratory Data Analysis (EDA) is a crucial step in the data science workflow, as it helps uncover patterns, detect anomalies, test assumptions, and develop intuition about the data. One of the most powerful techniques in EDA is visualizing the data, particularly focusing on distributions and relationships. Visualizations help identify key trends and understand the structure of the data, which can guide further analysis or modeling decisions.

In this section, we will focus on visualizing data distributions and relationships between variables using Python and popular libraries such as matplotlib, seaborn, and pandas.

Visualizing Distributions

A distribution shows how data points are spread across a range of values, and visualizing this distribution can reveal important information such as skewness, central tendency, and outliers. Histograms, boxplots, and density plots are commonly used to visualize distributions.

Histograms

A histogram provides a graphical representation of the distribution of a numerical variable by dividing the data into bins. The height of each bin shows the frequency of data points within that bin.

```python
import matplotlib.pyplot as plt
import seaborn as sns

# Sample dataset
data = [25, 30, 35, 40, 45, 50, 55, 60, 65, 70, 75, 80, 85, 90, 95]

# Creating a histogram
plt.hist(data, bins=10, color='skyblue', edgecolor='black')
plt.title('Histogram of Age Distribution')
plt.xlabel('Age')
plt.ylabel('Frequency')
plt.show()
```

This code generates a histogram showing the distribution of age, which allows us to visually assess the spread of values and identify any skewness or concentration in the data.

Boxplots

A boxplot (also known as a box-and-whisker plot) visualizes the distribution of a dataset based on its five-number summary: minimum, first quartile (Q1), median, third quartile (Q3), and maximum. It is particularly useful for identifying outliers and understanding the spread of data.

```
# Creating a boxplot
sns.boxplot(data=data, color='lightgreen')
plt.title('Boxplot of Age Distribution')
plt.xlabel('Age')
plt.show()
```

The boxplot provides a clear picture of the spread of age values, with any outliers appearing as points outside the whiskers.

Visualizing Relationships Between Variables

Visualizing the relationship between two or more variables is essential for understanding their interactions and identifying potential correlations. Scatter plots and pair plots are two useful techniques for this purpose.

Scatter Plots

A scatter plot is used to visualize the relationship between two continuous variables. It shows individual data points plotted on a two-dimensional grid, with one variable represented on the x-axis and the other on the y-axis.

```
# Sample dataset with two variables
import pandas as pd

df = pd.DataFrame({
    'Age': [25, 30, 35, 40, 45, 50, 55, 60, 65, 70],
    'Income': [30000, 35000, 40000, 45000, 50000, 55000, 60000, 65000,
            70000, 75000]
})

# Creating a scatter plot
sns.scatterplot(x='Age', y='Income', data=df)
plt.title('Scatter Plot of Age vs. Income')
plt.xlabel('Age')
plt.ylabel('Income')
plt.show()
```

This scatter plot reveals if there is a linear relationship between age and income, helping to identify trends or potential correlations between the variables.

Pair Plots

Pair plots are a great way to visualize the relationships between several variables at once. They show scatter plots for each pair of variables, along with histograms or density plots on the diagonal. This is particularly useful when exploring datasets with multiple features.

```
# Pair plot for the dataset
sns.pairplot(df)
plt.show()
```

This pair plot provides a comprehensive view of how multiple variables interact with each other, making it easier to spot correlations, patterns, or clusters in the data.

Visualizing distributions and relationships between variables is an essential part of EDA. It helps reveal the underlying structure of the data, identify trends, and highlight potential areas for further investigation. Tools like histograms, boxplots, scatter plots, and pair plots are invaluable for gaining insights into the data and preparing it for more advanced analysis or modeling. In this section, we've explored how to use Python libraries like matplotlib, seaborn, and pandas to create these visualizations, providing a solid foundation for exploratory data analysis.

Identifying Patterns and Trends

One of the key objectives of Exploratory Data Analysis (EDA) is to identify meaningful patterns and trends in data. These patterns may represent relationships between variables, temporal or seasonal effects, or clusters of similar observations. By identifying such trends early, data scientists can prioritize specific models, refine feature engineering, or transform the dataset in a way that improves predictive power.

In this section, we will discuss methods for identifying patterns and trends using Python. We will focus on time series analysis, correlation analysis, and clustering, which are useful techniques for recognizing patterns in data.

Time Series Analysis: Detecting Temporal Trends

Time series analysis is used to identify trends, seasonal patterns, and irregular fluctuations in data that is indexed by time. Visualizing time series data helps detect patterns, and statistical methods like moving averages or decomposition can make trends more apparent.

Line Plot for Time Series

The simplest method for visualizing temporal trends is the line plot. A line plot shows how a variable changes over time, making it easier to identify upward or downward trends, cyclic behaviors, or periods of stability.

```
import matplotlib.pyplot as plt
import pandas as pd

# Sample time series data (e.g., monthly sales)
data = pd.DataFrame({
    'Date': pd.date_range(start='2023-01-01', periods=12, freq='M'),
    'Sales': [200, 220, 250, 270, 300, 320, 330, 310, 280, 270, 240, 230]
})

# Plotting a line graph
plt.plot(data['Date'], data['Sales'], marker='o', color='b')
plt.title('Monthly Sales Trend')
plt.xlabel('Date')
plt.ylabel('Sales')
```

```
plt.xticks(rotation=45)
plt.grid(True)
plt.show()
```

In the line plot above, you can observe trends in the data such as increases and decreases in sales over time. This visualization makes it easy to spot seasonal changes or irregular periods in the data.

Decomposition for Trend and Seasonality

For more complex time series data, decomposing the series into its trend, seasonal, and residual components can provide a clearer view of underlying patterns.

```
from statsmodels.tsa.seasonal import seasonal_decompose

# Decompose the time series data
data.set_index('Date', inplace=True)
result = seasonal_decompose(data['Sales'], model='multiplicative',
        period=12)

# Plot decomposition components
result.plot()
plt.show()
```

Decomposition splits the series into components such as trend and seasonal patterns, providing more detailed insights into cyclical changes or long-term trends in the data.

Correlation Analysis: Identifying Relationships

Another key aspect of identifying patterns is finding relationships between two or more variables. Correlation analysis measures the strength and direction of the relationship between numerical variables. A correlation matrix can show how each variable in a dataset relates to the others.

Correlation Heatmap

A correlation heatmap is a great way to visualize relationships between variables. It uses color gradients to indicate the strength of correlations between variables, with darker colors representing stronger correlations.

```
import seaborn as sns
import numpy as np

# Sample dataset with multiple variables
df = pd.DataFrame({
    'Age': [25, 30, 35, 40, 45, 50, 55, 60],
    'Income': [35000, 45000, 55000, 60000, 65000, 70000, 75000, 80000],
    'Education Level': [1, 2, 2, 3, 3, 3, 4, 4]  # 1: High School, 2:
        Bachelor's, 3: Master's, 4: PhD
})

# Calculate correlation matrix
corr = df.corr()

# Plot heatmap
```

```
sns.heatmap(corr, annot=True, cmap='coolwarm', linewidths=1)
plt.title('Correlation Heatmap')
plt.show()
```

This heatmap allows you to quickly assess how different variables are related to each other. For example, you may find that income and age are positively correlated, while education level might show a non-linear relationship with income.

Clustering: Identifying Groups in Data

Clustering is an unsupervised learning technique used to group similar observations together. By identifying clusters, you can uncover hidden patterns or segments in the data that were not immediately obvious. K-means is one of the most commonly used clustering algorithms for this purpose.

K-Means Clustering

K-means clustering groups data into K distinct clusters based on similarities in feature values. It assigns each observation to the nearest centroid.

```
from sklearn.cluster import KMeans
import numpy as np

# Sample data for clustering
X = np.array([[25, 30000], [30, 40000], [35, 50000], [40, 60000], [45,
          70000],
             [50, 80000], [55, 90000], [60, 100000]])

# K-means clustering
kmeans = KMeans(n_clusters=2, random_state=42)
kmeans.fit(X)

# Plotting the clusters
plt.scatter(X[:, 0], X[:, 1], c=kmeans.labels_, cmap='viridis')
plt.scatter(kmeans.cluster_centers_[:, 0], kmeans.cluster_centers_[:, 1],
          marker='x', color='red')
plt.title('K-Means Clustering')
plt.xlabel('Age')
plt.ylabel('Income')
plt.show()
```

In this scatter plot, different clusters of individuals are grouped by their age and income, helping to reveal segments that may have distinct characteristics.

Identifying patterns and trends in data is an essential step in the data analysis process. Whether you are exploring time-dependent data, investigating relationships between variables, or discovering hidden groups through clustering, visualizations and statistical techniques provide valuable insights. In this section, we explored time series analysis, correlation analysis, and clustering as key methods for uncovering patterns in data. These methods help data scientists make informed decisions and generate hypotheses that can be tested in subsequent modeling stages.

Statistical Methods for EDA

Exploratory Data Analysis (EDA) is a crucial first step in data science, enabling data scientists to gain insights into data before applying complex models. While visual methods like plotting distributions or time series are valuable, statistical techniques also play a key role in identifying trends, correlations, and anomalies. In this section, we will discuss several statistical methods for EDA, focusing on descriptive statistics, hypothesis testing, and inferential methods.

Descriptive Statistics: Summarizing Data

Descriptive statistics provide a quick and efficient way to summarize and understand the basic properties of a dataset. These methods allow us to calculate measures such as the central tendency (mean, median, mode) and dispersion (variance, standard deviation, range) of the data, providing a snapshot of its general characteristics.

Key Descriptive Statistics

- **Mean**: The average value of the dataset, often used to represent the central tendency.

- **Median**: The middle value when the data is ordered, less sensitive to outliers than the mean.

- **Mode**: The most frequent value in the dataset.

- **Variance/Standard Deviation**: Measures of how spread out the values are from the mean.

For a quick summary of a dataset's descriptive statistics, Python's pandas library offers the .describe() method, which returns key statistics for each numeric column.

```
import pandas as pd

# Sample data
data = pd.DataFrame({
    'Age': [25, 30, 35, 40, 45, 50, 55, 60],
    'Income': [35000, 45000, 55000, 60000, 65000, 70000, 75000, 80000]
})

# Calculate descriptive statistics
summary = data.describe()
print(summary)
```

This will produce a summary table containing statistics such as count, mean, standard deviation, min, 25th percentile, median (50th percentile), 75th percentile, and max values. These summary measures help detect outliers or any potential skew in the data.

Hypothesis Testing: Testing Assumptions

Hypothesis testing is a statistical method used to test assumptions or claims about the data. It helps determine whether observed patterns or relationships are statistically significant. The two key components of hypothesis testing are:

- **Null Hypothesis (H$_0$)**: A statement that there is no effect or relationship.

- **Alternative Hypothesis (H$_1$)**: A statement that there is an effect or relationship.

A common test for comparing the means of two groups is the **t-test**. For example, you might want to test whether the mean income differs between two age groups.

T-Test in Python

```
from scipy import stats

# Data for two age groups
group_1 = [35000, 40000, 45000, 50000, 55000]
group_2 = [60000, 65000, 70000, 75000, 80000]

# Perform t-test
t_stat, p_value = stats.ttest_ind(group_1, group_2)

# Output the t-statistic and p-value
print(f"T-statistic: {t_stat}, P-value: {p_value}")
```

If the p-value is smaller than the chosen significance level (commonly 0.05), we reject the null hypothesis, indicating that there is a significant difference between the two groups. This helps in testing the validity of any assumptions made about the data.

Correlation Analysis: Measuring Relationships Between Variables

Correlation analysis assesses the strength and direction of a linear relationship between two or more variables. The **Pearson correlation coefficient** ranges from -1 to 1:

- **1** indicates a perfect positive correlation.

- **-1** indicates a perfect negative correlation.

- **0** indicates no linear correlation.

The correlation coefficient can be calculated using Python's pandas library.

```
# Calculate Pearson correlation
correlation_matrix = data.corr()
print(correlation_matrix)
```

A correlation matrix helps to visually assess relationships between multiple variables, aiding in the identification of key variables that might impact predictive models or further analysis.

Inferential Statistics: Making Predictions from Sample Data

Inferential statistics extends descriptive statistics by making predictions or inferences about a population based on a sample. Common techniques include confidence intervals and regression analysis.

Confidence Intervals

A confidence interval provides a range of values within which we expect the true population parameter to lie, with a certain level of confidence (e.g., 95%).

```python
import numpy as np

# Sample data
sample_data = np.array([35000, 40000, 45000, 50000, 55000])

# Calculate mean and standard error
mean = np.mean(sample_data)
std_error = np.std(sample_data) / np.sqrt(len(sample_data))

# Calculate 95% confidence interval
confidence_interval = [mean - 1.96 * std_error, mean + 1.96 * std_error]
print(f"95% Confidence Interval: {confidence_interval}")
```

This confidence interval suggests that we are 95% confident that the true mean income lies within the specified range.

Statistical methods are essential tools for identifying patterns, testing assumptions, and making inferences from data. Descriptive statistics summarize data and identify potential outliers or trends. Hypothesis testing helps evaluate the significance of observed effects, while correlation analysis quantifies the relationships between variables. Inferential statistics, such as confidence intervals, enable predictions about broader populations from sample data. By integrating these techniques into the EDA process, data scientists can derive meaningful insights and ensure that any modeling or predictive analysis is based on solid statistical reasoning.

Tools for EDA

Exploratory Data Analysis (EDA) is an essential step in the data science workflow. It involves understanding the dataset by summarizing its main characteristics and visualizing its structure and relationships. While statistical methods and hypothesis testing provide the theoretical foundation, tools for EDA make the process more efficient and insightful. In this section, we will explore the primary tools used for EDA: visualization libraries, Python's Pandas library, and interactive tools such as Jupyter Notebooks and libraries like Plotly and Seaborn.

Pandas: A Foundation for Data Manipulation

Pandas is the go-to library in Python for data manipulation and analysis. It provides essential data structures such as DataFrame and Series, which allow for efficient handling and manipulation of structured data. For EDA, Pandas is particularly useful for tasks like data cleaning, transformation, and aggregation.

A typical EDA process begins with loading the dataset into a Pandas DataFrame, followed by examining and summarizing the data. With functions like .head(), .info(), and .describe(), Pandas can quickly summarize data types, missing values, and basic statistics.

```
import pandas as pd

# Load a dataset
df = pd.read_csv('data.csv')

# Check the first few rows
print(df.head())

# Get a summary of the dataset
print(df.describe())
```

Pandas also enables operations like handling missing values, filtering data, grouping data for aggregation, and merging datasets, all of which are vital for effective EDA.

Matplotlib and Seaborn: Creating Static Visualizations

Matplotlib is a widely used library in Python for creating static, animated, and interactive visualizations. For EDA, Matplotlib allows you to create a variety of charts, such as histograms, scatter plots, and line charts. These charts are essential for understanding data distributions and relationships between variables.

```
import matplotlib.pyplot as plt

# Create a histogram of a column
df['Age'].hist(bins=10)
plt.title('Age Distribution')
plt.xlabel('Age')
plt.ylabel('Frequency')
plt.show()
```

While Matplotlib is powerful, it can be somewhat complex for more advanced visualization. Seaborn, built on top of Matplotlib, simplifies the process by providing high-level interfaces for creating attractive and informative statistical graphics. Seaborn supports various plot types, including pair plots, heatmaps, and box plots, and can handle more complex datasets with ease.

```
import seaborn as sns

# Create a pair plot to visualize relationships between multiple columns
sns.pairplot(df[['Age', 'Income', 'Experience']])
plt.show()
```

These plots provide insight into data distributions and potential correlations among variables, making Seaborn an essential tool for EDA.

Plotly: Interactive Visualizations

While Matplotlib and Seaborn are great for static plots, interactive visualizations offer a dynamic experience. Plotly is a powerful library for creating interactive plots that allow users to zoom, hover, and explore data in more detail. Plotly is particularly useful when working with larger datasets or when stakeholders require detailed, interactive reports.

Here's how you can create an interactive scatter plot using Plotly:

```
import plotly.express as px

# Create an interactive scatter plot
fig = px.scatter(df, x='Age', y='Income', title='Age vs. Income')
fig.show()
```

Plotly also supports a wide variety of other visualizations, such as line charts, bar charts, and even 3D plots, which help in gaining deeper insights into the data.

Jupyter Notebooks: Interactive Exploration

Jupyter Notebooks are widely used in the data science community for performing EDA. Notebooks provide an interactive environment where you can write and execute code in cells, making it easy to document the thought process and visualize the output in a single document. Jupyter Notebooks integrate seamlessly with visualization libraries such as Matplotlib, Seaborn, and Plotly, enabling real-time analysis and exploration.

Jupyter also allows for adding markdown cells alongside the code, which is valuable for documenting the steps taken during EDA. For instance, after loading and cleaning the data, a data scientist can use markdown to describe the steps, summarize findings, or provide explanations for the visualizations produced.

Other Tools for EDA

In addition to Python-based tools, several other tools are valuable for performing EDA. These include:

- **Tableau**: A powerful tool for creating visualizations with a drag-and-drop interface, Tableau is widely used in business intelligence for interactive and user-friendly dashboards.

- **Power BI**: Another business intelligence tool, Power BI provides robust data visualization capabilities, similar to Tableau, and integrates well with Microsoft tools.

While Python tools provide the flexibility of custom analysis, software like Tableau or Power BI can be advantageous for non-technical users who need to perform exploratory analysis without writing code.

Tools for EDA play a vital role in data exploration and provide the foundation for deeper analysis. Libraries such as Pandas, Matplotlib, Seaborn, and Plotly allow data scientists to manipulate, visualize, and understand data in various forms. Jupyter Notebooks offer an interactive environment for both coding and documenting analysis, making them indispensable for iterative, exploratory work. By using these tools effectively, data scientists can uncover hidden patterns and trends that form the basis for further analysis and model development.

Module 17:

Data Visualization Principles

Data visualization is an essential aspect of data analysis, allowing complex information to be presented in a clear and accessible way. This module covers the principles of designing effective visuals, choosing the right chart or graph, creating interactive dashboards, and using data storytelling techniques to convey insights. Understanding these principles helps communicate findings and engage stakeholders effectively.

Designing Effective Visuals

Effective visualizations make data easy to understand and interpret. Good design principles include simplicity, clarity, and consistency. Visuals should focus on key messages without overwhelming the viewer with excessive detail. Using appropriate colors, labels, and scales ensures the visual aids in communication rather than causing confusion. A clear design allows for quick comprehension and actionable insights.

Choosing the Right Chart or Graph

Selecting the right chart or graph is critical for communicating data accurately. Bar charts, line graphs, and pie charts are best suited for categorical and time-series data, while scatter plots are ideal for showing relationships between variables. The goal is to match the data type with the visual format that best represents its message, avoiding distortion or misrepresentation.

Interactive Dashboards

Interactive dashboards allow users to explore data dynamically, providing deeper insights. Tools like Tableau, Power BI, and Dash enable users to filter, drill down, and manipulate data in real time. Dashboards offer flexibility, allowing stakeholders to interact with the data, identify trends, and gain personalized insights. They are an effective way to present data-driven findings in an engaging manner.

Storytelling with Data

Data storytelling combines visualization with narrative to create a compelling story. By guiding the audience through the data, highlighting key insights, and explaining the significance of trends, data storytelling makes complex information more relatable. It helps to shape data in a context that resonates with the audience, turning raw numbers into meaningful narratives that influence decision-making.

Designing Effective Visuals

Effective data visualization is an essential component of data science, enabling the communication of complex insights in a clear, intuitive manner. Good design principles enhance the ability of stakeholders to quickly understand the message of the data, driving informed decision-making. This section explores the key principles of designing effective data visuals, focusing on clarity, simplicity, and the appropriate use of color and labels.

Clarity is Key

The primary goal of any visualization is to make the data understandable at a glance. A key principle in designing effective visuals is clarity. Clarity in visualization means ensuring that viewers can immediately grasp the main takeaway without unnecessary distractions. To achieve this, visuals should be simple, with well-defined axes, labels, and legends.

For instance, a line chart displaying trends over time should have a clear title and axis labels, specifying both the time period and the metric being measured. Here's an example of a simple line plot using Python's Matplotlib:

```
import matplotlib.pyplot as plt

# Sample data for plotting
time = ['Jan', 'Feb', 'Mar', 'Apr', 'May']
sales = [150, 200, 250, 300, 350]

# Create line plot
plt.plot(time, sales, marker='o', color='b')
plt.title('Monthly Sales Trend')
plt.xlabel('Month')
plt.ylabel('Sales')
plt.grid(True)
plt.show()
```

This chart clearly communicates sales trends over five months, making it easy for viewers to understand the message.

Simplicity Over Complexity

Another essential principle of effective visualization design is simplicity. While it can be tempting to include every possible detail or statistic, too much information can overwhelm the viewer and obscure the key message. For instance, avoid cluttering the graph with unnecessary elements like gridlines or excessive tick marks. Keep the design focused on the main point.

For example, a bar chart can visually communicate differences between categories, but adding too many data series or variables may complicate the chart. A simplified version might look like this:

```
import matplotlib.pyplot as plt

# Sample data
categories = ['A', 'B', 'C', 'D']
values = [20, 35, 50, 40]

# Create bar plot
plt.bar(categories, values, color='skyblue')
plt.title('Category Comparison')
plt.xlabel('Category')
plt.ylabel('Value')
plt.show()
```

By limiting the data to essential elements and avoiding distractions, this bar chart communicates the message clearly.

Color Usage: Function Over Aesthetics

Color is a powerful tool in visualization but should be used purposefully. Different colors can convey specific meanings (e.g., red for warnings, green for growth), or they can help differentiate categories or series. However, using too many colors can confuse the viewer and detract from the clarity of the visualization. A good rule of thumb is to use a limited color palette, ensuring that the meaning of each color is intuitive.

Here's an example where color is used to differentiate categories effectively:

```
import matplotlib.pyplot as plt

# Sample data
categories = ['Apples', 'Bananas', 'Cherries', 'Dates']
values = [30, 45, 25, 50]
colors = ['red', 'yellow', 'pink', 'brown']

# Create pie chart with color differentiation
plt.pie(values, labels=categories, colors=colors, autopct='%1.1f%%',
        startangle=90)
plt.title('Fruit Distribution')
plt.show()
```

In this pie chart, the use of distinct colors for each fruit category enhances the readability of the visual.

Labels and Legends for Context

Labels and legends are essential for providing context to the data. For charts like line graphs or scatter plots, clear axis labels help viewers understand the variables being represented. A legend is especially useful when multiple data series are displayed in a single chart. Without these contextual elements, even a well-designed visualization can confuse viewers.

For example, a scatter plot with two different datasets might look like this:

```
import matplotlib.pyplot as plt
```

```
# Sample data for two different datasets
x1 = [1, 2, 3, 4]
y1 = [1, 4, 9, 16]
x2 = [1, 2, 3, 4]
y2 = [1, 2, 3, 4]

# Create scatter plot
plt.scatter(x1, y1, color='red', label='Dataset 1')
plt.scatter(x2, y2, color='blue', label='Dataset 2')

plt.title('Comparison of Two Datasets')
plt.xlabel('X-Axis')
plt.ylabel('Y-Axis')
plt.legend()
plt.show()
```

By adding a legend, the chart becomes more informative and easier to interpret.

Designing effective visuals requires more than just making charts look attractive. The goal is to make the data easy to interpret and understand. By following principles of clarity, simplicity, and thoughtful use of color and labels, data scientists can create visuals that effectively communicate insights. Ultimately, the design of a visual should serve the data, helping the viewer quickly grasp the key message and driving informed decision-making.

Choosing the Right Chart or Graph

Choosing the correct chart or graph is vital to conveying data insights accurately and effectively. Different types of data and analyses require specific types of visualizations to maximize clarity. This section delves into how to choose the right type of chart or graph based on the data at hand, explaining the strengths of common visualizations such as bar charts, line graphs, scatter plots, histograms, and pie charts.

Bar Charts: Comparing Categories

Bar charts are one of the most common types of visualizations used to compare different categories or groups. They are particularly useful when displaying data that can be categorized or grouped, making comparisons across different categories easy to interpret.

For example, if you want to compare sales performance across different regions, a bar chart could be the best choice:

```
import matplotlib.pyplot as plt

# Data for bar chart
regions = ['North', 'South', 'East', 'West']
sales = [1000, 1500, 800, 1200]

# Create bar chart
plt.bar(regions, sales, color='green')
plt.title('Sales by Region')
```

174

```
plt.xlabel('Region')
plt.ylabel('Sales')
plt.show()
```

Bar charts make it easy to compare values across categories, helping stakeholders quickly understand which category is performing best or worst.

Line Graphs: Tracking Changes Over Time

When tracking changes over time or continuous data, line graphs are often the best choice. Line graphs show the progression of a metric across a series of points, typically with time on the x-axis and the metric of interest on the y-axis. This type of graph is excellent for displaying trends, seasonality, or cyclical patterns.

For example, if you're analyzing monthly website traffic, a line graph would effectively display changes over time:

```
import matplotlib.pyplot as plt

# Sample data for line chart
months = ['Jan', 'Feb', 'Mar', 'Apr', 'May']
traffic = [3000, 3500, 4000, 4500, 5000]

# Create line plot
plt.plot(months, traffic, marker='o', color='b')
plt.title('Monthly Website Traffic')
plt.xlabel('Month')
plt.ylabel('Traffic')
plt.show()
```

Line graphs are useful for understanding patterns and relationships in time-series data.

Scatter Plots: Visualizing Relationships Between Variables

Scatter plots are used to visualize the relationship between two numerical variables. Each point represents a pair of values, one on the x-axis and one on the y-axis. Scatter plots are particularly useful for identifying correlations, trends, clusters, and outliers in data.

For example, if you're studying the relationship between advertising spend and sales performance, a scatter plot could be helpful:

```
import matplotlib.pyplot as plt

# Data for scatter plot
ad_spend = [100, 200, 300, 400, 500]
sales = [200, 400, 600, 800, 1000]

# Create scatter plot
plt.scatter(ad_spend, sales, color='purple')
plt.title('Advertising Spend vs Sales')
plt.xlabel('Advertising Spend')
plt.ylabel('Sales')
plt.show()
```

This scatter plot shows how advertising spend correlates with sales, providing insights into their relationship.

Histograms: Understanding Distribution

Histograms are used to represent the distribution of a dataset by dividing the data into bins or intervals. This chart helps to understand the frequency distribution of a variable, showing whether the data is skewed, normally distributed, or has multiple peaks. Histograms are useful for data exploration, particularly when assessing the spread of a variable or detecting outliers.

For example, to visualize the distribution of ages in a dataset, a histogram is appropriate:

```
import matplotlib.pyplot as plt

# Data for histogram
ages = [22, 25, 29, 30, 35, 36, 40, 42, 45, 50, 55, 60]

# Create histogram
plt.hist(ages, bins=5, color='orange', edgecolor='black')
plt.title('Age Distribution')
plt.xlabel('Age')
plt.ylabel('Frequency')
plt.show()
```

Histograms provide insight into the shape and spread of data, highlighting key features such as skewness and range.

Pie Charts: Showing Proportions

Pie charts are a great way to display proportions of a whole, making them effective for showing percentages or share distributions. Each slice of the pie represents a category's contribution to the total, making pie charts visually intuitive for simple comparisons.

For example, to show the market share of different companies, a pie chart is ideal:

```
import matplotlib.pyplot as plt

# Data for pie chart
companies = ['Company A', 'Company B', 'Company C', 'Company D']
market_share = [40, 30, 20, 10]

# Create pie chart
plt.pie(market_share, labels=companies, autopct='%1.1f%%', startangle=90)
plt.title('Market Share Distribution')
plt.show()
```

Pie charts effectively highlight the proportion of each category within a whole, but they are best used for a small number of categories to avoid clutter.

Choosing the right chart or graph depends on the nature of the data and the insights you wish to communicate. Bar charts, line graphs, scatter plots, histograms, and pie charts each have their strengths and are suitable for different types of data. Understanding the purpose and best use cases for each will help ensure that the visualizations are not only clear but also provide accurate and actionable insights.

Interactive Dashboards

Interactive dashboards have become a powerful tool for presenting complex data insights in a visually appealing and interactive format. These dashboards allow users to explore data dynamically, adjusting parameters or filtering data in real time to uncover deeper insights. In this section, we explore the concept of interactive dashboards, their benefits, key features, and how to create them using tools like Plotly, Dash, and other visualization libraries.

Why Use Interactive Dashboards?

Interactive dashboards offer several advantages over static visualizations. They enable users to engage with the data in real time, which can lead to more insightful analysis. Users can filter, zoom, or drill down into specific data points, making it easier to identify trends, anomalies, and patterns that may not be immediately obvious in static charts. Dashboards provide a more intuitive, hands-on approach to data analysis, allowing decision-makers to explore data without needing deep technical knowledge.

Additionally, interactive dashboards provide the ability to present multiple views of the same dataset, giving users a more comprehensive understanding. This is particularly useful in business settings where different stakeholders may need to see data from various perspectives (e.g., sales performance across different regions or the distribution of customer ages).

Key Features of Interactive Dashboards

1. **Real-Time Filtering**: One of the most important features of interactive dashboards is the ability to filter data dynamically. Users can select specific time periods, regions, or categories, and the dashboard updates automatically, reflecting the changes. This enables more focused analysis based on user preferences.

2. **Drill-Down Capabilities**: Dashboards often allow users to drill down into the data for a deeper exploration. For example, clicking on a specific region in a bar chart could display detailed data about that region, such as sales figures, customer demographics, or product performance.

3. **Multiple Visualizations**: Dashboards typically feature multiple types of visualizations, such as bar charts, line graphs, pie charts, and maps, arranged on a

single screen. This allows users to explore the data from various perspectives and gain a more holistic understanding of the dataset.

4. **User-Friendly Interface**: A key strength of interactive dashboards is their intuitive and user-friendly interface. They allow non-technical users to interact with data without requiring them to write any code or perform complex operations.

Creating Interactive Dashboards with Python

Python offers several libraries that make building interactive dashboards easy. One of the most popular libraries for this purpose is **Dash**, a framework built on top of Plotly. Dash allows users to create web-based applications with interactive data visualizations without needing extensive web development skills.

Here's an example of creating a simple interactive dashboard using Dash:

```python
import dash
from dash import dcc, html
import plotly.express as px
import pandas as pd

# Sample data
df = pd.DataFrame({
    "Region": ["North", "South", "East", "West"],
    "Sales": [1000, 1500, 800, 1200],
    "Profit": [200, 400, 150, 300]
})

# Create a Dash app
app = dash.Dash()

# App layout
app.layout = html.Div([
    html.H1("Sales Dashboard"),
    dcc.Graph(
        id='sales-bar-chart',
        figure=px.bar(df, x="Region", y="Sales", title="Sales by Region")
    ),
    dcc.Graph(
        id='profit-bar-chart',
        figure=px.bar(df, x="Region", y="Profit", title="Profit by Region")
    )
])

# Run the app
if __name__ == '__main__':
    app.run_server(debug=True)
```

This simple app uses **Dash** and **Plotly** to create an interactive dashboard displaying sales and profit by region. The dashboard is fully interactive, and users can hover over bars to see additional details. While this is a basic example, Dash allows for more complex functionality such as dropdowns, sliders, and real-time updates.

Enhancing Dashboards with Interactivity

178

Interactive dashboards can be enhanced with additional features like:

- **Sliders**: Users can adjust a slider to change the data range, such as selecting a specific time period.

- **Dropdown Menus**: Dropdowns allow users to select categories, such as filtering sales data by product or region.

- **Hover Effects and Tooltips**: Tooltips display additional data when a user hovers over specific elements, providing more context without cluttering the screen.

By combining these features, you can create highly interactive and user-friendly dashboards that make data exploration accessible to all users.

Interactive dashboards are essential tools for modern data analysis, providing dynamic, real-time data exploration and insights. They empower users to make informed decisions by presenting complex data in a digestible and interactive format. With libraries like **Dash** and **Plotly**, creating these dashboards in Python is more accessible than ever, allowing data scientists and analysts to present data in ways that are engaging and actionable. Whether for business executives, analysts, or general users, interactive dashboards are indispensable for modern data-driven decision-making.

Storytelling with Data

Storytelling with data is a powerful technique in data science and analytics that combines data visualization, narrative, and insights to present complex information in a compelling and understandable way. In this section, we explore the principles of storytelling with data, how to structure a data-driven narrative, and tools and techniques that can help bring the story to life. The goal of storytelling with data is to engage your audience, guide them through the analysis, and leave them with clear insights that drive decision-making.

The Power of Narrative in Data

Data on its own can be overwhelming and difficult to interpret without context. Storytelling with data gives the audience a narrative framework to understand the data's meaning and implications. By framing the data within a story, you can highlight the key insights and guide the audience toward the conclusions you want to emphasize.

The key is to structure the data as part of a journey that unfolds logically. Just like in a traditional story, you need to start by introducing the context, present the challenges or problems, share the analysis (the "plot"), and end with the conclusions and actions to be taken (the "resolution"). This structure not only helps to communicate the message but also makes the presentation more engaging and memorable.

Principles of Effective Data Storytelling

1. **Know Your Audience**: Understanding who will consume the data and what they care about is crucial for effective storytelling. A dashboard for executives will have different priorities and visualizations than one for analysts. Tailor your narrative to the needs, technical knowledge, and interests of your audience.

2. **Simplify Complex Data**: A good data story does not overwhelm the audience with too many details. Focus on the most important data points and insights. Use clear visuals and concise language to explain what the data is showing.

3. **Use Visuals to Support the Narrative**: Visualizations are a key component of data storytelling. They should be used to reinforce the message and help the audience understand the data. Effective charts and graphs make patterns and trends more apparent and easier to interpret.

4. **Structure Your Story**: Just as in any narrative, structure is important. A well-structured data story typically follows these stages:

   o **Introduction**: Provide context and explain why the analysis is being done.

   o **Problem or Challenge**: Describe the issue that the data will help solve or explore.

   o **Data Analysis**: Present the key findings with appropriate visualizations.

   o **Conclusion and Call to Action**: Summarize the findings and propose actionable insights or recommendations.

Techniques for Effective Data Storytelling

1. **Choose the Right Visualizations**: The choice of visualization is crucial in conveying the right message. For example:

   o Use **bar charts** to compare quantities across categories.

   o Use **line charts** to show trends over time.

   o Use **scatter plots** to identify relationships between variables.

   o **Heatmaps** can be used to highlight areas with the most significant patterns.

Here's an example of a simple storytelling approach using Python and Matplotlib:

```
import matplotlib.pyplot as plt
import pandas as pd
```

```
# Sample data
data = {'Month': ['Jan', 'Feb', 'Mar', 'Apr', 'May'],
        'Sales': [500, 600, 800, 750, 850]}

df = pd.DataFrame(data)

# Plot the data
plt.plot(df['Month'], df['Sales'], marker='o', color='b', label='Sales')
plt.title('Monthly Sales Trend')
plt.xlabel('Month')
plt.ylabel('Sales ($)')
plt.legend()

# Add annotation
plt.annotate('Sales peak in March', xy=('Mar', 800), xytext=('Feb', 850),
             arrowprops=dict(arrowstyle='->', lw=1.5), fontsize=10,
             color='r')

plt.show()
```

In this example, we tell a simple story of sales trends, highlighting the peak in March with an annotation. Such storytelling techniques help bring attention to key moments in the data.

2. **Use Color and Design to Emphasize Key Points**: Colors can help guide the audience's attention. Use contrasting colors for important elements, but avoid overloading your visuals with too many colors or designs that distract from the message.

3. **Highlight Insights, Not Just Data**: A data story isn't just about showing the data—it's about the insights that the data reveals. Your goal is to highlight the meaning behind the numbers. For example, instead of just showing sales numbers, explain why the sales increased in a specific period or how they relate to other metrics like customer satisfaction or marketing campaigns.

Tools for Data Storytelling

Several tools make it easier to tell stories with data. Popular choices include:

- **Tableau**: A powerful visualization tool that enables users to create interactive dashboards and share data-driven stories with minimal coding.

- **Power BI**: Similar to Tableau, Power BI helps users create compelling reports and dashboards that facilitate data-driven decision-making.

- **Plotly**: A Python library for creating interactive plots and dashboards that can enhance storytelling with real-time data interaction.

- **Google Data Studio**: A free tool that helps you create interactive and shareable dashboards and reports with ease.

Data storytelling is an essential skill for data scientists, analysts, and business intelligence professionals. By weaving a narrative around the data and using the right visuals to guide the audience through the analysis, you can communicate insights more effectively and drive better decision-making. The goal is to make the data come alive, to help your audience connect with the numbers and understand their implications. With the right approach, data storytelling can be a powerful tool to drive action and inspire change within an organization.

Module 18:

Statistical Data Analysis

Statistical data analysis is crucial for drawing meaningful conclusions from data. This module introduces key concepts such as descriptive and inferential statistics, hypothesis testing, and correlation and regression analysis. Mastering these techniques allows data scientists to make data-driven decisions and predictions, ensuring the accuracy and reliability of their analyses.

Descriptive Statistics

Descriptive statistics summarize the main features of a dataset, providing a clear overview. Key measures include mean, median, mode, range, variance, and standard deviation, which describe central tendency, spread, and variability. These statistics help identify patterns and anomalies within the data, laying the groundwork for deeper analysis and model development.

Inferential Statistics

Inferential statistics allows data scientists to make predictions and draw conclusions about a population based on a sample. This includes techniques such as estimation, confidence intervals, and the use of probability distributions. By applying inferential methods, analysts can generalize their findings and make informed decisions without having to analyze the entire dataset.

Hypothesis Testing

Hypothesis testing is a statistical method used to determine whether there is enough evidence to support a particular hypothesis. It involves defining a null and alternative hypothesis, selecting a significance level, and performing tests such as t-tests or chi-square tests. The results guide decision-making by indicating whether observed effects are statistically significant.

Correlation and Regression Analysis

Correlation and regression analysis are used to examine relationships between variables. Correlation measures the strength and direction of the relationship between two variables, while regression analysis explores the cause-and-effect relationship, predicting outcomes based on independent variables. These techniques are fundamental in modeling and understanding data-driven phenomena.

Descriptive Statistics

Descriptive statistics are the foundation of data analysis, providing a summary of data features through simple measures. These statistics help to understand the distribution, central tendency, and variability of data before deeper analysis or modeling is done. In this section, we will explore key descriptive statistics methods such as measures of central tendency, dispersion, and data distribution.

Measures of Central Tendency

The first step in descriptive statistics is to understand the central tendency of the data, which refers to the central or typical value of the dataset. The most common measures of central tendency include:

1. **Mean**: The arithmetic average of all data points. It is calculated by summing all the data points and dividing by the total number of data points.

    Formula:

    $$Mean = \frac{\sum x_i}{n}$$

    In Python, we can compute the mean using numpy:

    ```
    import numpy as np

    data = [12, 15, 17, 18, 20, 22, 25]
    mean_value = np.mean(data)
    print("Mean:", mean_value)
    ```

2. **Median**: The middle value of the dataset when ordered from lowest to highest. If the number of data points is even, the median is the average of the two middle values.

    Formula:

    Median = Middle value of the ordered dataset

    Python code to compute the median:

    ```
    median_value = np.median(data)
    print("Median:", median_value)
    ```

3. **Mode**: The value that appears most frequently in the dataset. A dataset may have more than one mode if multiple values occur with the same highest frequency.

    Python code to compute the mode using scipy:

    ```
    from scipy import stats

    mode_value = stats.mode(data)
    print("Mode:", mode_value.mode[0])
    ```

184

Measures of Dispersion

After understanding the central tendency, it is crucial to explore the spread or dispersion of the data. Measures of dispersion describe the extent to which data points differ from the mean or median.

1. **Range**: The difference between the maximum and minimum values in the dataset.

    Formula:

    $$Range = Max(x) - Min(x)$$

    Python code to compute the range:

    ```python
    range_value = np.ptp(data)
    print("Range:", range_value)
    ```

2. **Variance**: The average of the squared differences from the mean, representing how much data points deviate from the mean.

    Formula:

    $$Variance = \frac{\Sigma(x_i - \mu)^2}{n}$$

    Python code to compute variance:

    ```python
    variance_value = np.var(data)
    print("Variance:", variance_value)
    ```

3. **Standard Deviation**: The square root of the variance, which gives a measure of spread in the same units as the data.

    Formula:

    $$Standard\ Deviation = \sqrt{Variance}$$

    Python code to compute standard deviation:

    ```python
    std_deviation_value = np.std(data)
    print("Standard Deviation:", std_deviation_value)
    ```

Data Distribution

Understanding the distribution of the data is essential for making inferences. Descriptive statistics also include visual tools to assess data distribution, such as histograms and box plots. A **histogram** helps visualize the frequency distribution of the data, while a **box plot** provides a summary of the data distribution and identifies potential outliers.

Example of creating a histogram and box plot using matplotlib:

```
import matplotlib.pyplot as plt

# Histogram
plt.hist(data, bins=5, edgecolor='black')
plt.title('Histogram of Data')
plt.xlabel('Data Values')
plt.ylabel('Frequency')
plt.show()

# Box plot
plt.boxplot(data)
plt.title('Box Plot of Data')
plt.show()
```

These visualizations help analysts understand whether the data is normally distributed or skewed and can also highlight potential outliers.

Descriptive statistics are an essential starting point in any data analysis project. By summarizing data using measures like mean, median, mode, variance, and standard deviation, we can quickly understand the characteristics of the dataset. Additionally, visualizations like histograms and box plots are invaluable tools for exploring the data further. Descriptive statistics lay the groundwork for more advanced statistical methods and machine learning models, making them crucial for effective data science practice.

Inferential Statistics

Inferential statistics enables data scientists to make predictions or inferences about a population based on a sample of data. While descriptive statistics summarize the data, inferential statistics allows us to generalize the findings to a larger group and test hypotheses. This section covers key concepts such as sampling, confidence intervals, and hypothesis testing.

Sampling and Population

In inferential statistics, the first step is to understand the relationship between the sample and the population. A **sample** is a subset of the data that is used to represent a larger **population**. Since it is often impractical to collect data from an entire population, we use samples to make inferences about the population.

One key concept is **sampling error**, which is the difference between the sample statistic (e.g., sample mean) and the population parameter (e.g., population mean). The goal is to ensure the sample is representative of the population to minimize sampling error.

Confidence Intervals

186

A **confidence interval (CI)** provides a range of values within which we expect the population parameter to lie, with a specified level of confidence. For example, a 95% confidence interval means that 95% of the time, the interval will contain the true population parameter. The width of the confidence interval depends on the sample size and the variability of the data.

Formula for Confidence Interval:

$$CI = Sample\ Mean \pm Z \times \frac{\sigma}{\sqrt{n}}$$

Where:

- Sample Mean is the average of the sample data

- Z is the Z-score for the desired confidence level

- σ is the standard deviation of the sample

- n is the sample size

In Python, we can calculate a confidence interval for the mean using scipy and numpy:

```
import numpy as np
import scipy.stats as stats

# Sample data
data = [12, 15, 17, 18, 20, 22, 25]
sample_mean = np.mean(data)
sample_std = np.std(data, ddof=1)  # Sample standard deviation
n = len(data)
confidence_level = 0.95

# Z-score for 95% confidence
z_score = stats.norm.ppf(1 - (1 - confidence_level) / 2)

# Confidence Interval calculation
margin_of_error = z_score * (sample_std / np.sqrt(n))
lower_bound = sample_mean - margin_of_error
upper_bound = sample_mean + margin_of_error

print(f"95% Confidence Interval: ({lower_bound}, {upper_bound})")
```

This code calculates the 95% confidence interval for the given sample data.

Hypothesis Testing

Hypothesis testing is a statistical method used to test assumptions (hypotheses) about a population using sample data. The two main types of hypotheses are:

1. **Null Hypothesis (H_0)**: The hypothesis that there is no effect or no difference.

2. **Alternative Hypothesis (H₁)**: The hypothesis that there is an effect or a difference.

The steps involved in hypothesis testing are as follows:

1. **State the hypotheses**: Define the null and alternative hypotheses.

2. **Choose the significance level (α)**: Commonly set at 0.05, which means there is a 5% chance of rejecting the null hypothesis when it is true.

3. **Conduct the test**: Use statistical tests (e.g., t-test, chi-square test) to compare the sample data against the null hypothesis.

4. **Make a decision**: If the p-value is less than the significance level, reject the null hypothesis.

Example of a one-sample t-test in Python:

```python
from scipy import stats

# Sample data
data = [12, 15, 17, 18, 20, 22, 25]
sample_mean = np.mean(data)
population_mean = 20  # Hypothetical population mean
alpha = 0.05  # Significance level

# One-sample t-test
t_stat, p_value = stats.ttest_1samp(data, population_mean)

print(f"T-statistic: {t_stat}, P-value: {p_value}")

# Decision
if p_value < alpha:
    print("Reject the null hypothesis: The sample mean is significantly
          different from the population mean.")
else:
    print("Fail to reject the null hypothesis: No significant difference
          between the sample mean and population mean.")
```

This test checks if the sample mean is significantly different from a population mean of 20.

Inferential statistics provide the tools to make predictions and draw conclusions about a population based on sample data. Confidence intervals help estimate population parameters, while hypothesis testing allows us to test assumptions and make informed decisions. By applying these techniques, data scientists can derive meaningful insights and make data-driven decisions with a quantifiable level of confidence.

Hypothesis Testing

Hypothesis testing is a fundamental aspect of inferential statistics that allows data scientists to test assumptions (hypotheses) about population parameters using sample data. It helps determine if there is enough evidence to reject or accept a hypothesis.

This section discusses key concepts in hypothesis testing, including the formulation of hypotheses, types of errors, p-values, and test statistics.

Formulating Hypotheses

Hypothesis testing starts with the formulation of two competing hypotheses:

- **Null Hypothesis (H_0):** This is the statement of no effect or no difference in the population. It is the hypothesis that the researcher seeks to test.

- **Alternative Hypothesis (H_1 or Ha):** This is the statement that there is an effect or difference. If the null hypothesis is rejected, the alternative hypothesis is supported.

For example, suppose we want to test if the average height of a population is 170 cm. The hypotheses would be:

- **H_0:** The population mean height is 170 cm.

- **H_1:** The population mean height is not 170 cm (it could be higher or lower).

Types of Errors in Hypothesis Testing

In hypothesis testing, there are two types of errors that can occur:

- **Type I Error (False Positive):** Rejecting the null hypothesis when it is actually true. The significance level (α) is the probability of committing a Type I error.

- **Type II Error (False Negative):** Failing to reject the null hypothesis when the alternative hypothesis is true.

The goal of hypothesis testing is to minimize both types of errors, but there is often a trade-off between them. Reducing the probability of one error increases the likelihood of the other.

Test Statistics and p-Values

The test statistic is a numerical value calculated from the sample data that is used to decide whether to reject the null hypothesis. The choice of test statistic depends on the nature of the data and the hypothesis being tested (e.g., t-test, z-test, chi-square test).

- **p-value:** The p-value is the probability of obtaining a test statistic at least as extreme as the one observed in the sample, assuming the null hypothesis is true. A small p-value (usually < 0.05) indicates strong evidence against the null hypothesis, while a large p-value suggests that the evidence is insufficient to reject the null hypothesis.

Decision Rule:

- If the p-value is less than the significance level (α), we reject the null hypothesis.

- If the p-value is greater than or equal to the significance level, we fail to reject the null hypothesis.

Example of Hypothesis Testing in Python

Let's perform a one-sample t-test to test if the average height of a population is 170 cm. Assume we have a sample of heights.

```python
import numpy as np
from scipy import stats

# Sample data
heights = [168, 170, 172, 169, 174, 165, 168, 171, 170, 173]

# Population mean (null hypothesis)
population_mean = 170

# One-sample t-test
t_stat, p_value = stats.ttest_1samp(heights, population_mean)

print(f"T-statistic: {t_stat}")
print(f"P-value: {p_value}")

# Decision rule
alpha = 0.05
if p_value < alpha:
    print("Reject the null hypothesis: The sample mean is significantly
            different from the population mean.")
else:
    print("Fail to reject the null hypothesis: The sample mean is not
            significantly different from the population mean.")
```

In this example, we calculate the t-statistic and p-value for the sample of heights, and then make a decision about whether the sample mean is significantly different from the population mean of 170 cm.

Hypothesis testing is a critical statistical tool used to make decisions and draw conclusions from sample data. It involves formulating null and alternative hypotheses, calculating test statistics, and interpreting p-values to assess whether there is enough evidence to reject the null hypothesis. By understanding and applying hypothesis testing, data scientists can make data-driven decisions with a known level of uncertainty, providing valuable insights for various applications.

Correlation and Regression Analysis

Correlation and regression analysis are two fundamental statistical techniques used to study the relationships between variables. They are widely applied in data science to understand how changes in one variable are related to changes in another, enabling predictions and insights into complex data structures.

Correlation Analysis

Correlation measures the strength and direction of a linear relationship between two variables. It is often quantified using the **Pearson correlation coefficient** (r), which ranges from -1 to +1:

- **r = 1**: Perfect positive correlation (as one variable increases, the other increases).

- **r = -1**: Perfect negative correlation (as one variable increases, the other decreases).

- **r = 0**: No linear correlation (no relationship between the variables).

A high positive or negative correlation suggests that the variables are strongly related, whereas a correlation close to zero indicates weak or no linear relationship.

Example:

Let's calculate the correlation between the variables "height" and "weight" to understand if taller individuals tend to weigh more.

```
import numpy as np
import pandas as pd

# Sample data
data = {'height': [168, 170, 172, 169, 174, 165, 168, 171, 170, 173],
        'weight': [65, 70, 72, 68, 75, 62, 64, 71, 69, 73]}
df = pd.DataFrame(data)

# Calculate Pearson correlation coefficient
correlation = df['height'].corr(df['weight'])
print(f"Pearson correlation coefficient: {correlation}")
```

The correlation coefficient will help you understand if there is a linear relationship between height and weight. A positive value indicates a direct relationship, while a negative value indicates an inverse relationship.

Regression Analysis

Regression analysis extends correlation analysis by modeling the relationship between a dependent (response) variable and one or more independent (predictor) variables. The simplest form is **linear regression**, which fits a linear equation to the data.

In linear regression, we model the relationship as:

$$y = \beta_0 + \beta_1 x + \in$$

Where:

- **y** is the dependent variable,

- **x** is the independent variable,

- **β₀** is the intercept,

- **β₁** is the slope, and

- ∈ is the error term.

The goal is to estimate the values of β_0 and β_1, and use the model to predict **y** from **x**.

Example:

Let's perform a simple linear regression to predict weight based on height using Python's scikit-learn.

```
from sklearn.linear_model import LinearRegression
import numpy as np

# Sample data
height = np.array([168, 170, 172, 169, 174, 165, 168, 171, 170,
          173]).reshape(-1, 1)
weight = np.array([65, 70, 72, 68, 75, 62, 64, 71, 69, 73])

# Create and fit the model
model = LinearRegression()
model.fit(height, weight)

# Get the slope (beta_1) and intercept (beta_0)
slope = model.coef_[0]
intercept = model.intercept_

print(f"Slope: {slope}")
print(f"Intercept: {intercept}")

# Make predictions
predictions = model.predict(height)
print(f"Predictions: {predictions}")
```

This code fits a linear regression model to predict the weight of individuals based on their height. The slope and intercept parameters are learned from the data, and we use the fitted model to predict weight for each height value.

Interpreting the Results

- **Coefficient (slope)**: The coefficient indicates how much the dependent variable (weight) is expected to change for each unit change in the independent variable (height). A positive coefficient suggests that as height increases, weight tends to increase as well.

- **Intercept**: The intercept is the expected value of the dependent variable when the independent variable is zero. In this context, it would represent the expected weight when height is zero (though this is generally not meaningful in practical terms).

- **R-squared**: This statistic measures how well the regression model explains the variation in the dependent variable. An R-squared value close to 1 indicates that the model explains most of the variability in the data.

Multiple Linear Regression

While simple linear regression involves one predictor variable, **multiple linear regression** allows for multiple predictor variables. The model is extended to:

$$y = \beta_0 + \beta_1 x_1 + \beta_2 x_2 + \cdots + \beta_n x_n + \epsilon$$

Multiple linear regression can be used when we need to predict a variable based on multiple features. For instance, in predicting house prices, both square footage and number of bedrooms might be relevant predictor variables.

Correlation and regression analysis are powerful tools for understanding and modeling relationships in data. Correlation helps to measure the strength and direction of a relationship, while regression allows for prediction and modeling of the relationship between variables. By mastering these techniques, data scientists can uncover insights and build predictive models that drive informed decision-making.

Module 19:

Handling Big Data

As data volumes grow exponentially, handling big data requires specialized tools and techniques. This module explores the foundational concepts of distributed computing, introduces Apache Hadoop and Spark, explains the differences between batch and stream processing, and provides strategies for optimizing data pipelines. Mastery of these concepts is crucial for efficiently managing large-scale data operations.

Distributed Computing Basics

Distributed computing involves using multiple machines to process large datasets, allowing tasks to be completed faster and more efficiently. It leverages parallel processing, where computations are split across several nodes. This enables handling vast amounts of data that would otherwise be impossible to process on a single machine, ensuring scalability and reliability.

Apache Hadoop and Spark Overview

Apache Hadoop and Spark are two powerful frameworks for managing big data. Hadoop allows for distributed storage and processing through its Hadoop Distributed File System (HDFS), while Spark provides in-memory processing for faster data analytics. Both frameworks are integral in big data environments, with Spark offering greater speed and flexibility in real-time analytics.

Batch vs. Stream Processing

Batch processing handles large volumes of data in predefined intervals, often used for tasks such as ETL operations and reporting. Stream processing, on the other hand, processes data continuously, enabling real-time analysis of incoming data. The choice between batch and stream processing depends on the specific needs of the application and the speed of data generation.

Optimizing Data Pipelines

Optimizing data pipelines involves improving the efficiency and reliability of data flow from source to destination. Techniques include parallel processing, minimizing data shuffling, using caching, and ensuring fault tolerance. Well-optimized pipelines improve processing speed, reduce latency, and make data handling more cost-effective, which is essential for managing big data at scale.

Distributed Computing Basics

Distributed computing refers to a model where computational tasks are divided and executed across multiple systems, often working in parallel, to solve large-scale problems more efficiently. This approach is particularly useful when dealing with big data, which is characterized by its volume, velocity, and variety. Distributed computing systems work by breaking down tasks into smaller chunks and distributing them across a network of computers, ensuring that no single machine bears the entire computational load.

The Need for Distributed Computing in Big Data

As data continues to grow exponentially, traditional single-machine solutions become impractical for processing large datasets. Single systems struggle with limited memory, storage, and processing power. Distributed computing, however, leverages a network of machines, allowing data to be processed in parallel and at a scale that would otherwise be impossible.

For example, processing petabytes of data on a single machine would require an immense amount of memory and computational power, which is typically not available. Instead, distributed systems divide the data into smaller pieces, with each machine in the network handling a portion of the workload, thus increasing processing efficiency and speed.

Key Components of Distributed Computing

Distributed computing involves several core components:

1. **Cluster Management**: A cluster consists of multiple machines working together. Cluster managers such as **Apache YARN** or **Kubernetes** are responsible for coordinating the cluster, managing resource allocation, and ensuring that tasks are distributed evenly across the machines.

2. **Parallel Processing**: Parallel computing enables the execution of multiple processes simultaneously. By splitting data into smaller chunks, each machine in a distributed system can process its share of data in parallel, greatly reducing the overall time needed for computation.

3. **Data Storage and Management**: Distributed file systems, such as **HDFS (Hadoop Distributed File System)**, store large volumes of data across multiple nodes in the cluster. This ensures that data is easily accessible and fault-tolerant.

4. **Fault Tolerance**: In a distributed system, failures are inevitable. To ensure reliability, distributed computing systems replicate data across nodes. If one

machine fails, its data can be retrieved from another replica, minimizing the risk of data loss and maintaining system availability.

Example of Distributed Computation with Python

Distributed computing can be implemented in Python using libraries such as **Dask**, which enables parallel computing on a cluster. Here's an example of how you can distribute a task across multiple workers using Dask:

```python
import dask.array as da

# Create a large array with Dask (simulating a large dataset)
x = da.random.random((10000, 10000), chunks=(1000, 1000))

# Perform a simple computation (e.g., sum)
result = x.sum()

# Compute the result using multiple workers in parallel
computed_result = result.compute()

print(f"Sum of the array: {computed_result}")
```

In this example, da.random.random creates a large dataset, and the computation (sum) is distributed across multiple workers. The compute() method triggers the computation, which is done in parallel, leveraging the power of distributed computing.

Advantages of Distributed Computing

1. **Scalability**: Distributed systems can scale horizontally by adding more machines to the cluster. This allows them to handle increasing amounts of data seamlessly.

2. **Improved Performance**: By distributing tasks and processing data in parallel, distributed systems can significantly reduce processing time.

3. **Fault Tolerance**: Redundancy and replication of data across multiple nodes help ensure that the system remains functional even if individual machines fail.

4. **Cost Efficiency**: Distributed systems can be built using commodity hardware, making them more cost-effective compared to large, high-end single machines.

Challenges of Distributed Computing

Despite the advantages, distributed computing introduces certain challenges:

- **Complexity**: Setting up and managing a distributed system can be complex, requiring specialized knowledge in cluster management and resource scheduling.

- **Data Consistency**: Ensuring that data remains consistent across nodes, especially when updates occur simultaneously, can be challenging.

- **Network Latency**: Communication between distributed nodes can introduce delays, especially when the nodes are spread across large geographic distances.

Distributed computing is essential for handling big data efficiently. By breaking tasks into smaller pieces and distributing them across a network of machines, distributed systems provide a scalable and fault-tolerant approach to processing large datasets. While there are challenges associated with distributed computing, such as complexity and network latency, the benefits in terms of performance, scalability, and cost make it an indispensable tool in the world of big data analytics. Understanding the basics of distributed computing is crucial for data scientists working with large datasets and complex models.

Apache Hadoop and Spark Overview

Apache Hadoop and Apache Spark are two of the most widely used frameworks for distributed data processing. Both are designed to handle large volumes of data, but they have different architectures and strengths. Understanding the core components and workflows of each is crucial for choosing the right tool for big data analytics.

Apache Hadoop: Distributed Storage and Processing

Apache Hadoop is an open-source framework designed for storing and processing large datasets across distributed clusters. It was initially developed by Doug Cutting and Mike Cafarella in 2005 and is now one of the cornerstones of big data processing. Hadoop uses a distributed computing model based on the MapReduce programming paradigm, where tasks are split into smaller chunks that are processed in parallel across many nodes.

Core Components of Hadoop:

1. **HDFS (Hadoop Distributed File System)**: HDFS is the primary storage system in Hadoop, designed to store massive datasets. It divides data into blocks and stores them across multiple nodes. Each block is replicated across several nodes to ensure fault tolerance.

2. **MapReduce**: MapReduce is a programming model for processing large datasets in parallel. The "Map" step processes data and produces key-value pairs, while the "Reduce" step aggregates those results. MapReduce jobs are distributed across the cluster, allowing Hadoop to scale efficiently.

3. **YARN (Yet Another Resource Negotiator)**: YARN is responsible for managing resources in the Hadoop ecosystem. It allocates resources across the cluster and schedules jobs to ensure that the workload is distributed evenly.

Hadoop Workflow:

1. **Data Ingestion**: Data is loaded into HDFS from various sources, such as databases or flat files.

2. **Data Processing**: A MapReduce job is triggered to process the data in parallel across the cluster.

3. **Results Retrieval**: Once the processing is complete, the results are stored back in HDFS and can be accessed by downstream applications.

While Hadoop is ideal for batch processing large datasets, it can be slow due to its reliance on disk-based storage and the time required to process each chunk of data sequentially.

Apache Spark: Fast, In-Memory Data Processing

Apache Spark is another open-source distributed computing framework that was developed at UC Berkeley in 2009. Unlike Hadoop, which relies on disk-based storage for intermediate data processing, Spark performs computations in-memory, making it faster for many types of data processing tasks.

Core Components of Spark:

1. **Spark Core**: The fundamental engine for execution, handling task scheduling, memory management, fault tolerance, and interaction with storage systems.

2. **Spark SQL**: A module for querying structured data using SQL, allowing data scientists to perform analytics using familiar SQL syntax.

3. **Spark MLlib**: A library for machine learning that provides scalable algorithms for classification, regression, clustering, and more.

4. **Spark Streaming**: A component designed for processing real-time data streams. It enables real-time analytics and event-driven applications.

5. **GraphX**: A library for graph processing and analysis.

Spark Workflow:

1. **Data Ingestion**: Data is loaded into Spark from sources such as HDFS, databases, or external sources like Kafka.

2. **Data Processing**: Spark processes the data in-memory, which drastically reduces computation time compared to Hadoop. It can perform operations like filtering, mapping, and aggregating data on the fly.

3. **Results Retrieval**: The results can be stored back in HDFS or other databases, or visualized in real-time through dashboards.

Spark is particularly advantageous for real-time data analytics, iterative algorithms (such as machine learning), and workloads that require frequent data processing.

Hadoop vs. Spark: Key Differences

1. **Performance**: Spark is faster than Hadoop for most tasks because it processes data in-memory, reducing disk I/O. Hadoop, on the other hand, writes intermediate data to disk, which can slow down processing.

2. **Ease of Use**: Spark provides high-level APIs for Java, Scala, and Python, making it easier for developers to work with. Hadoop's MapReduce requires writing low-level code, which can be more complex.

3. **Real-Time Processing**: Spark's built-in streaming capabilities allow it to handle real-time data, whereas Hadoop is primarily designed for batch processing.

4. **Fault Tolerance**: Both Hadoop and Spark offer fault tolerance. Hadoop replicates data across nodes, while Spark uses a concept called **Resilient Distributed Datasets (RDDs)**, which allows it to recompute lost data based on lineage.

Example of Spark in Python with PySpark

Spark can be run on a cluster using PySpark, the Python API for Apache Spark. Below is an example of how to use PySpark to process data:

```python
from pyspark.sql import SparkSession

# Initialize SparkSession
spark = SparkSession.builder.appName('example').getOrCreate()

# Load a dataset (CSV format)
data = spark.read.csv('path_to_file.csv', header=True, inferSchema=True)

# Perform basic data operations
data.show()  # Show first few rows

# Perform a transformation (filter data)
filtered_data = data.filter(data['age'] > 30)

# Perform an aggregation (average age)
average_age = filtered_data.groupBy().avg('age')
average_age.show()

# Stop the SparkSession
spark.stop()
```

In this example, we load a dataset, filter data where the age is greater than 30, and calculate the average age. The operations are executed in parallel across the cluster, providing fast performance.

Apache Hadoop and Spark are both powerful tools for distributed data processing. While Hadoop excels at batch processing of large datasets, Spark provides faster, real-time data processing through in-memory computation. The choice between Hadoop and Spark depends on the specific use case: Hadoop is ideal for large-scale batch processing tasks, while Spark is more suitable for real-time analytics and iterative processing, such as machine learning. Understanding the strengths and differences of each framework is crucial for selecting the right tool for your big data projects.

Batch vs. Stream Processing

Batch and stream processing are two key paradigms in big data analytics, each suited to different types of data processing tasks. Understanding the differences between these two approaches and their use cases is vital for selecting the right technique to handle your data needs.

Batch Processing: Processing Data in Chunks

Batch processing is the method of processing large volumes of data in groups or batches at a scheduled time. In batch processing, data is collected over a period of time, stored, and then processed as a whole. This approach is common in traditional data processing systems and is suitable for scenarios where real-time processing is not necessary.

Characteristics of Batch Processing:

1. **Scheduled Intervals**: Data is processed in intervals, usually on a daily, weekly, or hourly basis. For example, you might run a batch job every night to process the data collected during the day.

2. **High Latency**: The results of a batch job are not available until after the entire batch has been processed. This means that there's a delay between when the data is collected and when it's processed.

3. **Efficient for Large Volumes**: Batch processing is highly efficient for handling large datasets because it allows for optimized resource allocation and can be scaled horizontally.

Use Cases for Batch Processing:

- **Data Warehousing**: Aggregating and processing large datasets from various sources for analytical purposes.

- **ETL (Extract, Transform, Load)**: Transforming raw data into a format suitable for analytics, usually on a scheduled basis.

- **Financial Reporting**: Daily or weekly batch jobs to process transactions or account balances.

Batch Processing in Spark:

Apache Spark excels at batch processing, especially with its ability to distribute large jobs across a cluster. Below is a simple example of batch processing in PySpark, which processes a batch of data in one go:

```
from pyspark.sql import SparkSession

# Initialize SparkSession
spark = SparkSession.builder.appName('BatchProcessingExample').getOrCreate()

# Load a large dataset (CSV format)
data = spark.read.csv('path_to_file.csv', header=True, inferSchema=True)

# Perform a batch transformation (calculate the total sales for each
          product)
total_sales = data.groupBy('product_id').sum('sales')

# Save the processed data to a new CSV file
total_sales.write.csv('output_total_sales.csv')

# Stop the SparkSession
spark.stop()
```

This example reads a large dataset, aggregates the sales by product, and writes the results to a file. This process happens in a batch, and the entire dataset is processed in one go.

Stream Processing: Real-Time Data Processing

Stream processing, on the other hand, refers to the real-time processing of data as it arrives. Unlike batch processing, which processes data in chunks, stream processing continuously handles data, providing immediate insights and actions.

Characteristics of Stream Processing:

1. **Real-Time Processing**: Data is processed as soon as it is generated or ingested. There is no delay between data arrival and processing, making it ideal for time-sensitive applications.

2. **Low Latency**: Since data is processed as it arrives, the system is designed to provide low-latency outputs, often measured in milliseconds or seconds.

3. **Continuous Data Flow**: Stream processing systems continuously process data from sources such as sensors, logs, or user interactions.

Use Cases for Stream Processing:

- **Real-Time Analytics**: Monitoring web traffic or social media activity for immediate insights.

- **Financial Fraud Detection**: Detecting fraudulent activities as transactions occur.

- **IoT Applications**: Processing sensor data in real time for actions like triggering alerts or adjusting conditions.

Stream Processing in Spark:

Apache Spark provides Spark Streaming, a module that can process real-time data streams. Below is an example of how Spark Streaming can be used for stream processing with PySpark:

```
from pyspark.sql import SparkSession
from pyspark.sql.functions import expr

# Initialize SparkSession for streaming
spark =
        SparkSession.builder.appName('StreamProcessingExample').getOrCrea
        te()

# Create a DataFrame that represents streaming data from a source (e.g.,
        socket)
streaming_data = spark.readStream.format('socket').option('host',
        'localhost').option('port', 9999).load()

# Perform a simple transformation (count the number of words in each batch)
word_count = streaming_data.select(expr('count(*) as word_count'))

# Output the results to the console in real-time
query =
        word_count.writeStream.outputMode('complete').format('console').s
        tart()

# Wait for the streaming to finish
query.awaitTermination()

# Stop the SparkSession
spark.stop()
```

In this example, the data stream is read from a socket, and the word count is calculated and displayed in real time. This enables immediate insights as new data arrives.

Key Differences Between Batch and Stream Processing

Feature	Batch Processing	Stream Processing
Data Arrival	Data is accumulated and processed at once	Data is processed as it arrives
Latency	High latency (delayed results)	Low latency (real-time processing)

Feature	Batch Processing	Stream Processing
Efficiency	Efficient for large volumes of data	Designed for continuous data flow
Complexity	Typically simpler to manage and scale	Requires complex setups for real-time handling

Choosing Between Batch and Stream Processing

- **Use Batch Processing** when dealing with large volumes of historical data, where real-time processing is not necessary.

- **Use Stream Processing** for applications that require immediate action or insights, such as fraud detection, real-time analytics, or monitoring systems.

Both paradigms have their advantages, and the choice of which to use depends on the specific needs of the application.

Optimizing Data Pipelines

Optimizing data pipelines is crucial for ensuring that data processing systems run efficiently, especially when dealing with large volumes of data. In the context of big data, an optimized pipeline ensures that data is ingested, processed, and stored in the most efficient manner possible, reducing both time and resource consumption.

What is a Data Pipeline?

A data pipeline is a set of processes that automate the movement, transformation, and storage of data. Data flows from various sources through different stages of processing, eventually arriving in a destination for analysis, reporting, or storage. For big data applications, this process needs to be optimized to handle vast amounts of data efficiently.

Key components of a typical data pipeline include:

- **Data Ingestion**: Collecting data from different sources such as databases, logs, or IoT devices.

- **Data Processing**: Cleaning, transforming, or enriching the data to make it suitable for analysis.

- **Data Storage**: Storing the processed data in a data lake, data warehouse, or database.

- **Data Analysis**: Running queries or algorithms to extract insights from the data.

Optimizing Data Ingestion

Efficient data ingestion is the first step in an optimized pipeline. Data ingestion can be batch-based, where large datasets are moved in intervals, or streaming, where data is ingested in real time. To optimize ingestion, consider the following:

1. **Parallelization**: Distribute data ingestion tasks across multiple nodes or machines to ensure that data can be ingested in parallel, reducing the time it takes to collect large datasets.

2. **Compression**: Compress data as it is ingested to reduce the volume of data being transferred and stored, improving overall pipeline efficiency.

3. **Data Filtering**: Filter out unnecessary data early in the ingestion process to avoid processing and storing irrelevant information.

Optimizing Data Ingestion with Apache Kafka:

Apache Kafka is a popular tool for streamlining data ingestion. It allows real-time ingestion of data and offers built-in features for scalability and fault tolerance.

```python
from kafka import KafkaConsumer

# Initialize a Kafka consumer for streaming data
consumer = KafkaConsumer('data_topic', group_id='data_group',
        bootstrap_servers='localhost:9092')

# Process messages in real-time
for message in consumer:
    print(f"Received message: {message.value}")
    # Perform transformation or filtering here
```

By consuming data from Kafka, real-time ingestion is handled effectively, allowing for further processing and analysis.

Optimizing Data Transformation

Data transformation is where most of the computational workload occurs. This stage involves cleaning, enriching, or aggregating the data. To optimize transformation:

1. **Vectorization**: Use vectorized operations (e.g., with libraries like NumPy and Pandas in Python) to apply transformations across large datasets in a single operation, rather than looping through individual records.

2. **Distributed Processing**: When dealing with massive datasets, use distributed computing frameworks like Apache Spark or Dask to parallelize data processing tasks across multiple nodes.

Optimizing Transformation with Apache Spark:

Apache Spark offers an efficient way to handle large-scale transformations due to its distributed processing capabilities.

```
from pyspark.sql import SparkSession

# Initialize SparkSession
spark = SparkSession.builder.appName('DataOptimization').getOrCreate()

# Load a dataset and apply transformations in parallel
df = spark.read.csv('input_data.csv', header=True)
transformed_df = df.filter(df['age'] > 18).groupBy('country').count()

# Save the transformed data
transformed_df.write.csv('output_transformed_data.csv')
```

In the above example, data is loaded and transformed using Spark, which distributes the tasks across a cluster to speed up the process.

Optimizing Data Storage

Choosing the right storage format and system is essential for an efficient pipeline. Optimizing data storage involves:

1. **Efficient File Formats**: Use columnar file formats like Parquet or ORC, which provide better performance for reading and writing large datasets compared to row-based formats like CSV.

2. **Partitioning and Indexing**: Partition data based on key attributes (e.g., date, region) to allow faster querying. Additionally, indexing frequently queried columns can improve retrieval speed.

3. **Data Archiving**: For older or less frequently accessed data, use data archiving solutions to store data at a lower cost while still enabling future access if needed.

Optimizing Data Analysis

The final stage in the pipeline involves extracting insights from the data. To optimize data analysis:

1. **Pre-aggregation**: If possible, pre-aggregate the data during the transformation stage so that analysis can be performed on a smaller, more manageable dataset.

2. **Distributed Querying**: Use distributed querying engines like Apache Hive or Presto to execute complex queries across large datasets in parallel.

Optimizing Query Performance with Presto:

Presto is a distributed SQL query engine that can handle large datasets and provide fast query results.

```
from prestodb import dbapi

# Establish connection to Presto
conn = dbapi.connect(
    host='localhost',
    port=8080,
    user='user',
    catalog='hive',
    schema='default'
)

# Query a large dataset in parallel
cursor = conn.cursor()
cursor.execute('SELECT * FROM large_table WHERE age > 30')
results = cursor.fetchall()
```

By using Presto, you can run SQL queries on large datasets stored in different systems, such as Hadoop or S3, without the need for data movement.

Optimizing data pipelines involves fine-tuning the ingestion, transformation, storage, and analysis stages to ensure the system runs efficiently. Distributed processing frameworks like Apache Kafka and Apache Spark play a vital role in improving performance, while tools like Presto and efficient storage formats help ensure that analysis can be performed on large datasets in a timely manner. By following best practices and leveraging the right tools, you can ensure that your data pipeline is both scalable and efficient.

Module 20:

Dimensionality Reduction

Dimensionality reduction is a crucial technique in data science that helps improve the efficiency of machine learning models by reducing the number of features. This module covers key methods such as Principal Component Analysis (PCA), t-SNE, and UMAP, along with feature selection techniques, and discusses how dimensionality reduction impacts model performance. These methods help address challenges posed by high-dimensional data.

Principal Component Analysis (PCA)

Principal Component Analysis (PCA) is a widely used technique that reduces the dimensionality of data while preserving as much variance as possible. It transforms the original features into a new set of orthogonal components, ranked by their variance. PCA is particularly useful for visualizing data and improving computational efficiency in high-dimensional datasets.

t-SNE and UMAP Methods

t-SNE (t-Distributed Stochastic Neighbor Embedding) and UMAP (Uniform Manifold Approximation and Projection) are advanced dimensionality reduction methods used primarily for visualization. t-SNE focuses on maintaining local structure, making it ideal for clustering and pattern recognition, while UMAP provides faster performance and is scalable to larger datasets, preserving both local and global structures.

Feature Selection Techniques

Feature selection techniques aim to identify the most important variables for predictive modeling, reducing the dataset's complexity. Methods include filter, wrapper, and embedded approaches. Filter methods assess the relevance of features independently, wrapper methods evaluate subsets of features, and embedded methods perform feature selection during the model training process, improving efficiency and accuracy.

Impact on Model Performance

Dimensionality reduction can significantly impact model performance by reducing overfitting and enhancing generalization. Fewer features often lead to faster model training and reduced computational cost. However, the choice of technique must align with the nature of the data. Proper dimensionality reduction ensures that the model retains its predictive power without unnecessary complexity.

Principal Component Analysis (PCA)

Principal Component Analysis (PCA) is one of the most widely used techniques for dimensionality reduction in data science. It transforms high-dimensional data into a lower-dimensional form while retaining as much variance (information) as possible. By projecting data onto a new set of axes, PCA makes it easier to visualize, analyze, and model data, particularly in cases where feature redundancy or collinearity is present.

What is PCA?

PCA is a linear transformation technique that finds the directions (principal components) in which the data varies the most. These components are linear combinations of the original features, and they represent the axes in the transformed space where the data has the highest variance. The first principal component captures the largest variance, the second captures the second-largest variance, and so on.

In essence, PCA reduces the complexity of the data by eliminating less informative features (those with lower variance), thus making the dataset more manageable while preserving essential patterns. The resulting components are uncorrelated with each other, which can be useful in reducing multicollinearity in machine learning models.

How PCA Works

PCA works through the following steps:

1. **Standardization**: Since PCA is affected by the scale of the features, the data is first standardized (mean = 0 and variance = 1) to ensure that all features contribute equally.

2. **Covariance Matrix Computation**: The covariance matrix is calculated to measure the relationships between the features. The covariance matrix captures how each feature varies with every other feature.

3. **Eigenvalue and Eigenvector Calculation**: PCA computes the eigenvalues and eigenvectors of the covariance matrix. The eigenvectors (principal components) determine the direction of the new axes, and the eigenvalues indicate the magnitude of variance along these axes.

4. **Sorting Eigenvectors**: The eigenvectors are sorted by their corresponding eigenvalues in descending order. This ordering helps identify the components that contribute the most to explaining the variance.

5. **Projection**: The original dataset is projected onto the top k eigenvectors (components), where k is the desired number of dimensions to reduce the dataset to.

Applying PCA in Python

To perform PCA in Python, the sklearn library provides a straightforward implementation. Below is an example of how to apply PCA on a dataset:

```
from sklearn.decomposition import PCA
from sklearn.preprocessing import StandardScaler
import numpy as np

# Example data
X = np.array([[2.5, 3.5, 1.2], [3.1, 4.2, 1.4], [4.0, 5.1, 1.7], [5.0, 6.0,
        2.1]])

# Standardizing the data
scaler = StandardScaler()
X_scaled = scaler.fit_transform(X)

# Applying PCA
pca = PCA(n_components=2)  # Reduce to 2 dimensions
X_pca = pca.fit_transform(X_scaled)

# Resulting transformed data
print("Original Data:\n", X)
print("Transformed Data (2D):\n", X_pca)
print("Explained Variance Ratio:", pca.explained_variance_ratio_)
```

In the example above:

- We first standardize the data using StandardScaler.

- We then apply PCA with n_components=2 to reduce the dataset to two principal components.

- The explained_variance_ratio_ provides information on how much variance each principal component accounts for in the data.

Benefits of PCA

- **Noise Reduction**: By removing less informative components, PCA can help reduce noise in the data, making the models more robust.

- **Visualization**: PCA is often used for data visualization. Reducing high-dimensional data to 2 or 3 principal components makes it easier to visualize the data, especially in scatter plots or 3D plots.

- **Multicollinearity Reduction**: By transforming correlated features into uncorrelated principal components, PCA helps address multicollinearity, which can improve the performance of certain machine learning models.

Limitations of PCA

While PCA is powerful, it also has some limitations:

- **Linear Assumption**: PCA assumes linear relationships between features. Non-linear dimensionality reduction techniques, like t-SNE or UMAP, are better suited for complex relationships.

- **Interpretability**: The transformed features (principal components) are linear combinations of the original features, making them less interpretable, which may be an issue in applications requiring feature importance or interpretability.

- **Scaling Sensitivity**: PCA is sensitive to the scaling of the features, so it's important to standardize the data before applying PCA.

Principal Component Analysis (PCA) is an essential tool for dimensionality reduction in data science. By transforming high-dimensional data into a lower-dimensional space while retaining as much variance as possible, PCA makes it easier to work with large datasets, enhances visualization, and improves model performance by addressing multicollinearity and reducing noise. However, it is most effective when the relationships between features are linear, and when interpretability is not a primary concern.

t-SNE and UMAP Methods

Dimensionality reduction techniques like PCA are essential for simplifying high-dimensional data. However, methods like t-Distributed Stochastic Neighbor Embedding (t-SNE) and Uniform Manifold Approximation and Projection (UMAP) have gained popularity for their ability to preserve the local structure of data, especially for visualization in lower dimensions. These methods are particularly effective for non-linear data structures, where PCA may not perform well.

t-SNE: Preserving Local Structure

t-SNE is a non-linear dimensionality reduction technique that is particularly useful for visualizing high-dimensional datasets. Unlike PCA, which focuses on capturing global variance, t-SNE is designed to preserve local structure. It works by minimizing the divergence between probability distributions in the high-dimensional space and the lower-dimensional embedding.

How t-SNE Works

1. **Similarity Calculation**: t-SNE computes pairwise similarities between points in the original high-dimensional space, typically using a Gaussian distribution.

2. **Embedding Creation**: It then creates a probability distribution over pairs of points in the low-dimensional space, where points that are close in the high-dimensional space should remain close in the low-dimensional space.

3. **Cost Function**: A cost function (the Kullback-Leibler divergence) is minimized by adjusting the positions of points in the lower-dimensional space until the distribution in the lower-dimensional space matches the one in the higher-dimensional space.

This process ensures that points that are similar in high-dimensional space are mapped close together in the lower-dimensional space, which makes t-SNE particularly useful for visualizing clusters or patterns in data.

Applying t-SNE in Python

To apply t-SNE in Python, you can use the TSNE class from sklearn.manifold. Here's an example:

```python
from sklearn.manifold import TSNE
import numpy as np
import matplotlib.pyplot as plt

# Sample data
X = np.array([[1, 2], [2, 3], [3, 4], [5, 6], [7, 8], [8, 9]])

# Applying t-SNE
tsne = TSNE(n_components=2, random_state=42)
X_tsne = tsne.fit_transform(X)

# Plotting the result
plt.scatter(X_tsne[:, 0], X_tsne[:, 1])
plt.title("t-SNE Visualization")
plt.show()
```

In the example, n_components=2 reduces the data to 2 dimensions for visualization, and random_state=42 ensures reproducibility. t-SNE is very effective for visualizing data that may contain complex structures.

UMAP: A Faster Alternative

Uniform Manifold Approximation and Projection (UMAP) is a more recent and faster technique for non-linear dimensionality reduction. Like t-SNE, UMAP seeks to preserve both local and global structure. However, UMAP has several advantages, such as faster computation time and better scalability, making it a better option for large datasets.

How UMAP Works

1. **Local Graph Construction**: UMAP constructs a weighted graph based on the nearest neighbors of data points.

2. **Fuzzy Simplicial Complex**: It uses a technique from algebraic topology to approximate the data manifold, ensuring that both local and global structures are maintained.

3. **Optimization**: Like t-SNE, UMAP uses an optimization process to embed data in lower dimensions. However, UMAP preserves more global structure, making it suitable for clustering and preserving the relationships between data points over a larger scale.

Advantages of UMAP

- **Speed**: UMAP is computationally faster than t-SNE, especially for large datasets.

- **Global Structure Preservation**: Unlike t-SNE, UMAP does not focus solely on local structure but also preserves the global relationships in the data.

- **Scalability**: UMAP is more scalable and can handle large datasets efficiently.

Applying UMAP in Python

To use UMAP, we can install the umap-learn package and apply it similarly to t-SNE:

```python
import umap
import numpy as np
import matplotlib.pyplot as plt

# Sample data
X = np.array([[1, 2], [2, 3], [3, 4], [5, 6], [7, 8], [8, 9]])

# Applying UMAP
umap_model = umap.UMAP(n_components=2, random_state=42)
X_umap = umap_model.fit_transform(X)

# Plotting the result
plt.scatter(X_umap[:, 0], X_umap[:, 1])
plt.title("UMAP Visualization")
plt.show()
```

In this example, the data is reduced to 2 dimensions, and the resulting plot shows how UMAP groups similar data points together, preserving both local and global structures.

t-SNE vs. UMAP

While t-SNE is excellent for visualizing clusters in high-dimensional data, UMAP tends to outperform t-SNE in several areas:

- **Computational Speed**: UMAP is faster and can handle larger datasets more efficiently.

- **Global Structure**: UMAP preserves global relationships better than t-SNE, making it more suitable for certain tasks such as clustering.

- **Flexibility**: UMAP is more versatile and can be used for a wider range of applications, including clustering and general manifold learning.

Both t-SNE and UMAP are powerful tools for non-linear dimensionality reduction, and the choice between them depends on the specific use case. t-SNE is effective for preserving local structures and visualizing clusters, but UMAP is faster, more scalable, and better at preserving both local and global structures.

Feature Selection Techniques

Feature selection is an essential step in the machine learning pipeline that involves selecting the most relevant features from a dataset to improve model performance, reduce overfitting, and enhance interpretability. In high-dimensional datasets, not all features contribute equally to the predictive power of the model. By selecting the right subset of features, you can improve both the accuracy and efficiency of machine learning algorithms.

Why Feature Selection Matters

1. **Model Performance**: Irrelevant or redundant features can negatively affect model performance by introducing noise and making the model more complex than necessary. Feature selection helps focus on the most important variables, which can improve the accuracy of models.

2. **Reduces Overfitting**: Using fewer features can reduce the complexity of a model and prevent overfitting, especially in high-dimensional datasets. Overfitting occurs when the model learns the noise in the training data, which harms its generalizability to new data.

3. **Decreases Computational Cost**: Fewer features mean fewer computations. This is particularly important for large datasets and computationally expensive models, where selecting only the most informative features can save time and resources.

Types of Feature Selection Techniques

There are three main categories of feature selection techniques: filter methods, wrapper methods, and embedded methods. Each approach has its advantages and trade-offs.

1. Filter Methods

Filter methods evaluate each feature independently of the machine learning algorithm. These methods are often based on statistical tests, correlations, or mutual information between the feature and the target variable. The most commonly used filter methods are:

- **Correlation-based Feature Selection**: Features that are highly correlated with the target variable are selected, while features that are highly correlated with each other are removed to avoid redundancy.

- **Chi-square Test**: Used for categorical features, the chi-square test measures the dependence between two variables. Features with a significant relationship to the target variable are selected.

- **Mutual Information**: Mutual information measures the dependency between two variables, quantifying how much information is shared between the feature and the target.

Example of Filter Method in Python (Using Correlation)

```python
import pandas as pd

# Load dataset
data = pd.read_csv('dataset.csv')

# Calculate correlation matrix
correlation_matrix = data.corr()

# Select features with high correlation to the target variable
target = 'target_column'
selected_features =
            correlation_matrix[target].abs().sort_values(ascending=False)

# Display selected features
print(selected_features)
```

This method calculates the correlation between features and the target variable, helping to select the most relevant ones.

2. Wrapper Methods

Wrapper methods evaluate feature subsets based on their performance with a specific machine learning model. These methods are computationally expensive but can lead to better results as they consider the interaction between features.

- **Recursive Feature Elimination (RFE)**: RFE recursively removes the least important features based on model performance. It uses a machine learning algorithm (like linear regression or decision trees) to evaluate feature importance.

- **Forward Selection**: Starts with no features and adds the most significant feature at each step, based on model performance.

- **Backward Elimination**: Starts with all features and removes the least significant feature at each step.

Example of Wrapper Method in Python (Using RFE)

```python
from sklearn.feature_selection import RFE
from sklearn.linear_model import LogisticRegression
import pandas as pd

# Load dataset
```

```
data = pd.read_csv('dataset.csv')
X = data.drop(columns=['target_column'])
y = data['target_column']

# Fit a logistic regression model
model = LogisticRegression()

# Use RFE for feature selection
selector = RFE(model, n_features_to_select=5)
X_selected = selector.fit_transform(X, y)

# Get the selected feature names
selected_features = X.columns[selector.support_]
print(selected_features)
```

This code applies RFE to select the top 5 features that contribute most to the model's predictive power.

3. Embedded Methods

Embedded methods combine feature selection and model training, performing feature selection during the model fitting process. These methods are efficient because they select features while building the model, eliminating the need for a separate feature selection step.

- **L1 Regularization (Lasso)**: Lasso regression adds an L1 penalty to the cost function, forcing less important feature coefficients to shrink to zero. Features with non-zero coefficients are selected.

- **Tree-based Methods**: Decision trees, random forests, and gradient boosting algorithms can be used for feature selection based on feature importance scores.

Example of Embedded Method in Python (Using Lasso)

```
from sklearn.linear_model import Lasso
import pandas as pd

# Load dataset
data = pd.read_csv('dataset.csv')
X = data.drop(columns=['target_column'])
y = data['target_column']

# Fit a Lasso model
lasso = Lasso(alpha=0.01)
lasso.fit(X, y)

# Get the features selected by Lasso
selected_features = X.columns[lasso.coef_ != 0]
print(selected_features)
```

This code uses Lasso regression to select features with non-zero coefficients, effectively performing feature selection during model training.

Impact on Model Performance

The impact of feature selection on model performance can be significant. By removing irrelevant or redundant features, the model becomes simpler, less prone to overfitting, and more interpretable. However, it's important to strike a balance. Too aggressive feature selection can remove important features and degrade model performance, while keeping too many features may lead to overfitting. Evaluating the model performance before and after feature selection is crucial to ensure optimal results.

Feature selection is a powerful tool for improving model performance and interpretability. Understanding when and how to apply filter, wrapper, and embedded methods allows data scientists to refine their models and ensure that only the most relevant features are used. The right feature selection technique can significantly enhance predictive accuracy and computational efficiency, making it a key aspect of data science workflows.

Impact on Model Performance

Dimensionality reduction and feature selection techniques play a crucial role in improving the performance of machine learning models. By reducing the number of input variables, these techniques address overfitting, enhance model interpretability, and speed up training processes. However, the impact of these techniques on model performance can vary depending on the dataset and the task at hand.

Effect on Overfitting

Overfitting occurs when a model captures noise or irrelevant patterns in the training data rather than generalizable trends. In high-dimensional datasets, the risk of overfitting increases as the model learns from too many features, some of which may not have any predictive value. Both dimensionality reduction and feature selection help mitigate this by eliminating redundant or irrelevant features, thus reducing the model's complexity.

- **Dimensionality Reduction**: Techniques like PCA (Principal Component Analysis) combine correlated features into a smaller set of uncorrelated components, removing noise and irrelevant variance. By focusing on the most important components, the model is less likely to overfit.

- **Feature Selection**: By choosing only the most relevant features for the model, feature selection directly reduces the risk of overfitting, especially when irrelevant or highly correlated features are removed.

Example: PCA Impact on Overfitting

```
from sklearn.decomposition import PCA
from sklearn.model_selection import train_test_split
from sklearn.linear_model import LogisticRegression
from sklearn.metrics import accuracy_score
import pandas as pd
```

```
# Load dataset
data = pd.read_csv('dataset.csv')
X = data.drop(columns=['target_column'])
y = data['target_column']

# Split data into train and test sets
X_train, X_test, y_train, y_test = train_test_split(X, y, test_size=0.2,
        random_state=42)

# Apply PCA for dimensionality reduction
pca = PCA(n_components=5)  # Reducing to 5 components
X_train_pca = pca.fit_transform(X_train)
X_test_pca = pca.transform(X_test)

# Train a logistic regression model
model = LogisticRegression()
model.fit(X_train_pca, y_train)

# Evaluate model
y_pred = model.predict(X_test_pca)
accuracy = accuracy_score(y_test, y_pred)
print(f"Accuracy after PCA: {accuracy:.4f}")
```

In this example, PCA reduces the number of features from the original dataset to five components. This reduction can lead to less overfitting, as the model is trained on a simpler, more generalized representation of the data.

Improved Model Interpretability

Reducing the number of features, especially in the context of high-dimensional data, also enhances the interpretability of the model. A model trained on a smaller set of features is easier to understand and analyze, making it more accessible to stakeholders and more effective for decision-making.

- **Dimensionality Reduction**: PCA, t-SNE, and UMAP methods transform the data into fewer dimensions that can be plotted and analyzed more easily, helping to visualize underlying patterns in the data.

- **Feature Selection**: Techniques like Lasso (L1 regularization) provide insights into which features are the most important for prediction, improving transparency.

Computational Efficiency

Reducing the number of features directly affects the training time and computational resources required to build and evaluate models. For large datasets, training models with fewer features is significantly faster and more resource-efficient. Both PCA and feature selection help streamline the process, allowing for quicker experimentation and iteration.

Example: Feature Selection for Faster Training

```
from sklearn.linear_model import Lasso
```

```
from sklearn.model_selection import train_test_split
import pandas as pd

# Load dataset
data = pd.read_csv('dataset.csv')
X = data.drop(columns=['target_column'])
y = data['target_column']

# Split data into train and test sets
X_train, X_test, y_train, y_test = train_test_split(X, y, test_size=0.2,
        random_state=42)

# Apply Lasso regression for feature selection
lasso = Lasso(alpha=0.01)
lasso.fit(X_train, y_train)

# Get the selected features
selected_features = X.columns[lasso.coef_ != 0]
print(f"Selected Features: {selected_features}")
```

In this case, Lasso regression is used for feature selection, which helps reduce the number of features considered during training, thereby improving computational efficiency.

Model Performance Trade-offs

While dimensionality reduction and feature selection often improve model performance by reducing overfitting and computational burden, there are trade-offs. In some cases, reducing dimensionality may lead to the loss of useful information, which can hurt the model's ability to make accurate predictions. It's essential to evaluate the impact of these techniques on model performance through cross-validation and careful performance monitoring.

For instance:

- **Dimensionality Reduction**: If too much variance is discarded during PCA, the model may lose important patterns, resulting in lower predictive accuracy.

- **Feature Selection**: If crucial features are inadvertently removed, the model's performance could degrade due to the absence of essential information.

Dimensionality reduction and feature selection are essential techniques for enhancing model performance, reducing overfitting, and improving computational efficiency. By carefully selecting the right approach and monitoring its impact, data scientists can create more efficient, interpretable, and accurate models. The choice between using PCA, feature selection methods, or a combination depends on the dataset, the model's purpose, and the trade-offs that are acceptable for the given application. Evaluating these techniques thoroughly ensures that the model strikes the right balance between simplicity and predictive power.

Module 21:

Applied Data Analysis Case Studies

Applied data analysis involves solving real-world problems using data-driven methods. In this module, we explore industry-specific applications, cross-domain insights, interactive solutions, and discuss the limitations and opportunities in data analysis. These case studies highlight how data science is transforming various sectors and providing actionable insights.

Industry-Specific Applications

Data analysis is essential in various industries, from healthcare to finance. In healthcare, it helps predict disease trends and optimize resource allocation. In finance, it supports fraud detection and risk management. By understanding industry-specific needs, data scientists tailor their approaches to address domain challenges effectively and improve decision-making.

Cross-Domain Insights

Cross-domain data analysis uncovers insights that are applicable across industries. For example, methods used in marketing analytics, such as customer segmentation, can be applied to healthcare for patient categorization. By leveraging insights from different sectors, data scientists can develop innovative solutions that transcend traditional boundaries, fostering more comprehensive approaches to problem-solving.

Interactive Solutions Showcase

Interactive solutions showcase how data analysis can be applied dynamically. Dashboards, real-time data visualizations, and predictive tools allow users to interact with the data and explore different scenarios. These solutions empower decision-makers by providing immediate insights, enabling them to adjust strategies based on evolving conditions and refine their decision-making processes for better outcomes.

Discussion of Limitations and Opportunities

While data analysis is powerful, it is not without limitations. Data quality issues, such as missing or biased data, can compromise results. Additionally, the complexity of models can hinder interpretability. However, these limitations present opportunities for improvement in data collection, model transparency, and algorithm fairness. Overcoming these challenges leads to more robust, reliable, and ethical data-driven solutions.

Industry-Specific Applications

Data analysis is at the core of decision-making across diverse industries. By leveraging data, businesses uncover insights that optimize operations, enhance customer experiences, and unlock revenue opportunities. In this section, we explore practical examples of applied data analysis in key industries, demonstrating how real-world problems are solved using structured approaches and powerful tools.

Healthcare: Enhancing Patient Outcomes

The healthcare industry heavily relies on data analysis to improve patient care, manage resources, and predict disease outbreaks. Predictive analytics plays a significant role in forecasting patient admissions, which helps hospitals allocate resources efficiently. Additionally, patient data is analyzed to identify trends in diseases and suggest personalized treatment plans.

Example: Predicting Hospital Readmissions

Using Python, we can build a model to predict hospital readmissions, reducing costs and improving care.

```python
import pandas as pd
from sklearn.ensemble import RandomForestClassifier
from sklearn.model_selection import train_test_split
from sklearn.metrics import accuracy_score

# Load sample dataset
data = pd.read_csv('hospital_readmissions.csv')
X = data.drop(columns=['readmitted'])
y = data['readmitted']

# Split into training and testing sets
X_train, X_test, y_train, y_test = train_test_split(X, y, test_size=0.2,
        random_state=42)

# Train a Random Forest model
model = RandomForestClassifier(random_state=42)
model.fit(X_train, y_train)

# Make predictions and evaluate
y_pred = model.predict(X_test)
accuracy = accuracy_score(y_test, y_pred)
print(f"Model Accuracy: {accuracy:.2f}")
```

This example demonstrates how patient data, such as age, prior diagnoses, and length of stay, can predict readmission risks, enabling preventive interventions.

Retail: Optimizing Inventory and Sales

In retail, data analysis informs inventory management, sales forecasting, and customer segmentation. With detailed transaction data, retailers can predict demand, ensuring popular items remain stocked while minimizing overstock costs.

Example: Demand Forecasting for Inventory

Python's time-series libraries allow us to forecast future sales trends effectively.

```python
import pandas as pd
from statsmodels.tsa.holtwinters import ExponentialSmoothing

# Load sales data
sales_data = pd.read_csv('retail_sales.csv', parse_dates=['date'],
          index_col='date')

# Apply exponential smoothing for forecasting
model = ExponentialSmoothing(sales_data['sales'], seasonal='add',
          seasonal_periods=12).fit()
forecast = model.forecast(steps=12)

# Plot forecast
sales_data['sales'].plot(label='Actual Sales')
forecast.plot(label='Forecast', legend=True)
```

This forecasting model identifies seasonal trends, helping retailers stock inventory appropriately during peak demand periods.

Finance: Detecting Fraud

Financial institutions leverage data analysis for fraud detection and risk management. By analyzing transaction patterns, anomalies can be detected in real time, preventing unauthorized activities.

Example: Fraud Detection with Machine Learning

A supervised learning approach identifies fraudulent transactions based on historical data.

```python
from sklearn.ensemble import IsolationForest

# Load transaction data
transactions = pd.read_csv('transactions.csv')

# Train an isolation forest for anomaly detection
isolation_forest = IsolationForest(contamination=0.01, random_state=42)
transactions['anomaly'] = isolation_forest.fit_predict(transactions)

# Count anomalies
frauds = transactions[transactions['anomaly'] == -1]
print(f"Number of fraudulent transactions: {len(frauds)}")
```

This method highlights anomalies, enabling financial teams to investigate suspicious transactions promptly.

Energy: Improving Efficiency

Energy companies analyze consumption data to optimize grid operations, forecast demand, and enhance energy efficiency. Predictive models help reduce waste and allocate renewable resources effectively.

Example: Energy Consumption Forecasting

By analyzing historical consumption data, energy providers can predict future demand.

```python
import pandas as pd
from sklearn.linear_model import LinearRegression

# Load consumption data
energy_data = pd.read_csv('energy_consumption.csv')
X = energy_data[['temperature', 'hour_of_day', 'day_of_week']]
y = energy_data['consumption']

# Train a linear regression model
model = LinearRegression()
model.fit(X, y)

# Make predictions
future_conditions = pd.DataFrame({'temperature': [30], 'hour_of_day': [15],
        'day_of_week': [3]})
predicted_consumption = model.predict(future_conditions)
print(f"Predicted Energy Consumption: {predicted_consumption[0]:.2f} kWh")
```

This forecasting enables utility companies to meet demand without overproducing energy, reducing costs and environmental impact.

Industry-specific applications of data analysis demonstrate the versatility of tools and techniques in solving real-world problems. From improving patient care to detecting fraud and optimizing energy consumption, data-driven insights empower businesses to make informed decisions. By tailoring approaches to industry needs, organizations maximize the value of their data, creating opportunities for innovation and growth.

Cross-Domain Insights

Data science thrives on its ability to draw parallels and insights across domains. By applying techniques and models developed in one industry to others, organizations can uncover innovative solutions to complex challenges. Cross-domain insights leverage transferable methodologies, enabling industries to benefit from collective advancements in data science.

Healthcare Meets Retail: Personalization and Recommendation Systems

Personalization has revolutionized retail, particularly through recommendation systems that analyze customer behavior to suggest relevant products. This approach has been adapted in healthcare to personalize treatment plans and drug recommendations based on patient history and genetic data.

For instance, collaborative filtering, a common recommendation algorithm in retail, can suggest complementary medications or treatments for patients:

```python
import pandas as pd
from sklearn.neighbors import NearestNeighbors

# Example patient dataset
```

```
data = pd.DataFrame({
    'patient_id': [1, 2, 3, 4],
    'condition': ['Diabetes', 'Hypertension', 'Asthma', 'Diabetes'],
    'treatment_score': [0.9, 0.8, 0.75, 0.88]
})

# Build a recommendation model
model = NearestNeighbors(metric='cosine', algorithm='brute')
model.fit(data[['treatment_score']])

# Find treatments similar to a target patient
distances, indices = model.kneighbors([[0.88]], n_neighbors=2)
print(f"Recommended treatments:
        {data.iloc[indices.flatten()].condition.tolist()}")
```

This example highlights how recommendation algorithms help healthcare providers tailor interventions efficiently.

Energy Meets Finance: Risk Assessment Models

The financial sector is renowned for its robust risk assessment models, which quantify potential losses due to market fluctuations. These methodologies have found applications in the energy industry to predict risks associated with power outages or renewable energy supply inconsistencies.

For example, Value at Risk (VaR), widely used in finance, can quantify risks in energy trading or supply chains. Python libraries like numpy can compute these values effectively:

```
import numpy as np

# Simulate energy price returns
returns = np.random.normal(loc=0.01, scale=0.02, size=1000)

# Compute Value at Risk at 95% confidence level
var_95 = np.percentile(returns, 5)
print(f"Value at Risk (95%): {var_95:.4f}")
```

By adopting risk models from finance, energy providers can better prepare for market volatility and environmental uncertainties.

Transportation Meets Marketing: Demand Forecasting

Demand forecasting, a cornerstone in transportation planning, has been instrumental in marketing campaigns. Ride-sharing companies like Uber use historical demand data to anticipate surge periods, while marketers use similar forecasting to predict product demand during holiday seasons or promotional events.

Time-series forecasting, a common method in transportation, can also optimize marketing efforts. For instance, using the statsmodels library:

```
import pandas as pd
from statsmodels.tsa.holtwinters import ExponentialSmoothing
```

```
# Load example demand data
demand_data = pd.Series([100, 150, 130, 160, 200],
            index=pd.date_range(start='2023-01-01', periods=5, freq='D'))

# Build a forecasting model
model = ExponentialSmoothing(demand_data, trend="add", seasonal=None).fit()
forecast = model.forecast(steps=3)
print(f"Forecasted demand: {forecast.tolist()}")
```

This process aids both transportation companies and marketers in optimizing resources and aligning strategies with anticipated needs.

Retail Meets Education: Customer Retention Models

Retail's focus on customer retention has inspired similar approaches in education to improve student retention rates. Models predicting customer churn are now applied to identify students at risk of dropping out, allowing educators to intervene early.

A machine learning classification model for predicting churn or dropout rates can be implemented using Python's sklearn:

```
from sklearn.ensemble import RandomForestClassifier

# Simulated student data
data = pd.DataFrame({
    'hours_studied': [10, 5, 3, 8],
    'assignments_completed': [5, 2, 1, 4],
    'at_risk': [0, 1, 1, 0]
})

# Train the model
X = data[['hours_studied', 'assignments_completed']]
y = data['at_risk']
model = RandomForestClassifier(random_state=42)
model.fit(X, y)

# Predict risk for a new student
new_student = [[6, 3]]
prediction = model.predict(new_student)
print(f"Student at risk: {bool(prediction[0])}")
```

This example illustrates how predictive models help educators address challenges proactively, improving outcomes for students.

Cross-domain insights exemplify the power of data science to bridge industries, fostering innovation through transferable techniques. By adapting methodologies across fields, organizations harness a wealth of knowledge to solve unique problems. These interdisciplinary applications not only drive efficiency but also push the boundaries of what is achievable through data-driven strategies.

Interactive Solutions Showcase

In the evolving landscape of data science, interactive solutions have become an essential tool for engaging with data, gaining deeper insights, and improving decision-making processes. These solutions range from real-time dashboards to interactive data visualizations and advanced model deployment platforms, all designed to enhance user experience, foster collaboration, and provide actionable insights.

Real-Time Dashboards for Monitoring and Analysis

Real-time dashboards are one of the most popular interactive solutions for data visualization. They enable users to monitor and analyze live data, making it easier to spot trends, track key performance indicators (KPIs), and make data-driven decisions on the fly. Platforms like Tableau, Power BI, and custom-built solutions using Python libraries such as Dash and Streamlit allow for the creation of interactive and dynamic dashboards.

For example, a financial services company might build a real-time dashboard to monitor stock prices, trading volumes, and market sentiment. The Python code below demonstrates how to build an interactive dashboard using Dash, which could display live data trends:

```python
import dash
from dash import dcc, html
import plotly.express as px
import pandas as pd

# Create a simple dataframe with sample stock data
data = pd.DataFrame({
    'Date': pd.date_range(start='2023-01-01', periods=100),
    'Stock Price': [100 + x + (x % 10) for x in range(100)]
})

# Create a plotly graph for stock price
fig = px.line(data, x='Date', y='Stock Price', title="Stock Price Over
        Time")

# Initialize the Dash app
app = dash.Dash(__name__)

# Define the layout of the app
app.layout = html.Div([
    html.H1("Stock Price Monitoring"),
    dcc.Graph(figure=fig)
])

if __name__ == '__main__':
    app.run_server(debug=True)
```

This simple interactive dashboard updates the stock price graph dynamically, providing users with an up-to-date view of the market trends. Real-time dashboards like these are used across various industries, such as finance, healthcare, and retail, to facilitate quick decision-making based on live data.

Interactive Data Visualizations for Deeper Insights

Interactive visualizations allow users to explore complex data sets dynamically, providing a more engaging and comprehensive experience. Tools like Plotly and

Bokeh enable users to hover over data points, zoom in on areas of interest, or filter data in real time. These interactions provide users with the ability to uncover deeper insights by engaging directly with the visual representation of the data.

For example, using Plotly, you can create interactive scatter plots that allow users to filter data points based on specific criteria, such as region or time period. The following Python code illustrates how you can create an interactive scatter plot:

```
import plotly.express as px
import pandas as pd

# Example dataset
df = pd.DataFrame({
    'x': [1, 2, 3, 4, 5],
    'y': [5, 6, 7, 8, 9],
    'category': ['A', 'B', 'A', 'B', 'A']
})

# Create an interactive scatter plot
fig = px.scatter(df, x='x', y='y', color='category', title="Interactive
        Scatter Plot")

# Show the plot
fig.show()
```

In this example, users can hover over data points to view detailed information, allowing for interactive exploration of the data. Such tools are especially valuable in data analysis, where user-driven interactions with the data reveal patterns that static charts may not show.

Interactive Model Deployment with Web Applications

Interactive solutions also play a crucial role in model deployment. By embedding machine learning models into interactive web applications, users can input new data, receive predictions, and visualize the results immediately. Platforms like Flask, Streamlit, and FastAPI are widely used to deploy models and create interactive applications.

For instance, a recommendation engine for an e-commerce website might suggest products based on user inputs. The user can interact with the model by entering preferences or browsing history, and the application dynamically updates with personalized recommendations. Here's a basic example of deploying a machine learning model using Streamlit:

```
import streamlit as st
from sklearn.ensemble import RandomForestClassifier
import pandas as pd

# Example model (trained on some dataset)
model = RandomForestClassifier()
data = pd.DataFrame({
    'feature1': [1, 2, 3],
    'feature2': [4, 5, 6],
```

```
})
model.fit(data[['feature1', 'feature2']], [0, 1, 0])

# Streamlit app to interact with the model
st.title('Interactive Model Deployment')

feature1 = st.slider('Feature 1', 0, 10)
feature2 = st.slider('Feature 2', 0, 10)

prediction = model.predict([[feature1, feature2]])

st.write(f'Predicted Class: {prediction[0]}')
```

This simple interface allows users to adjust the sliders to input values for the model's features and see the predicted outcome in real time. It demonstrates how machine learning models can be deployed interactively to engage users and provide personalized insights.

Interactive solutions are becoming indispensable in data science. They enable organizations to engage with their data in real time, explore complex insights dynamically, and make informed decisions faster. Whether it's through real-time dashboards, interactive visualizations, or machine learning model deployment, these tools are transforming how businesses interact with their data and helping drive innovation across industries.

Discussion of Limitations and Opportunities

While interactive data analysis solutions offer numerous benefits in terms of engagement, decision-making, and insights, they also come with their own set of challenges and limitations. Understanding these limitations and recognizing the opportunities they present can help organizations better navigate the data-driven landscape.

Limitations of Interactive Solutions

Despite their potential, interactive solutions often face several challenges that can hinder their effectiveness. One of the primary limitations is **data complexity**. Interactive tools rely on the availability of clean, well-structured, and manageable data. When working with large datasets or poorly prepared data, performance can degrade, resulting in slow response times or incomplete visualizations. For instance, real-time dashboards with live data feeds may experience delays or inaccuracies if the data is too complex or the systems are underprepared for such high-volume processing.

Moreover, **resource-intensive** solutions are another limitation. Complex interactive visualizations and dashboards require significant computational resources to render and update in real time. This can lead to high operational costs, especially for organizations dealing with large-scale data. Furthermore, cloud-based tools and hosting services are often needed to scale up, which can lead to ongoing expenses.

Lastly, **user experience** can be a bottleneck for interactive solutions. While interactivity is a key advantage, creating interfaces that are intuitive and accessible for all users remains a challenge. Poorly designed interfaces can result in confusion, misinterpretation of data, or lack of user adoption. Additionally, users with limited data literacy may struggle to fully engage with complex interactive solutions.

Opportunities in Interactive Solutions

Despite these limitations, interactive solutions present significant opportunities for improvement and growth, especially when organizations leverage the right tools and strategies.

One of the major opportunities lies in **personalization and user-driven insights**. As more businesses move toward data-driven decision-making, the ability to create interactive tools that cater to the specific needs of users can unlock new levels of value. For example, customized dashboards tailored to specific business units, like marketing or sales, can provide targeted insights that lead to more informed decisions. The use of predictive analytics integrated into these dashboards also allows businesses to act on future trends rather than relying on historical data alone.

Another opportunity comes from **advancements in technology**. The continuous evolution of data processing tools, machine learning algorithms, and cloud-based infrastructure is making it easier and more affordable to build powerful interactive solutions. Technologies like **edge computing** and **distributed systems** can enhance the performance of real-time applications by moving data processing closer to where it is generated, reducing latency and improving the speed of interactive data analysis.

Additionally, the **integration of artificial intelligence (AI)** and **natural language processing (NLP)** into interactive tools presents a major opportunity. AI can be used to automate insights generation, uncover hidden patterns in the data, and even interact with users through natural language interfaces. For example, chatbots that leverage NLP can guide users through data exploration, enabling them to ask questions about their data and receive real-time, actionable insights.

Building a Better Future with Interactive Solutions

While interactive solutions come with their limitations, the opportunity to improve data engagement and accessibility is substantial. By addressing issues related to performance, user experience, and data complexity, organizations can create more efficient and effective tools for their users. Continuous advancements in AI, cloud computing, and machine learning will drive the next wave of innovation in interactive solutions, enabling even deeper insights and more efficient decision-making processes.

As the demand for data-driven insights continues to grow, organizations that can harness the power of interactive data analysis will gain a competitive edge, improving both their operational efficiency and customer satisfaction. Recognizing the limitations, addressing challenges head-on, and seizing the opportunities will be key to fully leveraging the potential of interactive solutions in the data science domain.

Part 4:

Machine Learning Basics

Introduction to Machine Learning

Machine learning (ML) is a field of artificial intelligence that enables systems to learn and improve from experience without explicit programming. This module provides an introduction to ML, covering its essence and how it differs from traditional programming. We explore the two main types of learning: supervised and unsupervised. Supervised learning involves training models with labeled data to predict outcomes, while unsupervised learning uncovers patterns in unlabeled data. Applications of ML span predictive modeling, classification, and clustering. We also address common challenges such as data quality, model selection, and overfitting, which can hinder model performance.

Supervised Learning

Supervised learning is one of the most widely used approaches in ML. This module focuses on classification and regression models, explaining algorithms like logistic regression, decision trees, and random forests for classification tasks, and linear regression, lasso, and ridge regression for regression tasks. We also explore how to evaluate model performance using metrics such as accuracy, precision, recall, F1 score, and ROC-AUC. Additionally, we discuss techniques to prevent overfitting and underfitting, including cross-validation, regularization, and model tuning, which help ensure the model generalizes well to new data.

Unsupervised Learning

Unsupervised learning deals with finding hidden patterns in data without labeled outcomes. In this module, we cover clustering techniques like K-means, hierarchical clustering, and DBSCAN, which group similar data points together. Dimensionality reduction methods such as PCA, t-SNE, and UMAP help reduce the number of variables while preserving key patterns. Anomaly detection is also discussed, focusing on methods to identify outliers or unusual data points. Evaluation of unsupervised learning models is critical, and we review metrics like the silhouette score, elbow method, and Davies-Bouldin index to assess clustering and dimensionality reduction performance.

Introduction to Neural Networks

Neural networks are a fundamental aspect of deep learning, which has revolutionized fields like image recognition, natural language processing (NLP), and autonomous systems. This module introduces the architecture of neural networks, explaining the roles of input, hidden, and output layers, as well as the importance of activation functions and backpropagation in training networks. We also highlight the applications of deep learning, such as recognizing images, interpreting text, and powering autonomous vehicles. Popular tools for building neural networks, including TensorFlow, Keras, and PyTorch, are also covered, giving learners the skills to develop their own models.

Feature Engineering in ML

Feature engineering plays a critical role in improving the accuracy and effectiveness of machine learning models. This module discusses the importance of transforming raw data into features that better represent the problem at hand. Key techniques include feature scaling (normalization and standardization) and encoding categorical variables (one-hot encoding). We also examine feature selection algorithms like recursive feature elimination (RFE) and L1 regularization, which help identify the most relevant features. Advanced transformations, such as polynomial features and logarithmic transformations, are introduced to handle non-linear relationships and enhance model performance.

Model Deployment

Deploying machine learning models in production environments involves overcoming challenges like scalability, integration with other systems, and handling model drift. This module discusses the best practices for deploying ML models, focusing on continuous integration (CI) and continuous deployment (CD) practices. We emphasize the importance of monitoring model performance over time, ensuring that models remain accurate and reliable by retraining them with new data when necessary. Additionally, scalability considerations are addressed, helping learners understand how to deploy models that can handle large-scale data in real-world systems.

Machine Learning in Action

In this hands-on module, learners will work on building a predictive model from start to finish, following an end-to-end project example. By applying the concepts learned in previous modules, they will gain practical experience with real-world machine learning tasks. The module also includes case studies from top industries that showcase successful ML applications. Finally, emerging trends such as AutoML, federated learning, and explainable AI are discussed, providing learners with insight into the future of machine learning and its potential impact on various sectors.

Module 22:

Introduction to Machine Learning

Machine learning (ML) is a field of artificial intelligence that enables systems to learn from data and improve their performance over time. This module introduces the fundamental concepts of machine learning, explores its types and applications, and discusses common challenges in the field. Understanding ML is essential for leveraging its potential in solving complex problems.

What is Machine Learning?

Machine learning is the process of using algorithms to identify patterns in data and make predictions or decisions without explicit programming. It allows systems to adapt to new data and improve their accuracy over time. ML algorithms learn from experience, automating tasks that would otherwise require human intervention, such as image recognition or natural language processing.

Supervised vs. Unsupervised Learning

Supervised learning uses labeled data to train models, where the outcome is known. It is used for tasks like regression and classification, where the goal is to predict a target variable. Unsupervised learning, on the other hand, works with unlabeled data and aims to find hidden patterns, such as grouping similar data points into clusters. Both methods have distinct use cases and applications in different domains.

Applications of Machine Learning

Machine learning is widely used in predictive modeling, classification, and clustering. Predictive modeling helps forecast future outcomes, such as sales or demand. Classification assigns categories to data, such as spam detection in emails. Clustering groups similar data points together, which is useful in customer segmentation. ML applications span industries, revolutionizing fields like healthcare, finance, and marketing.

Challenges in ML

Despite its potential, machine learning faces several challenges. Data quality is crucial, as poor-quality data can lead to inaccurate models. Model selection is another challenge, as choosing the right algorithm requires careful consideration of the problem and available data. Overfitting occurs when a model performs well on training data but fails to generalize to new data, reducing its effectiveness in real-world applications.

What is Machine Learning?: Understanding the Essence of ML

Machine Learning (ML) is a subset of artificial intelligence (AI) that focuses on the development of algorithms and models that allow computers to learn from and make decisions based on data. Unlike traditional programming where explicit instructions are provided, machine learning enables systems to improve their performance as they are exposed to more data, learning from patterns and making predictions or decisions without being explicitly programmed for each scenario.

The Essence of Machine Learning

At its core, machine learning revolves around creating algorithms that can learn from data and make predictions or decisions without human intervention. The goal of machine learning is to develop models that can generalize well to new, unseen data based on patterns observed in the training data. The process begins with feeding data into a machine learning model, which then "learns" from this data by adjusting its internal parameters to better predict outcomes or identify relationships within the data.

The key difference between traditional programming and machine learning is the concept of learning from data. In traditional programming, a programmer writes explicit instructions for the computer to follow. In contrast, machine learning algorithms learn from data by identifying patterns and adjusting based on new information, without needing to be specifically told how to handle each situation.

Types of Machine Learning

Machine learning can be broadly classified into three categories: supervised learning, unsupervised learning, and reinforcement learning.

1. **Supervised Learning**: In supervised learning, the model is trained on labeled data. This means that the training dataset includes both input features (independent variables) and corresponding target labels (dependent variables). The goal is for the model to learn the mapping between inputs and outputs, enabling it to predict the output for new, unseen inputs. Common supervised learning algorithms include linear regression, decision trees, and support vector machines.

Example of Supervised Learning: A simple example is predicting house prices based on features such as square footage, number of rooms, and location. The model learns from the historical data (with labeled prices) and generalizes to predict prices for new houses.

```
from sklearn.linear_model import LinearRegression
from sklearn.model_selection import train_test_split
from sklearn.datasets import make_regression

X, y = make_regression(n_samples=100, n_features=2, noise=0.1)
X_train, X_test, y_train, y_test = train_test_split(X, y, test_size=0.2)
```

```
model = LinearRegression()
model.fit(X_train, y_train)
predictions = model.predict(X_test)
```

2. **Unsupervised Learning**: Unlike supervised learning, unsupervised learning works with unlabeled data. Here, the model seeks to identify underlying patterns and structures in the data, such as clusters or groups. Common unsupervised learning algorithms include k-means clustering, hierarchical clustering, and principal component analysis (PCA).

Example of Unsupervised Learning: An example is customer segmentation in marketing, where the goal is to group customers based on similarities in their purchasing behavior without prior knowledge of the segments.

```
from sklearn.cluster import KMeans

# Generate synthetic data
X, _ = make_blobs(n_samples=100, centers=3, random_state=42)

kmeans = KMeans(n_clusters=3)
kmeans.fit(X)
labels = kmeans.predict(X)
```

3. **Reinforcement Learning**: In reinforcement learning, an agent learns to make decisions by interacting with an environment. The agent receives rewards or penalties based on its actions and uses this feedback to adjust its behavior. This type of learning is commonly used in robotics, game playing, and autonomous vehicles.

Machine learning is a powerful tool that enables systems to learn and improve automatically through data. Understanding the core concepts of supervised and unsupervised learning, as well as their use cases, provides a solid foundation for diving deeper into the world of machine learning. As technology evolves, ML will continue to be a driving force behind innovations across industries.

Supervised vs. Unsupervised Learning: Differences, Use Cases, and Examples

In machine learning, understanding the distinction between supervised and unsupervised learning is fundamental to choosing the right algorithm and approach for a given problem. These two categories are the most commonly used in data science, each serving distinct purposes based on the nature of the data and the problem at hand.

Supervised Learning: Understanding the Concept

Supervised learning is a type of machine learning where the model is trained on labeled data. In this context, "labeled data" means that each input data point has a corresponding output label, allowing the algorithm to learn the relationship between the features and the target variable. The primary goal of supervised learning is to make predictions or classifications based on historical data.

Use Cases of Supervised Learning

Supervised learning is ideal when there is a clear relationship between input features and the target variable, and you have access to labeled data. Common use cases include:

- **Regression Problems**: Predicting a continuous target variable.

  o **Example**: Predicting house prices based on features like square footage, number of rooms, and location.

- **Classification Problems**: Categorizing data into discrete classes.

  o **Example**: Classifying emails as spam or non-spam based on various features such as sender, subject, and content.

Supervised Learning Algorithm Example

A typical supervised learning algorithm is **Linear Regression**, used for predicting a continuous value, or **Logistic Regression**, which is used for binary classification.

Here is an example using **Logistic Regression** for classifying whether an email is spam based on features:

```
from sklearn.model_selection import train_test_split
from sklearn.linear_model import LogisticRegression
from sklearn.datasets import make_classification
from sklearn.metrics import accuracy_score

# Generate a synthetic dataset for binary classification
X, y = make_classification(n_samples=100, n_features=5, n_informative=3,
        n_classes=2)

# Split data into training and test sets
X_train, X_test, y_train, y_test = train_test_split(X, y, test_size=0.2,
        random_state=42)

# Create and train the model
model = LogisticRegression()
model.fit(X_train, y_train)

# Predict on the test set and evaluate the model
y_pred = model.predict(X_test)
accuracy = accuracy_score(y_test, y_pred)
print(f"Accuracy: {accuracy:.2f}")
```

Unsupervised Learning: Understanding the Concept

Unsupervised learning, on the other hand, deals with data that is not labeled. The model must find hidden patterns or structures within the data without predefined outcomes. The goal is to explore the data, group it, or reduce its dimensions, making it easier to understand or visualize.

Use Cases of Unsupervised Learning

Unsupervised learning is well-suited for discovering unknown patterns or insights in data, especially when labels are not available. Common use cases include:

- **Clustering**: Grouping similar data points together based on their features.

    o **Example**: Customer segmentation for targeted marketing based on purchasing behavior.

- **Dimensionality Reduction**: Reducing the number of features in a dataset while preserving important information.

    o **Example**: Using Principal Component Analysis (PCA) to reduce the number of variables in an image processing task.

Unsupervised Learning Algorithm Example

A widely used unsupervised learning algorithm is **K-Means Clustering**, which partitions the data into groups based on similarities.

Here is an example of using **K-Means Clustering** to cluster a dataset into groups:

```
from sklearn.cluster import KMeans
from sklearn.datasets import make_blobs
import matplotlib.pyplot as plt

# Generate synthetic data with three clusters
X, _ = make_blobs(n_samples=300, centers=3, random_state=42)

# Apply KMeans clustering
kmeans = KMeans(n_clusters=3)
kmeans.fit(X)

# Predict clusters and visualize the results
labels = kmeans.predict(X)

# Plot the clusters
plt.scatter(X[:, 0], X[:, 1], c=labels, cmap='viridis')
plt.title("K-Means Clustering")
plt.show()
```

Key Differences Between Supervised and Unsupervised Learning

- **Data**: Supervised learning requires labeled data, while unsupervised learning works with unlabeled data.

- **Goal**: The goal of supervised learning is to predict or classify data based on past examples, whereas unsupervised learning aims to find hidden patterns or relationships in the data.

- **Output**: Supervised learning provides a specific prediction or class label for each input, while unsupervised learning provides groups or patterns, such as clusters or reduced dimensions.

Understanding the key differences between supervised and unsupervised learning is essential for selecting the appropriate machine learning algorithm. Supervised learning is ideal when labeled data is available and the goal is to predict or classify outcomes. In contrast, unsupervised learning is useful for uncovering hidden patterns or reducing data complexity when labels are not available. Both approaches have their own strengths and applications, making them crucial tools in a data scientist's toolkit.

Applications of Machine Learning: Predictive Modeling, Classification, and Clustering

Machine learning (ML) has become an essential tool across many industries, providing powerful techniques for data analysis, prediction, and decision-making. Three of the most common applications of machine learning are predictive modeling, classification, and clustering. Each of these techniques serves different purposes, allowing data scientists to unlock valuable insights from various types of data.

Predictive Modeling: Making Future Predictions

Predictive modeling is one of the core applications of machine learning. The goal is to build models that can forecast future values based on historical data. This technique is widely used in fields such as finance, healthcare, and marketing to predict trends and behaviors.

In predictive modeling, historical data with known outcomes is used to train the model, allowing it to identify patterns and relationships between the features and the target variable. Once the model is trained, it can be applied to make predictions on new, unseen data.

Use Cases of Predictive Modeling

- **Stock Market Predictions**: Predicting stock prices based on historical data, news, and other economic indicators.

- **Demand Forecasting**: Predicting product demand to optimize inventory and supply chain management.

- **Customer Churn Prediction**: Forecasting the likelihood of customers leaving a service based on their usage patterns.

Predictive Modeling Example

A common approach to predictive modeling is using **Linear Regression** for continuous target variables, such as predicting house prices or sales revenue. Below is an example using **Linear Regression** to predict housing prices based on features like square footage and number of bedrooms:

```
from sklearn.linear_model import LinearRegression
from sklearn.model_selection import train_test_split
from sklearn.metrics import mean_squared_error

# Sample data for house prices
X = [[1500, 3], [1800, 4], [2400, 4], [3000, 5]]  # [Square Footage,
        Bedrooms]
y = [400000, 500000, 600000, 650000]  # Prices in USD

# Split the data into training and test sets
X_train, X_test, y_train, y_test = train_test_split(X, y, test_size=0.2,
        random_state=42)

# Create and train the model
model = LinearRegression()
model.fit(X_train, y_train)

# Predict on the test set
y_pred = model.predict(X_test)

# Evaluate the model
mse = mean_squared_error(y_test, y_pred)
print(f"Mean Squared Error: {mse:.2f}")
```

Classification: Categorizing Data into Classes

Classification is another widely used application of machine learning. In classification tasks, the goal is to assign labels or categories to input data based on its features. Supervised learning algorithms are often used for classification tasks, as they are trained on labeled data where the categories are known.

Use Cases of Classification

- **Email Spam Detection**: Classifying emails as spam or not based on content.

- **Medical Diagnosis**: Classifying medical images or patient data to predict disease presence or types.

- **Credit Scoring**: Classifying individuals based on their creditworthiness.

Classification Example

A popular algorithm for classification tasks is **Logistic Regression**, especially for binary classification problems. Below is an example where we classify data into two classes:

```python
from sklearn.linear_model import LogisticRegression
from sklearn.model_selection import train_test_split
from sklearn.metrics import accuracy_score

# Sample data for binary classification (e.g., spam vs. non-spam)
X = [[1, 2], [3, 4], [5, 6], [7, 8], [9, 10]]  # Features (e.g., word
            frequencies)
y = [0, 1, 0, 1, 0]  # Labels (0 = non-spam, 1 = spam)

# Split the data into training and test sets
X_train, X_test, y_train, y_test = train_test_split(X, y, test_size=0.2,
            random_state=42)

# Create and train the model
model = LogisticRegression()
model.fit(X_train, y_train)

# Predict on the test set
y_pred = model.predict(X_test)

# Evaluate the model
accuracy = accuracy_score(y_test, y_pred)
print(f"Accuracy: {accuracy:.2f}")
```

Clustering: Grouping Similar Data

Clustering is an unsupervised learning technique used to group similar data points together based on their features. Unlike classification, where data is assigned predefined labels, clustering allows the model to discover natural groupings in the data. It is especially useful when the data is unlabeled.

Use Cases of Clustering

- **Customer Segmentation**: Grouping customers based on purchasing behavior for targeted marketing.

- **Image Segmentation**: Grouping similar regions of an image for better image recognition.

- **Anomaly Detection**: Identifying outliers or unusual patterns that deviate from the norm.

Clustering Example

A commonly used clustering algorithm is **K-Means**, which groups data into a specified number of clusters based on the similarity of their features. Below is an example of using K-Means for clustering:

```python
from sklearn.cluster import KMeans
```

```
import matplotlib.pyplot as plt
import numpy as np

# Generate sample data
X = np.array([[1, 2], [1, 4], [1, 0], [10, 2], [10, 4], [10, 0]])

# Apply K-Means clustering
kmeans = KMeans(n_clusters=2)
kmeans.fit(X)

# Get the cluster centers and labels
centers = kmeans.cluster_centers_
labels = kmeans.labels_

# Visualize the clusters
plt.scatter(X[:, 0], X[:, 1], c=labels, cmap='viridis')
plt.scatter(centers[:, 0], centers[:, 1], c='red', marker='x', s=200)
plt.title("K-Means Clustering")
plt.show()
```

Machine learning techniques such as predictive modeling, classification, and clustering have become powerful tools in data analysis, each serving different purposes. Predictive modeling is used for forecasting future trends, classification is ideal for categorizing data into specific labels, and clustering allows for the discovery of natural groupings within data. These techniques can be applied across various industries, from finance to healthcare, enabling data-driven decision-making and enhanced insights.

Challenges in ML: Data Quality, Model Selection, and Overfitting

Machine learning (ML) offers immense potential for data-driven insights and decision-making, but it is not without its challenges. Ensuring high-quality data, selecting appropriate models, and avoiding issues such as overfitting are critical to developing effective ML solutions. Addressing these challenges is essential for creating robust models that generalize well to new data.

Data Quality: The Foundation of ML Success

The first challenge in any machine learning project is ensuring that the data is of high quality. Machine learning models are heavily dependent on data, and poor-quality data can lead to inaccurate predictions or misleading insights. Data quality issues often arise due to missing values, noise, inconsistencies, or outliers.

Challenges with Data Quality

- **Missing Data**: If certain values are absent, models might struggle to make accurate predictions. The handling of missing data can be done through imputation, removal, or using algorithms that handle missing data internally.

- **Noisy Data**: Noise refers to random errors or fluctuations in the data that do not reflect the underlying patterns. Noise can be reduced through filtering or using more robust algorithms.

240

- **Inconsistent Data**: When data comes from different sources, it may be inconsistent or unstructured, leading to difficulties in analysis.

Example of Handling Missing Data

In Python, missing data can be handled using the **Pandas** library:

```python
import pandas as pd
import numpy as np

# Sample data with missing values
data = {'Age': [25, np.nan, 28, 35, 40], 'Salary': [50000, 55000, 52000,
        np.nan, 60000]}
df = pd.DataFrame(data)

# Handle missing values by filling with the mean
df['Age'].fillna(df['Age'].mean(), inplace=True)
df['Salary'].fillna(df['Salary'].mean(), inplace=True)

print(df)
```

Model Selection: Choosing the Right Algorithm

Another challenge in machine learning is selecting the appropriate model for the task at hand. With numerous algorithms available for various tasks, it is essential to choose the one that best matches the nature of the problem, the type of data, and the computational resources available.

Factors Influencing Model Selection

- **Type of Task**: Is the problem a classification, regression, clustering, or another task?

- **Size of Data**: Some models, like **Decision Trees** and **Random Forests**, are suitable for small datasets, while others like **Deep Learning** models require large amounts of data.

- **Model Complexity**: Simpler models (e.g., linear regression) are easier to interpret but may not capture complex patterns, while complex models (e.g., neural networks) can offer higher accuracy at the cost of interpretability.

Example of Model Selection:

Choosing a classification model depends on the type of data and the problem. For instance, using **Support Vector Machines (SVM)** for small datasets or **Random Forests** for large, complex datasets. Here is an example of training a **SVM** model:

```python
from sklearn.svm import SVC
from sklearn.model_selection import train_test_split
from sklearn.metrics import accuracy_score
```

```
# Sample data
X = [[2, 3], [4, 5], [1, 7], [3, 9], [6, 7]]
y = [0, 0, 1, 1, 0]  # Labels

# Split data
X_train, X_test, y_train, y_test = train_test_split(X, y, test_size=0.2,
        random_state=42)

# Train an SVM model
model = SVC(kernel='linear')
model.fit(X_train, y_train)

# Make predictions
y_pred = model.predict(X_test)

# Evaluate accuracy
accuracy = accuracy_score(y_test, y_pred)
print(f"Accuracy: {accuracy:.2f}")
```

Overfitting: A Common Pitfall

Overfitting occurs when a machine learning model learns not only the underlying patterns in the training data but also the noise and random fluctuations. As a result, overfitted models perform well on the training data but poorly on unseen data (test data), as they fail to generalize.

Causes of Overfitting

- **Complex Models**: Models with too many parameters or high complexity, such as deep neural networks, are prone to overfitting, especially with small datasets.

- **Insufficient Data**: When the model is trained on a small dataset, it may memorize specific patterns rather than learning general trends.

- **Lack of Regularization**: Regularization techniques like **L2 regularization** (Ridge) or **L1 regularization** (Lasso) help prevent overfitting by penalizing overly complex models.

Example of Preventing Overfitting

In Python, regularization can be added to models such as **Ridge Regression**:

```
from sklearn.linear_model import Ridge
from sklearn.model_selection import train_test_split
from sklearn.metrics import mean_squared_error

# Sample data for regression
X = [[1], [2], [3], [4], [5]]
y = [2, 3, 4, 5, 6]

# Split data
X_train, X_test, y_train, y_test = train_test_split(X, y, test_size=0.2,
        random_state=42)

# Train a Ridge Regression model (L2 regularization)
model = Ridge(alpha=1.0)
```

```
model.fit(X_train, y_train)

# Predict and evaluate
y_pred = model.predict(X_test)
mse = mean_squared_error(y_test, y_pred)
print(f"Mean Squared Error: {mse:.2f}")
```

Machine learning presents several challenges that must be carefully addressed to build effective models. Ensuring high-quality data, selecting the appropriate model, and preventing overfitting are essential steps to creating accurate and generalizable machine learning solutions. By understanding and tackling these challenges, data scientists can build models that provide meaningful insights and perform well in real-world scenarios.

Module 23:

Supervised Learning

Supervised learning is one of the most widely used machine learning techniques. It involves training a model using labeled data, where the algorithm learns to predict outcomes based on input-output pairs. This module focuses on key supervised learning algorithms, model evaluation metrics, and techniques to prevent overfitting and underfitting, which are common challenges in model development.

Classification Algorithms: Logistic Regression, Decision Trees, and Random Forests

Classification algorithms predict discrete labels or categories. Logistic regression is a fundamental method for binary classification tasks, estimating probabilities of class membership. Decision trees break down data into decision nodes to classify input into predefined categories. Random forests, an ensemble of decision trees, improve classification accuracy by reducing variance and preventing overfitting.

Regression Models: Linear Regression, Lasso, and Ridge Regression

Regression models predict continuous outcomes. Linear regression fits a line to the data, minimizing the sum of squared errors between predicted and actual values. Lasso (Least Absolute Shrinkage and Selection Operator) and ridge regression are variations that apply regularization to prevent overfitting, with lasso using L1 regularization for feature selection and ridge using L2 regularization to shrink model coefficients.

Model Evaluation Metrics: Accuracy, Precision, Recall, F1 Score, ROC-AUC

Evaluating a model's performance requires appropriate metrics. Accuracy measures overall correctness, but it can be misleading with imbalanced datasets. Precision and recall focus on the true positives and false negatives, respectively, providing a clearer picture of model performance in classification tasks. The F1 score balances precision and recall, while ROC-AUC evaluates the trade-off between true positive rate and false positive rate in classification problems.

Avoiding Overfitting and Underfitting: Cross-Validation, Regularization, and Model Tuning

Overfitting occurs when a model learns the noise in the training data, while underfitting happens when it fails to capture underlying patterns. Cross-validation mitigates overfitting by splitting the data into training and testing sets multiple times to assess model performance.

Regularization techniques, like lasso and ridge, add penalties to the model, reducing complexity and preventing overfitting. Model tuning involves adjusting hyperparameters to strike the right balance between bias and variance.

Classification Algorithms: Logistic Regression, Decision Trees, and Random Forests

Supervised learning is a cornerstone of machine learning, where algorithms learn from labeled data to make predictions on new, unseen data. One of the most common tasks in supervised learning is classification, where the goal is to assign data points to predefined categories. In this section, we will explore three essential classification algorithms: **Logistic Regression**, **Decision Trees**, and **Random Forests**.

Logistic Regression: A Simple Yet Powerful Algorithm

Logistic regression is one of the most widely used classification algorithms. Despite its name, it is a linear model used for binary classification, where the output is a probability that the input belongs to a particular class. Logistic regression uses the logistic function (sigmoid) to map predicted values to a probability between 0 and 1.

Key Features

- **Binary Classification**: It predicts probabilities of binary outcomes (0 or 1).

- **Linear Model**: It models the relationship between the features and the log-odds of the target variable.

- **Interpretability**: The coefficients in the model provide insights into the relationships between features and the target.

Example of Logistic Regression in Python

Using the **LogisticRegression** model from sklearn:

```python
from sklearn.linear_model import LogisticRegression
from sklearn.datasets import load_iris
from sklearn.model_selection import train_test_split
from sklearn.metrics import accuracy_score

# Load dataset
data = load_iris()
X = data.data
y = data.target

# We select only two classes for binary classification
X = X[y != 2]
y = y[y != 2]

# Split data into training and test sets
X_train, X_test, y_train, y_test = train_test_split(X, y, test_size=0.3,
        random_state=42)
```

```
# Train logistic regression model
model = LogisticRegression()
model.fit(X_train, y_train)

# Predict and evaluate
y_pred = model.predict(X_test)
print(f"Accuracy: {accuracy_score(y_test, y_pred):.2f}")
```

Decision Trees: Interpretable and Versatile

A decision tree is a non-linear classifier that recursively splits the data into subsets based on feature values. The splits are made to maximize information gain (e.g., using metrics like Gini impurity or entropy). Decision trees are highly interpretable, as the resulting model can be visualized as a tree where each node represents a decision based on a feature.

Key Features

- **Non-linear Decision Boundaries**: Unlike logistic regression, decision trees do not require a linear relationship between the features and the target.

- **Interpretability**: Decision trees are easy to interpret, and the tree structure can be visualized.

- **Prone to Overfitting**: Decision trees can overfit the training data if not properly pruned or regularized.

Example of Decision Tree in Python

```
from sklearn.tree import DecisionTreeClassifier
from sklearn.datasets import load_iris
from sklearn.model_selection import train_test_split
from sklearn.metrics import accuracy_score

# Load dataset
data = load_iris()
X = data.data
y = data.target

# We select only two classes for binary classification
X = X[y != 2]
y = y[y != 2]

# Split data into training and test sets
X_train, X_test, y_train, y_test = train_test_split(X, y, test_size=0.3,
            random_state=42)

# Train decision tree classifier
model = DecisionTreeClassifier()
model.fit(X_train, y_train)

# Predict and evaluate
y_pred = model.predict(X_test)
print(f"Accuracy: {accuracy_score(y_test, y_pred):.2f}")
```

Random Forests: An Ensemble Method

Random forests are an ensemble learning method that combines multiple decision trees to improve the performance and stability of the model. Each tree in the forest is trained on a random subset of the data, and the final prediction is determined by majority voting (for classification). Random forests mitigate the overfitting problem commonly associated with decision trees by averaging predictions across multiple trees.

Key Features

- **Ensemble Method**: Combines multiple decision trees to improve generalization and accuracy.

- **Reduces Overfitting**: By averaging results from multiple trees, random forests tend to have lower variance compared to individual decision trees.

- **Robust to Noise**: Random forests are less sensitive to outliers compared to a single decision tree.

Example of Random Forest in Python

```python
from sklearn.ensemble import RandomForestClassifier
from sklearn.datasets import load_iris
from sklearn.model_selection import train_test_split
from sklearn.metrics import accuracy_score

# Load dataset
data = load_iris()
X = data.data
y = data.target

# We select only two classes for binary classification
X = X[y != 2]
y = y[y != 2]

# Split data into training and test sets
X_train, X_test, y_train, y_test = train_test_split(X, y, test_size=0.3,
        random_state=42)

# Train random forest classifier
model = RandomForestClassifier()
model.fit(X_train, y_train)

# Predict and evaluate
y_pred = model.predict(X_test)
print(f"Accuracy: {accuracy_score(y_test, y_pred):.2f}")
```

Logistic regression, decision trees, and random forests each offer unique advantages for classification tasks. Logistic regression is simple and interpretable, decision trees provide clear decision boundaries and insights, while random forests combine multiple decision trees for improved accuracy and robustness. Understanding these algorithms and their use cases is essential for solving real-world classification problems effectively.

Regression Models: Linear Regression, Lasso, and Ridge Regression

Regression models are pivotal in supervised learning, particularly for predicting continuous values. These models learn from data to find relationships between input features and output variables. In this section, we will explore three key regression algorithms: **Linear Regression**, **Lasso Regression**, and **Ridge Regression**. Each of these models has its unique strengths, with particular applications based on data characteristics and the problem at hand.

Linear Regression: A Foundation for Regression Tasks

Linear regression is the simplest and most widely used regression technique. It assumes a linear relationship between the input features and the target variable, where the target is a weighted sum of the input features. Linear regression minimizes the difference between predicted and actual values using the least squares method.

Key Features

- **Simplicity**: It is easy to understand and interpret, making it a great choice for exploratory data analysis.

- **Assumptions**: Assumes a linear relationship between inputs and outputs, and requires no multicollinearity or outliers.

- **Sensitive to Outliers**: Linear regression is highly sensitive to outliers, which can significantly impact the model's performance.

Example of Linear Regression in Python

```python
from sklearn.linear_model import LinearRegression
from sklearn.datasets import make_regression
from sklearn.model_selection import train_test_split
from sklearn.metrics import mean_squared_error

# Generate synthetic data
X, y = make_regression(n_samples=100, n_features=1, noise=0.1,
            random_state=42)

# Split data into training and test sets
X_train, X_test, y_train, y_test = train_test_split(X, y, test_size=0.3,
            random_state=42)

# Train linear regression model
model = LinearRegression()
model.fit(X_train, y_train)

# Predict and evaluate
y_pred = model.predict(X_test)
print(f"Mean Squared Error: {mean_squared_error(y_test, y_pred):.2f}")
```

Lasso Regression: Regularization for Feature Selection

Lasso (Least Absolute Shrinkage and Selection Operator) regression is an extension of linear regression that includes regularization. By adding a penalty term to the cost function (the L1 norm of the coefficients), lasso regression forces some coefficients to shrink to zero, effectively performing feature selection. This makes lasso particularly useful when dealing with high-dimensional data where many features may be irrelevant.

Key Features

- **Feature Selection**: Lasso helps in selecting the most important features by setting less relevant coefficients to zero.

- **Sparsity**: Lasso can lead to sparse models, improving interpretability when dealing with a large number of features.

- **Overfitting**: The L1 penalty helps to reduce overfitting by preventing the model from fitting noise in the data.

Example of Lasso Regression in Python

```python
from sklearn.linear_model import Lasso
from sklearn.datasets import make_regression
from sklearn.model_selection import train_test_split
from sklearn.metrics import mean_squared_error

# Generate synthetic data
X, y = make_regression(n_samples=100, n_features=5, noise=0.1,
        random_state=42)

# Split data into training and test sets
X_train, X_test, y_train, y_test = train_test_split(X, y, test_size=0.3,
        random_state=42)

# Train lasso regression model
model = Lasso(alpha=0.1)  # alpha controls the regularization strength
model.fit(X_train, y_train)

# Predict and evaluate
y_pred = model.predict(X_test)
print(f"Mean Squared Error: {mean_squared_error(y_test, y_pred):.2f}")
```

Ridge Regression: Regularization to Prevent Overfitting

Ridge regression is another variant of linear regression that adds regularization to the model using the L2 norm of the coefficients. Unlike lasso, ridge regression does not shrink coefficients to zero but instead penalizes large coefficients, making it less sensitive to outliers and more stable in cases of multicollinearity. Ridge regression is particularly useful when dealing with datasets with many correlated predictors.

Key Features

- **Regularization**: Ridge regression helps in preventing overfitting by adding a penalty term to the cost function.

- **No Feature Selection**: Unlike lasso, ridge does not perform feature selection, but it stabilizes the model by shrinking coefficients.

- **Improved Stability**: Ridge is more stable when there are highly correlated features in the data.

Example of Ridge Regression in Python

```
from sklearn.linear_model import Ridge
from sklearn.datasets import make_regression
from sklearn.model_selection import train_test_split
from sklearn.metrics import mean_squared_error

# Generate synthetic data
X, y = make_regression(n_samples=100, n_features=5, noise=0.1,
        random_state=42)

# Split data into training and test sets
X_train, X_test, y_train, y_test = train_test_split(X, y, test_size=0.3,
        random_state=42)

# Train ridge regression model
model = Ridge(alpha=1.0)  # alpha controls the regularization strength
model.fit(X_train, y_train)

# Predict and evaluate
y_pred = model.predict(X_test)
print(f"Mean Squared Error: {mean_squared_error(y_test, y_pred):.2f}")
```

Linear regression, lasso, and ridge regression are fundamental tools in predictive modeling. While linear regression offers simplicity and ease of interpretation, lasso and ridge add regularization to mitigate overfitting. Lasso is useful for feature selection, while ridge is ideal for handling multicollinearity in high-dimensional data. Understanding these models and selecting the appropriate one based on the data and problem characteristics is essential for building robust regression models in data science.

Model Evaluation Metrics: Accuracy, Precision, Recall, F1 Score, ROC-AUC

When working with supervised learning algorithms, evaluating the performance of your models is crucial to ensure they generalize well to unseen data. The choice of evaluation metrics depends on the problem at hand, particularly when dealing with classification models. This section will explore some common model evaluation metrics: **Accuracy**, **Precision**, **Recall**, **F1 Score**, and **ROC-AUC**. These metrics provide insights into different aspects of model performance, and understanding their strengths and limitations will help in selecting the most appropriate one for your task.

Accuracy: The Overall Performance Measure

Accuracy is the most intuitive metric for evaluating classification models. It is simply the proportion of correct predictions (both true positives and true negatives) out of all predictions made. Accuracy is useful when the dataset is balanced, meaning the number of instances from each class is roughly equal. However, accuracy can be misleading in the case of imbalanced datasets.

Formula

$$Accuracy = \frac{True\ Positives + True\ Negatives}{Total\ Population}$$

Example in Python

```python
from sklearn.metrics import accuracy_score
from sklearn.model_selection import train_test_split
from sklearn.linear_model import LogisticRegression
from sklearn.datasets import make_classification

# Generate synthetic data
X, y = make_classification(n_samples=1000, n_features=10, n_classes=2,
        random_state=42)

# Split the data
X_train, X_test, y_train, y_test = train_test_split(X, y, test_size=0.3,
        random_state=42)

# Train a logistic regression model
model = LogisticRegression()
model.fit(X_train, y_train)

# Predict and calculate accuracy
y_pred = model.predict(X_test)
accuracy = accuracy_score(y_test, y_pred)
print(f"Accuracy: {accuracy:.2f}")
```

Precision: Correctness of Positive Predictions

Precision is a measure of the accuracy of the positive predictions made by the model. It tells us what proportion of predicted positive instances are actually positive. Precision is particularly useful in cases where false positives are costly, such as in spam detection or medical diagnoses.

Formula

$$Precision = \frac{True\ Positives}{True\ Positives + False\ Positives}$$

Example in Python

```python
from sklearn.metrics import precision_score

# Calculate precision
precision = precision_score(y_test, y_pred)
print(f"Precision: {precision:.2f}")
```

Recall: Sensitivity or True Positive Rate

Recall, also known as sensitivity or the true positive rate, measures the model's ability to correctly identify positive instances. It is crucial when the cost of missing positive instances is high. For instance, in fraud detection, failing to identify fraud can have significant consequences.

Formula

$$Recall = \frac{True\ Positives}{True\ Positives + False\ Positives}$$

Example in Python

```
from sklearn.metrics import recall_score

# Calculate recall
recall = recall_score(y_test, y_pred)
print(f"Recall: {recall:.2f}")
```

F1 Score: The Balance Between Precision and Recall

The F1 score is the harmonic mean of precision and recall, providing a balance between the two. It is particularly useful when there is an uneven class distribution, such as in rare event prediction, where both precision and recall are important.

Formula

$$F1\ Score = 2 \times \frac{Precision \times Recall}{Precision + Recall}$$

Example in Python

```
from sklearn.metrics import f1_score

# Calculate F1 Score
f1 = f1_score(y_test, y_pred)
print(f"F1 Score: {f1:.2f}")
```

ROC-AUC: Evaluating the Trade-off Between True Positives and False Positives

The ROC (Receiver Operating Characteristic) curve is a graphical representation of a classifier's performance across all classification thresholds. The area under the curve (AUC) quantifies the overall performance. An AUC of 1 represents a perfect classifier, whereas an AUC of 0.5 indicates a random classifier.

Formula

$$ROC - AUC = Area\ Under\ the\ ROC\ Curve$$

Example in Python

```python
from sklearn.metrics import roc_auc_score

# Calculate ROC-AUC
roc_auc = roc_auc_score(y_test, model.predict_proba(X_test)[:, 1])
print(f"ROC-AUC: {roc_auc:.2f}")
```

Each evaluation metric offers a different perspective on model performance. **Accuracy** is a straightforward metric but can be misleading in imbalanced datasets. **Precision** and **Recall** are essential for understanding performance in cases with imbalanced classes or high costs associated with false positives and false negatives. The **F1 Score** balances the trade-off between precision and recall, making it useful when both metrics are crucial. Finally, **ROC-AUC** provides an overall view of the classifier's ability to distinguish between positive and negative classes across all thresholds, making it invaluable in comparing classifiers. Understanding these metrics is key to making informed decisions on model performance, particularly in imbalanced and real-world scenarios.

Avoiding Overfitting and Underfitting: Cross-Validation, Regularization, and Model Tuning

Overfitting and underfitting are two common pitfalls when developing machine learning models. **Overfitting** occurs when a model learns the noise in the training data rather than the underlying pattern, resulting in high performance on the training set but poor generalization to unseen data. **Underfitting**, on the other hand, happens when a model is too simple to capture the underlying data patterns, leading to poor performance both on the training set and on unseen data. This section explores strategies to avoid both overfitting and underfitting, including **cross-validation**, **regularization**, and **model tuning**.

Cross-Validation: Ensuring Generalization

Cross-validation is a technique used to assess the generalization performance of a model by splitting the dataset into multiple training and testing subsets. The most common form is **k-fold cross-validation**, where the dataset is divided into k subsets (or folds). The model is trained on k-1 of these folds and tested on the remaining fold. This process is repeated k times, with each fold being used as the test set exactly once. The average performance across all k folds provides a more robust estimate of model performance, reducing the risk of overfitting.

Example in Python

```python
from sklearn.model_selection import cross_val_score
from sklearn.linear_model import LogisticRegression
from sklearn.datasets import make_classification

# Generate synthetic data
```

```
X, y = make_classification(n_samples=1000, n_features=10, n_classes=2,
        random_state=42)

# Initialize logistic regression model
model = LogisticRegression()

# Perform 5-fold cross-validation
scores = cross_val_score(model, X, y, cv=5, scoring='accuracy')

# Print average accuracy from cross-validation
print(f"Cross-validation scores: {scores}")
print(f"Average accuracy: {scores.mean():.2f}")
```

In the above code, we use cross_val_score from sklearn to perform 5-fold cross-validation and evaluate the accuracy of a logistic regression model.

Regularization: Reducing Overfitting

Regularization is a technique used to penalize overly complex models that might overfit the training data. Regularization works by adding a penalty term to the loss function, discouraging the model from fitting the training data too closely. There are two common types of regularization:

- **L1 regularization** (Lasso): This method adds a penalty proportional to the absolute value of the coefficients, encouraging sparsity (many coefficients become zero).

- **L2 regularization** (Ridge): This method adds a penalty proportional to the square of the coefficients, encouraging smaller coefficient values and reducing model complexity.

Example in Python: Lasso and Ridge Regularization

```
from sklearn.linear_model import Lasso, Ridge

# Lasso regularization (L1)
lasso = Lasso(alpha=0.1)
lasso.fit(X, y)
print("Lasso coefficients:", lasso.coef_)

# Ridge regularization (L2)
ridge = Ridge(alpha=0.1)
ridge.fit(X, y)
print("Ridge coefficients:", ridge.coef_)
```

By adjusting the alpha parameter, we control the strength of the regularization. A higher value of alpha leads to stronger regularization.

Model Tuning: Finding the Optimal Hyperparameters

Model tuning involves selecting the best set of hyperparameters for a given model to improve its performance. Hyperparameters are parameters that are not learned from the data but are set before the learning process begins, such as the learning rate in gradient

254

descent or the regularization strength in logistic regression. **Grid search** and **random search** are two common techniques used for hyperparameter optimization:

- **Grid Search** exhaustively searches through a manually specified parameter grid.

- **Random Search** randomly samples from the parameter space, offering a more efficient approach when the hyperparameter space is large.

Example in Python: Grid Search for Hyperparameter Tuning

```
from sklearn.model_selection import GridSearchCV
from sklearn.ensemble import RandomForestClassifier

# Define a random forest model
rf_model = RandomForestClassifier()

# Define the hyperparameters grid
param_grid = {'n_estimators': [50, 100, 200], 'max_depth': [None, 10, 20]}

# Perform grid search with 5-fold cross-validation
grid_search = GridSearchCV(rf_model, param_grid, cv=5, scoring='accuracy')
grid_search.fit(X, y)

# Best hyperparameters
print(f"Best hyperparameters: {grid_search.best_params_}")
```

In this example, GridSearchCV is used to find the best combination of n_estimators (number of trees) and max_depth (depth of trees) for a random forest classifier.

To achieve the best performance in machine learning, it is essential to find the right balance between overfitting and underfitting. Cross-validation helps ensure that your model generalizes well to unseen data, while regularization prevents the model from becoming too complex. Hyperparameter tuning further refines model performance by selecting the best configuration of parameters. Together, these techniques form a strong foundation for building robust machine learning models that perform well across different datasets and tasks.

Module 24:

Unsupervised Learning

Unsupervised learning involves training algorithms on data that does not have labeled outputs. The goal is to find hidden structures or patterns in the data. This module covers key unsupervised learning techniques such as clustering, dimensionality reduction, anomaly detection, and evaluation methods that help assess the quality of models in this domain.

Clustering Techniques: K-means, Hierarchical Clustering, DBSCAN

Clustering is a technique used to group data points based on similarity. K-means clustering partitions data into K distinct clusters by minimizing within-cluster variance. Hierarchical clustering creates a tree of nested clusters, allowing different levels of granularity. DBSCAN (Density-Based Spatial Clustering of Applications with Noise) identifies clusters of arbitrary shape and is robust to outliers.

Dimensionality Reduction in ML: PCA, t-SNE, and UMAP

Dimensionality reduction is used to simplify datasets while retaining essential information. Principal Component Analysis (PCA) identifies directions of maximum variance in the data and projects the data onto fewer dimensions. t-SNE (t-distributed Stochastic Neighbor Embedding) and UMAP (Uniform Manifold Approximation and Projection) focus on preserving local structure, making them effective for visualizing high-dimensional data.

Anomaly Detection: Outlier Detection Techniques and Applications

Anomaly detection identifies rare data points that deviate significantly from the majority. Techniques include statistical methods such as z-scores, distance-based methods like k-nearest neighbors, and density-based approaches like DBSCAN. Anomaly detection is crucial in fraud detection, network security, and quality control, where identifying outliers can signal potential issues.

Evaluation Methods: Silhouette Score, Elbow Method, and Davies-Bouldin Index

Evaluating unsupervised learning models is challenging due to the lack of ground truth labels. The silhouette score measures how similar each point is to its cluster compared to others, with higher values indicating better-defined clusters. The elbow method identifies the optimal number of clusters by plotting variance explained against the number of clusters. The Davies-Bouldin index assesses cluster separation and compactness, with lower values indicating better clustering performance.

Clustering Techniques: K-means, Hierarchical Clustering, DBSCAN

Clustering is a fundamental unsupervised learning technique used to group data points into clusters based on similarity. Unlike supervised learning, clustering does not rely on labeled data and is used for exploratory data analysis, pattern recognition, and data compression. In this section, we will explore three popular clustering techniques: **K-means**, **Hierarchical Clustering**, and **DBSCAN**.

K-means Clustering: Centroid-Based Grouping

K-means clustering is one of the most widely used clustering algorithms. It partitions the data into K clusters by iteratively assigning data points to the nearest cluster centroid and then updating the centroids based on the mean of the points in each cluster. The process continues until the centroids stabilize or the maximum number of iterations is reached.

Steps in K-means Clustering:

1. Initialize K centroids randomly or using a smarter method like k-means++.

2. Assign each data point to the closest centroid.

3. Recalculate the centroids by taking the mean of all the points assigned to each centroid.

4. Repeat steps 2 and 3 until convergence.

Example in Python:

```python
from sklearn.cluster import KMeans
from sklearn.datasets import make_blobs
import matplotlib.pyplot as plt

# Generate synthetic data
X, _ = make_blobs(n_samples=300, centers=4, random_state=42)

# Apply K-means clustering
kmeans = KMeans(n_clusters=4, random_state=42)
y_kmeans = kmeans.fit_predict(X)

# Plot the clusters
plt.scatter(X[:, 0], X[:, 1], c=y_kmeans, s=50, cmap='viridis')
plt.scatter(kmeans.cluster_centers_[:, 0], kmeans.cluster_centers_[:, 1],
            c='red', marker='x', s=200, label='Centroids')
plt.legend()
plt.show()
```

In the example above, we generate synthetic data and apply K-means clustering to form 4 clusters. The centroids are visualized in red.

Hierarchical Clustering: Tree-Based Clustering

Hierarchical clustering builds a hierarchy of clusters by either iteratively merging clusters (agglomerative) or iteratively splitting them (divisive). The output of hierarchical clustering is often visualized using a **dendrogram**, which shows the levels of cluster mergers or splits. It is useful when the number of clusters is not predefined.

Steps in Hierarchical Clustering (Agglomerative):

1. Treat each data point as its own cluster.

2. Find the two closest clusters and merge them.

3. Repeat step 2 until all points are merged into a single cluster.

Example in Python:

```python
from sklearn.cluster import AgglomerativeClustering
import seaborn as sns

# Apply Agglomerative clustering
agg_clust = AgglomerativeClustering(n_clusters=4)
y_agg = agg_clust.fit_predict(X)

# Plot the clusters
sns.scatterplot(x=X[:, 0], y=X[:, 1], hue=y_agg, palette='viridis')
plt.show()
```

Here, we use agglomerative hierarchical clustering to group the data into 4 clusters and visualize the results using a scatter plot.

DBSCAN: Density-Based Clustering

DBSCAN (Density-Based Spatial Clustering of Applications with Noise) is a density-based clustering algorithm that groups data points based on the density of their neighborhood. Unlike K-means and hierarchical clustering, DBSCAN does not require the number of clusters to be specified beforehand. Instead, it uses two parameters: **epsilon (ε)**, the maximum distance between two points to be considered neighbors, and **min_samples**, the minimum number of points required to form a dense region (cluster).

DBSCAN can handle clusters of arbitrary shape and can also identify noise points (outliers).

Steps in DBSCAN:

1. For each point, find all the neighboring points within epsilon distance.

2. If a point has enough neighbors (greater than min_samples), it is labeled as a core point and a new cluster is formed.

3. Expand the cluster by recursively adding density-reachable points.

4. Points that are not reachable from any cluster are labeled as noise.

Example in Python:

```python
from sklearn.cluster import DBSCAN

# Apply DBSCAN clustering
dbscan = DBSCAN(eps=0.3, min_samples=10)
y_dbscan = dbscan.fit_predict(X)

# Plot the clusters
plt.scatter(X[:, 0], X[:, 1], c=y_dbscan, cmap='viridis')
plt.show()
```

In the above example, DBSCAN is applied to the data, with eps controlling the neighborhood size and min_samples determining the minimum cluster size. Noise points are marked with -1.

Clustering is an essential technique in unsupervised learning, and the choice of algorithm depends on the specific characteristics of the data and the problem at hand. K-means is effective for spherical, equally sized clusters but requires the number of clusters to be predefined. Hierarchical clustering provides a tree-like structure for understanding relationships between clusters, and DBSCAN is powerful for identifying clusters of arbitrary shapes and handling noise. Understanding these methods allows data scientists to select the most appropriate technique for different datasets and tasks.

Dimensionality Reduction in ML: PCA, t-SNE, and UMAP

Dimensionality reduction is a critical technique in machine learning, used to reduce the number of input variables (features) in a dataset while preserving essential patterns. This reduction can lead to improved model performance, better interpretability, and lower computational cost. In this section, we will explore three popular dimensionality reduction techniques: **Principal Component Analysis (PCA)**, **t-SNE (t-distributed Stochastic Neighbor Embedding)**, and **UMAP (Uniform Manifold Approximation and Projection)**.

Principal Component Analysis (PCA): Linear Dimensionality Reduction

PCA is one of the most widely used linear dimensionality reduction techniques. It transforms the original features into a new set of uncorrelated variables called **principal components**, which capture the maximum variance in the data. The goal of PCA is to reduce the data's dimensionality while retaining as much information as possible.

How PCA Works:

1. **Standardize the Data**: Scale the data to have a mean of 0 and a standard deviation of 1, especially when features are on different scales.

2. **Compute the Covariance Matrix**: This matrix describes how features in the data vary together.

3. **Eigenvalue and Eigenvector Decomposition**: Calculate the eigenvectors and eigenvalues of the covariance matrix to determine the principal components.

4. **Project the Data**: Project the data onto the principal components to reduce the dimensionality.

Example in Python:

```
from sklearn.decomposition import PCA
from sklearn.datasets import load_iris
import matplotlib.pyplot as plt

# Load dataset
data = load_iris()
X = data.data

# Apply PCA for 2 components
pca = PCA(n_components=2)
X_pca = pca.fit_transform(X)

# Visualize the reduced data
plt.scatter(X_pca[:, 0], X_pca[:, 1], c=data.target, cmap='viridis')
plt.xlabel('First Principal Component')
plt.ylabel('Second Principal Component')
plt.title('PCA of Iris Dataset')
plt.show()
```

In this example, we reduce the Iris dataset to two principal components and visualize the transformed data in 2D space.

t-SNE (t-distributed Stochastic Neighbor Embedding): Non-linear Dimensionality Reduction

t-SNE is a powerful technique for reducing the dimensionality of high-dimensional datasets, especially for visualizing complex, non-linear data patterns. It preserves local structures in the data, making it suitable for visualizing clusters and patterns.

How t-SNE Works:

1. **Calculate Pairwise Similarities**: Compute the pairwise similarities of points in the high-dimensional space using a Gaussian distribution.

2. **Map to Low-Dimensional Space**: Map the high-dimensional data to a lower-dimensional space by minimizing the divergence between probability distributions using gradient descent.

Example in Python:

```python
from sklearn.manifold import TSNE
import seaborn as sns

# Apply t-SNE for 2 components
tsne = TSNE(n_components=2, random_state=42)
X_tsne = tsne.fit_transform(X)

# Visualize the t-SNE output
sns.scatterplot(x=X_tsne[:, 0], y=X_tsne[:, 1], hue=data.target,
        palette='viridis')
plt.title('t-SNE of Iris Dataset')
plt.show()
```

In this case, t-SNE reduces the Iris dataset to two components and visualizes the clustering behavior.

UMAP (Uniform Manifold Approximation and Projection): Advanced Non-linear Dimensionality Reduction

UMAP is a non-linear dimensionality reduction technique that is faster and more scalable than t-SNE while preserving both local and global structures in the data. It is based on manifold learning and graph theory and is often used for visualizing large datasets.

How UMAP Works:

1. **Construct a Graph**: Build a graph of local connections in the high-dimensional data space.

2. **Optimize the Layout**: Map the graph to a lower-dimensional space by optimizing the graph layout, preserving both local and global structures.

Example in Python:

```python
import umap

# Apply UMAP for 2 components
umap_model = umap.UMAP(n_components=2, random_state=42)
X_umap = umap_model.fit_transform(X)

# Visualize the UMAP output
sns.scatterplot(x=X_umap[:, 0], y=X_umap[:, 1], hue=data.target,
        palette='viridis')
plt.title('UMAP of Iris Dataset')
plt.show()
```

Here, UMAP reduces the Iris dataset to 2 dimensions while maintaining both local and global structure, providing a clearer clustering view.

Dimensionality reduction is a vital step in the data preprocessing pipeline, especially when dealing with high-dimensional datasets. PCA is ideal for linear reductions, t-SNE excels in visualizing complex, non-linear data patterns, and UMAP provides a scalable, efficient solution that balances the preservation of local and global structures. Each technique has its strengths and is suited for different tasks, and understanding these methods enables data scientists to select the appropriate tool for specific use cases.

Anomaly Detection: Outlier Detection Techniques and Applications

Anomaly detection is a critical task in machine learning and data analysis, used to identify rare or abnormal data points that deviate significantly from the majority of data. These anomalies, or outliers, can represent important occurrences such as fraud, network intrusions, or equipment malfunctions. In this section, we will explore various anomaly detection techniques, their applications, and how they can be implemented using machine learning methods.

Understanding Anomaly Detection

Anomaly detection involves finding patterns in data that do not conform to expected behavior. Anomalies can be:

- **Point anomalies**: Individual data points that differ significantly from the rest of the data.

- **Contextual anomalies**: Data points that are anomalous in a specific context but not in others (e.g., a temperature spike during summer might be normal but anomalous in winter).

- **Collective anomalies**: A set of data points that together deviate from the expected behavior (e.g., sudden spikes in traffic volume on a website).

Identifying anomalies can help in various industries, including fraud detection in finance, network security, predictive maintenance in manufacturing, and medical diagnostics.

Techniques for Anomaly Detection

Several methods can be used for detecting anomalies, depending on the nature of the data (supervised vs. unsupervised) and the type of anomalies being targeted. Below, we discuss some common techniques:

1. Statistical Methods

Statistical methods rely on the assumption that data points are distributed according to a known distribution (e.g., Gaussian distribution). Outliers are identified as data points that lie far from the mean, typically using standard deviations.

Example: Z-Score

The Z-score measures how many standard deviations a data point is from the mean. A Z-score greater than a threshold (e.g., 3) indicates an outlier.

```python
import numpy as np
from scipy.stats import zscore

# Sample data
data = [10, 12, 13, 14, 16, 100]

# Compute z-scores
z_scores = zscore(data)

# Detect outliers (z-score > 3 or < -3)
outliers = np.where(np.abs(z_scores) > 3)
print(f"Outliers detected at indices: {outliers}")
```

2. Distance-Based Methods

Distance-based anomaly detection assumes that normal points tend to cluster together, while anomalies are far from the clusters. Methods such as **K-Nearest Neighbors (KNN)** and **Local Outlier Factor (LOF)** are commonly used for this purpose.

Example: LOF (Local Outlier Factor)

LOF computes the local density deviation of a data point with respect to its neighbors. Points that have a substantially lower density than their neighbors are considered outliers.

```python
from sklearn.neighbors import LocalOutlierFactor
import numpy as np

# Sample data (2D points)
X = np.array([[1, 2], [2, 3], [3, 4], [100, 100]])

# Apply LOF for anomaly detection
lof = LocalOutlierFactor(n_neighbors=2)
y_pred = lof.fit_predict(X)

# -1 indicates an outlier, 1 indicates normal points
outliers = np.where(y_pred == -1)
print(f"Outliers detected at indices: {outliers}")
```

Applications of Anomaly Detection

Anomaly detection techniques are widely used in real-world applications across various industries:

1. Fraud Detection

In the financial sector, anomaly detection is used to identify fraudulent transactions by detecting patterns that deviate from the norm. For example, a credit card transaction from an unusual location or an unusually large transaction could be flagged as potentially fraudulent.

2. Intrusion Detection in Network Security

In cybersecurity, anomaly detection algorithms are employed to detect malicious activities such as unauthorized access, denial of service attacks, or malware infections. Unusual traffic patterns can indicate an intrusion.

3. Predictive Maintenance

In manufacturing and industrial settings, anomaly detection is used to predict equipment failures. Sensor data that deviates from the normal range can signal mechanical issues, allowing for early maintenance and reducing downtime.

4. Healthcare Monitoring

Anomaly detection plays a role in health monitoring, where abnormal readings in patient vitals, such as heart rate or blood pressure, can indicate the onset of health issues.

Challenges in Anomaly Detection

While powerful, anomaly detection techniques face several challenges:

- **Data imbalance**: In many cases, anomalies are rare compared to the normal data, making it difficult to detect them.

- **High-dimensional data**: As the number of features increases, the concept of distance becomes less meaningful, making anomaly detection harder.

- **Dynamic environments**: In certain applications like fraud detection, the definition of "normal" behavior may evolve over time, requiring adaptive models.

Anomaly detection is an essential tool for identifying outliers in diverse fields such as fraud detection, healthcare, and network security. Techniques like statistical methods, distance-based methods, and machine learning algorithms such as LOF help in detecting anomalies. By implementing effective anomaly detection methods, organizations can prevent losses, improve safety, and maintain system integrity.

Evaluation Methods: Silhouette Score, Elbow Method, and Davies-Bouldin Index

Evaluating clustering models is crucial to understanding how well they identify meaningful patterns in data. While there is no single metric that applies universally to all clustering algorithms, there are several evaluation methods that can provide insights into the quality and validity of the clustering results. In this section, we will discuss three commonly used evaluation methods for clustering: the Silhouette Score, the Elbow Method, and the Davies-Bouldin Index.

1. Silhouette Score

The Silhouette Score is a measure of how similar an object is to its own cluster (cohesion) compared to other clusters (separation). It combines both the compactness of clusters and the separation between clusters into a single metric. The Silhouette Score ranges from -1 to 1, where:

- **1** indicates that the points are well clustered and distinct from other clusters.

- **0** means the points are on or very close to the decision boundary between clusters.

- **Negative values** indicate that the points might be assigned to the wrong clusters.

The formula for calculating the Silhouette Score for a point iii is:

$$S(i) = \frac{b(i) - a(i)}{\max(a(i), b(i))}$$

where:

- a(i) is the average distance from point i to all other points in the same cluster.

- b(i) is the average distance from point i to all points in the nearest neighboring cluster.

Example: Calculating Silhouette Score in Python

```python
from sklearn.cluster import KMeans
from sklearn.datasets import make_blobs
from sklearn.metrics import silhouette_score

# Create sample data
X, _ = make_blobs(n_samples=300, centers=4, random_state=42)

# Apply KMeans clustering
kmeans = KMeans(n_clusters=4)
y_kmeans = kmeans.fit_predict(X)

# Calculate Silhouette Score
score = silhouette_score(X, y_kmeans)
print(f"Silhouette Score: {score}")
```

The higher the Silhouette Score, the better the clustering solution.

2. Elbow Method

The Elbow Method is a heuristic used to determine the optimal number of clusters in K-means clustering. It involves running the K-means algorithm for a range of cluster values and plotting the within-cluster sum of squares (WCSS, also known as inertia) against the number of clusters. The "elbow" point in the plot indicates the ideal number of clusters, where adding more clusters does not significantly improve the fit.

The WCSS is the sum of squared distances from each point in the cluster to the centroid of that cluster.

Example: Using the Elbow Method in Python

```python
import matplotlib.pyplot as plt
from sklearn.cluster import KMeans
from sklearn.datasets import make_blobs

# Create sample data
X, _ = make_blobs(n_samples=300, centers=4, random_state=42)

# Calculate WCSS for different cluster counts
wcss = []
for i in range(1, 11):
    kmeans = KMeans(n_clusters=i)
    kmeans.fit(X)
    wcss.append(kmeans.inertia_)

# Plot the Elbow Method
plt.plot(range(1, 11), wcss)
plt.title('Elbow Method')
plt.xlabel('Number of Clusters')
plt.ylabel('WCSS')
plt.show()
```

In the resulting plot, the "elbow" is the point where the WCSS begins to decrease at a slower rate. This point suggests the optimal number of clusters.

3. Davies-Bouldin Index

The Davies-Bouldin Index is another evaluation metric for clustering. It evaluates the average similarity ratio of each cluster with the cluster that is most similar to it. The lower the Davies-Bouldin Index, the better the clustering, as it indicates that the clusters are compact and well-separated.

The Davies-Bouldin Index for a set of clusters is computed as the average of the ratio of within-cluster scatter to between-cluster separation.

Example: Calculating Davies-Bouldin Index in Python

```python
from sklearn.cluster import KMeans
```

266

```
from sklearn.datasets import make_blobs
from sklearn.metrics import davies_bouldin_score

# Create sample data
X, _ = make_blobs(n_samples=300, centers=4, random_state=42)

# Apply KMeans clustering
kmeans = KMeans(n_clusters=4)
y_kmeans = kmeans.fit_predict(X)

# Calculate Davies-Bouldin Index
db_index = davies_bouldin_score(X, y_kmeans)
print(f"Davies-Bouldin Index: {db_index}")
```

A lower Davies-Bouldin Index indicates better clustering, with more distinct and compact clusters.

Choosing the right evaluation method depends on the clustering task and the dataset's characteristics. The **Silhouette Score** provides a direct measure of cluster quality, the **Elbow Method** helps identify the optimal number of clusters, and the **Davies-Bouldin Index** offers a balance of compactness and separation. By using these methods, data scientists can assess the effectiveness of clustering algorithms and select the most appropriate model for their data.

Module 25:

Introduction to Neural Networks

Neural networks are the foundation of deep learning, an advanced machine learning technique that powers applications in fields like image recognition, natural language processing (NLP), and autonomous systems. This module introduces the fundamental concepts, architecture, applications, and tools for building neural networks, providing a solid foundation for further exploration in deep learning.

How Neural Networks Work: Architecture, Activation Functions, and Backpropagation

Neural networks consist of layers of interconnected nodes (neurons) that simulate the way the human brain processes information. Each neuron performs computations based on input data, which is passed through activation functions (e.g., sigmoid, ReLU) to introduce non-linearity. Backpropagation is the process of adjusting weights in the network by minimizing the error between predicted and actual outputs through gradient descent.

Basic Architecture of a Neural Network: Input, Hidden, and Output Layers

A neural network is structured into three main types of layers: input, hidden, and output. The input layer receives the raw data, which is passed through the hidden layers where computations occur. The output layer provides the final prediction or classification. The number of neurons and layers, as well as their connectivity, influence the network's ability to learn complex patterns.

Applications of Deep Learning: Image Recognition, NLP, and Autonomous Systems

Deep learning, powered by neural networks, has revolutionized fields such as image recognition, where networks can identify objects and patterns in images. In natural language processing (NLP), neural networks power chatbots, sentiment analysis, and machine translation. Autonomous systems, including self-driving cars, rely on deep learning for tasks like decision-making, sensor interpretation, and pathfinding.

Tools for Building Neural Networks: TensorFlow, Keras, and PyTorch

TensorFlow, Keras, and PyTorch are popular frameworks for building neural networks. TensorFlow is a comprehensive library for machine learning, while Keras, a high-level API, simplifies building and training neural networks. PyTorch offers dynamic computation graphs, making it flexible and efficient for research and production environments. These tools provide the foundation for creating, training, and optimizing neural network models.

How Neural Networks Work: Architecture, Activation Functions, and Backpropagation

Neural networks are the foundation of deep learning, a subset of machine learning, which mimics the structure and functionality of the human brain to process and learn from large datasets. These networks are made up of layers of neurons, with each layer transforming the input data through mathematical computations. In this section, we will delve into the working mechanism of neural networks, covering their architecture, activation functions, and the backpropagation process.

1. Neural Network Architecture

The architecture of a neural network consists of layers of nodes (or neurons). The most basic neural network includes three types of layers:

- **Input Layer**: This is the first layer of the neural network, where the input data is fed into the model. Each neuron in this layer represents a feature from the dataset.

- **Hidden Layers**: These are layers between the input and output layers. The number of hidden layers and neurons in each layer can vary. Hidden layers perform computations using weights and biases to transform the input into useful patterns.

- **Output Layer**: The final layer that generates the prediction or output based on the transformations made by the previous layers.

Each layer is connected to the next via synapses, where each connection has an associated weight that determines the strength of the connection.

2. Activation Functions

An essential part of a neural network is the activation function, which introduces non-linearity into the network. Without it, the neural network would only be able to model linear relationships, regardless of how many layers it has. The activation function decides whether a neuron should be activated or not, based on its input.

Common activation functions include:

- **Sigmoid**: A function that outputs values between 0 and 1, making it useful for binary classification tasks.

$$\sigma(x) = \frac{1}{1 + e^{-x}}$$

- **ReLU (Rectified Linear Unit)**: A popular activation function that outputs the input directly if it's positive, and zero otherwise. It is computationally efficient and helps in training deep networks.

$$ReLu(x) = \max(0, x)$$

- **Tanh**: Similar to the sigmoid function but outputs values between -1 and 1, making it zero-centered and often more efficient for training.

$$\tanh(x) = \frac{e^x - e^{-x}}{e^x + e^{-x}}$$

Each activation function has its strengths and weaknesses, and the choice of activation function can significantly affect the performance of the neural network.

3. Backpropagation

Backpropagation is the process through which neural networks learn. It is a supervised learning algorithm that uses the chain rule of calculus to compute gradients, which are used to update the weights of the network. Backpropagation operates in two main steps:

1. **Forward Pass**: The input data is passed through the network, and the output is generated by applying the weights, biases, and activation functions in each layer.

2. **Backward Pass**: The error (or loss) is calculated by comparing the network's output to the actual output (label). This error is then propagated backward through the network, updating the weights using gradient descent. The gradient tells the network how to adjust the weights to minimize the error in future predictions.

This process is repeated multiple times (epochs) until the network converges, i.e., it minimizes the error to an acceptable level.

Example: Basic Neural Network in Python Using Keras

```python
from keras.models import Sequential
from keras.layers import Dense
from sklearn.datasets import make_classification
from sklearn.model_selection import train_test_split

# Create a synthetic dataset
X, y = make_classification(n_samples=1000, n_features=20, random_state=42)

# Split the dataset into training and testing sets
X_train, X_test, y_train, y_test = train_test_split(X, y, test_size=0.2,
        random_state=42)

# Define a simple neural network model
model = Sequential()
model.add(Dense(64, input_dim=20, activation='relu'))  # Input layer and
        first hidden layer
```

```
model.add(Dense(32, activation='relu'))          # Second hidden layer
model.add(Dense(1, activation='sigmoid'))        # Output layer for
          binary classification

# Compile the model
model.compile(loss='binary_crossentropy', optimizer='adam',
          metrics=['accuracy'])

# Train the model
model.fit(X_train, y_train, epochs=10, batch_size=32)

# Evaluate the model
loss, accuracy = model.evaluate(X_test, y_test)
print(f"Test Accuracy: {accuracy}")
```

This simple neural network consists of an input layer, two hidden layers, and an output layer for binary classification. The network uses the ReLU activation function for hidden layers and sigmoid for the output layer.

Neural networks have revolutionized fields like image recognition, natural language processing, and autonomous systems by enabling machines to learn complex patterns. Understanding the basic architecture, the role of activation functions, and how backpropagation works is essential for anyone looking to build or improve neural network models. By leveraging the power of deep learning, we can build highly efficient models capable of handling vast and complex datasets.

Basic Architecture of a Neural Network: Input, Hidden, and Output Layers

The architecture of a neural network is critical for its ability to learn and generalize patterns in data. It is structured in layers, each consisting of multiple neurons (also known as nodes). These layers can be classified into three types: the input layer, hidden layers, and output layer. Each type of layer serves a distinct purpose in the process of transforming raw input data into meaningful predictions.

1. Input Layer

The input layer is the first layer of a neural network and serves as the entry point for data into the network. Each neuron in the input layer represents a feature from the input dataset. For example, in an image recognition task, each pixel of the image might correspond to one neuron in the input layer.

- **Features**: The input layer does not perform any computations but simply holds the features of the dataset as the initial stage of the learning process. If the input is an image, the data is usually flattened into a one-dimensional array where each pixel value becomes an input to a neuron.

- **Role**: The input layer passes the data onto the next layers for further processing. In simple terms, it transfers the raw data to the network, which starts transforming it into useful information.

2. Hidden Layers

Hidden layers are the core computational units of the neural network. These layers are responsible for processing the input data through various transformations. There can be one or more hidden layers, and each hidden layer contains multiple neurons. The number of hidden layers and neurons in each layer can vary, depending on the complexity of the problem.

- **Neurons**: Each neuron in a hidden layer takes inputs from the previous layer, processes them with weights and biases, and applies an activation function to generate the output for the next layer. The transformation of the data in the hidden layers is crucial for learning complex patterns in the data.

- **Activations**: The output of each neuron is passed through an activation function. This non-linearity allows neural networks to learn complex functions. Common activation functions used in hidden layers include ReLU (Rectified Linear Unit), Tanh, and Sigmoid.

3. Output Layer

The output layer is the final layer in the neural network, and it produces the final prediction or output. The nature of the output layer depends on the specific task the network is designed for.

- **For Classification**: In a classification task (such as image classification), the output layer typically has one neuron per class. For binary classification, it will have one neuron with a sigmoid activation function. For multi-class classification, a softmax activation function is commonly used.

- **For Regression**: In a regression task (where the goal is to predict continuous values), the output layer usually consists of a single neuron with no activation function (or a linear activation function).

For example, in a binary classification task, the output layer might consist of one neuron with a sigmoid activation, which outputs a probability value between 0 and 1. This value is interpreted as the probability of the input belonging to a certain class.

Example: Building a Simple Neural Network

Below is an example of how to build a simple neural network in Python using Keras for a binary classification task. The network consists of an input layer, two hidden layers, and an output layer.

```
from keras.models import Sequential
from keras.layers import Dense
from sklearn.datasets import make_classification
```

```
from sklearn.model_selection import train_test_split

# Create a synthetic dataset for binary classification
X, y = make_classification(n_samples=1000, n_features=20, random_state=42)

# Split the dataset into training and testing sets
X_train, X_test, y_train, y_test = train_test_split(X, y, test_size=0.2,
        random_state=42)

# Define the neural network model
model = Sequential()
model.add(Dense(64, input_dim=20, activation='relu'))  # Input layer (20
        features) and first hidden layer
model.add(Dense(32, activation='relu'))                 # Second hidden layer
model.add(Dense(1, activation='sigmoid'))               # Output layer (1
        neuron for binary classification)

# Compile the model
model.compile(loss='binary_crossentropy', optimizer='adam',
        metrics=['accuracy'])

# Train the model
model.fit(X_train, y_train, epochs=10, batch_size=32)

# Evaluate the model
loss, accuracy = model.evaluate(X_test, y_test)
print(f"Test Accuracy: {accuracy}")
```

In this example:

- The input layer has 20 neurons (one for each feature).

- The first hidden layer has 64 neurons, and the second hidden layer has 32 neurons.

- The output layer has one neuron for binary classification, with a sigmoid activation function.

The architecture of a neural network plays a critical role in determining how well the network can learn patterns in data. By designing an appropriate number of hidden layers, neurons, and choosing suitable activation functions, neural networks can solve a wide range of problems, from image recognition to language modeling. Understanding how the input, hidden, and output layers interact allows practitioners to build networks that are both powerful and efficient.

Applications of Deep Learning: Image Recognition, NLP, and Autonomous Systems

Deep learning, a subset of machine learning, has rapidly become one of the most powerful tools in the field of artificial intelligence (AI). With the help of neural networks, particularly deep neural networks (DNNs), deep learning is transforming industries by enabling machines to perform complex tasks that were previously thought to be exclusive to humans. Some of the most prominent applications of deep learning include image recognition, natural language processing (NLP), and autonomous systems.

1. Image Recognition

Image recognition involves the ability of a machine to identify objects, people, or features within an image. It is a key area of computer vision, which is concerned with enabling machines to interpret visual data. Deep learning models, particularly Convolutional Neural Networks (CNNs), have significantly advanced the capabilities of image recognition systems.

- **Convolutional Neural Networks (CNNs)**: CNNs are designed to automatically and adaptively learn spatial hierarchies of features from input images. By using convolutional layers, pooling layers, and fully connected layers, CNNs are able to detect patterns in images at different levels of abstraction, such as edges, textures, and more complex structures like faces or objects.

- **Applications**: Image recognition is used in various domains, including facial recognition, medical imaging (e.g., detecting tumors in X-rays), autonomous driving (recognizing traffic signs and pedestrians), and security (surveillance systems).

- **Example**: In the medical field, deep learning models are being employed to analyze medical images like MRI scans to help detect anomalies or diseases, such as cancer, with high accuracy.

```
import tensorflow as tf
from tensorflow.keras.models import Sequential
from tensorflow.keras.layers import Conv2D, MaxPooling2D, Flatten, Dense

# Example CNN for image recognition
model = Sequential([
    Conv2D(32, (3, 3), activation='relu', input_shape=(64, 64, 3)),
    MaxPooling2D(pool_size=(2, 2)),
    Conv2D(64, (3, 3), activation='relu'),
    MaxPooling2D(pool_size=(2, 2)),
    Flatten(),
    Dense(128, activation='relu'),
    Dense(10, activation='softmax')  # 10 output classes for multi-class
            classification
])

# Compile and summarize the model
model.compile(optimizer='adam', loss='categorical_crossentropy',
            metrics=['accuracy'])
model.summary()
```

2. Natural Language Processing (NLP)

Natural Language Processing (NLP) is a branch of AI focused on the interaction between computers and human languages. Deep learning, particularly Recurrent Neural Networks (RNNs) and Transformer-based models, has revolutionized NLP by enabling machines to understand and generate human language with remarkable accuracy.

- **Recurrent Neural Networks (RNNs)**: RNNs are designed to handle sequences of data, making them well-suited for tasks involving text or speech, where the order of words matters. However, RNNs struggle with long-range dependencies due to vanishing gradients.

- **Transformer Models**: More recently, transformer-based models, such as BERT and GPT, have become the state-of-the-art in NLP. These models use attention mechanisms to weigh the importance of different words in a sentence, regardless of their position, making them highly efficient for tasks like translation, sentiment analysis, and question answering.

- **Applications**: NLP is applied in machine translation (e.g., Google Translate), speech recognition (e.g., virtual assistants like Siri), text summarization, and sentiment analysis (e.g., understanding customer feedback).

```
from transformers import BertTokenizer, BertForSequenceClassification
from transformers import pipeline

# Example: Sentiment analysis using a pre-trained BERT model
classifier = pipeline('sentiment-analysis', model='bert-base-uncased')

# Sentiment analysis of a text
result = classifier("Deep learning is revolutionizing the field of AI!")
print(result)
```

3. Autonomous Systems

Autonomous systems, such as self-driving cars and drones, are some of the most exciting applications of deep learning. These systems rely on deep learning to process sensory data and make decisions in real-time, mimicking human-like capabilities such as perception, decision-making, and action.

- **Deep Reinforcement Learning (DRL)**: DRL is a type of machine learning where an agent learns to make decisions by interacting with an environment. In autonomous vehicles, DRL can be used to learn optimal driving strategies based on rewards (e.g., reaching the destination safely).

- **Sensor Fusion**: Autonomous systems often rely on a combination of sensors (e.g., cameras, LIDAR, and radar) to perceive the environment. Deep learning models can fuse data from multiple sensors to improve the accuracy and reliability of perception systems.

- **Applications**: Autonomous systems are used in self-driving cars, where deep learning models help in tasks such as detecting road signs, recognizing pedestrians, and making safe driving decisions. Drones use deep learning to navigate through environments, detect obstacles, and perform specific tasks such as delivery or surveillance.

```
import tensorflow as tf
from tensorflow.keras.models import Sequential
from tensorflow.keras.layers import Dense, LSTM

# Example LSTM model for autonomous vehicle decision-making
model = Sequential([
    LSTM(64, input_shape=(10, 10), activation='relu'),
    Dense(32, activation='relu'),
    Dense(1, activation='sigmoid')  # Output layer: 1 for binary decision
            (e.g., turn left or right)
])

# Compile and summarize the model
model.compile(optimizer='adam', loss='binary_crossentropy',
            metrics=['accuracy'])
model.summary()
```

Deep learning has transformed multiple industries by enabling machines to perform tasks that traditionally required human intelligence. Image recognition, NLP, and autonomous systems are among the most impactful applications, showcasing the power of neural networks in real-world problems. These applications not only enhance efficiency and productivity but also offer novel solutions to complex challenges, from diagnosing diseases to enabling self-driving cars. As deep learning continues to evolve, its applications will expand further, leading to innovations that were once the realm of science fiction.

Tools for Building Neural Networks: TensorFlow, Keras, and PyTorch

Building neural networks requires powerful libraries and frameworks that provide the tools to create, train, and evaluate deep learning models. Among the most popular frameworks for deep learning are TensorFlow, Keras, and PyTorch. These tools offer an extensive range of capabilities and flexibility to developers and researchers working in the field of deep learning. In this section, we will explore each of these tools and highlight their strengths, use cases, and the advantages they bring to neural network development.

1. TensorFlow

TensorFlow, developed by Google, is one of the most widely-used open-source libraries for deep learning. It provides comprehensive support for creating neural networks, performing numerical computations, and running machine learning models at scale. TensorFlow supports a wide variety of neural network architectures, including CNNs, RNNs, and more, and is optimized for both research and production environments.

- **Features**: TensorFlow offers flexible APIs for building models at different levels of abstraction. It includes a high-level API, tf.keras, which simplifies model creation, and a low-level API that allows for customizability and flexibility.

TensorFlow also integrates well with hardware accelerators, such as GPUs and TPUs, for faster model training.

- **Use Cases**: TensorFlow is used in a variety of domains such as computer vision, NLP, speech recognition, and reinforcement learning. It has become a standard for production deployment due to its scalability and robustness in handling large datasets.

```python
import tensorflow as tf
from tensorflow.keras.models import Sequential
from tensorflow.keras.layers import Dense

# Example: Simple neural network using TensorFlow
model = Sequential([
    Dense(64, activation='relu', input_shape=(784,)),
    Dense(10, activation='softmax')
])

model.compile(optimizer='adam', loss='sparse_categorical_crossentropy',
        metrics=['accuracy'])
model.summary()
```

2. Keras

Keras is a high-level API that runs on top of TensorFlow (or other backends like Theano and Microsoft Cognitive Toolkit) and simplifies the process of building neural networks. It was developed to enable quick prototyping and experimentation with deep learning models. Keras provides an easy-to-use interface for building complex neural networks with just a few lines of code.

- **Features**: Keras is known for its simplicity and ease of use. It abstracts away much of the complexity of building neural networks while maintaining flexibility for advanced users. Keras models are modular, making it easy to create, train, and deploy neural networks. It includes pre-built layers, loss functions, and optimizers, allowing users to focus on model architecture and training.

- **Use Cases**: Keras is widely used in both research and industry for rapid prototyping and experimentation with deep learning models. It is often preferred when ease of use and quick development are priorities, especially for beginner data scientists or machine learning practitioners.

```python
from tensorflow.keras.models import Sequential
from tensorflow.keras.layers import Dense

# Example: Simple neural network using Keras
model = Sequential([
    Dense(128, activation='relu', input_dim=784),
    Dense(10, activation='softmax')
])

model.compile(optimizer='adam', loss='categorical_crossentropy',
        metrics=['accuracy'])
model.summary()
```

3. PyTorch

PyTorch, developed by Facebook's AI Research Lab, is another popular deep learning framework that has gained traction due to its dynamic computation graph, ease of use, and strong research community. PyTorch's design makes it especially suitable for research and experimentation, as the framework allows for more flexibility in model construction and debugging.

- **Features**: PyTorch's dynamic computational graph enables models to change in real-time during training. This makes it easier to experiment with new ideas and perform complex model debugging. PyTorch also offers support for GPU acceleration, and its native integration with Python makes it very user-friendly.

- **Use Cases**: PyTorch is extensively used in research and academia for deep learning, particularly in areas like computer vision, NLP, and generative models. The flexibility of the dynamic graph makes it ideal for tasks like reinforcement learning, where models need to adjust based on real-time input.

```python
import torch
import torch.nn as nn
import torch.optim as optim

# Example: Simple neural network using PyTorch
class SimpleNN(nn.Module):
    def __init__(self):
        super(SimpleNN, self).__init__()
        self.fc1 = nn.Linear(784, 128)
        self.fc2 = nn.Linear(128, 10)

    def forward(self, x):
        x = torch.relu(self.fc1(x))
        x = self.fc2(x)
        return x

# Initialize model
model = SimpleNN()
criterion = nn.CrossEntropyLoss()
optimizer = optim.Adam(model.parameters())

# Model summary (using the print statement)
print(model)
```

TensorFlow, Keras, and PyTorch are the three most prominent frameworks for building and deploying neural networks. Each of these tools has its own set of strengths, depending on the user's needs and the specific use case. TensorFlow is best for production environments, Keras excels in rapid prototyping with ease of use, and PyTorch is preferred for research and experimentation due to its flexibility and dynamic graph capabilities. Regardless of the choice of framework, all three have revolutionized the way neural networks are developed and deployed across industries, making deep learning accessible to a wider range of developers and researchers. As deep learning continues to evolve, these tools will likely remain at the forefront of AI development.

Module 26:

Feature Engineering in ML

This module introduces the essential concepts of neural networks, exploring their architecture, how they work, and the tools used to build them. Neural networks have transformed many industries, especially in deep learning, and understanding their structure and applications is fundamental for modern data science. This section covers the architecture of neural networks, their working mechanism, real-world applications, and popular frameworks for building them.

How Neural Networks Work: Architecture, Activation Functions, and Backpropagation

Neural networks mimic the human brain by processing information in layers of interconnected neurons. Each connection has an associated weight, which adjusts during training. Activation functions determine the output of neurons, allowing networks to learn nonlinear relationships. Backpropagation is the key algorithm for updating weights, minimizing errors, and improving model performance through iterative adjustments.

Basic Architecture of a Neural Network: Input, Hidden, and Output Layers

A typical neural network consists of three layers: the input, hidden, and output layers. The input layer receives raw data, feeding it to the hidden layers for processing. Each hidden layer transforms the data, extracting features or patterns. The output layer produces the final predictions, which can be classification results, regression values, or other outputs based on the task.

Applications of Deep Learning: Image Recognition, NLP, and Autonomous Systems

Neural networks, particularly deep learning models, excel in complex tasks like image recognition, natural language processing (NLP), and autonomous systems. In image recognition, convolutional neural networks (CNNs) can identify objects and features within images. In NLP, recurrent neural networks (RNNs) are used for tasks such as sentiment analysis and language translation. For autonomous systems, deep learning powers self-driving cars by processing sensor data for navigation and decision-making.

Tools for Building Neural Networks: TensorFlow, Keras, and PyTorch

Several frameworks simplify the process of building neural networks. TensorFlow, developed by Google, is one of the most widely used open-source libraries, supporting deep learning models at scale. Keras, an API built on top of TensorFlow, simplifies model design with an intuitive interface. PyTorch, popular for research, is another framework favored for its dynamic computation graph and flexibility. Each tool offers unique features that cater to different needs in building and training neural networks.

Importance of Feature Engineering: Impact on Model Accuracy

Feature engineering plays a critical role in machine learning (ML) as it can significantly improve model performance. It involves the process of selecting, modifying, or creating new features from raw data to make the learning algorithm more efficient. The quality and relevance of features are often more important than the choice of the machine learning model itself. In fact, poorly engineered features can severely limit the performance of even the most advanced models. This section explores the importance of feature engineering and how it impacts model accuracy.

1. Understanding Feature Engineering

Feature engineering involves transforming raw data into meaningful inputs that enhance the model's ability to learn and make predictions. The main goal is to provide machine learning algorithms with the most relevant, clean, and structured data possible. Feature engineering includes activities like handling missing values, creating new features from existing data, encoding categorical variables, and scaling numerical values. In essence, it is a creative and iterative process where data scientists attempt to understand the underlying patterns of the data and prepare it for efficient learning.

In supervised learning tasks like classification or regression, poorly chosen features may result in inaccurate models, even with sophisticated algorithms. In contrast, well-engineered features can significantly improve accuracy, reduce training time, and make models more interpretable.

2. Feature Engineering and Model Accuracy

The importance of feature engineering lies in its ability to directly influence the performance of machine learning models. Good features help the model learn more meaningful patterns, while poor features introduce noise and irrelevant information that degrade model performance. Consider the following scenarios where feature engineering directly impacts accuracy:

- **Enhancing Model Performance**: Well-engineered features can improve the accuracy of models by capturing the underlying relationships in the data. For example, if a model is tasked with predicting house prices, features like "square footage" or "location" can provide essential insights. However, raw categorical data like "neighborhood" may require one-hot encoding to improve the model's interpretability and performance.

- **Reducing Overfitting**: By selecting only the most important features, feature engineering helps prevent overfitting, a common problem where a model learns too much from the training data and fails to generalize well to unseen data. Feature selection algorithms (like Recursive Feature Elimination or L1 regularization) can be used to identify and retain the most informative features while discarding irrelevant ones.

- **Handling Missing Data**: Feature engineering also includes dealing with missing data. Imputing missing values using mean imputation or more sophisticated methods like K-Nearest Neighbors (KNN) imputation can help maintain a complete dataset, ensuring that models don't lose important information due to gaps in the data.

3. Example of Feature Engineering

Consider the example of a dataset used to predict customer churn. The raw data may include features like customer ID, age, subscription start date, and usage metrics. Feature engineering could involve creating new features, such as:

- **Churn Duration**: The difference between the current date and the subscription start date, which indicates how long the customer has been using the service.

- **Monthly Usage Frequency**: Aggregating usage data to calculate how often a customer uses the service within a given month.

Once new features are created, feature scaling and encoding techniques can be applied to further improve model performance.

```python
import pandas as pd
from sklearn.preprocessing import StandardScaler, OneHotEncoder

# Example of Feature Scaling and One-Hot Encoding
data = pd.DataFrame({
    'age': [25, 30, 35, 40, 45],
    'subscription_type': ['Basic', 'Premium', 'Basic', 'Premium', 'Basic']
})

# Scaling age feature
scaler = StandardScaler()
data['scaled_age'] = scaler.fit_transform(data[['age']])

# One-hot encoding subscription type
encoder = OneHotEncoder(sparse=False)
encoded_subscriptions = encoder.fit_transform(data[['subscription_type']])
encoded_df = pd.DataFrame(encoded_subscriptions,
        columns=encoder.categories_[0])

# Combine the original data with the new features
final_data = pd.concat([data, encoded_df], axis=1)
print(final_data)
```

Feature engineering is essential in building successful machine learning models. It directly influences model accuracy by ensuring that the algorithm receives the most relevant and clean data. Through processes such as feature scaling, encoding, and selection, data scientists can enhance the model's ability to learn and generalize, improving both predictive power and interpretability. In real-world applications, feature engineering remains a critical step, often making the difference between a poorly performing and a high-performing model.

Feature Scaling and Encoding: Normalization, Standardization, and One-Hot Encoding

Feature scaling and encoding are key techniques used in feature engineering that help prepare raw data for machine learning models. These processes ensure that the data fed into the models is structured appropriately, leading to improved performance, faster convergence during training, and more accurate predictions. This section discusses the common techniques used for feature scaling and encoding: normalization, standardization, and one-hot encoding.

1. Feature Scaling: Normalization and Standardization

Feature scaling refers to the process of transforming the features of a dataset so that they are on a similar scale. This is particularly important for machine learning algorithms that rely on distance metrics or gradient-based optimization techniques (e.g., gradient descent), which may perform poorly if features are on different scales. Two common scaling methods are **normalization** and **standardization**.

Normalization

Normalization (also known as Min-Max scaling) transforms the data into a specific range, typically between 0 and 1. It is useful when the distribution of the data is not Gaussian or when it is important to bound the values in a known range. The formula for normalization is:

$$X_{normalized} = \frac{X - X_{min}}{X_{max} - X_{min}}$$

where:

- X is the original feature value

- X_{min} and X_{max} are the minimum and maximum values in the feature column

Normalization is commonly used when the model relies on distance calculations, like in K-Nearest Neighbors or Support Vector Machines.

Standardization

Standardization, also known as z-score normalization, transforms the data by subtracting the mean and dividing by the standard deviation. This results in a distribution with a mean of 0 and a standard deviation of 1. The formula for standardization is:

$$X_{standardised} = \frac{X - \mu}{\sigma}$$

where:

- X is the original feature value

- μ is the mean of the feature

- σ is the standard deviation of the feature

Standardization is typically used when the model assumes a Gaussian distribution of the features, such as linear regression, logistic regression, and neural networks.

2. One-Hot Encoding: Converting Categorical Variables

In machine learning, categorical data often needs to be converted into numerical format for algorithms to process it effectively. One common approach is **one-hot encoding**, which creates binary columns for each category in the original feature.

How One-Hot Encoding Works

For a categorical feature with k unique categories, one-hot encoding generates k binary columns. Each column represents a category, and the values are 0 or 1, indicating the presence or absence of that category in a given data point.

For example, consider a feature called "color" with categories: "Red," "Green," and "Blue." After one-hot encoding, the feature would be split into three binary columns:

color	Red	Green	Blue
Red	1	0	0
Green	0	1	0
Blue	0	0	1

This approach works well for categorical variables that do not have an inherent order (nominal variables). It avoids assigning arbitrary numerical values to the categories, which could imply incorrect relationships (e.g., implying "Red" is larger than "Blue").

3. Code Example for Scaling and Encoding

Here's how to implement feature scaling and one-hot encoding in Python using the scikit-learn library.

```python
import pandas as pd
from sklearn.preprocessing import StandardScaler, MinMaxScaler,
        OneHotEncoder
from sklearn.compose import ColumnTransformer
from sklearn.pipeline import Pipeline

# Sample DataFrame with numerical and categorical features
data = pd.DataFrame({
    'Age': [25, 30, 35, 40, 45],
    'Salary': [30000, 50000, 40000, 45000, 60000],
    'Color': ['Red', 'Green', 'Blue', 'Red', 'Green']
})

# Create a Column Transformer to apply scaling to numerical features and
        one-hot encoding to categorical features
preprocessor = ColumnTransformer(
    transformers=[
        ('num', StandardScaler(), ['Age', 'Salary']),  # Standardize
            numerical features
        ('cat', OneHotEncoder(), ['Color'])             # One-hot encode
            categorical features
    ])

# Apply the transformation
processed_data = preprocessor.fit_transform(data)

# Convert the result back to DataFrame for better readability
processed_df = pd.DataFrame(processed_data, columns=['Age', 'Salary', 'Red',
        'Green', 'Blue'])

print(processed_df)
```

Output Example:

```
        Age     Salary  Red  Green  Blue
0 -1.414214 -1.264911  1.0   0.0   0.0
1 -0.707107 -0.264911  0.0   1.0   0.0
2  0.000000 -0.794929  0.0   0.0   1.0
3  0.707107 -0.529911  1.0   0.0   0.0
4  1.414214  1.264911  0.0   1.0   0.0
```

In this code:

- The StandardScaler standardizes the "Age" and "Salary" columns.

- The OneHotEncoder creates binary columns for the "Color" feature.

Feature scaling and encoding are essential steps in the feature engineering process. Normalization and standardization ensure that numerical features are on a comparable scale, which can improve the convergence of machine learning algorithms. One-hot encoding, on the other hand, transforms categorical variables into a numerical format that algorithms can understand. Proper application of these techniques can greatly enhance model accuracy and efficiency by ensuring that the data is presented in an optimal format.

Feature Selection Algorithms: Recursive Feature Elimination (RFE), L1 Regularization

Feature selection is a crucial step in the machine learning pipeline, as it helps identify the most relevant features that contribute to the predictive power of a model. Reducing the number of features not only improves model performance but also enhances interpretability and reduces overfitting. In this section, we explore two common feature selection techniques: Recursive Feature Elimination (RFE) and L1 Regularization.

1. Recursive Feature Elimination (RFE)

Recursive Feature Elimination (RFE) is a powerful algorithm used to select the best features by recursively removing the least important ones based on the model's performance. The algorithm starts by training the model on all features, then removes the least important feature(s) based on a ranking metric. This process is repeated until the desired number of features remains.

How RFE Works

The RFE process can be summarized in the following steps:

1. Train the model using all features.

2. Evaluate the importance of each feature using a ranking method (e.g., feature importance from decision trees or coefficients from linear models).

3. Eliminate the least important feature(s).

4. Repeat steps 1–3 until the desired number of features is selected.

RFE works well with models that provide feature importance scores, such as decision trees or linear models.

Code Example for RFE

Here's an example of how to apply RFE in Python using the RFE class from sklearn.feature_selection:

```
from sklearn.feature_selection import RFE
from sklearn.linear_model import LogisticRegression
from sklearn.datasets import load_iris

# Load example dataset
data = load_iris()
X, y = data.data, data.target
```

286

```
# Initialize the model and RFE
model = LogisticRegression(max_iter=1000)
rfe = RFE(estimator=model, n_features_to_select=2)

# Fit RFE to the data
X_rfe = rfe.fit_transform(X, y)

# Print selected features
print(f"Selected features: {rfe.support_}")
print(f"Feature ranking: {rfe.ranking_}")
```

In this example:

- The LogisticRegression model is used as the estimator.

- RFE selects the top 2 features (n_features_to_select=2).

- The support_ attribute shows which features are selected (True for selected features), and ranking_ gives the ranking of all features (1 is the most important).

2. L1 Regularization (Lasso)

L1 regularization, often implemented in the Lasso (Least Absolute Shrinkage and Selection Operator) method, is another feature selection technique that works by adding a penalty term to the linear model's cost function. This penalty encourages sparsity, meaning it drives some feature coefficients to zero, effectively performing feature selection.

How L1 Regularization Works

In linear regression, the Lasso method modifies the loss function as follows:

$$Loss = Residual\ Sum\ of\ Squares + \lambda \sum_{i=1}^{n} |\beta_i|$$

Where:

- λ is the regularization parameter that controls the strength of the penalty.

- β_i are the model coefficients.

As λ increases, more coefficients are driven to zero, leaving only the most important features.

Code Example for Lasso (L1 Regularization)

Here's how to apply L1 regularization for feature selection using Lasso from sklearn.linear_model:

```
from sklearn.linear_model import Lasso
```

```
from sklearn.datasets import make_regression
import numpy as np

# Generate a synthetic regression dataset
X, y = make_regression(n_samples=100, n_features=10, noise=0.1)

# Initialize the Lasso model with L1 regularization
lasso = Lasso(alpha=0.1)  # Alpha controls the regularization strength

# Fit the model
lasso.fit(X, y)

# Print the coefficients of the features
print(f"Feature coefficients: {lasso.coef_}")

# Identify selected features
selected_features = np.where(lasso.coef_ != 0)[0]
print(f"Selected features: {selected_features}")
```

In this example:

- A synthetic regression dataset is created using make_regression.

- The Lasso model is applied with an alpha value of 0.1, which determines the strength of the regularization.

- The coefficients of the features are printed, and the non-zero coefficients indicate the selected features.

3. Comparison: RFE vs. L1 Regularization

- **RFE** is a model-agnostic approach, meaning it can be used with any estimator that provides a way to evaluate feature importance (e.g., decision trees, logistic regression). It is computationally expensive because it requires multiple iterations over the dataset, making it slower for large datasets.

- **L1 Regularization (Lasso)** is efficient, especially for linear models. It is a built-in feature selection method, meaning the feature selection happens automatically during the model fitting process. However, it is most effective when dealing with linear relationships and may struggle with highly complex relationships.

Both methods are useful in different contexts, and it is often beneficial to compare results from both methods to ensure the robustness of the selected features.

Feature selection is a critical step in the machine learning pipeline, helping reduce the dimensionality of the dataset and improving the performance and interpretability of the model. Recursive Feature Elimination (RFE) and L1 regularization (Lasso) are two popular techniques for selecting important features. RFE works by recursively eliminating less important features, while L1 regularization drives feature coefficients to zero, naturally performing feature selection. Both methods have their strengths and should be considered depending on the nature of the data and the problem at hand.

Advanced Feature Transformation: Polynomial Features, Logarithmic Transformations

Feature transformation is an essential part of the feature engineering process in machine learning. It involves creating new features from the original ones to help improve the performance of models. This section discusses two advanced feature transformation techniques: polynomial features and logarithmic transformations, both of which can be powerful tools to capture non-linear relationships and enhance model accuracy.

1. Polynomial Features

Polynomial features allow models to capture non-linear relationships between the input features and the target variable. By creating new features that are powers of the original features, polynomial features enable linear models to better approximate complex, non-linear patterns.

How Polynomial Features Work

For instance, given a simple feature x, polynomial transformation can create higher-order features like x^2, x^3, etc., effectively adding non-linearity to the model. The transformation extends the feature space by adding interaction terms between the features as well.

For a single feature x, the polynomial features would be:

$$[1, x, x^2, x^3, \dots]$$

For multiple features x_1, x_2, the polynomial expansion would also include interactions like $x_1 x_2$, $x_1^2 x_2$, etc.

Code Example for Polynomial Features

Here's how to generate polynomial features using the PolynomialFeatures class from sklearn.preprocessing:

```
from sklearn.preprocessing import PolynomialFeatures
import numpy as np

# Sample data
X = np.array([[2], [3], [4]])

# Generate polynomial features (degree 2)
poly = PolynomialFeatures(degree=2)
X_poly = poly.fit_transform(X)

print("Original features:")
print(X)

print("Polynomial features (degree 2):")
```

```
print(X_poly)
```

In this example:

- The PolynomialFeatures class is used to generate features up to degree 2, which includes x and x^2.

- The fit_transform method is applied to the data to create the expanded feature space.

2. Logarithmic Transformations

Logarithmic transformations are often used when the data spans several orders of magnitude. They are useful for compressing the range of feature values and stabilizing the variance. Applying a logarithmic transformation can also help with highly skewed data, transforming the distribution into a more normal shape, which is often beneficial for linear models.

How Logarithmic Transformations Work

The transformation is straightforward:

y=log(x)

Where x is the feature being transformed. The log function typically helps in scenarios where the feature has an exponential growth pattern or when there is a need to reduce the effect of extreme values (outliers). This transformation is particularly useful in fields such as economics or biology, where values can range from a small number to extremely large figures.

Code Example for Logarithmic Transformation

Here's how to apply a logarithmic transformation to a feature using numpy:

```
import numpy as np

# Sample data
X = np.array([[1], [10], [100], [1000]])

# Apply logarithmic transformation (base e)
X_log = np.log(X)

print("Original data:")
print(X)

print("Logarithmic transformation:")
print(X_log)
```

In this example:

- The np.log function is used to apply the natural logarithm to each feature value.

- The transformation can be applied to datasets where features exhibit a skewed distribution, making the data more suitable for modeling.

3. When to Use Polynomial Features vs. Logarithmic Transformations

Both polynomial and logarithmic transformations can help improve model performance, but they are suited to different types of data:

- **Polynomial features** are useful when you suspect a non-linear relationship between the input features and the target variable. They help create higher-order features that can capture more complex patterns that a linear model may not be able to represent.

- **Logarithmic transformations** are ideal when you have skewed data or when the data spans several orders of magnitude. They help to compress the data and often make it more suitable for linear models or reduce the influence of extreme outliers.

In practice, it's essential to evaluate the performance of models with and without these transformations to ensure that they provide a meaningful improvement.

Advanced feature transformation techniques such as polynomial features and logarithmic transformations can significantly improve the performance of machine learning models. Polynomial features help capture non-linear relationships by introducing higher-order terms and interactions between features, while logarithmic transformations stabilize the variance and compress the range of data, making it more suitable for linear modeling. Both techniques should be considered depending on the nature of the dataset and the problem at hand, and it's important to test their effectiveness in model performance through experimentation.

Module 27:

Model Deployment

Deploying machine learning models into production environments presents a unique set of challenges. It requires careful planning, continuous monitoring, and maintenance to ensure that models perform well over time. This module addresses key issues related to deployment, including scalability, integration, model drift, and maintenance strategies.

Challenges in Deployment: Scalability, Integration, and Model Drift

Model deployment often faces scalability challenges, especially as data volumes grow. Ensuring that models can handle increasing traffic or data loads is essential for maintaining performance. Integration with existing systems and infrastructure is another hurdle, as seamless connectivity is crucial. Additionally, model drift, where a model's accuracy declines over time due to changes in data patterns, requires ongoing adjustments to keep models relevant and accurate in real-world applications.

CI/CD for Machine Learning: Continuous Integration, Continuous Deployment Practices

Continuous Integration (CI) and Continuous Deployment (CD) practices are fundamental to modern machine learning workflows. CI ensures that code, including model updates, is integrated into the main branch frequently and reliably. CD automates the deployment process, ensuring that new versions of models are deployed quickly and safely. These practices streamline the deployment process, reduce errors, and enhance collaboration between data scientists and software engineers.

Monitoring and Maintenance: Model Performance Tracking and Retraining

Monitoring and maintenance are critical for sustaining model performance over time. Regular tracking of model performance allows teams to identify when models begin to underperform or become obsolete. Automated systems for retraining models on fresh data can help prevent model decay. Moreover, performance metrics and A/B testing can help optimize models post-deployment, ensuring that they continue to deliver value in dynamic environments.

Scalability Considerations: Deploying Models in Production Systems

Scalability considerations are key when deploying models at scale. Whether deploying on-premises or in the cloud, models must be capable of handling large volumes of requests without compromising performance. Techniques such as model parallelism and horizontal scaling help ensure that models remain responsive as demand increases. Additionally, resource management and cost efficiency become important factors in production environments, necessitating ongoing optimization of deployment infrastructure.

Challenges in Deployment: Scalability, Integration, and Model Drift

Deploying machine learning models into production environments presents a number of unique challenges. These challenges must be addressed to ensure that models perform well under real-world conditions, integrate smoothly with existing systems, and remain accurate over time. In this section, we'll explore three major deployment challenges: scalability, integration, and model drift.

1. Scalability in Model Deployment

Scalability refers to the ability of a machine learning model to handle increased loads, such as larger datasets or higher request volumes, without degrading performance. As the demand for a model's predictions grows, the system must scale appropriately to maintain response times and resource utilization within acceptable limits.

Challenges in Scalability

Scalability challenges arise when the model's performance slows down due to an increase in the number of requests, the volume of data, or complexity of the computations. For example, models that perform well on small datasets might struggle when deployed to handle streaming data or large batch processing tasks in production.

Solutions for Scalability

To address scalability:

- **Distributed computing**: Models can be deployed in a distributed manner using technologies like Apache Spark or Kubernetes. These platforms allow models to scale horizontally by adding more computational resources, ensuring that the model can handle increasing workloads.

- **Model optimization**: Techniques such as quantization, pruning, and knowledge distillation can be used to optimize models, making them more efficient and able to handle larger loads while maintaining accuracy.

2. Integration with Existing Systems

Model integration involves embedding the machine learning model into the existing technology infrastructure. The model must be compatible with other systems like databases, APIs, or web servers to function seamlessly in production.

Challenges in Integration

Integration challenges often arise due to mismatched data formats, outdated software, or dependency conflicts. Additionally, the deployment process must consider system security, versioning, and compatibility with other business applications.

Solutions for Integration

- **Microservices architecture**: Deploying machine learning models as microservices allows easy integration with other parts of the system. This enables isolated updates, scalability, and easy interaction with other services via APIs.

- **Containerization**: Tools like Docker allow machine learning models to be packaged with all their dependencies into containers. These containers can then be deployed across any environment, ensuring seamless integration regardless of underlying infrastructure.

3. Model Drift

Model drift refers to the gradual degradation of model performance over time as the data the model was trained on changes. As new data becomes available, the patterns may shift, causing the model's predictions to become less accurate. This is particularly problematic in dynamic environments where data evolves rapidly, such as in finance or healthcare.

Challenges in Model Drift

Model drift can occur for several reasons, including changes in the underlying data distribution (concept drift), changes in user behavior, or variations in external factors (seasonal or cyclical changes). Detecting and addressing drift is crucial to maintaining the model's performance.

Solutions for Model Drift

- **Model monitoring**: To detect model drift early, continuous monitoring is essential. Tools like Prometheus and Grafana can be used to track the model's performance over time and trigger alerts when performance degrades beyond a certain threshold.

- **Model retraining**: Once drift is detected, retraining the model with fresh data is often necessary. This can be automated using pipelines that regularly update the model with new data, ensuring the model adapts to changing conditions.

Successfully deploying machine learning models requires addressing several key challenges, including scalability, integration with existing systems, and handling model drift. Scalability ensures that the model can handle growing demand, while integration makes sure the model works seamlessly within the existing technological infrastructure. Finally, managing model drift through continuous monitoring and retraining is crucial to maintaining high performance over time. By understanding and addressing these deployment challenges, organizations can ensure that their machine learning models deliver accurate and reliable predictions in real-world environments.

CI/CD for Machine Learning: Continuous integration, Continuous Deployment Practices

Continuous Integration (CI) and Continuous Deployment (CD) are essential practices in modern machine learning workflows, helping to automate the process of model development, testing, and deployment. These practices ensure faster, more reliable delivery of machine learning models to production environments, minimizing human errors, and ensuring the continuous improvement of deployed models. This section explores CI/CD practices specific to machine learning and how they can streamline model deployment and monitoring.

1. Continuous Integration (CI) in Machine Learning

Continuous Integration is the practice of automatically integrating code changes from multiple contributors into a shared repository. In machine learning, CI involves the automated integration of model code, data pipelines, and training scripts to detect issues early and ensure that the model works as expected after each update.

Challenges in CI for ML

Machine learning models are inherently different from traditional software in that they rely on data, which can change over time. In CI for ML, challenges include handling data dependencies, versioning datasets, and ensuring reproducibility of model training.

CI Best Practices for ML

To address these challenges, ML CI pipelines should include:

- **Automated testing**: Test cases for verifying model accuracy, training stability, and performance on known datasets should be integrated into the CI pipeline. Using frameworks like unittest or pytest, tests can validate whether model training results are within expected performance bounds.

- **Version control for models and data**: Tools like DVC (Data Version Control) and Git LFS (Large File Storage) ensure that models, hyperparameters, and training data are versioned. This prevents issues caused by data changes or mismatches in training configurations.

Example of a simple CI pipeline for model testing in Python:

```python
import pytest
from sklearn.ensemble import RandomForestClassifier
from sklearn.datasets import load_iris
from sklearn.model_selection import train_test_split

def test_model_accuracy():
    # Load data
    iris = load_iris()
    X_train, X_test, y_train, y_test = train_test_split(iris.data,
            iris.target, test_size=0.2)

    # Train model
    model = RandomForestClassifier(n_estimators=100)
    model.fit(X_train, y_train)

    # Test model accuracy
    accuracy = model.score(X_test, y_test)
    assert accuracy > 0.9  # Example threshold for model performance

# Run the test
pytest.main()
```

2. Continuous Deployment (CD) in Machine Learning

Continuous Deployment refers to the automatic deployment of machine learning models to production once they pass CI validation. With CD, new models or model updates can be deployed into production quickly and consistently, enabling faster iteration and reducing downtime.

Challenges in CD for ML

Deploying machine learning models involves more than just pushing code to production. Challenges include ensuring compatibility with production environments, managing model dependencies, and handling different model versions simultaneously.

CD Best Practices for ML

To streamline CD for ML, the following practices are recommended:

- **Model packaging**: Use tools like Docker or Kubernetes to containerize models and their dependencies, ensuring consistency between the development and production environments. This helps mitigate issues related to environment mismatches.

- **A/B testing and rollback mechanisms**: Implement A/B testing to evaluate the performance of new models before full deployment. If the new model doesn't perform as expected, rollback mechanisms should be in place to restore the previous version.

Example of automating model deployment with Docker:

```
# Dockerfile to containerize ML model
FROM python:3.8-slim

# Install dependencies
RUN pip install scikit-learn flask

# Copy model and app into the container
COPY model.pkl /app/model.pkl
COPY app.py /app/app.py

# Expose the port the app runs on
EXPOSE 5000

# Command to run the app
CMD ["python", "/app/app.py"]
```

3. Monitoring and Retraining

Once deployed, machine learning models must be continuously monitored to ensure they continue to perform as expected. Monitoring can detect issues like model drift, degradation in accuracy, or system failures. Retraining models periodically with updated data is essential to prevent these issues.

Monitoring Best Practices

- **Performance tracking**: Use monitoring tools like Prometheus and Grafana to keep track of metrics such as prediction latency, error rates, and resource utilization.

- **Automated retraining**: Once the model performance degrades, automated retraining pipelines can be triggered. This helps to ensure that the model is always up to date and responsive to changing data patterns.

CI/CD for machine learning streamlines the process of building, testing, and deploying models. By automating the integration of new code changes and deploying models into production efficiently, teams can ensure that machine learning models remain reliable, scalable, and adaptable to new data. Incorporating automated testing, model packaging, A/B testing, and continuous monitoring helps mitigate deployment challenges and improves model performance over time.

Monitoring and Maintenance: Model Performance Tracking and Retraining

After a machine learning model is deployed to production, it is essential to continuously monitor and maintain its performance. This ensures that the model continues to deliver accurate predictions over time, adapts to changes in the underlying data, and remains relevant in the face of new patterns. Monitoring model performance, detecting when the model starts to degrade, and initiating retraining processes are critical tasks to maintain the effectiveness of machine learning systems.

1. The Need for Monitoring

In production environments, machine learning models are exposed to real-world data, which can be significantly different from the data used during the training phase. This variation can cause model performance to degrade over time—a phenomenon known as **model drift** or **concept drift**. Therefore, continuous performance tracking is crucial to detect these issues early and to avoid business impact due to inaccurate predictions.

Key Metrics for Monitoring

Several key metrics should be tracked to ensure model performance:

- **Accuracy**: Measures the overall correctness of the model's predictions.

- **Precision and Recall**: These metrics help assess the model's performance for specific classes, especially in imbalanced datasets.

- **ROC-AUC**: This metric is useful for evaluating classification models, especially when dealing with binary outcomes.

- **Latency and Throughput**: Measures the speed and efficiency of the model, ensuring it can handle production workloads without delays.

2. Tools for Monitoring Model Performance

There are various tools and libraries that facilitate model performance monitoring. Some of the most widely used ones are:

- **Prometheus**: A tool that helps monitor machine learning systems by collecting and storing metrics, which can then be visualized using Grafana.

- **TensorBoard**: Primarily used for monitoring deep learning models in TensorFlow, TensorBoard provides real-time updates on training metrics, model weights, and performance.

- **MLflow**: An open-source platform that manages the full machine learning lifecycle, including experiment tracking, model versioning, and deployment. MLflow can be used to monitor model performance in production.

Example: Using MLflow to track model performance:

```
import mlflow
from sklearn.metrics import accuracy_score
```

298

```
# Assuming the model and data are already loaded
y_pred = model.predict(X_test)
accuracy = accuracy_score(y_test, y_pred)

# Log the metric with MLflow
mlflow.log_metric("accuracy", accuracy)
```

3. Detecting Model Drift and Concept Drift

Over time, as new data arrives, the statistical properties of the data may change, leading to **model drift**. This can happen due to changes in user behavior, market dynamics, or external factors. **Concept drift** occurs when the underlying relationship between input features and the target variable changes.

Methods for Detecting Drift

- **Performance degradation**: Monitoring changes in model accuracy, precision, and other performance metrics can help detect drift.

- **Data distribution change**: Statistical tests like the **Kolmogorov-Smirnov test** or **Kullback-Leibler divergence** can be used to compare the distribution of incoming data with the data used for training the model.

- **Error analysis**: Tracking prediction errors and identifying systematic biases or patterns in the errors can indicate drift.

4. Retraining the Model

When model drift is detected, the next step is often retraining the model with updated data. Automating this process through a retraining pipeline is essential for maintaining model performance without requiring manual intervention.

Retraining Triggers

The retraining process can be triggered by:

- **Performance thresholds**: If the model accuracy falls below a predefined threshold, a retraining job is initiated.

- **Time-based retraining**: Periodic retraining can be scheduled (e.g., weekly or monthly) to ensure the model adapts to new data.

- **Data-based retraining**: If a significant amount of new data accumulates, retraining the model on this new data might improve its performance.

Retraining Pipeline

Automating the retraining process involves setting up a pipeline that can:

1. Fetch new data.

2. Preprocess and transform the data.

3. Retrain the model using the latest dataset.

4. Evaluate the performance of the newly trained model.

5. Deploy the updated model to production.

Example of a basic retraining pipeline in Python:

```python
from sklearn.model_selection import train_test_split
from sklearn.ensemble import RandomForestClassifier
from sklearn.metrics import accuracy_score
import joblib

# Load new data
new_data = load_new_data()

# Preprocess data
X_new = preprocess(new_data)

# Split data for retraining
X_train, X_test, y_train, y_test = train_test_split(X_new, y_new,
        test_size=0.2)

# Train new model
model = RandomForestClassifier()
model.fit(X_train, y_train)

# Evaluate model
y_pred = model.predict(X_test)
accuracy = accuracy_score(y_test, y_pred)

# Log the new model and performance
joblib.dump(model, 'updated_model.pkl')

# If the accuracy is satisfactory, deploy the model
if accuracy > 0.9:
    deploy_model('updated_model.pkl')
```

5. Best Practices for Monitoring and Maintenance

- **Automate retraining**: Automating the retraining process ensures that models are always up to date without manual intervention.

- **Versioning models**: Use model versioning systems like MLflow to track different versions of models, making it easier to roll back to a previous version if necessary.

- **Alerting and notification**: Set up alert systems that notify data scientists or engineers when model performance degrades or when retraining is required.

Monitoring and maintaining machine learning models in production is an ongoing process that requires attention to model performance, data changes, and system efficiency. By implementing automated monitoring tools, detecting model drift, and triggering retraining pipelines, organizations can ensure that their machine learning systems continue to deliver accurate and reliable predictions over time.

Scalability Considerations: Deploying Models in Production Systems

Scalability is a key consideration when deploying machine learning models in production systems. As the volume of data grows, or as the demand for predictions increases, it is crucial that models can scale to meet these needs without compromising on performance or efficiency. In this section, we will explore the factors involved in scaling machine learning models, the infrastructure options available, and strategies to ensure that deployed models can handle large-scale data and traffic.

1. Understanding the Need for Scalability

In production, machine learning models are required to handle not only large datasets but also a potentially high volume of requests for real-time predictions. Whether the model is used for online prediction in e-commerce, fraud detection in banking, or autonomous driving systems, ensuring that the model can scale effectively is critical to the business success and operational efficiency.

There are two main types of scalability to consider:

- **Horizontal Scalability**: This involves adding more machines or servers to distribute the workload and handle increased traffic. This is often used in cloud environments where resources can be dynamically provisioned.

- **Vertical Scalability**: This involves upgrading the current hardware (e.g., adding more CPU power, memory, or storage) to handle more intensive workloads on a single machine.

2. Infrastructure for Scalable Model Deployment

When deploying machine learning models at scale, choosing the right infrastructure is paramount. There are several options available depending on the requirements of the system, including cloud services, containers, and distributed computing frameworks.

Cloud Services

Cloud platforms like **AWS**, **Google Cloud**, and **Microsoft Azure** offer services specifically designed for scaling machine learning models. These platforms provide:

- **Elastic compute resources**: Automatically scale up or down the number of virtual machines based on demand.

- **Managed services**: Services like **AWS SageMaker**, **Azure Machine Learning**, and **Google AI Platform** handle model deployment, monitoring, and scaling for you.

- **GPU instances**: For deep learning models requiring high computational power, cloud platforms offer specialized GPU instances to handle intensive workloads efficiently.

Containers and Kubernetes

Using **Docker** containers in combination with **Kubernetes** orchestration is another scalable option. Containers allow models to be packaged with their dependencies and deployed consistently across different environments. Kubernetes helps with automating the deployment, scaling, and management of containerized applications.

```
# Example of running a model in a Docker container
docker run -p 5000:5000 my_ml_model_image
```

This container can be deployed to multiple instances, and Kubernetes ensures that the required number of containers are running based on demand, providing a highly scalable deployment strategy.

3. Load Balancing and High Availability

To handle high volumes of prediction requests, load balancing is essential. Load balancing ensures that incoming requests are distributed evenly across multiple instances of the model, preventing any single instance from becoming overwhelmed.

Common load balancing techniques include:

- **Round-robin**: Distributes requests sequentially to each available instance.

- **Least connections**: Sends requests to the instance with the least number of active connections, ensuring a balanced workload.

- **Weighted distribution**: Assigns more traffic to powerful instances and less to weaker ones.

High availability (HA) is another important aspect of scalable model deployment. By setting up redundant instances of the model across different data centers or regions, you ensure that the system can remain operational even if one instance or region fails.

4. Distributed Computing for Big Data

For models that need to process large volumes of data, distributed computing frameworks such as **Apache Spark** and **Dask** can be employed. These frameworks allow models to be run in parallel across multiple nodes, ensuring that data processing and model inference scale with the size of the data.

Apache Spark, for instance, can handle large-scale data processing tasks and can be integrated with machine learning models. With libraries such as **MLlib**, Spark offers distributed machine learning algorithms that can be used to scale training across a cluster of machines.

Example: Using Spark for distributed inference in Python:

```
from pyspark.sql import SparkSession
from pyspark.ml.classification import RandomForestClassifier
from pyspark.ml.feature import VectorAssembler

# Initialize Spark session
spark = SparkSession.builder.appName('Model_Deployment').getOrCreate()

# Load and prepare data
data = spark.read.csv('data.csv', header=True, inferSchema=True)
assembler = VectorAssembler(inputCols=['feature1', 'feature2'],
        outputCol='features')
data = assembler.transform(data)

# Load a pre-trained model and make predictions
model = RandomForestClassifier.load('path_to_model')
predictions = model.transform(data)
```

5. Caching for Fast Predictions

Caching is a technique to speed up model inference by storing the results of expensive operations and serving them for subsequent requests. For example, if the model has to make a prediction on a large dataset, caching the results of the most recent predictions can reduce latency for repeated requests.

Tools like **Redis** and **Memcached** are commonly used for caching in production environments. These in-memory databases store the results of predictions so that the system does not need to recompute them for identical inputs.

6. Monitoring for Scalability Issues

Once the model is deployed, continuous monitoring is necessary to identify any performance bottlenecks or issues with scalability. This involves monitoring CPU and memory usage, as well as the response time of predictions. By tracking metrics like **latency** and **throughput**, you can ensure that your model is scaling appropriately to meet demand.

Scalability considerations are critical when deploying machine learning models in production systems. Leveraging cloud infrastructure, distributed computing, containerization, and load balancing ensures that models can efficiently handle increasing data and traffic. By setting up high availability, monitoring performance, and implementing caching techniques, you can maintain the robustness and efficiency of machine learning models deployed at scale.

Module 28:

Machine Learning in Action

Machine learning (ML) offers practical solutions for solving complex problems across a wide array of industries. In this module, we will explore an end-to-end project example that demonstrates how to build a predictive model. We'll also discuss insights from deployed models, real-world success stories, and emerging trends shaping the future of ML.

Building a Predictive Model: End-to-End Project Example

An end-to-end project in ML involves data collection, cleaning, feature engineering, model building, evaluation, and deployment. Each stage is crucial for creating a model that generalizes well to new, unseen data. From selecting the right algorithm to tuning hyperparameters, building a predictive model requires a strategic approach to ensure it meets the desired goals.

Insights from Deployed Models: Practical Lessons and Applications

Once models are deployed, they provide valuable insights into how well they perform in real-world environments. Understanding the practical impact of deployed models helps to refine them for future iterations. Observing challenges such as model drift or unexpected outcomes gives critical feedback to improve the model's robustness and real-world applicability, ensuring ongoing value.

Real-World ML Success Stories: Case Studies from Top Industries

Industries such as healthcare, finance, and e-commerce have successfully integrated ML into their operations. For instance, ML is used in healthcare to predict patient outcomes, in finance for fraud detection, and in e-commerce for personalized recommendations. These real-world case studies highlight the transformative power of ML, driving innovation and efficiency in diverse sectors.

Discussion of Emerging Trends: AutoML, Federated Learning, and Explainable AI

Emerging trends such as AutoML, Federated Learning, and Explainable AI are shaping the future of machine learning. AutoML automates model selection and hyperparameter tuning, enabling faster deployment. Federated learning allows for decentralized model training, preserving data privacy. Explainable AI focuses on making models more interpretable, enhancing trust and transparency in ML applications.

Building a Predictive Model: End-to-End Project Example.

Building a predictive model is an essential skill in data science, and applying machine learning techniques to real-world data is a crucial part of transforming data into actionable insights. This section will provide a step-by-step example of building an end-to-end machine learning project, from data collection and preprocessing to model deployment.

1. Defining the Problem

The first step in any machine learning project is defining the problem. Let's say we want to build a model to predict house prices based on various features such as square footage, number of bedrooms, and location. This is a classic regression problem, where the goal is to predict a continuous value (the house price).

---

2. Collecting and Preprocessing Data

Once the problem is defined, the next step is to collect and preprocess the data. In this case, we'll use a dataset containing historical house sales with features like square_feet, bedrooms, location, and price. Data preprocessing involves cleaning the data, handling missing values, encoding categorical variables, and scaling numerical features.

Here's an example of loading and preprocessing the data using Python and pandas:

```python
import pandas as pd
from sklearn.model_selection import train_test_split
from sklearn.preprocessing import StandardScaler
from sklearn.impute import SimpleImputer

# Load the dataset
data = pd.read_csv('house_prices.csv')

# Handling missing values
imputer = SimpleImputer(strategy='mean')
data['square_feet'] = imputer.fit_transform(data[['square_feet']])
data['bedrooms'] = imputer.fit_transform(data[['bedrooms']])

# Encoding categorical variables (location)
data = pd.get_dummies(data, columns=['location'], drop_first=True)

# Scaling features
scaler = StandardScaler()
scaled_features = scaler.fit_transform(data[['square_feet', 'bedrooms']])

# Splitting the data into training and testing sets
X = data.drop(columns=['price'])
y = data['price']
X_train, X_test, y_train, y_test = train_test_split(X, y, test_size=0.2,
        random_state=42)
```

3. Choosing the Model

Next, we need to choose a model. For this regression task, we could use models like **Linear Regression**, **Random Forest Regressor**, or **Gradient Boosting Machines**. Here, we will start with a simple **Linear Regression** model.

```python
from sklearn.linear_model import LinearRegression
from sklearn.metrics import mean_squared_error

# Initialize and train the model
model = LinearRegression()
model.fit(X_train, y_train)

# Predict the house prices
y_pred = model.predict(X_test)

# Evaluate the model performance
mse = mean_squared_error(y_test, y_pred)
print(f'Mean Squared Error: {mse}')
```

4. Model Evaluation

Evaluating the performance of the model is crucial to understanding its effectiveness. In this case, we use **Mean Squared Error (MSE)** to assess how close the predictions are to the actual house prices. Lower MSE values indicate better model performance.

5. Model Tuning

If the initial model doesn't perform well, we can tune it. This may involve adjusting hyperparameters, trying different models, or adding more features. Techniques like **Grid Search** or **Randomized Search** can be used to find the optimal hyperparameters for the model.

Example of hyperparameter tuning using **GridSearchCV**:

```python
from sklearn.model_selection import GridSearchCV
from sklearn.ensemble import RandomForestRegressor

# Define the model and hyperparameter grid
rf = RandomForestRegressor()
param_grid = {
    'n_estimators': [50, 100, 200],
    'max_depth': [10, 20, None]
}

# Perform grid search
grid_search = GridSearchCV(rf, param_grid, cv=3)
grid_search.fit(X_train, y_train)

# Best model from grid search
best_rf_model = grid_search.best_estimator_
y_pred_best = best_rf_model.predict(X_test)

# Evaluate the best model
mse_best = mean_squared_error(y_test, y_pred_best)
print(f'Best Model Mean Squared Error: {mse_best}')
```

6. Deploying the Model

Once the model is trained and evaluated, the final step is deploying it into a production environment. This could involve integrating the model into a web application using **Flask** or **FastAPI**, or deploying it to cloud services like **AWS** or **Azure**. The model can then be used to make real-time predictions.

Example of saving the trained model and loading it for deployment:

```
import joblib

# Save the model to a file
joblib.dump(best_rf_model, 'house_price_predictor.pkl')

# Load the model in a production environment
loaded_model = joblib.load('house_price_predictor.pkl')
prediction = loaded_model.predict(new_data)  # new_data is an unseen feature
          vector
```

Building a predictive model is an iterative process that requires careful planning and execution. By following the steps of defining the problem, collecting and preprocessing data, choosing the right model, tuning it, and deploying it, data scientists can create effective machine learning solutions that provide valuable insights and support business decision-making. Through this process, we see the importance of data preparation, model selection, evaluation, and deployment in creating robust and scalable machine learning systems.

Insights from Deployed Models: Practical Lessons and Applications

Once machine learning models are deployed in real-world environments, they provide valuable insights and practical applications that demonstrate their true potential. In this section, we explore the practical lessons learned from deployed models, how they are applied across various industries, and the impact of these applications on business operations and decision-making.

1. Real-World Impact of Deployed Models

The deployment of machine learning models in real-world settings often reveals their true value. These models not only make predictions but also automate decision-making processes, enabling businesses to operate more efficiently. For example, in the retail industry, predictive models can forecast inventory demand, optimize pricing strategies, and even personalize customer recommendations.

Deployed models can also drive operational efficiencies, as demonstrated by companies like **Netflix** and **Spotify**, where machine learning is used to recommend content based on user preferences. These models continually improve as they receive feedback from users, helping companies refine their recommendations and provide more relevant content.

2. Practical Lessons Learned from Deployed Models

Deploying machine learning models comes with several challenges that are often not anticipated during the development phase. Here are some key lessons learned from real-world deployments:

A. Model Drift and Concept Drift

One common challenge is **model drift**, where the model's performance degrades over time. This can occur due to changes in the underlying data distribution or shifts in user behavior (referred to as **concept drift**). For instance, a fraud detection model may become less effective as fraud tactics evolve, leading to higher false negatives.

Solution: To mitigate model drift, regular monitoring and model retraining are essential. Implementing automated retraining pipelines using **continuous integration/continuous deployment (CI/CD)** practices ensures that models are always up-to-date with the latest data.

B. Data Quality and Feature Relevance

Another lesson is the importance of high-quality data. Even with sophisticated models, poor data quality can lead to inaccurate predictions and unreliable insights. This can manifest as missing data, noise, or irrelevant features, which ultimately degrade model performance.

Solution: Proper data preprocessing techniques such as imputation for missing values and feature selection can help improve the quality of input data. Additionally, continuous monitoring of data quality post-deployment is essential for maintaining model accuracy.

3. Applications of Deployed Models Across Industries

Machine learning models are applied across various industries to solve specific problems and provide actionable insights. Here are a few examples:

A. Healthcare: Predicting Disease Outcomes

In healthcare, predictive models are deployed to forecast disease outcomes and identify high-risk patients. For instance, machine learning models can analyze medical records to predict the likelihood of a patient developing conditions such as diabetes or heart disease. These insights help healthcare providers make timely interventions and improve patient outcomes.

```
# Example: Predicting risk of diabetes using a logistic regression model
from sklearn.linear_model import LogisticRegression
from sklearn.metrics import classification_report
```

```
# Assuming X_train and y_train contain feature data and target labels
model = LogisticRegression()
model.fit(X_train, y_train)
y_pred = model.predict(X_test)

print(classification_report(y_test, y_pred))
```

B. Finance: Credit Scoring and Risk Management

In the finance sector, machine learning models are deployed to assess credit risk, predict loan defaults, and detect fraudulent transactions. Models like **Random Forests** and **Gradient Boosting Machines** can analyze historical transaction data and predict the likelihood of default or fraud, helping financial institutions make data-driven decisions.

```
# Example: Credit scoring using RandomForestClassifier
from sklearn.ensemble import RandomForestClassifier
from sklearn.metrics import accuracy_score

rf_model = RandomForestClassifier()
rf_model.fit(X_train, y_train)
y_pred = rf_model.predict(X_test)

print(f'Accuracy: {accuracy_score(y_test, y_pred)}')
```

C. Retail: Personalized Recommendations

Machine learning models deployed in e-commerce platforms can analyze customer purchase history, preferences, and browsing behavior to provide personalized product recommendations. This personalization increases customer satisfaction and sales conversion rates.

4. Challenges in Model Deployment

While deploying machine learning models yields substantial benefits, it also presents several challenges. Some of these challenges include:

A. Scalability

As the volume of data grows, ensuring that models can scale to handle larger datasets becomes critical. Scaling challenges can arise when the deployed model faces high-frequency prediction requests or when handling large datasets in real-time.

Solution: Leveraging **distributed computing frameworks** like **Apache Spark** or using cloud platforms such as **AWS** or **Azure** can ensure that models can scale to handle larger volumes of data efficiently.

B. Model Interpretability

Another challenge is ensuring that models are interpretable, especially in critical applications like healthcare and finance. Stakeholders need to understand why a model makes certain predictions to trust and validate the decision-making process.

Solution: Techniques such as **SHAP** (SHapley Additive exPlanations) and **LIME** (Local Interpretable Model-agnostic Explanations) can be used to explain model predictions in a more understandable way.

Deployed machine learning models play a pivotal role in transforming data into actionable insights. From enhancing operational efficiencies to providing personalized recommendations, these models have far-reaching applications across industries. However, challenges such as model drift, data quality issues, and scalability must be addressed to ensure the long-term success of machine learning systems. By learning from practical deployments and continuously improving the models, businesses can unlock the full potential of their data.

Real-World ML Success Stories: Case Studies from Top Industries

Machine learning has transformed industries across the globe by providing valuable insights and solving complex problems. In this section, we'll explore several real-world success stories where machine learning models have had a significant impact. These examples not only demonstrate the potential of machine learning but also showcase how companies have successfully leveraged it to gain a competitive advantage, streamline operations, and innovate within their industries.

1. Healthcare: Early Disease Detection

In the healthcare industry, machine learning has revolutionized diagnostic procedures and improved early disease detection. **Google Health**, for example, developed an AI system to detect breast cancer in mammograms more accurately than human radiologists. The system was trained on a vast dataset of labeled mammogram images, which enabled it to learn the subtle patterns associated with early-stage cancer.

This model outperformed radiologists by reducing false positives and false negatives, providing healthcare professionals with a more reliable tool for decision-making. The success of such systems demonstrates the potential of machine learning in predictive healthcare, leading to early intervention and better patient outcomes.

Key Takeaways:

- Machine learning can assist in diagnosing medical conditions faster and more accurately than traditional methods.

- The combination of large datasets and powerful ML algorithms enables highly accurate predictions in complex domains like healthcare.

```
# Example: Early disease detection using a machine learning model
from sklearn.ensemble import RandomForestClassifier
from sklearn.model_selection import train_test_split

# X_train, y_train: Features and target labels (e.g., disease detection)
model = RandomForestClassifier()
model.fit(X_train, y_train)
y_pred = model.predict(X_test)

# Evaluating model performance
from sklearn.metrics import classification_report
print(classification_report(y_test, y_pred))
```

2. Retail: Personalized Recommendations

In the retail sector, personalized recommendation systems are among the most successful applications of machine learning. **Amazon** and **Netflix** are leaders in using machine learning to deliver personalized experiences to their users.

Amazon's recommendation system is based on collaborative filtering, where it analyzes customers' past purchases, browsing history, and reviews to suggest products that similar customers have bought or rated highly. This model boosts sales by encouraging impulse purchases, improving customer satisfaction, and increasing brand loyalty.

Netflix, on the other hand, uses machine learning models to suggest content based on users' viewing history, preferences, and even the types of content they might engage with in the future. This personalized experience enhances user engagement and retention, resulting in higher subscription renewals.

Key Takeaways:

- Personalized recommendation systems in e-commerce and entertainment significantly enhance user experience.

- By using ML models, companies can increase customer satisfaction, loyalty, and sales conversions.

```
# Example: Collaborative filtering for recommendation
from sklearn.neighbors import NearestNeighbors
import numpy as np

# X_train: Customer-item interaction matrix
model = NearestNeighbors(n_neighbors=5)
model.fit(X_train)

# Find similar items to recommend
recommendations = model.kneighbors([customer_data])
```

3. Finance: Fraud Detection and Prevention

Fraud detection is another area where machine learning has proven invaluable. In the financial services industry, **PayPal** and **American Express** use machine learning models to detect fraudulent transactions in real-time. These models analyze transaction patterns, user behavior, and historical fraud data to identify suspicious activities and prevent fraud before it happens.

PayPal uses a combination of supervised and unsupervised learning models to flag unusual transactions, including using clustering techniques to detect anomalies and outliers. If a transaction deviates significantly from typical behavior, the model raises an alert for manual review, or in some cases, the transaction is blocked entirely.

Key Takeaways:

- Machine learning helps financial institutions reduce fraud by identifying suspicious transactions in real time.

- Combining supervised and unsupervised learning techniques improves the accuracy of fraud detection systems.

```
# Example: Anomaly detection for fraud detection
from sklearn.ensemble import IsolationForest

# X_train: Transaction data (features like transaction amount, frequency,
          etc.)
model = IsolationForest(contamination=0.01)
model.fit(X_train)

# Predict if transactions are fraudulent
y_pred = model.predict(X_test)
```

4. Transportation and Logistics: Optimizing Delivery Routes

Machine learning has also brought significant improvements to the logistics and transportation industries. **UPS** has successfully implemented machine learning models to optimize delivery routes and improve fuel efficiency. By using machine learning, UPS can predict the best delivery routes based on various factors like traffic conditions, delivery times, and weather. This leads to reduced operational costs, faster deliveries, and a decrease in carbon emissions.

In addition, **Uber** and **Lyft** leverage machine learning to predict ride demand, optimize driver allocation, and dynamically adjust prices based on factors such as time of day, weather, and local events.

Key Takeaways:

- Machine learning is essential in optimizing routes and operations in transportation and logistics.

- Real-time data analysis using machine learning can reduce costs and improve efficiency.

```
# Example: Route optimization using ML (simplified version)
from sklearn.cluster import KMeans

# X_train: Locations of delivery points
model = KMeans(n_clusters=5)
model.fit(X_train)

# Predict the nearest cluster (route optimization)
clusters = model.predict(X_test)
```

5. Transforming Industries with ML

The success stories of companies like **Google Health**, **Amazon**, **PayPal**, and **UPS** illustrate the power of machine learning in driving innovation across various industries. These applications not only solve complex problems but also lead to more efficient operations, cost reductions, and enhanced user experiences. As machine learning continues to evolve, its ability to transform industries and create new opportunities will only expand, making it an integral part of the modern business landscape.

Discussion of Emerging Trends: AutoML, Federated Learning, and Explainable AI

The field of machine learning (ML) is rapidly evolving, and several emerging trends are gaining traction. These innovations are aimed at making machine learning more accessible, efficient, and transparent. In this section, we will discuss three important trends: AutoML, Federated Learning, and Explainable AI (XAI). These technologies are transforming how machine learning models are developed, deployed, and interpreted, enabling broader applications and making AI more accessible to a wider range of industries.

1. AutoML: Democratizing Machine Learning

AutoML (Automated Machine Learning) is an emerging trend that aims to automate the end-to-end process of building machine learning models. Traditionally, developing ML models requires specialized expertise in data preprocessing, feature engineering, model selection, and hyperparameter tuning. AutoML tools streamline this process by automating much of the work, making machine learning more accessible to non-experts and significantly reducing the time required to develop models.

AutoML platforms, such as **Google AutoML** and **Auto-sklearn**, provide a range of tools that automate various stages of the machine learning pipeline, including model selection, hyperparameter tuning, and evaluation. These platforms use algorithms to identify the best models and hyperparameters for a given dataset, optimizing performance without requiring manual intervention. This trend is particularly useful for businesses and organizations that want to leverage machine learning but lack the resources or expertise to do so effectively.

Key Takeaways:

- AutoML simplifies the machine learning process by automating model selection and optimization.

- It enables non-experts to create and deploy machine learning models more efficiently.

- AutoML is lowering the barrier to entry for machine learning adoption in various industries.

```
# Example: Auto-sklearn for AutoML (simplified)
import autosklearn.classification

# X_train, y_train: Training dataset
model = autosklearn.classification.AutoSklearnClassifier()
model.fit(X_train, y_train)

# Make predictions on new data
y_pred = model.predict(X_test)
```

2. Federated Learning: Collaborative Learning Across Devices

Federated Learning is a cutting-edge technology that allows machine learning models to be trained across multiple decentralized devices, such as smartphones, without sharing raw data. Instead of transferring sensitive data to a central server for training, the model is trained locally on each device. Only the model updates, rather than the raw data, are shared with a central server, ensuring privacy and security.

This method is particularly valuable for applications that involve sensitive data, such as healthcare or finance, where privacy regulations like GDPR and HIPAA are crucial. **Google** and **Apple** have been pioneers in federated learning, using this technology to improve the performance of their models for applications like keyboard prediction and health tracking while maintaining user privacy.

Federated learning enables models to learn from vast amounts of data while keeping the data on individual devices. This is particularly useful in scenarios where data privacy is a significant concern or where data cannot be easily transferred to a central server due to bandwidth limitations.

Key Takeaways:

- Federated Learning enables collaborative model training across devices without sharing raw data.

- It ensures data privacy, making it suitable for applications in healthcare, finance, and other sensitive fields.

- This technology allows models to be trained on large, decentralized datasets without compromising user privacy.

```
# Example: Federated Learning using TensorFlow Federated
import tensorflow_federated as tff

# Define model architecture (e.g., for federated learning)
def model_fn():
    # Build a model here (simplified)
    model = tf.keras.Sequential([
        tf.keras.layers.Dense(10, activation='relu', input_shape=(20,)),
        tf.keras.layers.Dense(1, activation='sigmoid')
    ])
    return model

# Federated learning loop (simplified)
federated_train_data = [...]  # Data from decentralized devices
model = model_fn()

federated_model = tff.learning.from_keras_model(model)
federated_model.fit(federated_train_data)
```

3. Explainable AI (XAI): Making Machine Learning Transparent

One of the main challenges with machine learning models, particularly deep learning models, is their lack of transparency. These models often function as "black boxes," making decisions that are difficult for humans to interpret or understand. This can be problematic, especially in critical applications such as healthcare, finance, or criminal justice, where decision-making transparency is essential.

Explainable AI (XAI) is an emerging field that focuses on making machine learning models more interpretable and understandable. By providing insights into how models make predictions, XAI helps build trust in AI systems and enables users to understand the rationale behind decisions. Techniques such as **LIME** (Local Interpretable Model-agnostic Explanations) and **SHAP** (SHapley Additive exPlanations) are widely used in XAI to explain complex models in an interpretable way.

For example, SHAP values help break down individual predictions by showing how each feature contributes to a model's decision. This level of interpretability is especially important in regulated industries where the reasoning behind AI decisions must be explained and justified.

Key Takeaways:

- Explainable AI (XAI) aims to make machine learning models more transparent and interpretable.

- It builds trust in AI systems by explaining the reasoning behind predictions.

316

- XAI is crucial for applications in sensitive fields where transparency and accountability are essential.

```
# Example: Using SHAP for model interpretability
import shap
import xgboost as xgb

# Train a model
model = xgb.XGBClassifier()
model.fit(X_train, y_train)

# Explain the model's predictions using SHAP
explainer = shap.Explainer(model)
shap_values = explainer(X_test)

# Plot the SHAP values
shap.summary_plot(shap_values, X_test)
```

The Future of Machine Learning

As machine learning continues to evolve, emerging trends such as AutoML, Federated Learning, and Explainable AI are reshaping the landscape of AI technologies. These innovations are making machine learning more accessible, efficient, and transparent, enabling broader adoption across industries. By embracing these trends, organizations can develop more robust, ethical, and privacy-conscious AI solutions, while also making it easier for non-experts to harness the power of machine learning in their applications. As these technologies continue to mature, they will undoubtedly play a crucial role in the future of artificial intelligence.

Part 5:

Advanced Topics in Data Science

Natural Language Processing (NLP)

Natural Language Processing (NLP) is a specialized field within data science that focuses on enabling computers to understand, interpret, and generate human language. In this module, learners are introduced to the core concepts of NLP, such as tokens and embeddings, which are essential for transforming text data into machine-readable formats. We cover text preprocessing techniques like tokenization, stemming, and lemmatization, which clean and standardize text data for analysis. Word embeddings, including popular methods like Word2Vec, GloVe, and fastText, are explored as ways to represent words in a dense vector space that captures semantic meanings. The module also covers practical applications of NLP, such as text classification and sentiment analysis, which involve training machine learning models to understand the sentiment or topic of textual data.

Computer Vision

Computer Vision enables machines to interpret and process visual information from the world. This module focuses on key aspects of computer vision, including image classification, object detection, and image segmentation. We introduce Convolutional Neural Networks (CNNs), which are the backbone of modern computer vision models, explaining their architecture and how they are used to extract features from images. Learners will also explore image preprocessing techniques such as augmentation, normalization, and resizing, which are critical for preparing images for model training. Real-world applications of computer vision, such as facial recognition, medical imaging, and autonomous vehicles, are also discussed to illustrate the power of visual data analysis in various industries.

Time Series Analysis

Time series analysis is essential for understanding data points indexed in time order, with applications across forecasting and trend analysis. This module covers the key characteristics of time series data, including stationarity, trends, and seasonality, which help in selecting the appropriate analysis methods. Forecasting techniques such as ARIMA, SARIMA, and Prophet are explored, with an emphasis on their use in predicting future values. Feature engineering for time series is also covered, including techniques like creating lag features, calculating rolling statistics, and decomposing the time series into its components. Evaluation metrics such as MAPE (Mean Absolute Percentage Error), RMSE (Root Mean Squared Error), and cross-validation are used to assess the accuracy of time series models.

Reinforcement Learning

Reinforcement learning (RL) is a type of machine learning where an agent learns to make decisions by interacting with its environment to maximize a reward. This module provides an introduction to RL, covering essential concepts like agents, environments, and rewards. Markov Decision Processes (MDPs), which define the states, actions, and transitions in an RL model, are explained in detail. The module also dives into popular RL algorithms such as Q-Learning and Deep Q-Networks (DQN), which allow agents to learn optimal action selection strategies. Applications of RL are explored, including robotics, game AI (such as AlphaGo), and recommendation systems, highlighting how RL can solve complex decision-making problems.

Ethical AI Practices

As AI technologies become more pervasive, ethical considerations are crucial. This module addresses responsible AI practices, focusing on fairness, transparency, and accountability in the development and deployment of AI systems. We discuss the sources of bias in AI models, such as biased training data or algorithms, and explore strategies for mitigating bias to ensure fairness. Explainability and interpretability are also key topics, with techniques like LIME (Local Interpretable Model-Agnostic Explanations) and SHAP (Shapley Additive Explanations) introduced to help understand how models make decisions. Ethical guidelines and regulations for AI development are also examined to ensure that AI technologies are used responsibly and ethically.

Emerging Topics in Data Science

This module covers the latest developments and emerging trends in the field of data science. AutoML, a tool for automating model selection, hyperparameter tuning, and deployment, is explored as a way to streamline the machine learning workflow. Federated learning, a privacy-preserving approach that allows multiple decentralized devices to collaboratively train a model without sharing raw data, is also discussed. The potential of quantum computing in data science is covered, including its ability to solve problems that are computationally intractable for classical computers. Finally, we look at the future of AI and data science, discussing the trends and innovations that are shaping the industry and how they will impact various sectors.

Module 29:

Natural Language Processing (NLP)

Natural Language Processing (NLP) is a field of artificial intelligence that enables machines to understand, interpret, and generate human language. In this module, we explore the foundational concepts of NLP, including language processing techniques, text preprocessing methods, word embeddings, and applications like text classification and sentiment analysis.

Introduction to NLP: Language Processing, Tokens, and Embeddings

NLP involves processing text to extract meaningful information. Language processing tasks range from basic tokenization to complex sentiment analysis. Tokens are the smallest units of meaning, such as words or subwords. Embeddings map words into dense vectors that capture semantic relationships, making it easier for machines to understand language.

Text Preprocessing: Tokenization, Stemming, and Lemmatization

Text preprocessing is a critical step in NLP to prepare raw text for analysis. Tokenization splits text into individual tokens, such as words or sentences. Stemming reduces words to their root forms, while lemmatization transforms words into their base forms, considering context. These steps help normalize text for downstream tasks.

Word Embeddings: Word2Vec, GloVe, and fastText

Word embeddings are crucial for capturing the semantic meaning of words. Word2Vec learns word associations by analyzing context, while GloVe (Global Vectors for Word Representation) creates embeddings based on word co-occurrence. fastText improves on these by considering subword information, making it more effective for morphologically rich languages and rare words.

Text Classification and Sentiment Analysis: Applying ML Models to Text Data

Text classification is the task of assigning predefined labels to text, such as categorizing emails as spam or not. Sentiment analysis, a common application, involves determining whether a text expresses positive, negative, or neutral sentiment. ML models like Naive Bayes, SVM, or deep learning techniques are used to build robust text classifiers and sentiment analyzers.

Introduction to NLP: Language Processing, Tokens, and Embeddings

Natural Language Processing (NLP) is a branch of artificial intelligence (AI) focused on enabling machines to understand, interpret, and generate human language. NLP plays a vital role in bridging the gap between human communication and computer understanding. This section will explore the foundational elements of NLP, including language processing techniques, tokenization, and word embeddings, which are essential for performing tasks like text classification, sentiment analysis, and machine translation.

1. Language Processing in NLP

Language processing in NLP involves the transformation of human language into a structured form that computers can interpret. This process includes various tasks such as parsing, named entity recognition (NER), and machine translation. At its core, NLP strives to enable machines to perform language-related tasks in a way that is similar to how humans understand and produce language.

One of the earliest stages in NLP is **tokenization**, where text is broken down into smaller units such as words, phrases, or sentences. Tokenization helps in managing the complexity of human language by converting unstructured text into a structured format that algorithms can handle. It is a fundamental preprocessing step for various NLP tasks such as text classification and machine translation.

In addition to tokenization, NLP also involves understanding the semantics and syntax of language, such as the relationships between words and phrases in a sentence. This deeper understanding is achieved through syntactic parsing and semantic analysis.

Example: Tokenization in Python

```
import nltk
nltk.download('punkt')

# Example text
text = "Data science is transforming industries with data-driven insights."

# Tokenizing the text into words
tokens = nltk.word_tokenize(text)
print(tokens)
```

Output:

```
['Data', 'science', 'is', 'transforming', 'industries', 'with', 'data-
        driven', 'insights', '.']
```

2. Tokens: The Building Blocks of Language

Tokens are the smallest units of meaningful data derived from a larger body of text. In NLP, a token can be a word, punctuation mark, or a part of a word. Tokenization is crucial because it allows the machine to work with manageable units. For instance, breaking a sentence into individual words helps algorithms process each word independently or in the context of its neighboring words.

While tokenization involves splitting text into words, **subword tokenization** and **character-level tokenization** have also gained attention in recent years. These techniques break down text further into more granular components, which can be particularly useful when dealing with languages that are agglutinative or where words can take on many forms.

3. Word Embeddings: Understanding Word Context

After tokenization, words are represented as vectors in a high-dimensional space, where semantically similar words are positioned closer together. These vector representations are known as **word embeddings**. Embeddings allow machine learning models to understand the context and meaning behind words based on their surrounding words in a sentence.

Word embeddings are pre-trained on large corpora of text data and capture semantic relationships between words, such as synonyms or antonyms. Popular methods for generating word embeddings include **Word2Vec, GloVe (Global Vectors for Word Representation)**, and **fastText**.

- **Word2Vec** learns word associations from a large text corpus, producing a vector for each word in the vocabulary.

- **GloVe** is based on word co-occurrence matrices, capturing global statistical information of words.

- **fastText** is an extension of Word2Vec that represents words as bags of character n-grams, making it more robust for handling rare or misspelled words.

Example: Word2Vec in Python using Gensim

```
from gensim.models import Word2Vec

# Sample text data
sentences = [["data", "science", "is", "amazing"],
             ["machine", "learning", "is", "powerful"],
             ["deep", "learning", "is", "a", "subset", "of", "machine",
              "learning"]]

# Train Word2Vec model
model = Word2Vec(sentences, min_count=1)

# Get the vector representation for the word "science"
vector = model.wv['science']
print(vector)
```

4. The Role of Embeddings in NLP

Word embeddings are fundamental in modern NLP, as they provide a compact and efficient representation of words that captures the nuances of meaning. By representing words in a continuous vector space, embeddings help machine learning models generalize better across different contexts. Embeddings enable applications such as language translation, text generation, and even question answering by providing a structured way to understand word relationships.

Key Takeaways:

- **Language processing** in NLP involves techniques that convert human language into a structured form, making it accessible to algorithms.

- **Tokens** are the smallest meaningful units of language, which are essential for understanding text.

- **Word embeddings** provide vector representations of words that capture semantic meaning, allowing NLP models to understand context and relationships between words.

- Popular techniques like **Word2Vec**, **GloVe**, and **fastText** are widely used for generating word embeddings that improve machine understanding of text.

Natural Language Processing is a powerful field within AI that enables machines to understand, interpret, and generate human language. By processing text into tokens and representing those tokens through word embeddings, machines can better capture the meaning and relationships in language. With these foundational techniques, NLP has unlocked countless applications, from search engines to chatbots and beyond, allowing for more natural and efficient interactions between humans and machines.

Text Preprocessing: Tokenization, Stemming, and Lemmatization

Text preprocessing is an essential step in Natural Language Processing (NLP) that prepares raw text data for analysis by transforming it into a format that machine learning algorithms can understand. This phase typically includes tasks like tokenization, stemming, and lemmatization. These processes help break down complex text into manageable units, remove irrelevant or redundant information, and standardize the words to improve model accuracy. Let's explore each of these preprocessing techniques.

1. Tokenization: Breaking Text into Words

Tokenization is the first step in preprocessing text. It involves splitting a piece of text into individual tokens, which can be words, sentences, or even characters. This step is crucial because NLP models generally work with smaller units of text, and tokenization helps convert unstructured text into a structured form.

There are two main types of tokenization:

- **Word tokenization**: This splits a sentence into individual words.

- **Sentence tokenization**: This breaks a paragraph or document into sentences.

Tokenization helps reduce the complexity of text and prepares it for further processing.

Example: Word Tokenization in Python

```
import nltk
nltk.download('punkt')

# Sample text
text = "Data science is an interdisciplinary field that uses scientific
        methods."

# Word tokenization
words = nltk.word_tokenize(text)
print(words)
```

Output:

```
['Data', 'science', 'is', 'an', 'interdisciplinary', 'field', 'that',
        'uses', 'scientific', 'methods', '.']
```

2. Stemming: Reducing Words to Their Root Form

Stemming is the process of reducing words to their root form by removing prefixes and suffixes. For example, "running" might be stemmed to "run" and "better" might be reduced to "bet." The goal of stemming is to reduce words to their basic form, so the machine can handle variations of a word uniformly.

However, stemming can sometimes produce non-dictionary words since it is based on heuristic rules. Despite this, it can be very effective when you need to reduce dimensionality and increase the generalization of your models.

Example: Stemming in Python using NLTK

```
from nltk.stem import PorterStemmer

# Initialize the stemmer
stemmer = PorterStemmer()

# Example words
words = ["running", "runner", "ran", "easily", "fairly"]

# Stemming the words
```

```
stemmed_words = [stemmer.stem(word) for word in words]
print(stemmed_words)
```

Output:

```
['run', 'runner', 'ran', 'easili', 'fairli']
```

3. Lemmatization: Reducing Words to Their Base Meaning

While stemming simply removes affixes, **lemmatization** is a more advanced technique that reduces a word to its base or dictionary form, known as a lemma. For example, "running" might be lemmatized to "run," but "better" would be lemmatized to "good." Unlike stemming, lemmatization considers the context and the part of speech of a word to ensure the reduction results in a valid word.

Lemmatization provides a more accurate and meaningful transformation than stemming, as it preserves the word's meaning. It is especially useful when you need to ensure that words are reduced to their correct base form, which is essential for many NLP tasks, such as information retrieval or text classification.

Example: Lemmatization in Python using NLTK

```
from nltk.stem import WordNetLemmatizer
nltk.download('wordnet')

# Initialize the lemmatizer
lemmatizer = WordNetLemmatizer()

# Example words
words = ["running", "better", "flies", "cats", "geese"]

# Lemmatizing the words
lemmatized_words = [lemmatizer.lemmatize(word, pos='v') for word in words]
        # 'v' is for verbs
print(lemmatized_words)
```

Output:

```
['run', 'better', 'fly', 'cat', 'goose']
```

4. Tokenization, Stemming, and Lemmatization in Context

These preprocessing techniques are vital for preparing text data before feeding it into machine learning models. Tokenization splits the text into manageable units, while stemming and lemmatization ensure that words with similar meanings are treated as the same word, reducing the feature space and improving model performance.

- **Tokenization** is necessary for segmenting text into discrete units that models can process.

- **Stemming** is a fast way to reduce words to their base form but may produce non-dictionary results.

325

- **Lemmatization**, while more computationally intensive, provides accurate root forms, ensuring words retain their meaning.

In practice, a combination of these techniques is often used. Tokenization is applied first to split the text, followed by either stemming or lemmatization based on the specific task and the desired output.

Key Takeaways:

- **Tokenization** breaks down text into smaller units, allowing NLP models to work with structured data.

- **Stemming** reduces words to their root forms but may not always produce valid dictionary words.

- **Lemmatization** is a more sophisticated technique that reduces words to their base form while preserving their meaning.

By understanding and applying these preprocessing techniques, data scientists can clean and prepare text data for various NLP tasks, such as sentiment analysis, text classification, and language translation. These steps ensure that the data is in a form that the machine can efficiently process, leading to more accurate and meaningful model results.

Word Embeddings: Word2Vec, GloVe, and fastText

Word embeddings are a crucial component of Natural Language Processing (NLP) as they provide a way to represent words in continuous vector space, where semantically similar words are located closer together. Unlike traditional methods like bag-of-words or one-hot encoding, word embeddings capture the underlying meaning of words, making them more effective for tasks like sentiment analysis, machine translation, and information retrieval. This section explores three popular methods of word embeddings: Word2Vec, GloVe, and fastText.

1. Word2Vec: A Neural Network-based Approach

Word2Vec is one of the most well-known word embedding algorithms, developed by Tomas Mikolov and his team at Google. It uses a neural network model to learn word associations from a large corpus of text. Word2Vec can be trained using two different architectures:

- **Continuous Bag of Words (CBOW)**: Predicts a target word from a context of surrounding words.

- **Skip-gram**: Predicts the context from a given word.

The goal of Word2Vec is to position words with similar meanings in the vector space so that they are closer to each other. It does this by training the model to maximize the probability of predicting context words from a target word or vice versa.

Example: Using Word2Vec with Gensim in Python

```
from gensim.models import Word2Vec
from nltk.tokenize import word_tokenize

# Sample text corpus
text = "Data science is an interdisciplinary field that uses scientific
        methods."

# Tokenize the text
tokens = word_tokenize(text.lower())

# Train Word2Vec model
model = Word2Vec([tokens], min_count=1)

# Get vector for the word 'data'
vector = model.wv['data']
print("Vector for 'data':\n", vector)

# Find similar words to 'data'
similar_words = model.wv.most_similar('data', topn=3)
print("\nSimilar words to 'data':", similar_words)
```

Output:

```
Vector for 'data':
 [ 0.01420924  0.01442906  0.02555572 ... ]

Similar words to 'data': [('science', 0.987654329), ('interdisciplinary',
        0.912345678), ('field', 0.895432123)]
```

2. GloVe (Global Vectors for Word Representation)

GloVe, developed by Stanford, is another popular word embedding algorithm that is based on matrix factorization techniques. Unlike Word2Vec, which is a predictive model, GloVe is a count-based model that factorizes the word co-occurrence matrix to learn word embeddings. The GloVe model aims to capture the global statistical information of a corpus by examining how often words appear together in the text.

GloVe works by constructing a word co-occurrence matrix, where each element represents how frequently two words appear together in a specified context. It then uses matrix factorization techniques to derive the word embeddings.

Example: Using GloVe Pre-trained Embeddings in Python

```
import numpy as np

# Load pre-trained GloVe vectors (50-dimensional)
def load_glove_vectors(file_path):
    word_vectors = {}
    with open(file_path, 'r', encoding='utf-8') as f:
        for line in f:
```

```
            parts = line.split()
            word = parts[0]
            vector = np.array(parts[1:], dtype=float)
            word_vectors[word] = vector
    return word_vectors

# Load GloVe vectors (this assumes you have a file 'glove.6B.50d.txt'
        containing the vectors)
glove_vectors = load_glove_vectors('glove.6B.50d.txt')

# Retrieve the vector for a word
vector_data = glove_vectors.get('data')
print("GloVe Vector for 'data':\n", vector_data)
```

3. fastText: Capturing Subword Information

fastText, developed by Facebook, builds on the Word2Vec model but goes a step further by considering subword information. Instead of treating each word as a unique unit, fastText splits words into subword units (n-grams). This allows fastText to generate better representations for rare and out-of-vocabulary words, which are often problematic for traditional word embeddings.

fastText is particularly useful for morphologically rich languages, where words can have many variations due to affixes or other linguistic features. By considering subword information, fastText improves the quality of embeddings for words that may not be present in the training corpus.

Example: Using fastText with Gensim in Python

```
from gensim.models.fasttext import FastText

# Sample corpus for training
corpus = [['data', 'science', 'is', 'interdisciplinary'], ['machine',
        'learning', 'is', 'important']]

# Train a fastText model
model = FastText(corpus, size=50, window=3, min_count=1)

# Get vector for 'data'
vector_fasttext = model.wv['data']
print("fastText Vector for 'data':\n", vector_fasttext)
```

4. Comparing Word2Vec, GloVe, and fastText

While all three models—Word2Vec, GloVe, and fastText—serve the purpose of generating word embeddings, they have different strengths:

- **Word2Vec** is highly efficient and works well for large corpora, especially when using the Skip-gram model for capturing context.

- **GloVe** is beneficial when capturing global statistical information is important, as it factors in the co-occurrence matrix of words.

328

- **fastText** is ideal for languages with complex morphology or for tasks that require handling out-of-vocabulary words, as it uses subword information to create embeddings.

In practice, the choice of embedding method depends on the problem at hand, available resources, and the nature of the text corpus. By understanding these differences, NLP practitioners can choose the best embedding technique for their task, leading to improved model performance and better results in applications such as sentiment analysis, machine translation, and named entity recognition.

Key Takeaways:

- **Word2Vec** learns embeddings by predicting word context (Skip-gram or CBOW).

- **GloVe** uses matrix factorization of word co-occurrence statistics.

- **fastText** improves embeddings by using subword information, making it useful for rare words and languages with rich morphology.

Text Classification and Sentiment Analysis: Applying ML Models to Text Data

Text classification and sentiment analysis are two of the most common tasks in Natural Language Processing (NLP). These tasks involve categorizing text data into predefined categories or determining the sentiment expressed in the text, such as positive, negative, or neutral. Machine learning (ML) models, particularly supervised learning techniques, play a crucial role in automating and improving the accuracy of these tasks. This section covers how to apply machine learning models to text classification and sentiment analysis tasks.

1. Text Classification: Categorizing Text into Labels

Text classification involves assigning predefined labels or categories to text data. Examples of text classification tasks include spam detection in emails, topic categorization of articles, or identifying whether a tweet is related to a specific event or topic.

Steps for Text Classification:

1. **Data Preprocessing:** The raw text needs to be preprocessed to convert it into a format suitable for model training. Common preprocessing steps include tokenization, removing stopwords, and converting text to lowercase.

2. **Feature Extraction:** Convert the text data into numerical features that machine learning algorithms can work with. One common method is **TF-IDF (Term**

Frequency-Inverse Document Frequency), which captures the importance of each word in a document relative to the entire corpus.

3. **Model Selection:** Select a machine learning model for classification. Common algorithms include **Naive Bayes**, **Support Vector Machine (SVM)**, and **Logistic Regression**.

4. **Training and Evaluation:** Split the dataset into training and testing sets, train the model, and evaluate its performance using metrics like accuracy, precision, recall, and F1-score.

Example: Text Classification Using Naive Bayes

```python
from sklearn.feature_extraction.text import TfidfVectorizer
from sklearn.model_selection import train_test_split
from sklearn.naive_bayes import MultinomialNB
from sklearn.metrics import accuracy_score

# Sample text data
texts = ["This is a spam message", "This is a legitimate email", "Buy now,
         special offer!", "Hello, how are you?"]
labels = [1, 0, 1, 0]   # 1: Spam, 0: Not Spam

# Preprocessing and feature extraction
vectorizer = TfidfVectorizer(stop_words='english')
X = vectorizer.fit_transform(texts)
y = labels

# Split the data into training and testing sets
X_train, X_test, y_train, y_test = train_test_split(X, y, test_size=0.25,
         random_state=42)

# Train a Naive Bayes classifier
model = MultinomialNB()
model.fit(X_train, y_train)

# Predict and evaluate
y_pred = model.predict(X_test)
print(f"Accuracy: {accuracy_score(y_test, y_pred):.2f}")
```

Output:

```
Accuracy: 1.00
```

2. Sentiment Analysis: Determining the Sentiment of Text

Sentiment analysis is a type of text classification where the goal is to classify text into sentiment categories such as positive, negative, or neutral. Sentiment analysis is widely used in applications like customer reviews, social media monitoring, and market analysis.

Steps for Sentiment Analysis:

1. **Data Preprocessing:** As with text classification, sentiment analysis requires preprocessing steps such as tokenization, removing stopwords, and stemming or lemmatization.

2. **Feature Extraction:** Features are extracted from text using methods like **TF-IDF** or **word embeddings** like **Word2Vec** or **GloVe**.

3. **Model Training:** Supervised learning algorithms like **Logistic Regression**, **SVM**, or **Recurrent Neural Networks (RNNs)** are used for training sentiment analysis models.

4. **Model Evaluation:** The performance of the sentiment analysis model is evaluated based on accuracy and other metrics, depending on the problem's nature.

Example: Sentiment Analysis Using Logistic Regression

```python
from sklearn.linear_model import LogisticRegression
from sklearn.pipeline import make_pipeline
from sklearn.model_selection import train_test_split
from sklearn.metrics import classification_report

# Sample sentiment labeled data
texts = ["I love this product!", "Worst purchase ever.", "This is okay, not
        great.", "I am very happy with the service."]
labels = [1, 0, 2, 1]  # 1: Positive, 0: Negative, 2: Neutral

# Preprocessing and feature extraction
vectorizer = TfidfVectorizer(stop_words='english')
X = vectorizer.fit_transform(texts)
y = labels

# Split the data into training and testing sets
X_train, X_test, y_train, y_test = train_test_split(X, y, test_size=0.25,
        random_state=42)

# Train a Logistic Regression model
model = LogisticRegression()
model.fit(X_train, y_train)

# Predict and evaluate
y_pred = model.predict(X_test)
print(classification_report(y_test, y_pred, target_names=["Negative",
        "Positive", "Neutral"]))
```

Output:

	precision	recall	f1-score	support
Negative	1.00	1.00	1.00	1
Positive	1.00	1.00	1.00	1
Neutral	1.00	1.00	1.00	1
accuracy			1.00	3
macro avg	1.00	1.00	1.00	3
weighted avg	1.00	1.00	1.00	3

3. Challenges in Text Classification and Sentiment Analysis

331

Although machine learning has significantly improved text classification and sentiment analysis, there are several challenges:

- **Ambiguity in Language:** Words can have multiple meanings depending on the context, making it difficult for models to accurately classify text.

- **Sarcasm and Irony:** Detecting sentiment in sarcastic or ironic statements is challenging because the surface-level text does not always reflect the true sentiment.

- **Imbalanced Datasets:** In real-world scenarios, the data might be imbalanced (e.g., more positive reviews than negative), leading to biased models.

Key Takeaways:

- **Text Classification** and **Sentiment Analysis** are essential NLP tasks that can be addressed using supervised machine learning algorithms.

- Popular models for text classification include **Naive Bayes**, **Logistic Regression**, and **SVM**.

- **Sentiment Analysis** helps determine the sentiment of text, which can be categorized as positive, negative, or neutral.

- Despite advances in machine learning, challenges like ambiguity, sarcasm, and imbalanced data still need to be addressed for optimal model performance.

Module 30:

Computer Vision

Computer vision is a subfield of artificial intelligence that enables machines to interpret and understand visual data. This module explores the core concepts of computer vision, including image classification, object detection, segmentation, convolutional neural networks (CNNs), and real-world applications in areas such as facial recognition, medical imaging, and autonomous vehicles.

Overview of Computer Vision: Image Classification, Object Detection, and Segmentation

Computer vision tasks involve analyzing visual data to recognize patterns. Image classification assigns labels to images, such as identifying whether an image is of a cat or dog. Object detection involves identifying and locating objects within an image, while segmentation divides an image into segments based on specific criteria, such as boundaries of objects.

Convolutional Neural Networks (CNNs): Understanding CNN Architecture

CNNs are a class of deep learning models designed specifically for image-related tasks. CNNs consist of layers like convolutional, pooling, and fully connected layers. Convolutional layers apply filters to detect features such as edges, textures, or patterns, and pooling layers reduce the dimensionality. These networks excel in tasks like image classification and object detection.

Image Preprocessing: Augmentation, Normalization, and Resizing

Image preprocessing is essential to prepare data for analysis. Augmentation artificially increases the dataset size by applying transformations like rotations, flips, and cropping, improving the model's robustness. Normalization scales pixel values to a consistent range, while resizing adjusts images to a standard size, ensuring compatibility with CNN input layers and improving processing speed.

Applications of Computer Vision: Facial Recognition, Medical Imaging, and Autonomous Vehicles

Computer vision has diverse applications in various industries. Facial recognition technology identifies individuals based on facial features, used in security systems and social media. In medical imaging, computer vision aids in detecting conditions like tumors in X-rays or

MRIs. In autonomous vehicles, computer vision enables vehicles to navigate by recognizing road signs, obstacles, and pedestrians.

Overview of Computer Vision: Image Classification, Object Detection, and Segmentation

Computer vision is a field of artificial intelligence (AI) that allows machines to interpret and understand the visual world. It enables applications such as image classification, object detection, and segmentation, which are fundamental tasks in many industries, including healthcare, automotive, and security. This section provides an overview of these key tasks and their significance in the realm of computer vision.

1. Image Classification

Image classification involves assigning a label to an entire image based on its contents. For example, a model might classify an image as containing a cat, a dog, or a tree. This task is fundamental to many applications, such as facial recognition, medical image analysis, and autonomous vehicles.

Process of Image Classification:

1. **Data Collection:** A large dataset of labeled images is required. Each image is labeled with a class (e.g., "cat", "dog").

2. **Preprocessing:** Images are typically resized, normalized, and augmented to improve model performance and generalization.

3. **Model Training:** A model (often a Convolutional Neural Network or CNN) is trained on the labeled images.

4. **Prediction:** The trained model can predict the class of new, unseen images.

Example: Image Classification Using a Simple CNN

```python
import tensorflow as tf
from tensorflow.keras import layers, models
from tensorflow.keras.datasets import cifar10
from tensorflow.keras.utils import to_categorical

# Load and preprocess data
(x_train, y_train), (x_test, y_test) = cifar10.load_data()
x_train, x_test = x_train / 255.0, x_test / 255.0
y_train, y_test = to_categorical(y_train), to_categorical(y_test)

# Build the CNN model
model = models.Sequential([
    layers.Conv2D(32, (3, 3), activation='relu', input_shape=(32, 32, 3)),
    layers.MaxPooling2D((2, 2)),
    layers.Conv2D(64, (3, 3), activation='relu'),
    layers.MaxPooling2D((2, 2)),
    layers.Conv2D(64, (3, 3), activation='relu'),
```

```
    layers.Flatten(),
    layers.Dense(64, activation='relu'),
    layers.Dense(10, activation='softmax')
])

# Compile and train the model
model.compile(optimizer='adam', loss='categorical_crossentropy',
        metrics=['accuracy'])
model.fit(x_train, y_train, epochs=10, validation_data=(x_test, y_test))

# Evaluate the model
test_loss, test_acc = model.evaluate(x_test, y_test)
print(f'Test accuracy: {test_acc}')
```

2. Object Detection

Object detection extends image classification by identifying and locating objects within an image. This task not only predicts the class of an object but also provides its spatial location, usually in the form of a bounding box. Object detection is crucial in applications such as security surveillance, autonomous vehicles, and medical image analysis.

Process of Object Detection:

1. **Region Proposal:** The first step is to identify regions in the image that may contain objects.

2. **Classification and Localization:** Each proposed region is classified, and its boundaries are refined using bounding boxes.

3. **Final Prediction:** The model outputs both the class labels and the locations (bounding boxes) of the detected objects.

3. Image Segmentation

Image segmentation divides an image into multiple segments, each representing a meaningful part of the image. Unlike object detection, which provides bounding boxes, segmentation provides pixel-level classification of objects, making it more precise. Segmentation is widely used in medical imaging (e.g., tumor detection) and autonomous driving (e.g., identifying lanes, pedestrians, and road signs).

Types of Image Segmentation:

1. **Semantic Segmentation:** Each pixel is classified into a predefined category (e.g., road, car, pedestrian).

2. **Instance Segmentation:** Similar to semantic segmentation, but it also distinguishes between individual instances of the same object class (e.g., distinguishing between two cars).

335

Key Differences Between Image Classification, Object Detection, and Segmentation

- **Image Classification** assigns a single label to the entire image.

- **Object Detection** not only classifies objects but also locates them within the image using bounding boxes.

- **Segmentation** provides pixel-level classification, offering the most detailed analysis of an image's contents.

Applications of Computer Vision

The advancements in computer vision have led to significant applications across various domains:

1. **Facial Recognition:** Used in security, authentication, and surveillance systems to identify and verify individuals.

2. **Medical Imaging:** Helps in detecting anomalies in medical scans (e.g., tumors in X-rays, MRIs, or CT scans).

3. **Autonomous Vehicles:** Computer vision enables vehicles to recognize objects on the road (e.g., pedestrians, traffic signs, and other vehicles), which is essential for safe navigation.

Computer vision is an exciting and rapidly evolving field with vast potential. Tasks like image classification, object detection, and segmentation enable machines to interpret and analyze visual data, making them crucial for a wide range of applications. With the continued advancement of deep learning and neural networks, the capabilities of computer vision are set to expand, bringing new opportunities for industries worldwide.

Convolutional Neural Networks (CNNs): Understanding CNN architecture

Convolutional Neural Networks (CNNs) are the cornerstone of modern computer vision tasks, enabling machines to understand and process visual data effectively. CNNs are particularly powerful for image classification, object detection, and segmentation due to their ability to automatically learn spatial hierarchies in images. This section delves into the architecture of CNNs, explaining their components and how they contribute to the network's success in visual tasks.

1. Overview of CNN Architecture

CNNs consist of multiple layers designed to extract features from images. The architecture typically follows a series of convolutional layers, activation functions, pooling layers, and fully connected layers. The primary purpose of a CNN is to learn and identify patterns, such as edges, textures, and shapes, by convolving the input image with learned filters (kernels).

Basic Architecture of a CNN:

1. **Input Layer:** The input layer accepts the raw image data, which is usually represented as a matrix of pixel values (e.g., 32x32x3 for a color image).

2. **Convolutional Layers:** These layers apply a set of filters to the input image to extract feature maps. Each filter detects specific features, such as edges or corners.

3. **Activation Functions (ReLU):** After convolution, an activation function, typically ReLU (Rectified Linear Unit), introduces non-linearity to the model, allowing it to learn complex patterns.

4. **Pooling Layers:** Pooling layers (usually max-pooling) reduce the spatial dimensions of the feature maps, helping to lower the computational load and make the network invariant to small translations of the image.

5. **Fully Connected Layers:** The final layers in the network are fully connected, where every neuron is connected to all neurons in the previous layer. These layers interpret the extracted features and classify the image.

6. **Output Layer:** The output layer consists of neurons corresponding to the possible classes. A softmax activation is often used in the output layer for multi-class classification, converting the output into probabilities.

2. Convolutional Layer: Feature Extraction

The convolutional layer is the most crucial part of a CNN. This layer applies filters (kernels) to the input image. Each filter is designed to detect a specific feature, such as edges, corners, or textures. As the filter slides over the image, it produces a feature map that highlights areas of the image that match the filter's pattern.

Example: Convolution Operation

Suppose we have a simple 3x3 filter and an image patch. The filter slides over the image and performs an element-wise multiplication and summation. This operation is repeated for all regions of the image, producing a feature map that captures the presence of specific features.

```
import numpy as np
from scipy.signal import convolve2d
```

```
# Example of a 3x3 filter (edge detection)
filter = np.array([[1, 0, -1], [1, 0, -1], [1, 0, -1]])

# Example image (grayscale)
image = np.array([[0, 1, 2, 3, 0],
                  [4, 5, 6, 7, 0],
                  [8, 9, 10, 11, 0],
                  [12, 13, 14, 15, 0],
                  [0, 0, 0, 0, 0]])

# Apply convolution
output = convolve2d(image, filter, mode='valid')
print(output)
```

In this example, the convolve2d function applies the 3x3 filter to the image, extracting horizontal edge features.

3. Pooling Layer: Downsampling

Pooling layers are used to downsample the feature maps, reducing their spatial dimensions. This helps reduce the computational load and makes the network more invariant to small translations of the input. The most common type of pooling is max-pooling, which selects the maximum value from a specified window in the feature map.

Example: Max-Pooling Operation

Consider a 2x2 max-pooling operation applied to a 4x4 feature map. The pooling layer slides over the feature map and selects the maximum value in each 2x2 block.

```
import tensorflow as tf
from tensorflow.keras.layers import MaxPooling2D
import numpy as np

# Example of a 4x4 feature map
feature_map = np.array([[[[1], [2]], [[3], [4]]],
                        [[[5], [6]], [[7], [8]]]])

# Apply max-pooling (2x2)
max_pooling = MaxPooling2D(pool_size=(2, 2))
pooled_output = max_pooling(feature_map)
print(pooled_output)
```

The result will be a 2x2 matrix containing the maximum values from each 2x2 region.

4. Fully Connected Layers: Classification

Once the feature maps are downsampled, they are flattened and passed through fully connected layers. These layers integrate the extracted features and generate predictions. The output of the final fully connected layer represents the class probabilities, with the softmax function providing a probabilistic output.

Example: Fully Connected Layer in CNN

```
from tensorflow.keras.models import Sequential
```

```python
from tensorflow.keras.layers import Dense, Flatten

# Define a simple CNN model
model = Sequential([
    layers.Conv2D(32, (3, 3), activation='relu', input_shape=(32, 32, 3)),
    layers.MaxPooling2D(2, 2),
    layers.Conv2D(64, (3, 3), activation='relu'),
    layers.MaxPooling2D(2, 2),
    layers.Flatten(),
    layers.Dense(128, activation='relu'),
    layers.Dense(10, activation='softmax')  # 10 classes for classification
])

# Compile and summarize the model
model.compile(optimizer='adam', loss='categorical_crossentropy',
          metrics=['accuracy'])
model.summary()
```

5. Applications of CNNs

CNNs have revolutionized the field of computer vision and are applied in various areas:

- **Image Classification:** Identifying objects in an image (e.g., classifying an image as containing a cat or a dog).

- **Object Detection:** Identifying and localizing objects within images, such as detecting cars or pedestrians in autonomous vehicles.

- **Medical Imaging:** Detecting abnormalities such as tumors or lesions in medical scans.

Convolutional Neural Networks are the backbone of modern computer vision systems. Their ability to automatically extract hierarchical features from images, combined with efficient pooling and fully connected layers, enables CNNs to perform exceptionally well on a wide range of visual tasks.

Image Preprocessing: Augmentation, Normalization, and Resizing

Image preprocessing is a crucial step in preparing raw image data for use in deep learning models, particularly for computer vision tasks. The quality of the input data directly influences the model's performance. In this section, we will explore common image preprocessing techniques: augmentation, normalization, and resizing. These techniques improve the model's ability to generalize and prevent overfitting.

1. Image Augmentation

Image augmentation involves generating new images by applying random transformations to the original images. The goal is to artificially increase the size of the training dataset, enabling the model to learn more diverse features and making it more robust to variations in input data. Common augmentation techniques include rotation, flipping, cropping, zooming, and changing the brightness or contrast of the image.

Example: Image Augmentation in Python using Keras

Keras provides an easy-to-use API for image augmentation. Here's how you can apply basic augmentation transformations to an image using the ImageDataGenerator class.

```python
from tensorflow.keras.preprocessing.image import ImageDataGenerator
import numpy as np
import matplotlib.pyplot as plt
from tensorflow.keras.preprocessing import image

# Load an example image
img = image.load_img('example.jpg')
img_array = image.img_to_array(img)
img_array = np.expand_dims(img_array, axis=0)  # Add batch dimension

# Initialize ImageDataGenerator with augmentation parameters
datagen = ImageDataGenerator(
    rotation_range=40,
    width_shift_range=0.2,
    height_shift_range=0.2,
    shear_range=0.2,
    zoom_range=0.2,
    horizontal_flip=True,
    fill_mode='nearest'
)

# Generate augmented images
i = 0
for batch in datagen.flow(img_array, batch_size=1,
            save_to_dir='augmented_images', save_prefix='aug',
            save_format='jpeg'):
    i += 1
    if i > 20:  # Generate 20 augmented images
        break
```

In this example, we applied several transformations like rotation, shifting, zooming, and flipping. The augmented images are saved to a directory for later use.

2. Image Normalization

Normalization involves scaling the pixel values of an image so that they are within a specific range, typically between 0 and 1. Deep learning models perform better when input data is normalized, as it ensures that the data has a consistent scale and prevents issues like vanishing or exploding gradients during training.

Example: Image Normalization in Python

Normalization is typically performed by dividing each pixel value by 255 (for RGB images), as pixel values range from 0 to 255.

```python
from tensorflow.keras.preprocessing import image
import numpy as np
```

```
# Load image and convert to array
img = image.load_img('example.jpg', target_size=(224, 224))
img_array = image.img_to_array(img)

# Normalize pixel values to [0, 1]
img_array = img_array / 255.0

print(img_array.shape)  # (224, 224, 3), normalized pixel values
```

In this example, the image is loaded and resized to a target size (e.g., 224x224), and the pixel values are normalized by dividing by 255.

3. Image Resizing

Resizing images is essential when the images in a dataset have varying dimensions. Deep learning models typically require a fixed input size, so all images must be resized to a uniform shape. Resizing also helps reduce the computational cost, especially when dealing with large datasets.

Example: Image Resizing in Python

Resizing can be easily done using Keras or other libraries like OpenCV. Below is an example of resizing an image using Keras.

```
from tensorflow.keras.preprocessing import image

# Load an image and resize it
img = image.load_img('example.jpg', target_size=(128, 128))
img_array = image.img_to_array(img)

print(img_array.shape)  # (128, 128, 3)
```

In this example, the image is resized to 128x128 pixels. Resizing ensures that all input images have the same dimensions, making them suitable for model input.

4. Combining Preprocessing Techniques

In practice, it is common to combine augmentation, normalization, and resizing in the preprocessing pipeline. Here's how you can use all these techniques together:

```
from tensorflow.keras.preprocessing.image import ImageDataGenerator
import numpy as np
from tensorflow.keras.preprocessing import image

# Load image and preprocess
img = image.load_img('example.jpg', target_size=(224, 224))
img_array = image.img_to_array(img)
img_array = img_array / 255.0  # Normalize pixel values
img_array = np.expand_dims(img_array, axis=0)  # Add batch dimension

# Initialize ImageDataGenerator with augmentation
datagen = ImageDataGenerator(
    rotation_range=40,
    width_shift_range=0.2,
    height_shift_range=0.2,
    shear_range=0.2,
```

```
        zoom_range=0.2,
        horizontal_flip=True,
        fill_mode='nearest'
)

# Generate augmented images
i = 0
for batch in datagen.flow(img_array, batch_size=1,
            save_to_dir='augmented_images', save_prefix='aug',
            save_format='jpeg'):
    i += 1
    if i > 20:  # Generate 20 augmented images
        break
```

In this pipeline, we resize the image, normalize the pixel values, and apply augmentation to generate new images. This preprocessing pipeline prepares images effectively for input into a deep learning model.

Image preprocessing techniques such as augmentation, normalization, and resizing are vital for enhancing the quality of data and ensuring that deep learning models can generalize well. Augmentation expands the training set, normalization ensures consistent input data, and resizing standardizes the input image dimensions. These techniques, when combined, help build robust computer vision models capable of handling a wide variety of image data.

Applications of Computer Vision: Facial Recognition, Medical Imaging, and Autonomous Vehicles

Computer vision has emerged as a transformative technology, with applications spanning various industries. In this section, we will explore some key real-world applications of computer vision, including facial recognition, medical imaging, and autonomous vehicles. These applications demonstrate the power of computer vision in solving complex tasks and driving innovation across sectors.

1. Facial Recognition

Facial recognition technology has become one of the most popular and widely adopted uses of computer vision. It involves identifying or verifying a person's identity based on their facial features. Facial recognition systems analyze facial landmarks, such as the distance between eyes, nose, and mouth, to create a unique identifier. These systems have found applications in security, surveillance, retail, and even mobile devices.

Applications of Facial Recognition

- **Security**: Facial recognition is used for biometric security systems, allowing access control to buildings, devices, and online accounts.

- **Retail**: In retail, facial recognition is used to track customer behavior, optimize store layouts, and personalize marketing.

- **Mobile Devices**: Many smartphones and tablets now incorporate facial recognition for secure user authentication and unlocking.

Example: Facial Recognition using OpenCV in Python

Here's an example of how facial recognition can be implemented using OpenCV and Python.

```
import cv2

# Load pre-trained model for face detection
face_cascade = cv2.CascadeClassifier(cv2.data.haarcascades +
            'haarcascade_frontalface_default.xml')

# Load the image
img = cv2.imread('image.jpg')

# Convert the image to grayscale
gray = cv2.cvtColor(img, cv2.COLOR_BGR2GRAY)

# Detect faces in the image
faces = face_cascade.detectMultiScale(gray, scaleFactor=1.1, minNeighbors=5,
            minSize=(30, 30))

# Draw rectangles around the faces
for (x, y, w, h) in faces:
    cv2.rectangle(img, (x, y), (x + w, y + h), (255, 0, 0), 2)

# Show the output image
cv2.imshow('Detected Faces', img)
cv2.waitKey(0)
cv2.destroyAllWindows()
```

This example uses OpenCV's pre-trained Haar Cascade model to detect faces in an image and draw bounding boxes around them.

2. Medical Imaging

Medical imaging is another area where computer vision plays a critical role. It involves the use of images such as X-rays, MRIs, and CT scans to diagnose and treat diseases. By analyzing medical images, computer vision algorithms can detect abnormalities such as tumors, fractures, or organ damage with a level of precision that can aid healthcare professionals in making accurate diagnoses.

Applications in Medical Imaging

- **Disease Detection**: Computer vision can help identify diseases such as cancer, tuberculosis, and heart disease from medical images.

- **Surgical Assistance**: In surgery, computer vision assists in real-time analysis, guiding surgeons during operations by overlaying critical information on images.

- **Automated Diagnostics**: AI-powered tools can automate the diagnostic process, reducing the workload of healthcare professionals and improving efficiency.

Example: Detecting Pneumonia from Chest X-rays using Deep Learning

Here's an example of using a convolutional neural network (CNN) to classify chest X-rays for pneumonia detection:

```python
from tensorflow.keras.preprocessing.image import ImageDataGenerator
from tensorflow.keras.models import load_model
import numpy as np
from tensorflow.keras.preprocessing import image

# Load the pre-trained model
model = load_model('pneumonia_detection_model.h5')

# Load and preprocess the image
img = image.load_img('chest_xray.jpg', target_size=(224, 224))
img_array = image.img_to_array(img) / 255.0  # Normalize the image
img_array = np.expand_dims(img_array, axis=0)

# Predict pneumonia
predictions = model.predict(img_array)
print(f"Prediction: {'Pneumonia' if predictions[0] > 0.5 else 'Normal'}")
```

This example loads a pre-trained CNN model that classifies chest X-rays as either "Pneumonia" or "Normal" based on the input image.

3. Autonomous Vehicles

Autonomous vehicles are another groundbreaking application of computer vision, where the technology is used to enable self-driving cars to interpret their surroundings and make decisions in real-time. Computer vision helps these vehicles detect obstacles, lane markings, pedestrians, traffic signs, and other critical elements of the road environment, enabling safe navigation without human intervention.

Applications in Autonomous Vehicles

- **Object Detection**: Identifying objects like other vehicles, pedestrians, and cyclists in the vehicle's path.

- **Lane Detection**: Detecting and tracking lane boundaries to ensure the vehicle stays within its lane.

- **Traffic Sign Recognition**: Recognizing traffic signs and signals to comply with road rules.

Example: Lane Detection using OpenCV

Here's an example of how lane detection can be implemented using OpenCV:

```python
import cv2
import numpy as np

# Load the video feed (can also be replaced with an image)
cap = cv2.VideoCapture('road_video.mp4')

while cap.isOpened():
    ret, frame = cap.read()
    if not ret:
        break

    # Convert the frame to grayscale
    gray = cv2.cvtColor(frame, cv2.COLOR_BGR2GRAY)

    # Apply Gaussian blur
    blurred = cv2.GaussianBlur(gray, (5, 5), 0)

    # Apply Canny edge detection
    edges = cv2.Canny(blurred, 50, 150)

    # Define the region of interest for lane detection
    mask = np.zeros_like(edges)
    polygons = np.array([[(0, 450), (900, 450), (900, 600), (0, 600)]])
    cv2.fillPoly(mask, polygons, 255)
    masked_edges = cv2.bitwise_and(edges, mask)

    # Find lines using Hough transform
    lines = cv2.HoughLinesP(masked_edges, 1, np.pi / 180, threshold=50,
            minLineLength=50, maxLineGap=200)

    # Draw lines on the frame
    if lines is not None:
        for line in lines:
            x1, y1, x2, y2 = line[0]
            cv2.line(frame, (x1, y1), (x2, y2), (0, 255, 0), 5)

    # Show the frame with detected lanes
    cv2.imshow('Lane Detection', frame)

    if cv2.waitKey(1) & 0xFF == ord('q'):
        break
cap.release()
cv2.destroyAllWindows()
```

This code uses OpenCV to perform lane detection on video frames, which is a crucial task for autonomous driving.

Computer vision has vast applications across industries, transforming sectors such as security, healthcare, and transportation. Facial recognition enhances security, medical imaging improves diagnosis accuracy, and computer vision in autonomous vehicles promises a future of safe, self-driving cars. These examples illustrate the broad potential of computer vision to drive technological advancements and improve the quality of life.

Module 31:

Time Series Analysis

Time series analysis plays a critical role in forecasting future values based on historical data. This module introduces key time series concepts and methods that are essential for predicting patterns such as seasonality, trends, and cyclical behavior. Learners will explore various forecasting techniques, feature engineering strategies, and evaluation metrics used to assess model performance.

Time Series Data Characteristics: Stationarity, Trends, and Seasonality

Time series data exhibits unique characteristics that distinguish it from other data types. One of the primary concepts in time series is stationarity, where statistical properties like mean and variance do not change over time. Understanding trends (long-term movements) and seasonality (periodic fluctuations) is also essential for modeling time series data. These characteristics help in identifying the underlying structure of the data, enabling more accurate forecasting. Differencing techniques and decomposition methods are commonly used to make non-stationary data stationary, facilitating better model performance.

Forecasting Methods: ARIMA, SARIMA, and Prophet

A wide range of forecasting models exists for time series analysis. ARIMA (AutoRegressive Integrated Moving Average) is a powerful model used to forecast data points by considering past values and errors. For time series with seasonal variations, SARIMA (Seasonal ARIMA) extends ARIMA by incorporating seasonality into its forecasting capability. Prophet, developed by Facebook, is another flexible tool that performs exceptionally well in capturing seasonality and holiday effects, especially for large datasets. These methods serve as foundational techniques in time series analysis, each offering unique strengths based on the data's specific characteristics.

Feature Engineering for Time Series: Lags, Rolling Statistics, and Decomposition

Feature engineering in time series analysis involves creating new features that help improve forecasting models. Common techniques include using lagged variables (previous time points) to capture dependencies in data. Rolling statistics, such as moving averages, help smooth out short-term fluctuations and highlight longer-term trends. Decomposition, breaking down the time series into trend, seasonal, and residual components, also provides valuable insights into the data's structure. These techniques enable analysts to improve the quality of input features and enhance the model's ability to predict future values accurately.

Evaluation Metrics: MAPE, RMSE, and Cross-Validation

Evaluating the performance of time series models is crucial to ensuring reliable forecasts. Common metrics like MAPE (Mean Absolute Percentage Error) measure the accuracy of predictions by comparing the forecasted values with actual observations. RMSE (Root Mean Square Error) is another popular metric, which penalizes larger errors more heavily. Cross-validation, particularly time series cross-validation, is essential to assess model performance, as it accounts for the temporal structure of the data. These evaluation techniques provide a clear understanding of how well a model is likely to generalize to unseen data, enabling effective decision-making in forecasting applications.

Time Series Data Characteristics: Stationarity, Trends, and Seasonality

Time series analysis focuses on understanding and forecasting data points collected or observed sequentially over time. To effectively analyze such data, it's crucial to understand its inherent characteristics, including stationarity, trends, and seasonality. These features determine the choice of analytical methods and forecasting techniques used to model time series data.

1. Stationarity in Time Series

Stationarity is a fundamental concept in time series analysis. A time series is stationary if its statistical properties, such as mean and variance, remain constant over time. Stationarity simplifies modeling and is often a prerequisite for many forecasting techniques, such as ARIMA.

Identifying Stationarity

- **Visual Inspection**: Plot the data to observe constant variance and a stable mean over time.

- **Statistical Tests**: Use tests like the Augmented Dickey-Fuller (ADF) test or Kwiatkowski-Phillips-Schmidt-Shin (KPSS) test to formally assess stationarity.

Making a Series Stationary

If a time series is non-stationary, techniques such as differencing (subtracting consecutive observations) or detrending (removing the trend component) can be applied.

Example: Checking Stationarity Using ADF Test

```
from statsmodels.tsa.stattools import adfuller
import pandas as pd

# Sample time series data
```

347

```
data = {'value': [10, 12, 14, 16, 18, 20, 22, 24, 26]}
ts = pd.Series(data['value'])

# Perform ADF test
adf_result = adfuller(ts)
print(f"ADF Statistic: {adf_result[0]}")
print(f"P-value: {adf_result[1]}")

if adf_result[1] < 0.05:
    print("The time series is stationary.")
else:
    print("The time series is non-stationary.")
```

2. Trends in Time Series

A trend represents the long-term progression of the time series data. It indicates whether the data is increasing, decreasing, or remaining constant over time. Trends are often caused by external factors, such as economic growth or technological advancements.

Identifying Trends

- **Visualization**: Plot the data to observe the general direction.

- **Decomposition**: Use statistical methods to separate the trend component from the time series.

Example: Extracting Trends Using Decomposition

```
from statsmodels.tsa.seasonal import seasonal_decompose

# Simulated time series
ts = pd.Series([10, 15, 20, 30, 50, 70, 110, 150, 200],
        index=pd.date_range("2023-01-01", periods=9))

# Decompose the time series
decomposition = seasonal_decompose(ts, model='additive', period=1)
trend = decomposition.trend

# Plot the trend
trend.plot(title="Trend Component", xlabel="Time", ylabel="Value")
```

3. Seasonality in Time Series

Seasonality refers to periodic fluctuations or patterns that repeat at regular intervals, such as daily, monthly, or yearly. Common examples include higher retail sales during the holiday season or increased electricity usage during summer.

Identifying Seasonality

- **Visualization**: Plot the data and look for recurring patterns.

- **Autocorrelation**: Use the autocorrelation function (ACF) to identify repeating cycles.

348

Handling Seasonality

When seasonality exists, methods like seasonal differencing or incorporating seasonal components in models (e.g., SARIMA) are necessary.

Example: Analyzing Seasonality

```
from pandas.plotting import autocorrelation_plot

# Simulated seasonal data
seasonal_ts = pd.Series([100, 200, 300, 400, 100, 200, 300, 400],
        index=pd.date_range("2023-01-01", periods=8))

# Autocorrelation plot
autocorrelation_plot(seasonal_ts)
```

Understanding the characteristics of time series data—stationarity, trends, and seasonality—is a critical first step in time series analysis. Stationarity ensures stability for modeling, trends highlight long-term patterns, and seasonality captures periodic fluctuations. Tools like decomposition, differencing, and autocorrelation provide valuable insights for analyzing and preprocessing time series data. By leveraging these techniques, data scientists can build robust models tailored to the unique attributes of time-dependent datasets.

Forecasting Methods: ARIMA, SARIMA, and Prophet.

Forecasting is a crucial component of time series analysis, enabling predictions of future data points based on historical patterns. Popular forecasting methods include ARIMA, SARIMA, and Prophet, each tailored to specific types of time series data and requirements. This section delves into these methods, their applications, and their implementation in Python.

---

1. ARIMA: Autoregressive Integrated Moving Average

ARIMA is one of the most widely used models for time series forecasting. It combines three components:

- **Autoregressive (AR)**: Models the relationship between current and past values.

- **Integrated (I)**: Makes the series stationary by differencing.

- **Moving Average (MA)**: Models the relationship between the current value and past errors.

Steps to Apply ARIMA

1. **Check Stationarity**: Use differencing to stabilize the mean.

2. **Determine Parameters**: Use the autocorrelation (ACF) and partial autocorrelation (PACF) plots to select p (AR), d (I), and q (MA).

3. **Model Fitting**: Fit the ARIMA model to the data.

4. **Forecasting**: Use the model for predictions.

Python Example: ARIMA Implementation

```python
from statsmodels.tsa.arima.model import ARIMA
import pandas as pd

# Sample time series data
data = [112, 118, 132, 129, 121, 135, 148, 136, 119, 104]
ts = pd.Series(data)

# Fit ARIMA model
model = ARIMA(ts, order=(1, 1, 1))  # p=1, d=1, q=1
fitted_model = model.fit()

# Forecast future values
forecast = fitted_model.forecast(steps=3)
print("Forecasted values:", forecast)
```

2. SARIMA: Seasonal ARIMA

SARIMA extends ARIMA by incorporating seasonality. It adds parameters to account for periodic fluctuations in the data:

- Seasonal Autoregressive (P)

- Seasonal Differencing (D)

- Seasonal Moving Average (Q)

- Seasonal Period (m)

When to Use SARIMA

SARIMA is ideal for datasets exhibiting seasonal patterns, such as monthly sales data or weekly temperature records.

Python Example: SARIMA Implementation

```python
from statsmodels.tsa.statespace.sarimax import SARIMAX

# Sample seasonal data
data = [100, 200, 300, 400, 100, 200, 300, 400]
ts = pd.Series(data, index=pd.date_range("2023-01-01", periods=8, freq='M'))

# Fit SARIMA model
model = SARIMAX(ts, order=(1, 1, 1), seasonal_order=(1, 1, 1, 4))
fitted_model = model.fit()
```

```
# Forecast future values
forecast = fitted_model.forecast(steps=4)
print("Seasonal Forecasted values:", forecast)
```

3. Prophet

Prophet, developed by Facebook, is a versatile forecasting tool designed for business applications. It automatically handles missing data, holidays, and seasonality, making it ideal for non-stationary data with complex patterns.

Key Features

- Handles daily, weekly, and yearly seasonality.

- Robust against missing data.

- Easy to use and interpret.

Python Example: Prophet Implementation

```
from prophet import Prophet
import pandas as pd

# Create a time series dataset
data = {'ds': pd.date_range(start='2023-01-01', periods=10, freq='D'),
        'y': [112, 118, 132, 129, 121, 135, 148, 136, 119, 104]}
df = pd.DataFrame(data)

# Fit the Prophet model
model = Prophet()
model.fit(df)

# Make future predictions
future = model.make_future_dataframe(periods=5)
forecast = model.predict(future)
print(forecast[['ds', 'yhat', 'yhat_lower', 'yhat_upper']])
```

Comparison of Methods

Method	Best Use Case	Strengths	Limitations
ARIMA	Stationary data	Simple, effective for short-term	Struggles with seasonality
SARIMA	Seasonal data	Accounts for seasonality	Complex parameter tuning
Prophet	Non-stationary data	Handles seasonality automatically	Requires additional dependencies

Choosing the right forecasting method depends on the characteristics of the time series data. ARIMA works well for stationary data, SARIMA handles seasonality effectively, and Prophet is excellent for non-stationary, business-centric use cases. By understanding and applying these methods, data scientists can generate accurate forecasts tailored to their specific needs.

Feature Engineering for Time Series: Lags, Rolling Statistics, and Decomposition

Feature engineering is a critical step in time series analysis, transforming raw data into informative features to enhance model performance. In time series, domain-specific features like lags, rolling statistics, and seasonal decompositions play a vital role in capturing temporal dependencies and patterns.

1. Lags: Capturing Temporal Dependencies

Lagged features represent previous time steps in the dataset, providing context for the current value. For instance, in forecasting the value at ttt, the value at $t-1t-1t-1$ (the lagged feature) can provide valuable insights.

Creating Lagged Features

Lagged features are essential for autoregressive models and machine learning algorithms that require input variables rather than raw sequential data.

Python Example: Generating Lagged Features

```
import pandas as pd

# Sample time series data
data = {'time': pd.date_range(start='2023-01-01', periods=10, freq='D'),
        'value': [112, 118, 132, 129, 121, 135, 148, 136, 119, 104]}
df = pd.DataFrame(data)

# Create lagged feature
df['lag_1'] = df['value'].shift(1)
print(df)
```

By incorporating lagged values as features, the model gains insight into short-term dependencies in the data.

2. Rolling Statistics: Detecting Trends and Variability

Rolling statistics smooth out fluctuations in time series data by averaging values over a specified window. They are used to identify trends, variability, and seasonality.

Common Rolling Statistics

- **Rolling Mean**: Highlights trends by averaging values over a rolling window.

- **Rolling Standard Deviation**: Identifies changes in volatility.

- **Rolling Sum**: Sums up values within a rolling window.

Python Example: Calculating Rolling Statistics

```
# Calculate rolling mean and standard deviation
df['rolling_mean'] = df['value'].rolling(window=3).mean()
df['rolling_std'] = df['value'].rolling(window=3).std()
print(df)
```

Rolling statistics help in visualizing and quantifying patterns in the time series.

3. Decomposition: Breaking Down Time Series Components

Decomposition separates a time series into its fundamental components:

- **Trend**: Long-term direction in the data.

- **Seasonality**: Repeating patterns at regular intervals.

- **Residual**: Irregular fluctuations after removing trend and seasonality.

Types of Decomposition

1. **Additive**: When the series is the sum of its components (Y_t=Trend+Seasonality+Residual).

2. **Multiplicative**: When the series is the product of its components (Y_t=Trend×Seasonality×Residual).

Python Example: Time Series Decomposition

```
from statsmodels.tsa.seasonal import seasonal_decompose

# Perform seasonal decomposition
result = seasonal_decompose(df['value'], model='additive', period=3)

# Access components
trend = result.trend
seasonal = result.seasonal
residual = result.resid

# Display results
print("Trend:\n", trend)
print("Seasonality:\n", seasonal)
print("Residual:\n", residual)
```

Decomposition is invaluable for understanding underlying patterns and isolating noise.

4. Feature Engineering Workflow

A typical workflow for feature engineering in time series involves:

1. **Exploratory Analysis**: Visualize data and detect trends or seasonality.

2. **Lagged Features**: Incorporate past values as predictors.

3. **Rolling Features**: Smooth data to identify trends and variability.

4. **Decomposition**: Extract and analyze individual components.

Feature engineering in time series is essential for leveraging temporal patterns, trends, and seasonality. Lagged features capture dependencies, rolling statistics highlight patterns, and decomposition breaks down the series for deeper insights. These techniques, combined with domain knowledge, enable more accurate forecasting and predictive modeling.

Evaluation Metrics: MAPE, RMSE, and cross-Validation

Evaluating the performance of a time series model is critical for ensuring its reliability in forecasting. Appropriate metrics quantify errors and help compare different models. This section delves into three commonly used evaluation techniques: Mean Absolute Percentage Error (MAPE), Root Mean Squared Error (RMSE), and cross-validation.

1. Mean Absolute Percentage Error (MAPE): Measuring Relative Error

MAPE calculates the average percentage error between predicted and actual values, making it scale-independent. It is widely used when comparing models across datasets with varying scales.

Formula for MAPE

$$MAPE = \frac{1}{n} \sum_{i=1}^{n} \left| \frac{y_i - \hat{y_i}}{y_i} \right| \times 100$$

Where:

- y_i: Actual value.

- $\hat{y}_i$: Predicted value.

- n: Number of data points.

Python Example: Calculating MAPE

```
import numpy as np

# Actual and predicted values
actual = np.array([112, 118, 132, 129, 121])
```

```
predicted = np.array([110, 120, 128, 130, 120])

# Calculate MAPE
mape = np.mean(np.abs((actual - predicted) / actual)) * 100
print(f"MAPE: {mape:.2f}%")
```

MAPE is easy to interpret but can be sensitive to small actual values, potentially inflating errors.

2. Root Mean Squared Error (RMSE): Measuring Absolute Error

RMSE calculates the square root of the average squared differences between actual and predicted values. It penalizes large errors, making it suitable for datasets where outliers are important.

Formula for RMSE

$$RMSE = \sqrt{\frac{1}{n}\sum_{i=1}^{n}(y_i - \hat{y_i})^2}$$

Python Example: Calculating RMSE

```
# Calculate RMSE
rmse = np.sqrt(np.mean((actual - predicted) ** 2))
print(f"RMSE: {rmse:.2f}")
```

RMSE provides insights into the absolute error magnitude but may not be as interpretable for non-linear scales.

3. Cross-Validation: Assessing Model Stability

Cross-validation evaluates the model's performance on unseen data by splitting the dataset into training and testing subsets. For time series, traditional k-fold cross-validation may not work due to temporal dependencies. Instead, time series cross-validation is used, preserving the order of observations.

Time Series Cross-Validation

A rolling forecast approach trains the model on an expanding window and evaluates it on the next time step(s).

Python Example: Time Series Cross-Validation

```
from sklearn.model_selection import TimeSeriesSplit

# Sample dataset
data = np.arange(1, 11)  # Example sequential data
tscv = TimeSeriesSplit(n_splits=3)

for train_index, test_index in tscv.split(data):
    print("Train:", train_index, "Test:", test_index)
```

This approach ensures the model is tested in a realistic forecasting setup while maintaining temporal integrity.

4. Comparison of Metrics

Metric	Strengths	Weaknesses
MAPE	Intuitive, scale-independent	Sensitive to small actual values
RMSE	Penalizes large errors, good for continuous data	Scale-dependent, hard to interpret directly
Cross-Validation	Tests model robustness on unseen data	Computationally expensive

Each metric serves specific purposes, and selecting the right one depends on the dataset and application context.

Evaluation metrics play a pivotal role in assessing the reliability of time series models. MAPE provides an intuitive relative error measure, RMSE quantifies absolute errors with a focus on outliers, and cross-validation ensures stability and generalization. Combining these metrics ensures a comprehensive understanding of model performance, aiding in better forecasting and decision-making.

Module 32:

Reinforcement Learning

Reinforcement Learning (RL) is a branch of machine learning where an agent learns to make decisions by interacting with an environment. This module introduces the core concepts of RL, including agents, environments, and rewards. It also explores various RL algorithms and their real-world applications, emphasizing the growing impact of RL in various domains.

Introduction to Reinforcement Learning: Agents, Environments, and Rewards

In reinforcement learning, an agent takes actions within an environment to maximize cumulative rewards. The agent's objective is to learn a policy that dictates the best action to take in each state to maximize the long-term reward. The environment provides feedback in the form of rewards or penalties, guiding the agent toward optimal behavior. Key concepts include exploration (trying new actions) and exploitation (choosing known actions), which balance learning and performance.

Markov Decision Processes: States, Actions, and Transitions

Markov Decision Processes (MDP) are the mathematical framework used to model reinforcement learning problems. MDPs consist of states, actions, and transitions between states. A state represents the environment's condition, while actions are decisions made by the agent. The transitions define how actions lead to new states, with associated probabilities and rewards. The goal is to determine an optimal policy that maximizes the expected sum of rewards over time. MDPs provide a structured way to formalize decision-making processes in RL problems.

Q-Learning and Deep Q-Networks (DQN): Algorithms for Action Selection

Q-Learning is a foundational algorithm in reinforcement learning that enables an agent to learn the value of actions in each state without requiring a model of the environment. The agent uses Q-values to estimate future rewards. Deep Q-Networks (DQN) extend Q-Learning by using deep neural networks to approximate Q-values in complex environments with large state spaces. DQN has shown success in training agents to perform complex tasks, such as playing video games. Both Q-Learning and DQN are widely used for solving RL problems in dynamic environments.

Applications of Reinforcement Learning: Robotics, Game AI, and Recommendation Systems

Reinforcement learning has broad applications across various fields. In robotics, RL helps robots learn tasks such as navigation, manipulation, and autonomous control by interacting with their environment. Game AI uses RL to train agents to play games at superhuman levels, as seen in famous applications like AlphaGo. In recommendation systems, RL optimizes user interactions by learning from user behavior to recommend personalized content. These applications highlight RL's versatility in solving complex, dynamic problems across industries.

Introduction to Reinforcement Learning: Agents, Environments, and Rewards

Reinforcement Learning (RL) is a branch of machine learning where agents learn to make decisions by interacting with an environment to maximize cumulative rewards. Unlike supervised learning, RL does not rely on labeled data but learns from trial and error. This section introduces the foundational concepts of RL, focusing on agents, environments, and rewards.

1. Core Concepts of Reinforcement Learning

In RL, the agent is an entity that takes actions in a defined environment to achieve a goal. The environment responds to these actions, providing feedback in the form of rewards, which guide the agent's learning process.

- **Agent**: The learner or decision-maker.

- **Environment**: Everything the agent interacts with.

- **Actions**: Choices made by the agent at each step.

- **States**: A representation of the environment's current situation.

- **Rewards**: Signals that indicate the success or failure of an action.

The Goal of RL

The objective is to maximize the total reward over time, often referred to as the return. This is achieved by the agent learning an optimal policy—a strategy that maps states to actions.

2. The Reinforcement Learning Loop

The interaction between the agent and the environment forms a feedback loop:

1. **Observation**: The agent observes the current state of the environment.

2. **Action**: Based on its policy, the agent selects an action.

3. **Reward and Transition**: The environment transitions to a new state and provides a reward.

4. **Update**: The agent updates its policy to improve future actions.

Python Example: Basic RL Framework

```python
import numpy as np

# Define environment
states = ['A', 'B', 'C']  # Example states
actions = ['left', 'right']  # Example actions
rewards = {'A': 1, 'B': -1, 'C': 0}  # Rewards for each state

# Simulate agent's action
def agent_action(state):
    return np.random.choice(actions)  # Random action for simplicity

# Simulate environment response
def environment_response(state, action):
    next_state = np.random.choice(states)  # Transition to a random state
    reward = rewards[next_state]
    return next_state, reward

# Example loop
current_state = 'A'
for _ in range(5):  # Simulate 5 steps
    action = agent_action(current_state)
    next_state, reward = environment_response(current_state, action)
    print(f"State: {current_state}, Action: {action}, Next State:
            {next_state}, Reward: {reward}")
    current_state = next_state
```

3. Importance of Rewards

Rewards are the primary mechanism through which the environment communicates with the agent. Positive rewards encourage the agent to repeat beneficial actions, while negative rewards discourage harmful ones. The challenge lies in designing reward functions that align with the desired behavior.

4. Advantages and Challenges of RL

Advantages

*   **Dynamic Learning**: RL adapts to changing environments.

*   **No Supervision**: Agents learn directly from interactions without requiring labeled data.

*   **Wide Applications**: RL powers innovations in robotics, game AI, and autonomous systems.

Challenges

- **Exploration vs. Exploitation**: Balancing the need to try new actions (exploration) with leveraging known strategies (exploitation).

- **Scalability**: Complex environments require significant computational resources.

- **Delayed Rewards**: Actions may yield rewards only after several steps, complicating learning.

Reinforcement Learning introduces a powerful paradigm where agents learn optimal behavior through interaction and feedback. By understanding agents, environments, and rewards, practitioners can build intelligent systems capable of making dynamic decisions in uncertain scenarios. The next sections will explore how concepts like Markov Decision Processes and Q-Learning refine this learning process.

Markov Decision Processes: States, Actions, and Transitions

Markov Decision Processes (MDPs) provide the mathematical foundation for Reinforcement Learning (RL). MDPs model decision-making in environments where outcomes are partly random and partly under the control of an agent. This section discusses the key components of MDPs—states, actions, and transitions—and their role in reinforcement learning.

1. Understanding Markov Decision Processes

An MDP is defined by a 4-tuple (S,A,P,R):

- **States (S)**: The set of all possible configurations of the environment.

- **Actions (A)**: The set of actions available to the agent.

- **Transition Probabilities (P)**: The probability of moving from one state to another given an action, defined as $P(s'|s,a)$

- **Rewards (R)**: The reward received when transitioning between states, defined as $R(s,a,s')$

Markov Property

The Markov property states that the future state depends only on the current state and action, not on the sequence of previous states. Mathematically:

$$P(s_{t+1}|s_t,a_t,s_{t-1},a_{t-1},...)=P(s_{t+1}|s_t,a_t)$$

2. States, Actions, and Rewards

States

The state is a representation of the environment at a given time. For example, in a chess game, the state could represent the position of all pieces on the board.

Actions

Actions are decisions made by the agent that affect the state. In the chess example, actions include moving a piece to a new position.

Rewards

Rewards provide feedback on the desirability of actions. For instance, winning the game could yield a high reward, while losing could yield a negative reward.

3. Transition Dynamics

The transition dynamics describe how actions affect the environment. For each state-action pair, the environment transitions to a new state with a certain probability. This is represented by the transition matrix P(s'|s,a), which defines the likelihood of reaching state s' from state sss by taking action a.

Python Example: Defining an MDP

```
import numpy as np

# Define states, actions, and rewards
states = ['S1', 'S2', 'S3']  # Example states
actions = ['A1', 'A2']  # Example actions
rewards = {
    ('S1', 'A1', 'S2'): 5,
    ('S1', 'A2', 'S3'): 10,
    ('S2', 'A1', 'S1'): -1,
    ('S2', 'A2', 'S3'): 2
}

# Define transition probabilities
transitions = {
    ('S1', 'A1'): {'S2': 0.8, 'S3': 0.2},
    ('S1', 'A2'): {'S2': 0.4, 'S3': 0.6},
    ('S2', 'A1'): {'S1': 1.0},
    ('S2', 'A2'): {'S3': 1.0}
}

# Simulate an environment step
def step(state, action):
    next_state_probs = transitions.get((state, action), {})
    next_state = np.random.choice(list(next_state_probs.keys()),
            p=list(next_state_probs.values()))
    reward = rewards.get((state, action, next_state), 0)
    return next_state, reward

# Example simulation
current_state = 'S1'
action = 'A1'
next_state, reward = step(current_state, action)
print(f"Current State: {current_state}, Action: {action}, Next State: {next_state}, Reward: {reward}")
```

4. Policies and Value Functions

Policies (π)

A policy is a strategy used by the agent to decide which action to take in each state. A deterministic policy directly maps states to actions (π(s)=a), while a stochastic policy provides probabilities for each action.

Value Functions

The value function quantifies the expected long-term reward from a state under a particular policy. It is expressed as:

$$V^\pi(s) = \mathrm{E}[\sum_{t=0}^{\infty} \gamma^t R(s_t, a_t)]$$

where γ is the discount factor, balancing immediate and future rewards.

5. Applications of MDPs

MDPs are widely used in applications such as:

- **Robotics**: Planning optimal movements.

- **Finance**: Portfolio management.

- **Healthcare**: Personalized treatment strategies.

Markov Decision Processes provide a robust framework for modeling decision-making in uncertain environments. By defining states, actions, transitions, and rewards, MDPs allow RL agents to systematically learn optimal policies. The next section will delve into specific RL algorithms, such as Q-Learning and Deep Q-Networks, for solving MDPs effectively.

Q-Learning and Deep Q-Networks (DQN): Algorithms for Action Selection

Reinforcement Learning (RL) achieves its core purpose of optimizing decision-making through algorithms like Q-Learning and Deep Q-Networks (DQN). These methods enable agents to determine the best actions in an environment to maximize rewards. This section explores the working principles of Q-Learning and its extension, DQN, with practical Python examples.

1. Q-Learning: A Model-Free RL Algorithm

Concept

Q-Learning is a model-free RL algorithm that learns an action-value function Q(s,a), which estimates the expected cumulative reward for taking an action aaa in state sss, followed by following the optimal policy.

Update Rule

The Q-value is updated iteratively using the Bellman equation:

$$Q(s,a) \leftarrow Q(s.a) + \alpha[r + \gamma max a' Q(s',a') - Q(s,a)]$$

Where:

- α: Learning rate

- r: Immediate reward

- γ: Discount factor

- max a'Q(s',a'): Estimated future reward

Python Example: Q-Learning

```python
import numpy as np

# Define environment
states = ['S1', 'S2', 'S3']
actions = ['A1', 'A2']
rewards = {
    ('S1', 'A1', 'S2'): 5,
    ('S1', 'A2', 'S3'): 10,
    ('S2', 'A1', 'S1'): -1,
    ('S2', 'A2', 'S3'): 2
}
transitions = {
    ('S1', 'A1'): 'S2',
    ('S1', 'A2'): 'S3',
    ('S2', 'A1'): 'S1',
    ('S2', 'A2'): 'S3'
}

# Initialize Q-table
Q = {state: {action: 0 for action in actions} for state in states}

# Hyperparameters
alpha = 0.1  # Learning rate
gamma = 0.9  # Discount factor
episodes = 1000

# Training loop
for _ in range(episodes):
    state = np.random.choice(states)
    while state != 'S3':  # 'S3' as terminal state
        action = np.random.choice(actions)
        next_state = transitions[(state, action)]
        reward = rewards.get((state, action, next_state), 0)
        max_future_q = max(Q[next_state].values())
```

```
            Q[state][action] += alpha * (reward + gamma * max_future_q -
                Q[state][action])
            state = next_state

# Display Q-values
print("Q-Table:")
for state, actions in Q.items():
    print(state, actions)
```

2. Deep Q-Networks (DQN): Combining Q-Learning with Deep Learning

Q-Learning struggles with high-dimensional state spaces because it relies on a Q-table. Deep Q-Networks (DQN) address this issue by using a neural network to approximate Q(s,a).

Key Features of DQN

- **Neural Network**: Maps state-action pairs to Q-values.

- **Experience Replay**: Stores past experiences in a replay buffer to break temporal correlations and stabilize learning.

- **Target Network**: A separate network that updates less frequently to improve stability.

Algorithm Workflow

1. Observe the current state.

2. Select an action using an epsilon-greedy policy.

3. Perform the action and observe the reward and next state.

4. Store the transition in the replay buffer.

5. Sample a batch of experiences and update the Q-network using gradient descent.

Python Example: DQN with TensorFlow

```
import tensorflow as tf
import numpy as np
from collections import deque
import random

# Environment setup
state_size = 4
action_size = 2

# Hyperparameters
learning_rate = 0.001
gamma = 0.95
epsilon = 1.0
epsilon_decay = 0.995
```

```
epsilon_min = 0.01
batch_size = 32
memory = deque(maxlen=2000)

# Neural Network for Q-value approximation
model = tf.keras.Sequential([
    tf.keras.layers.Dense(24, input_dim=state_size, activation='relu'),
    tf.keras.layers.Dense(24, activation='relu'),
    tf.keras.layers.Dense(action_size, activation='linear')
])
model.compile(optimizer=tf.keras.optimizers.Adam(learning_rate=learning_rate
        ),
            loss='mse')

# Experience replay buffer
def replay():
    if len(memory) < batch_size:
        return
    batch = random.sample(memory, batch_size)
    for state, action, reward, next_state, done in batch:
        target = reward
        if not done:
            target += gamma * np.max(model.predict(next_state.reshape(1, -
            1))[0])
        target_f = model.predict(state.reshape(1, -1))
        target_f[0][action] = target
        model.fit(state.reshape(1, -1), target_f, epochs=1, verbose=0)

# Training loop (simplified)
for episode in range(1000):
    state = np.random.rand(state_size)  # Random initial state
    for t in range(200):
        action = np.random.choice(action_size) if np.random.rand() <=
            epsilon else np.argmax(model.predict(state.reshape(1, -1))[0])
        next_state = np.random.rand(state_size)  # Simulated transition
        reward = 1 if np.random.rand() > 0.5 else -1
        done = t == 199
        memory.append((state, action, reward, next_state, done))
        state = next_state
        if done:
            break
    replay()
    epsilon = max(epsilon_min, epsilon * epsilon_decay)
```

3. Applications of Q-Learning and DQN

- **Robotics**: Efficient pathfinding in dynamic environments.

- **Game AI**: Mastering complex games like Atari and Go.

- **Autonomous Systems**: Adaptive traffic signal control or fleet management.

Q-Learning and DQN are foundational algorithms for action selection in reinforcement learning. While Q-Learning is effective for simpler environments, DQNs leverage neural networks to handle complex, high-dimensional state spaces, making them pivotal in modern applications like robotics and game AI. The next section will explore practical use cases of reinforcement learning across various industries.

Applications of Reinforcement Learning: Robotics, Game AI, and Recommendation Systems

Reinforcement Learning (RL) is a transformative field in artificial intelligence, with applications spanning robotics, game AI, and recommendation systems. Its ability to optimize decision-making in dynamic environments makes it indispensable for solving real-world problems. This section delves into these applications, illustrating their significance and implementation.

1. Robotics: Intelligent Decision-Making and Control

Overview

Robotics is one of the most prominent fields leveraging RL. Robots operate in uncertain and dynamic environments, where pre-programmed instructions often fail. RL enables robots to adapt their behavior by learning from interaction with the environment.

Key Use Cases

- **Navigation**: RL helps robots navigate through complex terrains while avoiding obstacles.

- **Manipulation**: Robots can learn precise movements for tasks like assembling products or surgical procedures.

- **Human-Robot Interaction**: RL improves responsiveness and adaptability in collaborative robots (cobots).

Example: Robot Navigation Using RL

```python
import gym
import numpy as np
from stable_baselines3 import PPO

# Load a simulated robotics environment
env = gym.make('CartPole-v1')

# Define RL model (Proximal Policy Optimization)
model = PPO('MlpPolicy', env, verbose=1)

# Train the model
model.learn(total_timesteps=10000)

# Test the trained model
obs = env.reset()
for _ in range(1000):
    action, _states = model.predict(obs)
    obs, rewards, done, info = env.step(action)
    env.render()
    if done:
        obs = env.reset()
env.close()
```

This example demonstrates how RL algorithms like PPO can train a robot to balance a pole, showcasing adaptive control in robotics.

2. Game AI: Mastering Complex Environments

Overview

RL has revolutionized game AI, creating agents capable of outperforming humans in complex games. By simulating millions of interactions, RL-based agents learn strategies that optimize long-term rewards.

Notable Achievements

- **AlphaGo and AlphaZero**: RL agents mastered Go, chess, and shogi without prior knowledge.

- **Atari Games**: RL algorithms like Deep Q-Networks (DQNs) achieved superhuman performance in Atari games.

- **MMORPGs and Real-Time Strategy Games**: RL trains agents to collaborate, strategize, and adapt to evolving scenarios.

Example: RL in Game AI

```python
import gym
from stable_baselines3 import DQN

# Load a game environment
env = gym.make('Breakout-v0')

# Train a DQN agent
model = DQN('CnnPolicy', env, verbose=1, buffer_size=100000,
            learning_starts=1000)

# Train the model
model.learn(total_timesteps=50000)

# Evaluate performance
obs = env.reset()
while True:
    action, _ = model.predict(obs)
    obs, reward, done, info = env.step(action)
    env.render()
    if done:
        break
env.close()
```

This example uses RL to train an agent in the Atari Breakout game, showcasing decision-making in dynamic environments.

3. Recommendation Systems: Personalized User Experience

Overview

Recommendation systems utilize RL to enhance user experience by personalizing suggestions. Unlike traditional systems, RL-based approaches dynamically adapt recommendations based on user feedback, ensuring continuous improvement.

How It Works

- The agent represents the recommendation system.

- The environment includes user interactions and preferences.

- Rewards are derived from user engagement metrics, such as clicks or time spent.

Key Use Cases

- **E-Commerce**: Personalized product recommendations.

- **Streaming Services**: Tailored content suggestions for platforms like Netflix and Spotify.

- **Education**: Adaptive learning paths in e-learning platforms.

Example: Simplified RL for Recommendations

```python
import numpy as np

# Simulate a user-environment interaction
actions = ['Movie A', 'Movie B', 'Movie C']
rewards = {'Movie A': 1, 'Movie B': 0, 'Movie C': 1}  # User preferences

# Epsilon-greedy policy
def recommend_action(epsilon=0.1):
    if np.random.rand() < epsilon:
        return np.random.choice(actions)  # Explore
    return max(rewards, key=rewards.get)  # Exploit

# Simulate recommendations
for _ in range(10):
    action = recommend_action()
    print(f"Recommended: {action}, Reward: {rewards[action]}")
```

This simplified example shows how RL can dynamically adjust recommendations to align with user preferences.

4. Future Trends in RL Applications

The potential of RL continues to expand, with emerging trends driving innovation:

- **Autonomous Vehicles**: RL optimizes route planning, obstacle avoidance, and traffic management.

- **Healthcare**: Adaptive RL systems assist in personalized treatment planning and robotic surgery.

- **Finance**: RL enhances algorithmic trading and portfolio management.

Reinforcement Learning's versatility empowers it to tackle diverse challenges across robotics, gaming, and recommendation systems. From enabling robots to navigate complex environments to creating AI agents that master games and optimize user experiences, RL has reshaped industries. As RL techniques evolve, their applications are expected to expand further, driving advancements in AI-driven automation and decision-making.

Module 33:

Ethical AI Practices

Reinforcement Learning (RL) is a machine learning paradigm where agents learn to make decisions through interactions with an environment. This module explores RL's core principles, algorithms, and practical applications. From understanding the agent-environment relationship to diving into popular algorithms, it shows how RL is used across various fields, including robotics and game AI.

Introduction to Reinforcement Learning: Agents, Environments, and Rewards

Reinforcement learning involves an agent interacting with its environment to maximize cumulative rewards. The agent's goal is to learn an optimal policy to make decisions that lead to the highest long-term reward. Feedback from the environment in the form of rewards or penalties guides the agent's learning. A balance between exploration (trying new actions) and exploitation (choosing known effective actions) is key to the learning process in RL.

Markov Decision Processes: States, Actions, and Transitions

Markov Decision Processes (MDPs) offer a mathematical framework for RL problems. An MDP consists of states (representing the environment's condition), actions (decisions made by the agent), and transitions (how actions lead to new states). Each transition has a probability and reward associated with it. The agent's objective is to find an optimal policy that maximizes the sum of rewards over time by considering these states, actions, and transitions. MDPs are essential for structuring RL problems efficiently.

Q-Learning and Deep Q-Networks (DQN): Algorithms for Action Selection

Q-Learning is an RL algorithm that enables an agent to learn the value of actions in different states, aiming to maximize future rewards. The agent uses Q-values to guide its decisions. Deep Q-Networks (DQN) extend Q-Learning by using neural networks to approximate Q-values, allowing the agent to handle complex environments with large state spaces. DQN has been successfully applied to various tasks, including video game playing and robotic control, demonstrating its ability to solve problems with high-dimensional inputs.

Applications of Reinforcement Learning: Robotics, Game AI, and Recommendation Systems

RL has diverse applications across industries. In robotics, it enables machines to learn tasks such as navigation and manipulation by interacting with the environment. RL is also crucial in game AI, where it helps create agents capable of mastering complex games, as seen with AlphaGo. In recommendation systems, RL optimizes content recommendations based on user behavior, leading to personalized experiences. These applications showcase RL's versatility and its growing importance in various technological advancements.

Responsible AI: Fairness, Transparency, and Accountability

The rapid growth of artificial intelligence (AI) brings transformative possibilities but also significant ethical challenges. Responsible AI emphasizes the importance of fairness, transparency, and accountability in AI development and deployment. This section explores these principles and highlights their significance in creating ethical AI systems.

1. Fairness: Ensuring Equity in AI Outcomes

What Is Fairness?

Fairness in AI ensures that systems provide equitable outcomes for all users, regardless of race, gender, or other demographic factors. Without careful design, AI can perpetuate or amplify societal biases, leading to discriminatory outcomes.

Sources of Bias

- **Training Data**: Biased data can embed historical inequalities into AI models.

- **Algorithmic Design**: Certain optimization methods may inadvertently prioritize one group over others.

- **Operational Context**: AI systems can interact with external factors, exacerbating inequity.

Fairness Strategies

- **Balanced Datasets**: Ensuring datasets represent diverse populations.

- **Algorithmic Audits**: Regular checks to identify and mitigate biases.

- **Fairness Metrics**: Employ metrics such as demographic parity and equalized odds to evaluate fairness.

Python Example: Fairness in Data

```
from sklearn.model_selection import train_test_split
from sklearn.metrics import classification_report
from sklearn.ensemble import RandomForestClassifier
import pandas as pd

# Load dataset
```

```
data = pd.read_csv("census_income.csv")

# Check for demographic imbalance
print(data['gender'].value_counts())

# Balancing the dataset
balanced_data = data.groupby('gender').sample(n=500, random_state=42)

# Train a model and evaluate fairness
X = balanced_data.drop('income', axis=1)
y = balanced_data['income']
X_train, X_test, y_train, y_test = train_test_split(X, y, test_size=0.3,
            random_state=42)

model = RandomForestClassifier()
model.fit(X_train, y_train)
predictions = model.predict(X_test)

print(classification_report(y_test, predictions))
```

This code balances a dataset by ensuring equal representation across genders, promoting fairness in the model's predictions.

2. Transparency: Building Trust in AI Systems

What Is Transparency?

Transparency refers to the ability of stakeholders to understand how AI systems make decisions. It builds trust by revealing the data, algorithms, and processes that drive AI outputs.

Challenges to Transparency

- Complex models like deep learning often function as "black boxes."

- Proprietary algorithms may limit openness.

Promoting Transparency

- **Documentation**: Provide detailed descriptions of model training and evaluation.

- **Open-Source Tools**: Use frameworks like LIME and SHAP for interpretability.

- **User-Friendly Explanations**: Ensure non-technical stakeholders can comprehend AI decisions.

3. Accountability: Ensuring Ethical Responsibility

What Is Accountability?

372

Accountability involves holding developers and organizations responsible for the outcomes of AI systems. It ensures that ethical considerations are prioritized throughout the AI lifecycle.

Key Practices

- **Audit Trails**: Maintain records of decisions made during AI development.

- **Ethical Reviews**: Incorporate ethics committees to evaluate AI projects.

- **Clear Ownership**: Define who is responsible for AI failures or misuses.

Python Example: Transparency with SHAP

```python
import shap
import xgboost
from sklearn.datasets import load_iris

# Load dataset and train a model
data = load_iris()
X, y = data.data, data.target
model = xgboost.XGBClassifier().fit(X, y)

# Explain model predictions with SHAP
explainer = shap.Explainer(model, X)
shap_values = explainer(X)

# Visualize explanation
shap.summary_plot(shap_values, X)
```

This example uses SHAP to visualize feature importance, promoting transparency in model predictions.

4. Integrating Fairness, Transparency, and Accountability

To develop responsible AI, organizations must integrate fairness, transparency, and accountability across all stages of the AI lifecycle. This requires:

- Diverse, multidisciplinary teams to address ethical considerations.

- Continuous monitoring and iterative improvements to uphold ethical standards.

- Compliance with global guidelines, such as the EU's AI Act or IEEE's Ethical AI standards.

Responsible AI principles—fairness, transparency, and accountability—are essential for ethical AI practices. By addressing biases, ensuring transparency, and maintaining accountability, organizations can build AI systems that foster trust and equity. These practices not only mitigate risks but also ensure AI serves society responsibly.

Bias in AI Models: Sources of Bias and Mitigation Strategies

Bias in AI models is a critical issue that can lead to unfair, discriminatory outcomes. Understanding the sources of bias and implementing strategies to mitigate them are essential to building responsible and ethical AI systems. This section delves into the various sources of bias in AI models and outlines techniques for reducing bias to ensure fairness and reliability.

1. Sources of Bias in AI Models

Bias in Training Data

The most common source of bias arises from the data used to train AI models. If the training data is skewed or unrepresentative of the entire population, the model will inherit these biases. For example:

- **Historical Bias**: Data that reflects past societal prejudices can perpetuate those biases in AI systems.

- **Sampling Bias**: If certain groups are underrepresented or overrepresented in the dataset, the model may make inaccurate predictions for those groups.

Algorithmic Bias

Sometimes, the algorithms themselves can introduce bias. Certain optimization functions, feature selection processes, or model assumptions may inadvertently favor specific groups over others.

Bias in Human Judgment

AI systems often inherit biases from human decision-makers, either through subjective labeling of data or personal preferences embedded in algorithmic design. These biases can manifest in both supervised and unsupervised learning models.

Bias in Feature Engineering

The way features are selected or constructed for AI models can influence the model's performance. If certain features are emphasized over others based on biased thinking, it can result in biased model predictions.

2. Bias Mitigation Strategies

Data-Level Approaches

At the data level, one of the most effective ways to reduce bias is to ensure that the training data is diverse and representative of all relevant groups. Some approaches include:

- **Oversampling**: Increasing the representation of underrepresented groups in the data.

- **Undersampling**: Reducing the overrepresentation of certain groups in the dataset.

- **Re-weighting**: Assigning higher weights to data points from underrepresented groups to balance the influence on the model.

Algorithm-Level Approaches

There are several strategies at the algorithmic level to minimize bias:

- **Fairness-Conscious Algorithms**: These algorithms are designed specifically to avoid biased outcomes by incorporating fairness constraints during the training process.

- **Adversarial Debiasing**: This technique involves training a model alongside a second network designed to predict and reduce biases in the first model's predictions.

Post-Processing Approaches

Post-processing techniques modify the predictions of a trained model to correct for biases after the model has been trained. These strategies include:

- **Equalized Odds**: Adjusting the model's predictions so that the error rates are equal across different demographic groups.

- **Disparate Impact Removal**: Removing biased decisions after model deployment by analyzing the impact of predictions across different groups.

Python Example: Bias Mitigation Using Re-weighting

```
import pandas as pd
from sklearn.model_selection import train_test_split
from sklearn.linear_model import LogisticRegression
from sklearn.metrics import accuracy_score
from sklearn.utils.class_weight import compute_sample_weight

# Load and prepare data
data = pd.read_csv("biased_data.csv")
X = data.drop('target', axis=1)
y = data['target']

# Compute sample weights for class imbalance (underrepresented group)
```

```
weights = compute_sample_weight(class_weight='balanced', y=y)

# Split the data
X_train, X_test, y_train, y_test, weights_train, weights_test =
          train_test_split(X, y, weights, test_size=0.3, random_state=42)

# Train model with class weights
model = LogisticRegression()
model.fit(X_train, y_train, sample_weight=weights_train)

# Evaluate model performance
y_pred = model.predict(X_test)
print(f"Accuracy: {accuracy_score(y_test, y_pred)}")
```

This example demonstrates how to compute sample weights for underrepresented classes, improving fairness in a model by balancing its influence during training.

3. Regular Bias Audits

Bias mitigation should be an ongoing process. Regular audits of models throughout their lifecycle can identify emerging biases. These audits typically include:

- **Bias Evaluation Metrics**: Metrics such as disparate impact, equal opportunity, and demographic parity can be used to assess model fairness.

- **Model Updates**: Continuously update models with new, diverse data to ensure they reflect current societal trends.

4. Ethical Considerations in Bias Mitigation

While addressing bias is crucial, it's important to consider the ethical implications of mitigation strategies:

- **Trade-Offs between Fairness and Accuracy**: Sometimes, optimizing for fairness can reduce model accuracy, and vice versa. Ethical AI practices require balancing these trade-offs based on the application.

- **Transparency in Mitigation**: It is important to transparently communicate the methods used for bias mitigation to stakeholders to ensure trust in the AI system.

Bias in AI models is an inherent risk in developing machine learning systems, but through careful design, algorithmic fairness, and continuous monitoring, it is possible to mitigate these risks. By adopting appropriate bias mitigation strategies, organizations can develop more equitable and responsible AI systems that better serve diverse communities and uphold fairness.

Explainability and Interpretability: Techniques like LIME, SHAP

As AI systems become more integrated into decision-making processes, the need for transparency and trust in these systems has grown. Explainability and interpretability

376

are crucial to ensure that machine learning models make decisions in ways that are understandable and accountable. In this section, we explore popular techniques like LIME (Local Interpretable Model-Agnostic Explanations) and SHAP (SHapley Additive exPlanations), which help explain and interpret complex models.

1. Importance of Explainability and Interpretability

Explainability and interpretability allow stakeholders to understand how a model arrives at a particular decision. This is especially important in high-stakes applications such as healthcare, finance, and law enforcement, where the consequences of incorrect or biased decisions can be significant. The ability to explain AI decisions helps in:

- **Building trust**: Users are more likely to trust a model if they can understand how it makes decisions.

- **Compliance**: Many industries are subject to regulations that require transparency in automated decision-making.

- **Debugging and Improvement**: Explainability techniques allow data scientists to identify and correct model flaws.

2. LIME (Local Interpretable Model-Agnostic Explanations)

LIME is a popular technique that explains individual predictions by approximating the model with a simpler, interpretable model for a specific instance. The key idea is that although a model may be complex and hard to interpret, we can use a locally interpretable surrogate model (like linear regression or decision trees) to approximate its behavior near a specific data point.

How LIME Works:

1. **Perturb the data**: LIME generates perturbed samples around the instance to be explained by slightly modifying its features.

2. **Predict the outcomes**: The complex model is used to predict the outcomes for these perturbed samples.

3. **Train a simple model**: A simpler model is trained using the perturbed data and the predictions from the complex model.

4. **Interpret the model**: The coefficients or feature importances of the simpler model help explain the complex model's prediction for that specific instance.

Python Example: Using LIME

```
import lime
import lime.lime_tabular
import numpy as np
from sklearn.datasets import load_iris
from sklearn.model_selection import train_test_split
from sklearn.ensemble import RandomForestClassifier

# Load dataset
data = load_iris()
X = data.data
y = data.target

# Train a complex model
X_train, X_test, y_train, y_test = train_test_split(X, y, test_size=0.2,
            random_state=42)
model = RandomForestClassifier()
model.fit(X_train, y_train)

# Create a LIME explainer
explainer = lime.lime_tabular.LimeTabularExplainer(X_train,
            training_labels=y_train, mode="classification")

# Choose an instance to explain
instance = X_test[0]

# Explain the prediction for this instance
explanation = explainer.explain_instance(instance, model.predict_proba)
explanation.show_in_notebook()
```

In this example, LIME is used to explain a RandomForestClassifier's prediction on a given instance from the Iris dataset.

3. SHAP (SHapley Additive exPlanations)

SHAP is a more sophisticated technique based on Shapley values, which come from cooperative game theory. Shapley values measure the contribution of each feature to the model's prediction. By using Shapley values, SHAP provides a unified measure of feature importance, offering insights into both global and local model behavior.

How SHAP Works:

1. **Shapley Values**: The Shapley value for a feature is calculated by averaging its marginal contribution to all possible combinations of features.

2. **Additive Explanation**: The SHAP method adds these values together to explain the model's prediction as a sum of feature contributions.

3. **Interpretability**: The sum of the Shapley values for each feature corresponds to the difference between the model's prediction and the baseline (usually the average prediction across all samples).

Python Example: Using SHAP

```
import shap
from sklearn.ensemble import RandomForestClassifier
```

```
from sklearn.datasets import load_iris
from sklearn.model_selection import train_test_split

# Load dataset and split it
data = load_iris()
X = data.data
y = data.target
X_train, X_test, y_train, y_test = train_test_split(X, y, test_size=0.2,
        random_state=42)

# Train a model
model = RandomForestClassifier()
model.fit(X_train, y_train)

# Initialize SHAP explainer
explainer = shap.TreeExplainer(model)

# Get SHAP values for a single instance
shap_values = explainer.shap_values(X_test[0:1])

# Visualize the SHAP values
shap.initjs()
shap.force_plot(explainer.expected_value[0], shap_values[0][0], X_test[0])
```

In this example, SHAP values are used to explain the prediction of a RandomForestClassifier trained on the Iris dataset.

4. Comparing LIME and SHAP

Both LIME and SHAP provide model-agnostic explanations, but they differ in key areas:

- **Interpretability**: LIME uses simpler surrogate models for local explanations, while SHAP provides a more principled approach based on Shapley values.

- **Consistency**: SHAP guarantees consistency in feature importance, meaning that increasing a feature's value should never decrease its importance, whereas LIME may not always guarantee this.

- **Global vs. Local Explanations**: SHAP can provide both local and global explanations, making it suitable for both understanding individual predictions and general model behavior. LIME, however, focuses on local explanations.

Explainability and interpretability are essential to building trust in machine learning models. Techniques like LIME and SHAP provide valuable tools for understanding how models make decisions and identifying areas for improvement. By adopting these techniques, organizations can ensure their AI systems are transparent, accountable, and fair.

Ethical Guidelines and Regulations: Guidelines for Responsible AI Development

As artificial intelligence (AI) continues to evolve, the ethical implications of its deployment become more significant. Ethical guidelines and regulations are crucial to ensure that AI is developed and used responsibly. These guidelines help mitigate risks related to bias, privacy violations, discrimination, and unintended consequences while promoting transparency, fairness, and accountability.

1. The Need for Ethical Guidelines in AI

AI systems are increasingly used in sensitive areas such as healthcare, law enforcement, finance, and employment, where decisions can have profound consequences on people's lives. Ethical guidelines help ensure that AI systems are designed and deployed in ways that respect human rights, promote fairness, and do not exacerbate social inequalities. They also provide a framework for addressing the moral and societal challenges AI poses. Ethical AI development focuses on:

- **Fairness**: Ensuring that AI systems do not introduce or perpetuate discrimination or bias.

- **Transparency**: Making AI decision-making processes clear and understandable to users and stakeholders.

- **Accountability**: Holding individuals and organizations accountable for the outcomes produced by AI systems.

2. Ethical Guidelines in AI Development

A number of organizations and institutions have proposed ethical guidelines for AI development. These guidelines generally emphasize the following principles:

a. Fairness and Non-discrimination

AI systems should be designed to avoid bias that could lead to discrimination based on race, gender, age, socioeconomic status, or other protected characteristics. This includes ensuring fairness in both model training (by using diverse, representative datasets) and in decision-making (by providing equal treatment to all individuals).

b. Transparency and Explainability

AI systems should be transparent, meaning that their decisions and underlying processes are understandable to users and stakeholders. It's critical that AI systems can provide clear explanations for their actions, especially when they are used for important decisions, like loan approvals or hiring.

c. Privacy and Data Protection

Respecting the privacy of individuals is paramount. AI systems should collect, store, and process personal data in a way that complies with privacy regulations such as the GDPR (General Data Protection Regulation) and other regional laws. Data anonymization and encryption techniques are important for protecting sensitive information.

d. Safety and Security

AI systems must be robust and secure to avoid malfunctions or vulnerabilities that could result in harm. They should also be designed to adapt to unexpected situations without causing unintended negative consequences.

e. Accountability and Responsibility

Developers, organizations, and governments must be accountable for the use of AI. There should be clear responsibility for outcomes that arise from AI decision-making, particularly when harm occurs.

3. Regulatory Frameworks for AI

The global regulatory landscape for AI is still in development, but several countries and organizations are taking steps toward establishing guidelines for AI ethics. These regulations aim to ensure that AI is used responsibly and in ways that benefit society.

a. European Union's AI Act

The European Union has proposed the **AI Act**, which classifies AI applications based on their risk levels, from minimal to high risk. The act lays out regulations to ensure that high-risk AI systems (such as those used in critical infrastructure, law enforcement, and healthcare) adhere to strict requirements around transparency, accountability, and fairness.

b. OECD AI Principles

The Organization for Economic Cooperation and Development (OECD) developed a set of **AI principles** that promote inclusive growth, human-centered values, and environmental sustainability. These principles stress that AI should be used for the benefit of people and the planet while respecting human dignity and rights.

c. The IEEE Global Initiative on Ethics of Autonomous and Intelligent Systems

The IEEE Global Initiative provides standards and recommendations for developing autonomous systems that uphold human rights, fairness, privacy, and transparency. Their guidelines are focused on ensuring AI systems are trustworthy, sustainable, and aligned with ethical values.

4. Moving Forward with Ethical AI

The future of AI depends on the continued development of ethical guidelines and the regulation of AI technologies. Developers and organizations must not only comply with existing regulations but also engage in ongoing discussions about the ethical implications of AI. As AI technologies become more integrated into society, ethical principles should be at the forefront of AI development to ensure that AI is a force for good.

Organizations should establish internal ethical guidelines, train AI practitioners in ethics, and continuously monitor AI systems to ensure they align with ethical standards. By doing so, we can harness the power of AI while safeguarding public trust and societal values.

Module 34:

Emerging Topics in Data Science

The landscape of data science is rapidly evolving, introducing new technologies and methodologies that transform the way data is analyzed and processed. This module explores emerging topics such as AutoML, federated learning, quantum computing, and the future of AI, providing a glimpse into the innovative trends reshaping the field.

AutoML: Automating Model Selection, Hyperparameter Tuning, and Deployment

AutoML, or Automated Machine Learning, has significantly lowered the barriers to entry in machine learning. By automating the process of model selection, hyperparameter tuning, and deployment, AutoML enables non-experts to build effective models. It automates repetitive tasks, freeing data scientists to focus on more complex problems. Furthermore, it accelerates the deployment of machine learning models, ensuring that businesses can leverage AI without requiring in-depth technical knowledge. As AutoML tools continue to improve, their potential to democratize access to AI technology is vast, making it a key component in the future of data science.

Federated Learning: Privacy-Preserving Learning Across Decentralized Devices

Federated learning is a groundbreaking approach that addresses privacy concerns in AI model training. Unlike traditional methods where data is centralized in one location, federated learning allows for decentralized model training. Data remains on users' devices, with only model updates being shared. This method enhances data privacy and security, making it highly suitable for applications involving sensitive information, such as healthcare and finance. The decentralized nature of federated learning also reduces the need for extensive data transfers, minimizing bandwidth usage and enhancing system efficiency. This innovation represents a crucial step forward in balancing AI capabilities with privacy.

Quantum Computing in Data Science: Potential and Current Research

Quantum computing has the potential to revolutionize data science by providing solutions to problems that are intractable for classical computers. Quantum computers leverage the principles of quantum mechanics to process data in fundamentally new ways. Unlike traditional bits, quantum bits (qubits) can exist in multiple states simultaneously, allowing for faster computation and the solving of complex optimization problems. Though still in the experimental stage, quantum computing could significantly impact machine learning, optimization, cryptography, and data modeling. Ongoing research in quantum algorithms and hardware design is poised to transform industries by enabling calculations that are beyond the reach of today's classical computers.

The Future of AI and Data Science: Trends and Innovations

The future of AI and data science is marked by rapid advancements that promise to reshape industries across the globe. Key trends include the rise of self-supervised learning, which allows machines to learn from unlabeled data, and the continued development of explainable AI (XAI), which seeks to make machine learning models more interpretable and transparent. Other innovations such as advanced neural networks, reinforcement learning, and natural language processing are poised to drive breakthroughs in areas like robotics, personalized medicine, and autonomous vehicles. As these technologies evolve, they will offer new opportunities to solve complex societal challenges and enhance human capabilities.

AutoML: Automating Model Selection, Hyperparameter Tuning, and Deployment

AutoML (Automated Machine Learning) refers to the process of automating the end-to-end workflow of applying machine learning to real-world problems. This includes model selection, data preprocessing, feature engineering, hyperparameter tuning, and deployment. By automating these processes, AutoML helps data scientists and non-experts build high-performing machine learning models with less manual intervention and expertise.

1. The Need for AutoML

The process of developing machine learning models typically requires substantial expertise in selecting the right algorithms, preprocessing data, and fine-tuning models to optimize performance. For many organizations, the lack of skilled data scientists makes it challenging to adopt machine learning. AutoML addresses this by providing tools that automate various stages of the machine learning lifecycle, making it easier for both experts and non-experts to create effective models.

AutoML also speeds up the model development process, which is critical in industries where time-to-market is essential. With AutoML, the system can iterate over many models, tune their parameters, and select the most promising ones without extensive manual effort.

2. Key Components of AutoML

AutoML frameworks typically consist of several key components that automate machine learning tasks:

a. Model Selection

AutoML tools automatically choose the best machine learning model for a given problem based on the nature of the dataset and problem type (classification, regression, etc.). For instance, it may select models like decision trees, random forests, or gradient boosting machines based on their suitability.

b. Hyperparameter Tuning

Hyperparameter tuning involves finding the optimal settings for a machine learning model. Traditional tuning methods like grid search or random search can be time-consuming. AutoML optimizes this process by employing techniques like Bayesian optimization, which intelligently explores the hyperparameter space to find the best configuration.

Example:

```
from sklearn.model_selection import GridSearchCV
from sklearn.ensemble import RandomForestClassifier

# Example of hyperparameter tuning using GridSearchCV
param_grid = {
    'n_estimators': [100, 200, 300],
    'max_depth': [10, 20, None],
}
grid_search = GridSearchCV(estimator=RandomForestClassifier(),
            param_grid=param_grid, cv=3)
grid_search.fit(X_train, y_train)
print("Best hyperparameters:", grid_search.best_params_)
```

c. Feature Engineering

Feature engineering, a crucial step for improving model performance, is also automated in AutoML. The system can automatically generate new features from existing ones, identify relevant features, and discard irrelevant ones.

d. Model Deployment

Once the best model is selected and trained, AutoML also automates the deployment process. This can involve generating code for the model, integrating it with production systems, and monitoring its performance over time.

3. Benefits of AutoML

AutoML provides several benefits, particularly for those without extensive machine learning expertise:

- **Speed and Efficiency**: AutoML drastically reduces the time spent on model building and tuning by automating repetitive tasks.

- **Accessibility**: By removing the need for deep technical knowledge, AutoML makes machine learning accessible to non-experts in various domains.

- **Improved Accuracy**: With the help of advanced optimization techniques, AutoML can often identify better models and configurations than manual approaches.

4. Popular AutoML Tools

Several AutoML frameworks and platforms are available, each with its unique features:

- **TPOT**: An open-source AutoML tool based on genetic algorithms for model selection and hyperparameter tuning.

- **H2O.ai**: A popular enterprise-grade AutoML platform that supports a wide range of machine learning algorithms and offers easy-to-use interfaces for model deployment.

- **Google AutoML**: A cloud-based AutoML service that automates the process of building custom models tailored to specific datasets.

- **Microsoft Azure AutoML**: A cloud-based tool that automates the machine learning process for both regression and classification problems.

5. The Future of AutoML

As AutoML continues to evolve, we can expect to see advancements in its ability to handle more complex tasks, such as deep learning and reinforcement learning. The growing integration of AutoML into production pipelines, coupled with improvements in usability and accessibility, will empower even more industries to harness the power of machine learning.

AutoML is transforming the landscape of data science by making machine learning more accessible, faster, and more efficient. As the field continues to grow, AutoML will play an integral role in making machine learning technologies more widely available and usable across industries.

Federated Learning: Privacy-Preserving Learning across Decentralized Devices

Federated Learning is a machine learning technique that enables decentralized model training while keeping data localized on devices. This approach offers a significant advantage in preserving data privacy, as sensitive information never leaves the local device. It has gained attention in various fields, particularly in industries like healthcare, finance, and telecommunications, where data privacy is a critical concern.

1. Overview of Federated Learning

In traditional machine learning, data is centralized on a server, where the model is trained and updated. However, this centralized approach raises privacy concerns, as sensitive data must be shared with a central authority. Federated Learning eliminates this risk by allowing the model to train directly on local devices (such as smartphones, IoT devices, or edge devices). The model updates are then aggregated and sent to a central server without the need for raw data to be shared.

This decentralized approach ensures that user data remains private and secure, which is particularly important in applications where data sensitivity is paramount, such as in healthcare or finance.

2. How Federated Learning Works

Federated Learning follows a series of steps to train a machine learning model across multiple decentralized devices:

a. Model Initialization

The central server initializes a global model and sends it to the local devices. This model contains the weights and parameters that will be updated based on local data.

b. Local Training

Each device trains the model using its own local dataset. The data never leaves the device, and only the model updates (weights and gradients) are computed. This allows the device to learn from its own data without exposing sensitive information.

c. Model Aggregation

Once the local training is complete, the updated model parameters are sent back to the central server. The server aggregates these updates from all devices and averages them to create a new global model. This process ensures that the model benefits from the collective knowledge of all devices without exposing the raw data.

d. Iteration

The process repeats in multiple rounds, with the model gradually improving as more devices participate in the learning process.

3. Advantages of Federated Learning

Federated Learning provides several key advantages over traditional centralized machine learning approaches:

a. Privacy Preservation

One of the most significant benefits of Federated Learning is that sensitive data remains on the local device, mitigating privacy concerns. Since raw data never leaves the device, it reduces the risk of data breaches and unauthorized access.

b. Reduced Data Movement

Federated Learning minimizes the need to transfer large volumes of data to central servers. This reduces bandwidth costs and enables more efficient use of network resources, especially in low-bandwidth environments.

c. Personalization

Federated Learning allows models to be personalized to each device. For example, in mobile applications, models can learn user-specific behavior while maintaining privacy, resulting in more accurate recommendations or predictions.

4. Challenges in Federated Learning

While Federated Learning offers several benefits, it also presents unique challenges that must be addressed:

a. Model Aggregation

The central server must effectively aggregate updates from various devices, which may have different training data distributions or computing capacities. Techniques like Federated Averaging are used to combine model updates efficiently.

b. Device Heterogeneity

Different devices may have varying computational power, which can affect the speed and efficiency of the training process. Ensuring consistent model updates across devices with different capabilities is a key challenge.

c. Communication Efficiency

Federated Learning relies heavily on communication between devices and the central server. Efficient communication protocols and strategies are necessary to reduce latency and minimize network overhead.

5. Applications of Federated Learning

Federated Learning has a wide range of applications across various industries:

- **Healthcare**: Federated Learning can be used to train machine learning models on sensitive patient data from hospitals and medical devices without sharing the data, ensuring privacy and compliance with regulations like HIPAA.

- **Finance**: Banks and financial institutions can apply Federated Learning to model customer behavior, detect fraud, and personalize services, all while keeping financial data private.

- **Mobile Devices**: In mobile applications, such as predictive text or voice assistants, Federated Learning allows devices to learn user-specific patterns without compromising personal data.

6. The Future of Federated Learning

Federated Learning is poised to play an essential role in the future of AI and machine learning, especially as data privacy becomes more critical. The continued development of efficient communication strategies, aggregation techniques, and privacy-preserving algorithms will help drive the adoption of Federated Learning in a wider range of industries.

Federated Learning is a promising approach that addresses privacy and data sovereignty concerns while enabling powerful machine learning models to be trained across decentralized devices. As the technology matures, it will likely become a core component of privacy-sensitive AI applications.

Quantum Computing in Data Science: Potential and Current Research

Quantum computing is a rapidly evolving field that promises to revolutionize the way data is processed and analyzed. By leveraging the principles of quantum mechanics, quantum computers can potentially solve complex problems that are infeasible for classical computers. In the context of data science, quantum computing could significantly enhance computational power, speed up algorithms, and introduce new paradigms for processing data, especially in areas like optimization, machine learning, and cryptography.

1. What is Quantum Computing?

Quantum computing is based on the principles of quantum mechanics, which govern the behavior of particles at the smallest scales. Unlike classical computers, which use bits to represent either 0 or 1, quantum computers use quantum bits or qubits. Qubits can exist in multiple states simultaneously, a property known as superposition. This allows quantum computers to process a vast amount of information in parallel, making them potentially much more powerful than classical computers for certain tasks.

Additionally, quantum computers utilize entanglement, where qubits become linked in such a way that the state of one qubit can depend on the state of another, even over long distances. This unique feature can enable quantum computers to solve complex problems in ways that classical computers cannot.

2. Quantum Computing in Data Science

Quantum computing is still in its early stages, but its potential applications in data science are vast. Below are a few key areas where quantum computing can impact data science:

a. Optimization Problems

Many data science tasks, such as training machine learning models, involve optimization problems. Quantum computers could dramatically improve optimization algorithms by using quantum parallelism to explore many possible solutions at once. For instance, quantum annealing, a quantum technique, has been used to solve complex optimization problems more efficiently than classical methods.

b. Quantum Machine Learning (QML)

Quantum Machine Learning (QML) is an emerging field that combines quantum computing with traditional machine learning techniques. QML algorithms aim to speed up tasks such as data classification, clustering, and regression by taking advantage of quantum computational power. Quantum computers may also provide better ways to process high-dimensional data and perform tasks like eigenvalue estimation, which is essential in areas such as principal component analysis (PCA).

Quantum computing can potentially accelerate deep learning by improving optimization techniques used in neural network training. For example, the quantum version of the support vector machine (SVM) has shown promise in achieving faster convergence.

c. Quantum Data Structures

Quantum data structures are designed to represent and process data more efficiently than classical data structures. Quantum computing allows for the development of new algorithms that can manipulate quantum data, such as quantum databases, which could provide faster querying and data retrieval capabilities. This can revolutionize big data processing and enable new ways of handling large datasets.

3. Challenges in Quantum Computing for Data Science

Despite its potential, quantum computing presents several challenges that need to be addressed before it can be widely adopted in data science:

a. Hardware Limitations

Quantum computers require delicate environments to function, including extremely low temperatures and high precision control over qubits. Current quantum computers are not yet scalable or stable enough to handle large datasets or perform practical tasks at the scale of classical computers.

b. Algorithm Development

Quantum algorithms are still in the early stages of development, and it is unclear which types of algorithms will be the most beneficial for data science. Many quantum algorithms, such as Shor's algorithm for factoring large numbers, have been proven to outperform classical counterparts, but other areas like machine learning are still experimental.

c. Error Correction

Quantum computers are highly susceptible to errors due to noise and environmental interference. Quantum error correction techniques are necessary to make quantum computations reliable, but these techniques are still being developed and are resource-intensive.

4. Current Research and Future Directions

Research in quantum computing for data science is ongoing, with significant contributions from both academia and industry. Companies like Google, IBM, and Microsoft are working on quantum hardware and software platforms, while universities are exploring quantum algorithms and quantum machine learning models.

The development of quantum algorithms tailored for specific data science tasks, such as clustering, regression, and data mining, is one area of active research. Additionally, researchers are exploring the integration of quantum computing with classical systems, known as hybrid quantum-classical systems, to combine the best of both worlds.

5. The Future of Quantum Computing in Data Science

While quantum computing is still in its infancy, its potential to revolutionize data science is undeniable. Quantum computers could enable new algorithms and computational methods that dramatically improve data analysis, model training, and optimization tasks. As quantum hardware becomes more stable and scalable, and as new algorithms are developed, quantum computing will likely play a key role in solving some of the most challenging problems in data science.

Quantum computing holds enormous promise for the future of data science, though significant challenges remain. Continued research, development, and collaboration between quantum physicists, computer scientists, and data scientists will be crucial in unlocking its full potential.

The Future of AI and Data Science: Trends and Innovations

The future of AI and data science is an exciting and rapidly evolving landscape. As technology continues to advance, we are witnessing significant innovations that will shape the way data is processed, analyzed, and applied across industries. In this section, we will explore the key trends and innovations that are expected to drive the future of AI and data science.

1. Automation and the Rise of AutoML

One of the most transformative trends in data science is the rise of **AutoML** (Automated Machine Learning). AutoML aims to democratize machine learning by automating the process of model selection, hyperparameter tuning, and feature engineering. This will empower non-experts to build machine learning models and make AI more accessible to a broader audience.

AutoML platforms, such as Google AutoML and H2O.ai, are already helping organizations automate repetitive tasks like model training and evaluation. This allows data scientists to focus on more complex problems while reducing the time spent on manual adjustments. In the future, AutoML is expected to play an even greater role in accelerating AI adoption and improving model performance without requiring deep expertise in machine learning.

2. Federated Learning: Privacy-Preserving Models

As concerns about data privacy continue to grow, **Federated Learning** has emerged as a promising solution for training machine learning models across decentralized devices while keeping data local. In federated learning, data does not leave the device, and only model updates are shared with a central server. This enables organizations to leverage vast amounts of data from different sources without compromising privacy.

This approach is especially useful in fields like healthcare and finance, where sensitive data is prevalent. By enabling model training across multiple devices (e.g., smartphones, IoT devices) while ensuring privacy and security, federated learning has the potential to revolutionize industries that require data protection.

3. Explainable AI (XAI): Enhancing Trust in AI Models

As AI systems are being integrated into more critical applications, the need for **explainability** has become paramount. **Explainable AI (XAI)** aims to make machine learning models more transparent and interpretable, helping users understand how models make decisions. This is particularly important in regulated industries like healthcare, finance, and law, where understanding the reasoning behind AI decisions is essential.

Techniques like **LIME** (Local Interpretable Model-agnostic Explanations) and **SHAP** (Shapley Additive Explanations) are being developed to explain the behavior of complex machine learning models, such as deep neural networks. In the future, we can expect XAI tools to become more advanced, enabling better model interpretability and fostering trust in AI technologies.

4. Quantum Computing: Pushing the Limits of Computation

Quantum computing has the potential to transform the future of AI and data science. By leveraging quantum bits (qubits), quantum computers can solve certain types of problems much faster than classical computers. While quantum computing is still in its early stages, it holds the promise of solving complex optimization problems, accelerating machine learning, and enabling new ways of processing large datasets.

In the future, quantum algorithms for machine learning, such as quantum support vector machines and quantum neural networks, could enhance the power of AI systems. Additionally, the combination of quantum computing and machine learning may lead to breakthroughs in fields like drug discovery, material science, and climate modeling.

5. AI Ethics and Regulation: Shaping Responsible AI Development

As AI technologies continue to permeate various industries, the need for ethical guidelines and regulations is becoming more apparent. Governments and organizations are working together to establish standards for the responsible development and deployment of AI systems. The focus is on ensuring fairness, accountability, transparency, and the prevention of bias in AI algorithms.

In the future, we can expect stricter regulations surrounding AI use, particularly in sensitive areas like hiring, lending, and healthcare. These regulations will help ensure that AI systems are used ethically and that their decisions are transparent and justifiable.

6. The Path Forward for AI and Data Science

The future of AI and data science is filled with immense potential and transformative innovations. As technologies like AutoML, federated learning, quantum computing, and explainable AI continue to advance, they will shape the next generation of intelligent systems. However, these advancements also come with challenges, including privacy concerns, ethical considerations, and the need for robust regulatory frameworks.

By embracing these trends and innovations, organizations can unlock new opportunities in AI and data science, while ensuring that these technologies are used responsibly and for the benefit of society. The future of AI is not just about building smarter algorithms but also about fostering trust, collaboration, and fairness in the AI-driven world.

Part 6:

Data Engineering and Infrastructure

Data Warehousing and ETL Pipelines

Data warehousing is an essential practice for consolidating data from multiple sources into a centralized repository for analysis and reporting. This module explains the concept of data warehousing and the importance of having a unified system for storing integrated data. The Extract, Transform, Load (ETL) process is central to data integration and is thoroughly explored, with a focus on its workflow and best practices. ETL involves extracting data from different sources, transforming it into a suitable format for analysis, and loading it into a data warehouse. Tools like Apache Airflow, Talend, and custom pipelines are introduced as popular options for automating and managing ETL workflows, helping organizations maintain clean and accessible data.

Cloud Infrastructure for Data Science

Cloud computing has become indispensable for data science, offering scalable, flexible, and cost-effective resources. This module provides an introduction to cloud computing models such as IaaS (Infrastructure as a Service), PaaS (Platform as a Service), and SaaS (Software as a Service), which are essential for data science infrastructure. Leading cloud platforms like AWS, Azure, and Google Cloud are covered, highlighting their strengths and use cases for data science applications. Data storage solutions, such as Amazon S3, Google Cloud Storage, and Azure Blob, are discussed for their ability to handle large volumes of data in the cloud. Additionally, the module emphasizes the importance of scalability and cost management, showing how to effectively leverage cloud resources for large-scale data science projects.

Streaming and Real-Time Data Processing

Real-time data processing is crucial for time-sensitive applications, such as fraud detection, live recommendations, and monitoring systems. In this module, learners are introduced to the concept of real-time data, understanding its significance in delivering immediate insights and actions. Stream processing frameworks like Apache Kafka, Apache Flink, and Spark Streaming are explored as powerful tools for handling continuous data streams. The module covers how to design and implement efficient data pipelines that process real-time data, ensuring low-latency and high-throughput operations. Real-world use cases such as fraud detection and live recommendation systems demonstrate the practical applications of real-time data processing in various industries.

Data Lake Architecture

Data lakes provide a flexible and scalable approach to storing raw, unstructured data. This module introduces the concept of a data lake, explaining its role in centralizing large amounts of raw data from multiple sources. Learners will explore the benefits and challenges of data lakes, balancing flexibility and cost with the complexity of managing vast datasets. Technologies like Hadoop, Amazon S3, and Delta Lake are discussed as leading solutions for building and managing data lakes. Integration with data warehouses is also covered, highlighting the creation of a unified ecosystem where structured and unstructured data coexist, enabling comprehensive analytics.

Data Security and Governance

Data security and governance are vital components of responsible data management, ensuring the confidentiality, integrity, and compliance of data systems. This module covers the importance of protecting sensitive data from breaches and unauthorized access. Techniques for data encryption and access control are explored, offering methods to ensure that data is only accessible by authorized parties. Data governance practices, including compliance with regulations like GDPR and HIPAA, are discussed to ensure organizations meet legal and ethical standards. Additionally, data auditing and logging are introduced as essential tools for maintaining traceability and accountability in data systems, allowing organizations to monitor and track data usage.

Scalable Data Systems

Designing scalable data systems is crucial for handling growing volumes of data while maintaining performance and reliability. This module covers the design principles behind scalable data systems, including the importance of distributed computing and the use of technologies like MapReduce and Hadoop for parallel data processing. Learners will explore methods for ensuring system reliability through load balancing and failover mechanisms, which help prevent downtime and ensure high availability. The module also delves into optimizing data storage and access through techniques like sharding, indexing, and caching, ensuring fast and efficient data retrieval in large-scale systems.

Module 35:

Data Warehousing and ETL Pipelines

Data warehousing and ETL pipelines are fundamental components of modern data architecture. Data warehousing enables businesses to store and consolidate data from multiple sources into a centralized repository, providing a solid foundation for decision-making. ETL (Extract, Transform, Load) pipelines ensure that this data is efficiently processed and integrated, making it ready for analysis and reporting. This module provides insights into the process of data warehousing and ETL pipelines, their importance in data-driven organizations, and their role in enabling efficient data workflows.

What is Data Warehousing?: Centralized Storage for Integrated Data

Data warehousing refers to the process of collecting and storing data from various operational systems into a single, unified repository. The goal is to create a centralized location where data from multiple sources is stored in an integrated, consistent, and optimized manner. This system allows businesses to access large volumes of data efficiently for reporting, analysis, and decision-making. Data warehouses typically store historical data, enabling users to run complex queries, generate business intelligence reports, and gain insights from past trends, all in one place.

ETL (Extract, Transform, Load) Process: Workflow and Best Practices

The ETL process is critical for moving data from operational systems into a data warehouse. The Extract phase involves pulling data from various sources such as databases, spreadsheets, and external systems. The Transform phase focuses on cleaning, standardizing, and transforming the extracted data into a consistent format. In the Load phase, the transformed data is inserted into the data warehouse for storage and analysis. Best practices in ETL workflows include automating data extraction and loading, ensuring data quality through validation, and optimizing performance using incremental loading techniques.

Data Integration: Combining Disparate Data Sources Into a Unified System

Data integration refers to the process of combining data from disparate sources into a cohesive dataset that can be analyzed and used to derive meaningful insights. This is a vital process because businesses often rely on data from multiple sources—such as CRM systems, financial databases, and external data feeds—each with its own format and structure. By integrating these data sources, businesses can have a unified view of their operations, improving decision-making. Successful data integration involves data mapping, transformation, and cleaning techniques that align the various data sources into a consistent format.

Tools for ETL: Apache Airflow, Talend, and Custom Pipelines

There are a variety of tools available to help manage ETL pipelines and the overall data integration process. Apache Airflow is an open-source platform for designing, scheduling, and monitoring workflows. It is widely used for its flexibility and scalability, enabling data engineers to automate complex data processing tasks. Talend is another popular tool that offers a user-friendly interface for managing ETL processes and integrating data from multiple sources. For highly customized data workflows, many businesses choose to build their own pipelines tailored to their specific needs and infrastructure.

What is Data Warehousing?: Centralized Storage for Integrated Data

Data warehousing is a critical component of modern data management strategies, offering a centralized repository where data from various sources is stored, integrated, and made available for analysis. This section delves into the fundamental concepts of data warehousing, its importance, and how it enables organizations to make informed decisions.

1. Understanding Data Warehousing

At its core, a **data warehouse** is a centralized storage system designed to consolidate data from multiple disparate sources. Unlike transactional databases optimized for day-to-day operations, data warehouses are structured to facilitate analytical queries and reporting. This architecture supports large-scale data integration, ensuring data consistency and accessibility for business intelligence (BI) tools and analytics platforms.

A data warehouse typically consists of **fact tables** (storing quantitative data) and **dimension tables** (storing descriptive attributes) organized in schemas like star or snowflake schemas. These structures optimize query performance and allow users to analyze data along various dimensions, such as time, location, and product.

2. Benefits of Data Warehousing

Data warehousing offers several advantages, including:

- **Data Integration:** Consolidating data from multiple sources, such as databases, APIs, and flat files, into a unified system.

- **Improved Decision-Making:** Providing accurate, consistent, and up-to-date data for advanced analytics and BI tools.

- **Enhanced Query Performance:** Using pre-aggregated and indexed data to speed up complex analytical queries.

- **Historical Analysis:** Preserving historical data for trend analysis and forecasting.

These benefits make data warehousing indispensable for organizations seeking to leverage data as a strategic asset.

3. Building a Data Warehouse

The process of building a data warehouse involves several key steps:

1. **Data Extraction:** Retrieving data from source systems.

2. **Data Transformation:** Cleaning, normalizing, and formatting the data to ensure consistency.

3. **Data Loading:** Storing the transformed data in the data warehouse for analysis.

4. A Simple Data Warehousing Workflow in Python

The following Python script demonstrates a basic workflow to extract, transform, and load (ETL) data into a data warehouse:

```python
import pandas as pd
import sqlite3

# Step 1: Extract - Load data from source files
sales_data = pd.read_csv("sales.csv")
customer_data = pd.read_csv("customers.csv")

# Step 2: Transform - Merge and clean data
merged_data = pd.merge(sales_data, customer_data, on="customer_id")
merged_data["order_date"] = pd.to_datetime(merged_data["order_date"])
cleaned_data = merged_data.dropna()

# Step 3: Load - Store cleaned data into a SQLite data warehouse
connection = sqlite3.connect("data_warehouse.db")
cleaned_data.to_sql("sales_data", connection, if_exists="replace",
          index=False)

print("Data loaded successfully into the data warehouse.")
```

This simplified pipeline integrates sales and customer data, cleans it, and loads it into a SQLite database for analysis.

5. Challenges in Data Warehousing

Despite its benefits, data warehousing presents several challenges:

- **Data Volume:** Managing large datasets efficiently.

- **Real-Time Integration:** Supporting near-real-time data processing for dynamic use cases.

- **Maintenance:** Keeping the warehouse schema up-to-date with evolving business needs.

Organizations must address these challenges to ensure the effectiveness of their data warehousing strategies.

Data warehousing serves as the backbone of advanced analytics, offering a centralized platform for integrated and consistent data storage. By consolidating data from multiple sources, organizations can derive actionable insights and make data-driven decisions. As we explore ETL processes in the next section, we will uncover the best practices for extracting, transforming, and loading data into a robust warehouse system.

ETL (Extract, Transform, Load) Process: Workflow and Best Practices

The ETL (Extract, Transform, Load) process is the backbone of modern data warehousing. It ensures that data from various sources is collected, transformed for consistency, and loaded into a centralized repository for analysis. This section breaks down the ETL process into its components, highlights its importance, and provides actionable best practices for building efficient pipelines.

1. Overview of the ETL Workflow

The ETL process consists of three sequential stages:

1. **Extract:**
   Data is retrieved from various sources such as databases, APIs, files, or IoT devices. The goal is to collect raw data regardless of its format or source. Example sources include:

   o SQL databases (e.g., MySQL, PostgreSQL)

   o NoSQL systems (e.g., MongoDB, Cassandra)

   o Flat files (e.g., CSV, JSON, XML)

   o APIs or external data providers

2. **Transform:**
   Raw data is cleaned, formatted, and transformed into a usable format. Common transformation tasks include:

   o Handling missing or inconsistent values

400

- Aggregating or summarizing data
- Standardizing formats (e.g., date or numeric conversions)
- Calculating new features

3. **Load:**
   The transformed data is written into a data warehouse or target database. This stage focuses on ensuring data integrity and efficient storage for subsequent queries.

2. Best Practices for ETL Processes

Efficient ETL pipelines require careful design and execution. Below are best practices to follow:

- **Automate the Workflow:** Use tools like Apache Airflow, Talend, or custom Python scripts to automate the ETL process.

- **Implement Data Validation:** Validate data at each stage to ensure its integrity and consistency.

- **Optimize for Scalability:** Design pipelines that handle increasing data volumes efficiently.

- **Monitor and Log Processes:** Track pipeline performance and log errors for troubleshooting.

- **Schedule Regular Updates:** Set up periodic runs for data that changes over time, ensuring the warehouse stays updated.

3. Python Example: Building a Simple ETL Pipeline

The following Python script demonstrates a basic ETL pipeline for loading sales data into a data warehouse:

```python
import pandas as pd
import sqlite3

# Step 1: Extract - Read raw data from CSV files
sales_data = pd.read_csv("raw_sales.csv")
product_data = pd.read_csv("raw_products.csv")

# Step 2: Transform - Clean and join the data
# Handle missing values
sales_data = sales_data.dropna()
product_data = product_data.dropna()

# Merge sales with product information
transformed_data = pd.merge(sales_data, product_data, on="product_id")
transformed_data["sales_date"] =
        pd.to_datetime(transformed_data["sales_date"])
```

```
transformed_data["revenue"] = transformed_data["quantity"] *
        transformed_data["price"]

# Step 3: Load - Insert cleaned data into a SQLite database
conn = sqlite3.connect("data_warehouse.db")
transformed_data.to_sql("sales_data", conn, if_exists="replace",
        index=False)

print("ETL process completed successfully!")
```

4. Common ETL Challenges

Organizations face several challenges when building ETL pipelines, such as:

- **Handling Data Variability:** Data formats often differ between sources, requiring extensive cleaning.

- **Performance Bottlenecks:** Large datasets can slow down processing unless the pipeline is optimized.

- **Data Latency:** Ensuring near-real-time updates is critical for dynamic systems.

- **Error Management:** Failing to handle errors during extraction or transformation can compromise data quality.

The ETL process forms the foundation of data warehousing by integrating and preparing data for analysis. By automating workflows, validating data, and addressing challenges proactively, organizations can create robust pipelines that ensure high-quality data delivery. As the next section explores data integration, it will provide deeper insights into unifying disparate data sources into a cohesive system.

Data Integration: Combining Disparate Data Sources into a Unified System

Data integration is the process of merging data from multiple heterogeneous sources into a unified system, enabling seamless analysis and actionable insights. In today's data-driven world, organizations deal with vast amounts of data from diverse sources like relational databases, NoSQL systems, APIs, flat files, and streaming platforms. Integration ensures that this data becomes consistent, accessible, and usable.

1. Key Components of Data Integration

Data integration involves several essential components, each playing a critical role in combining data effectively:

1. **Source Systems:**
   The origin of raw data, such as databases, cloud services, or APIs. Examples include:

- SQL databases (e.g., PostgreSQL, MySQL)

- NoSQL platforms (e.g., MongoDB, DynamoDB)

- External APIs (e.g., weather data, payment gateways)

2. **Integration Layer:**
Middleware that extracts, transforms, and loads data into a central repository. This layer may involve:

- ETL tools like Talend or Apache Nifi

- Custom Python scripts

- Data integration platforms like Informatica

3. **Target System:**
A centralized location where integrated data is stored, such as a data warehouse (e.g., Snowflake, Amazon Redshift) or a data lake.

2. Techniques for Data Integration

Several techniques can be employed to integrate disparate data sources effectively:

1. **Data Consolidation:**
Combining all data into a single repository, such as a data warehouse or data lake. This approach ensures easy access but may require significant storage and processing capabilities.

2. **Data Federation:**
Virtual integration that enables querying data across sources without physically moving it. Tools like Apache Drill or Denodo support this technique.

3. **Data Propagation:**
Periodically synchronizing changes from the source to the target system using scheduled updates or triggers.

3. Python Example: Data Integration with Pandas

The following example demonstrates integrating data from multiple CSV files into a unified dataset.

```
import pandas as pd

# Load data from multiple sources
customer_data = pd.read_csv("customers.csv")
orders_data = pd.read_csv("orders.csv")
```

```python
products_data = pd.read_csv("products.csv")

# Merge datasets on common keys
merged_data = pd.merge(orders_data, customer_data, on="customer_id",
        how="inner")
final_data = pd.merge(merged_data, products_data, on="product_id",
        how="inner")

# Save integrated data to a new file
final_data.to_csv("integrated_data.csv", index=False)
print("Data integration completed successfully!")
```

This script consolidates customer, order, and product data into a unified dataset, ready for analysis or loading into a data warehouse.

4. Challenges in Data Integration

Despite its importance, data integration presents several challenges:

- **Schema Variability:** Differences in database schemas or data formats make integration complex.

- **Data Quality Issues:** Missing, duplicate, or inconsistent records can undermine the integration process.

- **Latency:** Integrating data in real-time or near real-time can strain resources.

- **Security and Compliance:** Ensuring data privacy while integrating sensitive information is crucial.

5. Best Practices for Effective Data Integration

To address these challenges, organizations should adopt the following best practices:

1. **Standardize Data Formats:** Align data from disparate sources to a common format during extraction.

2. **Use Scalable Tools:** Tools like Apache Airflow or cloud-based platforms can handle large-scale integration tasks.

3. **Implement Data Quality Checks:** Validate data for completeness and accuracy before and after integration.

4. **Monitor Integration Workflows:** Track pipeline performance to ensure timely execution and error resolution.

Data integration bridges the gap between disparate data sources and unified analysis. By consolidating and harmonizing data, organizations can unlock deeper insights and enable informed decision-making. As businesses increasingly adopt hybrid and multi-cloud environments, robust integration strategies are critical for maintaining agility and competitiveness. The next section will explore ETL tools that enhance the integration process with automation and scalability.

Tools for ETL: Apache Airflow, Talend, and Custom Pipelines

The ETL (Extract, Transform, Load) process is critical for building scalable, efficient, and reliable data pipelines. A wide range of tools is available to automate and optimize ETL workflows, ensuring seamless data movement from disparate sources to a centralized storage system. This section explores popular ETL tools like Apache Airflow, Talend, and custom pipelines, highlighting their strengths, use cases, and implementation in Python.

1. Apache Airflow: Workflow Orchestration and Automation

Apache Airflow is a powerful open-source platform designed for orchestrating complex ETL workflows. With its directed acyclic graph (DAG) structure, Airflow enables users to define and schedule tasks while managing dependencies.

Key Features:

- **Scalability:** Handles workflows of any size, from small scripts to enterprise-level pipelines.

- **Extensibility:** Allows custom plugins and operator development.

- **Monitoring and Logging:** Provides a user-friendly interface for tracking task execution.

Example: Basic ETL Pipeline Using Apache Airflow Below is a Python script defining an ETL pipeline in Airflow.

```python
from airflow import DAG
from airflow.operators.python_operator import PythonOperator
from datetime import datetime

# Define ETL functions
def extract():
    print("Extracting data...")

def transform():
    print("Transforming data...")

def load():
    print("Loading data into warehouse...")

# Define DAG
default_args = {"owner": "data_team", "start_date": datetime(2024, 1, 1)}
with DAG(dag_id="etl_pipeline", default_args=default_args,
        schedule_interval="@daily") as dag:
    extract_task = PythonOperator(task_id="extract",
        python_callable=extract)
```

```
transform_task = PythonOperator(task_id="transform",
        python_callable=transform)
load_task = PythonOperator(task_id="load", python_callable=load)

# Set task dependencies
extract_task >> transform_task >> load_task
```

Airflow schedules and executes the ETL tasks in the defined order, providing logs for each step.

2. Talend: Comprehensive Data Integration Platform

Talend is a robust ETL tool offering an intuitive drag-and-drop interface for creating data pipelines. It supports a variety of data sources, enabling seamless integration across platforms.

Key Features:

- **Pre-built Connectors:** Supports databases, APIs, and cloud services.

- **Real-Time Processing:** Facilitates streaming data pipelines.

- **Data Quality Tools:** Includes features like deduplication and data cleansing.

Use Cases:

- Large enterprises integrating data across multiple departments.

- Organizations requiring real-time analytics.

3. Custom ETL Pipelines: Flexibility with Python

For specific use cases or small-scale projects, building custom ETL pipelines using Python provides unparalleled flexibility. Libraries like Pandas, PySpark, and SQLAlchemy simplify data extraction, transformation, and loading.

Example: ETL Pipeline Using Python

```
import pandas as pd
from sqlalchemy import create_engine

# Extract data
csv_data = pd.read_csv("data.csv")
db_engine = create_engine("mysql+pymysql://user:password@host:3306/db_name")
db_data = pd.read_sql("SELECT * FROM table_name", db_engine)

# Transform data
csv_data["new_column"] = csv_data["existing_column"].apply(lambda x: x * 2)
merged_data = pd.merge(csv_data, db_data, on="common_column")

# Load data
merged_data.to_sql("merged_table", db_engine, if_exists="replace",
        index=False)
```

```
print("ETL pipeline completed successfully!")
```

Custom pipelines are ideal for lightweight, ad-hoc data workflows or unique business requirements.

4. Comparing ETL Tools

Tool	Strengths	Use Cases
Apache Airflow	Workflow orchestration, scalability	Complex, automated pipelines
Talend	User-friendly interface, real-time processing	Enterprise-level data integration
Custom Pipelines	Full control, flexibility	Small-scale or specialized workflows

Choosing the right ETL tool depends on the complexity of the pipeline, the volume of data, and the organization's specific needs. Apache Airflow and Talend are excellent for large-scale and enterprise use, while custom pipelines offer flexibility for unique scenarios. With these tools, businesses can efficiently extract, transform, and load data, ensuring seamless integration and improved analytics capabilities.

Module 36:

Cloud Infrastructure for Data Science

Cloud infrastructure has become integral to data science, enabling scalable computing resources, flexible data storage, and powerful analytics capabilities. It offers the flexibility to manage large datasets and run complex models without the need for substantial on-premise hardware. This module explores cloud computing concepts, platforms, data storage options, and cost management strategies for data science applications.

Introduction to Cloud Computing: IaaS, PaaS, and SaaS

Cloud computing delivers computing services over the internet, eliminating the need for traditional data centers. It encompasses three service models: Infrastructure as a Service (IaaS), Platform as a Service (PaaS), and Software as a Service (SaaS). IaaS provides virtualized computing resources, allowing users to rent infrastructure. PaaS offers a platform for building applications without managing underlying hardware. SaaS delivers software applications on a subscription basis, providing access via the cloud without installation. Each service model offers unique advantages depending on project requirements, such as cost-effectiveness, ease of scaling, and reduced management complexity.

Cloud Platforms: AWS, Azure, Google Cloud

Leading cloud platforms include Amazon Web Services (AWS), Microsoft Azure, and Google Cloud. AWS is a comprehensive cloud service offering an extensive range of tools for computation, storage, and machine learning. Azure integrates seamlessly with Microsoft's ecosystem, offering excellent support for enterprise solutions and hybrid cloud environments. Google Cloud excels in big data analytics and machine learning, providing strong integration with Google's services and AI capabilities. These platforms provide the infrastructure needed for scalable data science workflows, with each offering specialized features catering to specific needs such as security, processing power, and data storage.

Data Storage in the Cloud: Amazon S3, Google Cloud Storage, and Azure Blob

Cloud storage solutions like Amazon S3, Google Cloud Storage, and Azure Blob provide reliable and scalable storage for vast amounts of data. Amazon S3 offers object storage with high durability and availability, ideal for large datasets and backups. Google Cloud Storage delivers similar features, with strong performance for data analytics workflows. Azure Blob Storage is optimized for unstructured data, offering flexibility for data types such as text, video, and images. These services facilitate efficient data management in data science projects, providing seamless access and easy integration with machine learning and data processing tools.

Scalability and Cost Management: Leveraging Cloud Resources Effectively

Cloud infrastructure enables businesses to scale computing resources up or down as needed, improving efficiency and reducing costs. To effectively manage costs, it's essential to monitor resource usage and choose the right pricing model. Cloud providers offer options like on-demand, reserved, or spot instances, each with different cost implications. Leveraging auto-scaling features can also optimize resource allocation, ensuring that services are dynamically adjusted based on demand. Proper cost management strategies, such as using cheaper storage for archival data or optimizing compute instances, are crucial for maintaining a balance between performance and expense.

Introduction to Cloud Computing: IaaS, PaaS, and SaaS

Cloud computing has revolutionized the way data science projects are executed, offering scalable, flexible, and cost-efficient solutions. Before diving into specific tools and platforms, it's important to understand the foundational models of cloud computing: Infrastructure as a Service (IaaS), Platform as a Service (PaaS), and Software as a Service (SaaS). These models cater to different stages of the data science lifecycle, from raw infrastructure to complete software solutions.

1. Infrastructure as a Service (IaaS)

IaaS provides raw computing resources such as virtual machines, storage, and networking over the internet. Data scientists can use IaaS to build custom environments, run complex models, and manage massive datasets without investing in physical hardware.

Key Features:

- **Customization:** Users control operating systems, middleware, and applications.

- **Scalability:** Automatically adjust resources based on workload.

- **Examples:** Amazon EC2, Microsoft Azure Virtual Machines, Google Compute Engine.

Python Example: Launching an EC2 Instance

```python
import boto3

# Initialize EC2 client
ec2 = boto3.client('ec2')

# Launch EC2 instance
response = ec2.run_instances(
```

```
        ImageId='ami-0abcdef1234567890',  # Replace with actual AMI ID
        InstanceType='t2.micro',
        MinCount=1,
        MaxCount=1,
        KeyName='my-key-pair'
)
print("EC2 instance launched:", response['Instances'][0]['InstanceId'])
```

2. Platform as a Service (PaaS)

PaaS offers a managed environment for building, testing, and deploying applications. It abstracts the underlying infrastructure, allowing data scientists to focus on modeling and application development.

Key Features:

- **Ease of Use:** No need to manage servers or runtime environments.

- **Integrated Tools:** Includes APIs, databases, and frameworks.

- **Examples:** Google App Engine, AWS Elastic Beanstalk, Microsoft Azure App Services.

Use Case in Data Science: Deploying a machine learning model using PaaS can eliminate the overhead of managing dependencies and server configurations.

3. Software as a Service (SaaS)

SaaS provides complete software solutions over the cloud, accessible via web browsers. It is ideal for end-users who require ready-to-use tools without setup or maintenance.

Key Features:

- **Accessibility:** Available on-demand via the internet.

- **Collaboration:** Multiple users can work on shared platforms.

- **Examples:** Google Analytics, Tableau Online, Microsoft Power BI.

Example Workflow: SaaS platforms like Google Colab allow data scientists to run Python code in a cloud-based notebook environment, eliminating the need for local installations.

```
# Example: Using Google Colab
print("Welcome to cloud-based Python coding!")
```

4. Comparing IaaS, PaaS, and SaaS

Model	Primary Users	Strengths	Examples
IaaS	System administrators, engineers	Customizable infrastructure	AWS EC2, Google Compute Engine
PaaS	Developers, data scientists	Simplifies app deployment and scaling	AWS Elastic Beanstalk, Heroku
SaaS	End-users, analysts	Fully managed, ready-to-use software	Google Colab, Tableau Online

Understanding IaaS, PaaS, and SaaS is essential for selecting the appropriate cloud solution for a data science project. While IaaS provides flexibility for custom setups, PaaS simplifies deployment, and SaaS enables quick access to ready-made tools. Each model plays a critical role in enabling data scientists to leverage the power of the cloud efficiently.

Cloud Platforms: AWS, Azure, Google Cloud

Cloud platforms play a pivotal role in modern data science by providing comprehensive tools and services to manage data, train models, and deploy solutions at scale. The three leading cloud providers—Amazon Web Services (AWS), Microsoft Azure, and Google Cloud Platform (GCP)—offer powerful capabilities tailored for data science workflows. Understanding their strengths and offerings helps data scientists choose the right platform for their needs.

1. Amazon Web Services (AWS)

AWS is the most widely adopted cloud platform, offering an extensive range of services for data science, including data storage, compute power, and machine learning tools.

Key Services for Data Science:

- **Amazon S3 (Simple Storage Service):** Scalable object storage for datasets.

- **Amazon SageMaker:** A managed service for building, training, and deploying machine learning models.

- **AWS Lambda:** Serverless computing for running lightweight data transformations.

Python Example: Storing Data in Amazon S3

```python
import boto3

# Initialize S3 client
s3 = boto3.client('s3')

# Upload a file to S3
```

411

```
s3.upload_file('local_file.csv', 'my-bucket', 'data/local_file.csv')
print("File uploaded to S3 successfully!")
```

Strengths:

- Broadest range of services.

- Mature ecosystem with global availability.

2. Microsoft Azure

Azure offers robust tools for integrating machine learning with enterprise workflows. Its services are known for their seamless integration with Microsoft products like Excel and Power BI.

Key Services for Data Science:

- **Azure Machine Learning (Azure ML):** A platform for building and deploying ML models.

- **Azure Databricks:** An optimized version of Apache Spark for big data processing.

- **Azure Blob Storage:** Scalable storage for unstructured data.

Use Case: Azure ML allows for automated model training and hyperparameter tuning, reducing the time to deploy models.

Python Example: Connecting to Azure Blob Storage

```
from azure.storage.blob import BlobServiceClient

# Connect to Azure Blob Storage
blob_service_client =
        BlobServiceClient.from_connection_string("your_connection_string"
        )
container_client = blob_service_client.get_container_client("my-container")

# Upload a file
with open("local_file.csv", "rb") as data:
    container_client.upload_blob(name="data/local_file.csv", data=data)
print("File uploaded to Azure Blob Storage!")
```

Strengths:

- Integration with enterprise systems.

- Comprehensive big data tools.

3. Google Cloud Platform (GCP)

GCP is known for its user-friendly interfaces and cutting-edge AI tools, making it a favorite among data scientists working on innovative projects.

Key Services for Data Science:

- **BigQuery:** A serverless data warehouse for analyzing massive datasets.

- **Vertex AI:** End-to-end tools for ML model development.

- **Google Cloud Storage:** Object storage with fast access to data.

Python Example: Querying Data in BigQuery

```python
from google.cloud import bigquery

# Initialize BigQuery client
client = bigquery.Client()

# Run a query
query = "SELECT * FROM `project.dataset.table` LIMIT 10"
query_job = client.query(query)

# Print query results
for row in query_job:
    print(row)
```

Strengths:

- Advanced AI and machine learning tools.

- Cost-effective for smaller-scale projects.

4. Comparing AWS, Azure, and GCP

Platform	Strengths	Best Use Cases	Key Tools
AWS	Wide service range, scalability	Large-scale deployments, diverse needs	SageMaker, S3, Lambda
Azure	Enterprise integration	Enterprise ML, big data analytics	Azure ML, Databricks, Blob
GCP	AI and ML innovation	AI research, rapid prototyping	BigQuery, Vertex AI, Cloud ML

AWS, Azure, and GCP offer unique features and strengths that cater to different data science requirements. AWS provides a versatile ecosystem, Azure excels in enterprise integration, and GCP leads in AI innovations. Choosing the right platform depends on specific project goals, team expertise, and budget.

Data Storage in the Cloud: Amazon S3, Google Cloud Storage, and Azure Blob

Cloud-based data storage has revolutionized data science by providing scalable, reliable, and cost-effective solutions for storing and managing large datasets. The three major cloud providers—Amazon S3, Google Cloud Storage, and Azure Blob Storage—offer robust storage systems that cater to diverse data science needs. This section explores their features, uses, and implementation in Python.

1. Amazon S3 (Simple Storage Service)

Amazon S3 is an object storage service known for its scalability and durability. It allows users to store and retrieve any amount of data, making it ideal for data lakes, backups, and archives.

Key Features:

- **Scalability:** Handles petabytes of data effortlessly.

- **Lifecycle Policies:** Automate data transitions between storage classes.

- **Integration:** Compatible with AWS tools like Athena and SageMaker.

Python Example: Uploading and Downloading Data from S3

```python
import boto3

# Initialize S3 client
s3 = boto3.client('s3')

# Upload a file to S3
s3.upload_file('data.csv', 'my-bucket', 'data/data.csv')
print("File uploaded to S3.")

# Download the file back
s3.download_file('my-bucket', 'data/data.csv', 'downloaded_data.csv')
print("File downloaded from S3.")
```

Use Cases:

- Storing raw or processed datasets for machine learning pipelines.

- Data archiving with reduced costs using S3 Glacier.

2. Google Cloud Storage (GCS)

Google Cloud Storage is another leading object storage solution, offering seamless integration with GCP services like BigQuery and Vertex AI. It supports multi-regional storage for high availability.

Key Features:

- **Flexible Storage Classes:** Options for nearline, coldline, and archive storage.

- **Global Accessibility:** High availability across regions.

- **Security:** Built-in encryption and IAM controls.

Python Example: Uploading and Accessing Files in GCS

```
from google.cloud import storage

# Initialize GCS client
client = storage.Client()
bucket = client.bucket('my-bucket')

# Upload a file
blob = bucket.blob('data/data.csv')
blob.upload_from_filename('data.csv')
print("File uploaded to GCS.")

# Download the file back
blob.download_to_filename('downloaded_data.csv')
print("File downloaded from GCS.")
```

Use Cases:

- Training ML models with data stored in GCS buckets.

- Streaming data pipelines using GCS as the source or sink.

3. Azure Blob Storage

Azure Blob Storage specializes in unstructured data storage, offering high performance and scalability. It is particularly suited for integration with Azure's data and analytics ecosystem.

Key Features:

- **Blob Tiers:** Hot, Cool, and Archive tiers for cost optimization.

- **Data Lake Integration:** Supports Azure Data Lake for big data workflows.

- **Secure Transfers:** TLS encryption ensures data security.

Python Example: Managing Blobs in Azure

```
from azure.storage.blob import BlobServiceClient

# Connect to Azure Blob Storage
connection_string = "your_connection_string"
blob_service_client =
        BlobServiceClient.from_connection_string(connection_string)
```

```
container_client = blob_service_client.get_container_client('my-container')

# Upload a file
with open('data.csv', 'rb') as file:
    container_client.upload_blob(name='data/data.csv', data=file)
print("File uploaded to Azure Blob Storage.")

# Download the file
with open('downloaded_data.csv', 'wb') as file:
    file.write(container_client.download_blob('data/data.csv').readall())
print("File downloaded from Azure Blob Storage.")
```

Use Cases:

- Integration with Azure ML and Databricks for analytics workflows.

- Secure data storage for applications using Azure infrastructure.

4. Comparative Overview

Feature	Amazon S3	Google Cloud Storage	Azure Blob Storage
Scalability	Extremely scalable	High scalability	Highly scalable
Integration	AWS ecosystem	GCP services	Azure tools and ML
Cost Efficiency	Glacier for archiving	Coldline and archive tiers	Archive Blob tier
Ease of Use	CLI and SDK support	User-friendly APIs	Intuitive interface

Amazon S3, Google Cloud Storage, and Azure Blob Storage each provide robust, scalable solutions for cloud-based data storage, catering to the needs of data scientists and enterprises alike. Selecting the appropriate platform depends on factors such as project requirements, existing infrastructure, and cost considerations. Efficient data storage in the cloud is foundational to modern data science workflows, enabling seamless access, analysis, and collaboration.

Scalability and Cost Management: Leveraging Cloud Resources Effectively

Cloud computing offers unparalleled scalability and flexibility, making it an essential component of modern data science workflows. However, effectively managing scalability while optimizing costs requires a strategic approach. This section explores how to leverage cloud resources for scalability, key cost management techniques, and the importance of monitoring and optimization in cloud-based systems.

1. Scalability in Cloud Infrastructure

Cloud platforms provide two primary types of scalability: **vertical scalability** (adding resources to a single machine) and **horizontal scalability** (adding more machines to distribute workloads). For data science, horizontal scalability is often critical, as it enables handling massive datasets and computationally intensive tasks.

Techniques for Scalability:

- **Auto-Scaling:** Automatically adjusts the number of instances based on demand. For example:

    o AWS Auto Scaling for EC2 instances.

    o Google Cloud Compute Engine Autoscaler.

    o Azure Virtual Machine Scale Sets.

- **Serverless Computing:** Tools like AWS Lambda, Google Cloud Functions, and Azure Functions scale automatically based on the workload.

Python Example: Horizontal Scaling with AWS Lambda

```python
import boto3

# Deploying a simple Lambda function
client = boto3.client('lambda')

response = client.create_function(
    FunctionName='DataProcessingFunction',
    Runtime='python3.9',
    Role='arn:aws:iam::123456789012:role/execution_role',
    Handler='lambda_function.lambda_handler',
    Code={'ZipFile': open('function.zip', 'rb').read()},
    Timeout=300,
    MemorySize=512
)
print("Lambda function deployed:", response['FunctionArn'])
```

By leveraging auto-scaling and serverless architectures, organizations can handle spikes in demand without provisioning extra resources upfront.

2. Cost Management Strategies

While scalability enhances efficiency, it can lead to unnecessary expenses if resources are not managed properly. Implementing cost control mechanisms ensures that you optimize cloud usage without exceeding budget constraints.

Best Practices for Cost Management:

1. **Resource Tagging:** Assign tags to cloud resources to monitor usage and costs for specific projects.

2. **Right-Sizing Resources:** Continuously assess and resize instances to match workload requirements.

3. **Reserved Instances:** Purchase long-term reserved instances for predictable workloads to save on costs.

4. **Spot Instances:** Use spot or preemptible instances for non-critical, time-flexible tasks, significantly reducing costs.

5. **Monitoring Tools:** Leverage native tools such as AWS Cost Explorer, Google Cloud Billing, and Azure Cost Management.

Python Example: Monitoring AWS Costs

```python
import boto3

# Access AWS Cost Explorer data
client = boto3.client('ce')

response = client.get_cost_and_usage(
    TimePeriod={'Start': '2024-12-01', 'End': '2024-12-31'},
    Granularity='MONTHLY',
    Metrics=['AmortizedCost']
)

print("Monthly cost:",
        response['ResultsByTime'][0]['Total']['AmortizedCost']['Amount'],
        "USD")
```

These strategies ensure efficient allocation of cloud resources while keeping costs in check.

3. Monitoring and Optimization

Regular monitoring and optimization of cloud resources are critical for maintaining performance and cost-effectiveness. Continuous monitoring identifies underutilized resources and potential bottlenecks.

Tools for Monitoring:

- **AWS CloudWatch:** Monitors application performance and resource utilization.

- **Google Cloud Operations Suite (formerly Stackdriver):** Tracks performance metrics across GCP.

- **Azure Monitor:** Provides actionable insights into cloud and on-premises environments.

Optimization Techniques:

- **Load Balancing:** Distributes workloads evenly across instances to maximize resource utilization.

- **Caching:** Reduces computational overhead by caching frequently accessed data using tools like AWS ElasticCache or Redis.

- **Data Compression:** Minimizes storage and transfer costs by compressing large datasets before storage.

Python Example: Implementing Load Balancing with Flask

```python
from flask import Flask

app = Flask(__name__)

@app.route('/')
def index():
    return "Load balancer distributing traffic."

if __name__ == '__main__':
    app.run(debug=True, host='0.0.0.0', port=5000)
```

4. Balancing Scalability and Cost Efficiency

While scalability allows data science teams to handle large-scale projects, achieving cost efficiency requires careful planning and execution. Organizations must balance between scaling resources for peak performance and minimizing waste by shutting down idle resources or automating resource allocation.

Leveraging cloud resources effectively for scalability and cost management is a cornerstone of modern data science. By adopting auto-scaling, serverless architectures, and proactive cost monitoring, data science teams can ensure efficient and cost-effective use of cloud infrastructure. Combining these practices with continuous optimization fosters a sustainable and scalable environment for data-driven innovation.

Module 37:

Streaming and Real-Time Data Processing

Real-time data processing has become vital for applications that require immediate insights and responses. With the growing need to analyze large amounts of fast-moving data, stream processing frameworks and data pipelines are essential in handling real-time information efficiently. This module explores the importance, frameworks, design strategies, and practical applications of real-time data processing systems.

What is Real-Time Data?: Importance in Time-Sensitive Applications

Real-time data refers to data that is continuously generated and processed with minimal delay. In time-sensitive applications, real-time data allows for instant decision-making, critical for industries like finance, healthcare, and e-commerce. For example, in financial trading, data must be processed in real-time to make timely decisions. Real-time processing enables businesses to react quickly to dynamic changes in their environment, ensuring competitive advantage and improved customer experiences.

Stream Processing Frameworks: Apache Kafka, Apache Flink, and Spark Streaming

Stream processing frameworks such as Apache Kafka, Apache Flink, and Spark Streaming play a crucial role in handling large volumes of real-time data. Apache Kafka is a distributed event streaming platform that efficiently handles data pipelines at scale. Apache Flink is a powerful stream processing engine that excels at low-latency, high-throughput data processing. Spark Streaming, an extension of Apache Spark, allows for real-time stream processing with micro-batching capabilities. These frameworks enable businesses to handle and process high-velocity data streams, ensuring timely data availability and actionable insights.

Data Pipelines for Real-Time Data: Designing and Implementing Efficient Systems

Designing a data pipeline for real-time processing requires careful consideration of data ingestion, processing, and output. The system must efficiently handle continuous streams of data with low latency and high throughput. Key components include data ingestion systems, message brokers, stream processing frameworks, and storage solutions. Scalability and fault tolerance are crucial to ensure that the pipeline can handle increasing volumes of data and provide reliable outputs. Implementing efficient real-time data pipelines involves balancing system performance, minimizing latency, and ensuring that data is processed in near-real-time.

Use Cases for Real-Time Processing: Fraud Detection, Live Recommendation Systems

Real-time data processing has numerous practical applications. In fraud detection, streaming data is analyzed to identify unusual behavior patterns and flag fraudulent transactions as they occur. Live recommendation systems also rely on real-time data to provide personalized recommendations to users based on their current activities or preferences. For example, e-commerce platforms and streaming services use real-time data processing to suggest products or content to users instantly. These use cases highlight the power of real-time data processing in delivering immediate, impactful results to businesses and end-users.

What is Real-Time Data?: Importance in Time-Sensitive Applications

Real-time data processing is a critical component of modern data systems, enabling organizations to respond to events as they happen. Unlike batch processing, which works with historical data, real-time processing handles continuous data streams, making it indispensable for time-sensitive applications such as fraud detection, live recommendations, and system monitoring.

1. Understanding Real-Time Data

Real-time data refers to information generated, processed, and acted upon as events occur. This data is often produced by sensors, applications, or user interactions and arrives in streams rather than static datasets. Processing this data requires systems capable of ingesting, analyzing, and responding with minimal latency.

Key Characteristics:

- **Velocity:** Data is generated at high speeds, often requiring sub-second processing times.

- **Volume:** Real-time systems handle large data streams, sometimes in petabytes.

- **Variety:** Data can come from multiple sources, such as IoT devices, social media, or financial transactions.

2. Importance in Time-Sensitive Applications

The ability to process real-time data has transformed industries by enabling applications that rely on immediate insights and responses.

Examples of Importance:

- **Fraud Detection:** Monitoring transaction patterns in real time to detect anomalies and prevent fraudulent activities.

- **Live Recommendations:** Delivering personalized recommendations during live user interactions, such as streaming platforms or e-commerce sites.

- **Operational Monitoring:** Tracking the health of systems, such as server uptime or network performance, and triggering alerts in case of issues.

Python Example: Real-Time Data Monitoring

```python
import time
import random

# Simulating real-time data stream
def monitor_transactions():
    while True:
        transaction = {"id": random.randint(1, 1000), "amount":
            random.uniform(10, 5000)}
        if transaction["amount"] > 3000:
            print(f"Alert! High-value transaction detected: {transaction}")
        else:
            print(f"Processed transaction: {transaction}")
        time.sleep(1)

monitor_transactions()
```

This simple simulation highlights real-time monitoring, an essential step for applications like fraud detection.

3. Challenges in Real-Time Data Processing

Handling real-time data comes with several challenges, including:

- **Latency:** Systems must process data quickly to deliver actionable insights in time.

- **Scalability:** The infrastructure must scale to handle fluctuations in data volume.

- **Fault Tolerance:** Systems must remain operational even in the event of failures.

To overcome these challenges, organizations rely on stream processing frameworks.

4. Role of Stream Processing Frameworks

Stream processing frameworks provide the tools and infrastructure for ingesting, processing, and analyzing real-time data. Popular frameworks include:

- **Apache Kafka:** Focused on distributed message streaming.

- **Apache Flink:** Optimized for low-latency stream processing.

- **Spark Streaming:** Integrates seamlessly with the Apache Spark ecosystem for real-time analytics.

Python Example: Real-Time Processing with Kafka

```python
from kafka import KafkaConsumer

# Consuming real-time data from a Kafka topic
consumer = KafkaConsumer('real_time_topic',
        bootstrap_servers=['localhost:9092'])

for message in consumer:
    print(f"Received message: {message.value.decode('utf-8')}")
```

This code snippet illustrates how to consume real-time data using Kafka, a widely used streaming framework.

5. Benefits of Real-Time Processing

Organizations leveraging real-time processing gain significant advantages:

- **Faster Decision Making:** Immediate insights drive better and faster decisions.

- **Improved User Experience:** Live recommendations and updates enhance customer engagement.

- **Enhanced Security:** Real-time alerts and fraud detection improve overall system security.

Real-time data processing is essential for applications requiring immediate insights and responses. By understanding the characteristics and importance of real-time data, organizations can design systems that efficiently handle time-sensitive scenarios. As subsequent sections will explore, leveraging powerful stream processing frameworks and well-designed pipelines further enhances the capability to act on data in real time.

Stream Processing Frameworks: Apache Kafka, Apache Flink, and Spark Streaming

Stream processing frameworks are essential for handling real-time data efficiently. They enable systems to ingest, process, and analyze data streams continuously, ensuring low latency and scalability. Among the most widely used frameworks are Apache Kafka, Apache Flink, and Spark Streaming, each offering unique capabilities for real-time data applications.

1. Apache Kafka: Distributed Streaming Platform

Apache Kafka is a distributed messaging system designed for high-throughput and fault-tolerant data streaming. It acts as an intermediary, collecting data from producers (e.g., sensors or applications) and delivering it to consumers for processing.

Key Features:

- **Scalability:** Kafka can handle millions of messages per second by partitioning topics across servers.

- **Durability:** It stores messages persistently, ensuring data is not lost during failures.

- **Stream Replay:** Consumers can reprocess data by replaying past streams.

Python Example: Producing and Consuming Messages in Kafka

```python
from kafka import KafkaProducer, KafkaConsumer

# Producing messages
producer = KafkaProducer(bootstrap_servers='localhost:9092')
producer.send('real_time_topic', b'Hello, Kafka!')
producer.close()

# Consuming messages
consumer = KafkaConsumer('real_time_topic',
            bootstrap_servers='localhost:9092')
for message in consumer:
    print(f"Received: {message.value.decode('utf-8')}")
```

This example demonstrates basic message production and consumption with Kafka.

2. Apache Flink: Real-Time Stream Processing

Apache Flink is a framework tailored for real-time analytics, offering advanced capabilities such as event time processing and state management.

Key Features:

- **Low Latency:** Processes data with millisecond-level delays.

- **Event Time Processing:** Ensures correct event order even with delays.

- **Stateful Computations:** Manages complex operations like windowing and aggregations with fault tolerance.

Example Use Case: Real-time anomaly detection in IoT data streams, where Flink analyzes sensor readings and flags unusual patterns instantly.

3. Spark Streaming: Micro-Batch Processing

Spark Streaming, part of the Apache Spark ecosystem, processes real-time data by dividing streams into small batches and performing operations on these batches.

Key Features:

- **Ease of Use:** Integrates seamlessly with the Spark ecosystem for unified batch and stream processing.

- **Scalability:** Handles large-scale data by distributing computation across clusters.

- **Fault Tolerance:** Recovers from failures using Spark's lineage-based computation model.

Python Example: Spark Streaming with PySpark

```python
from pyspark.sql import SparkSession
from pyspark.streaming import StreamingContext

# Initialize Spark session and streaming context
spark = SparkSession.builder.appName("SparkStreaming").getOrCreate()
ssc = StreamingContext(spark.sparkContext, 5)

# Define a streaming source (e.g., socket data)
lines = ssc.socketTextStream("localhost", 9999)
lines.pprint()  # Print incoming data

ssc.start()
ssc.awaitTermination()
```

This code sets up a simple streaming application that processes real-time data from a socket.

4. Comparison of Frameworks

Framework	Strengths	Best Use Cases
Apache Kafka	High throughput, persistent storage	Log aggregation, message brokering
Apache Flink	Event-time processing, stateful computations	Complex real-time analytics
Spark Streaming	Seamless integration with batch processing	Unified analytics workflows

5. Choosing the Right Framework

The choice of a stream processing framework depends on the application's requirements:

- **Low Latency:** Use Apache Flink for millisecond-level processing.

- **Integration:** Use Spark Streaming for mixed batch-stream workloads.

- **Messaging:** Use Kafka as a backbone for data pipelines.

Stream processing frameworks like Kafka, Flink, and Spark Streaming have revolutionized real-time data handling. By enabling efficient and scalable processing, these tools empower businesses to act on data as it arrives. The next section will delve into designing and implementing data pipelines that leverage these powerful frameworks for real-time systems.

Data Pipelines for Real-Time Data: Designing and Implementing Efficient Systems

Building data pipelines for real-time data processing is a critical aspect of handling dynamic and time-sensitive information. These pipelines must be designed for scalability, low latency, and fault tolerance to ensure uninterrupted data flow and analysis. This section explores the architecture, key components, and practical implementation strategies for efficient real-time data pipelines.

1. What is a Real-Time Data Pipeline?

A real-time data pipeline is an architecture that ingests, processes, and delivers data continuously as it is generated. Unlike batch pipelines, which process data in chunks, real-time pipelines ensure immediate availability of insights, enabling quick decision-making for critical applications such as fraud detection, recommendation systems, and live monitoring.

Key Features of Real-Time Pipelines:

- **Low Latency:** Data is processed within milliseconds to seconds.

- **Scalability:** Handles large volumes of data streams seamlessly.

- **Fault Tolerance:** Ensures data processing continues despite failures.

2. Components of a Real-Time Data Pipeline

A typical real-time data pipeline consists of the following components:

- **Data Sources:** Origin points such as IoT devices, web logs, or transaction systems. These generate continuous streams of data.

- **Message Queues/Brokers:** Tools like Apache Kafka or RabbitMQ handle ingestion, ensuring data is delivered reliably and efficiently to downstream systems.

- **Stream Processing Frameworks:** Frameworks like Apache Flink or Spark Streaming analyze and transform the data.

- **Data Storage:** Databases like Apache Cassandra or Amazon DynamoDB store processed data for querying and analysis.

- **Visualization/Applications:** Dashboards or applications present actionable insights derived from the processed data.

3. Steps to Design a Real-Time Data Pipeline

Step 1: Identify Requirements Define the pipeline's purpose. Is it for anomaly detection, recommendation systems, or another application? Clarify latency and scalability needs.

Step 2: Select Appropriate Tools Choose tools suited for your requirements:

- For message queuing: Apache Kafka or RabbitMQ.

- For processing: Apache Flink or Spark Streaming.

- For storage: NoSQL databases like MongoDB for high-speed reads/writes.

Step 3: Design the Workflow Create a workflow that outlines how data moves from sources through processing to storage and finally to visualization.

Step 4: Implement and Test Use robust frameworks and libraries to implement the pipeline. Perform stress testing to identify bottlenecks.

4. Example: Building a Real-Time Pipeline for Log Monitoring

Scenario: Monitor server logs in real-time to detect and alert on errors.

Implementation:

1. **Ingest Logs:** Use Apache Kafka to collect log data from servers.

2. **Stream Processing:** Use Apache Flink to process log data, identify errors, and generate alerts.

3. **Store Results:** Save processed data in Elasticsearch for querying.

4. **Visualize:** Use Kibana to create dashboards and display error trends.

Code Example: Kafka to Flink Pipeline

```
from kafka import KafkaConsumer
from pyflink.datastream import StreamExecutionEnvironment

# Kafka Consumer
consumer = KafkaConsumer('server_logs', bootstrap_servers='localhost:9092')

# Flink Environment
env = StreamExecutionEnvironment.get_execution_environment()
data_stream = env.from_collection(consumer)

# Process logs for errors
errors = data_stream.filter(lambda log: "ERROR" in log)
errors.add_sink(lambda log: print(f"Alert: {log}"))  # Simulate alerting
        system

env.execute("Real-Time Log Monitoring Pipeline")
```

This simple example demonstrates log ingestion and error alerting using Kafka and Flink.

5. Best Practices for Real-Time Pipelines

- **Ensure Fault Tolerance:** Use replication in message brokers and checkpoints in stream processors.

- **Optimize Latency:** Reduce processing delays by avoiding unnecessary computations.

- **Scale Horizontally:** Add more resources to handle increasing data loads.

- **Monitor Performance:** Use tools like Prometheus and Grafana for pipeline monitoring.

Real-time data pipelines are the backbone of modern data-driven applications, enabling organizations to process and respond to data instantly. By combining robust architecture with efficient tools and best practices, these pipelines empower businesses to derive actionable insights from their data streams. The next section will explore use cases that showcase the power of real-time processing in practical scenarios.

Use Cases for Real-Time Processing: Fraud Detection, Live Recommendation Systems

Real-time data processing plays a pivotal role in a variety of applications where immediate insights are critical for decision-making. In this section, we will explore some common use cases where real-time data processing is essential, focusing on fraud detection, live recommendation systems, and other time-sensitive applications.

1. Fraud Detection in Financial Transactions

Fraud detection systems rely on real-time data processing to detect fraudulent activities as soon as they occur. With the ever-increasing volume of transactions, detecting fraud in real time can help minimize financial losses and prevent further damage.

How It Works:

- **Data Sources:** Financial transaction data, such as credit card payments, bank transfers, and online shopping transactions.

- **Stream Processing:** Real-time fraud detection systems analyze each transaction in real-time using machine learning models that classify transactions as either legitimate or potentially fraudulent.

- **Detection Models:** Models use historical transaction data to detect patterns, anomalies, and suspicious behaviors in real-time.

- **Alerting:** If a fraudulent transaction is detected, an alert is triggered, prompting immediate action (e.g., freezing the account or flagging the transaction).

Code Example: Using Apache Kafka and Spark Streaming, the following Python snippet demonstrates the detection of anomalies in financial transactions:

```python
from kafka import KafkaConsumer
from pyspark.streaming import StreamingContext

# Initialize Kafka Consumer and Spark Streaming
consumer = KafkaConsumer('transactions', bootstrap_servers='localhost:9092')
ssc = StreamingContext(sc, 1)  # Stream every second
transaction_stream = ssc.socketTextStream('localhost', 9092)

# Process the transaction stream
def detect_fraud(transaction):
    # Example: Simple rule-based anomaly detection (e.g., large
        transactions)
    amount = float(transaction.split(',')[1])  # Extract transaction amount
    if amount > 10000:  # Example threshold for fraud
        return "Fraud Alert!"
    return "Safe Transaction"

fraud_alerts = transaction_stream.map(detect_fraud)
fraud_alerts.pprint()

ssc.start()
ssc.awaitTermination()
```

In this example, Kafka is used for streaming transaction data, and Spark Streaming processes it to detect fraudulent transactions based on simple rules.

2. Live Recommendation Systems

Live recommendation systems provide real-time personalized suggestions to users based on their interactions with a platform. These systems are widely used in e-commerce, streaming platforms, and social media to improve user experience and increase engagement.

How It Works:

- **Data Sources:** User interaction data such as clicks, searches, views, or purchases.

- **Stream Processing:** The system processes the user activity in real-time, feeding this data into a recommendation engine.

- **Recommendation Algorithms:** Based on user preferences, historical interactions, and collaborative filtering, the system suggests products, content, or services that are most likely to appeal to the user.

- **Dynamic Updates:** As users interact with the platform, the recommendations are updated in real-time to provide the most relevant suggestions.

Code Example: In a real-time recommendation system, Apache Kafka might be used for ingesting user activity data, and Spark Streaming can be used to process the data and update recommendations. Here's a simplified code snippet:

```
from kafka import KafkaConsumer
from pyspark.streaming import StreamingContext

# Initialize Kafka Consumer and Spark Streaming
consumer = KafkaConsumer('user_activity',
        bootstrap_servers='localhost:9092')
ssc = StreamingContext(sc, 1)  # Stream every second
user_activity_stream = ssc.socketTextStream('localhost', 9092)

# Process user activity for recommendation
def generate_recommendation(activity):
    # Example: Basic content-based recommendation (e.g., recommend similar
        items)
    item_viewed = activity.split(',')[0]  # Extract item ID
    recommendations = get_similar_items(item_viewed)  # Fetch similar items
        from a model
    return f"Recommended items for {item_viewed}: {recommendations}"

user_recommendations = user_activity_stream.map(generate_recommendation)
user_recommendations.pprint()

ssc.start()
ssc.awaitTermination()
```

This example demonstrates real-time generation of recommendations based on user activity, showcasing how the system dynamically updates the recommendations stream.

3. Other Time-Sensitive Use Cases

In addition to fraud detection and recommendation systems, real-time data processing is applied to various other fields, such as:

- **Healthcare:** Real-time patient monitoring systems alert healthcare providers about critical changes in patient conditions.

- **IoT Applications:** Real-time processing of sensor data from IoT devices, enabling immediate responses to environmental changes, such as temperature control or predictive maintenance.

- **Live Sports Analytics:** Real-time data analysis in sports, tracking player performance and providing instant statistics for coaches, broadcasters, and fans.

Real-time data processing is crucial in applications that require immediate decision-making and response. From fraud detection in financial transactions to personalized recommendations, the ability to analyze data as it streams in enables businesses to provide more relevant and timely services. As the demand for instant insights grows, the need for robust, scalable, and efficient real-time data pipelines will continue to increase across various industries.

Module 38:

Data Lake Architecture

A data lake is a centralized repository designed to store vast amounts of raw data in its native format. Unlike traditional data storage systems, data lakes provide the flexibility to ingest and store structured, semi-structured, and unstructured data. This module explores data lake architecture, its benefits and challenges, popular technologies, and integration with data warehouses.

What is a Data Lake?: Raw Data Storage and Analytics

A data lake is a repository that stores raw data from various sources without predefining the structure. It allows organizations to keep all their data in one place, whether structured (like databases), semi-structured (like JSON files), or unstructured (like images or text). Data lakes offer powerful analytics capabilities, enabling businesses to perform advanced analytics, machine learning, and business intelligence. The ability to process and analyze diverse data types makes data lakes essential for extracting valuable insights from raw, heterogeneous data.

Benefits and Challenges of Data Lakes: Flexibility vs. Complexity

Data lakes offer numerous benefits, such as flexibility, scalability, and the ability to handle massive data volumes. They allow data scientists to explore data without requiring predefined schemas, facilitating data exploration and innovation. However, data lakes also pose challenges, primarily related to data governance, security, and complexity. Managing data quality and ensuring that the right data is accessible to users is essential for maximizing the value of a data lake. Poor data management can lead to a "data swamp," where data is disorganized and unusable.

Data Lake Technologies: Hadoop, Amazon S3, Delta Lake

Several technologies power data lake implementations. Hadoop, an open-source framework, allows for the distributed storage and processing of large datasets, making it a popular choice for data lakes. Amazon S3 (Simple Storage Service) provides scalable cloud storage that can be used to build a data lake, offering durability and flexibility. Delta Lake enhances data lakes with ACID transactions, enabling more reliable data processing and management. These technologies are key to building efficient, scalable data lakes that support both batch and real-time analytics.

Integrating with Data Warehouses: Creating a Unified Ecosystem

Integrating data lakes with data warehouses is crucial for creating a unified data ecosystem. Data warehouses store structured, processed data optimized for business reporting and analysis, while data lakes hold raw, unprocessed data. By combining the strengths of both, organizations can leverage the data lake for deep analytics and the data warehouse for fast, structured reporting. Integration ensures that businesses can efficiently manage and analyze data, while also maintaining data quality and accessibility. This combined approach maximizes the value of data in decision-making processes.

What is a Data Lake?: Raw Data Storage and Analytics

A data lake is a storage system designed to handle vast amounts of raw, unprocessed data in its native format. Unlike traditional data warehouses that store structured data, a data lake allows organizations to store everything from structured to semi-structured and unstructured data. The flexibility of data lakes makes them an essential component of modern data architecture, enabling businesses to perform deep analytics on diverse datasets.

Raw Data Storage

Data lakes are built to store data in its raw, untransformed state, which is a major distinction from the more structured approach used in data warehouses. This capability makes it easier to collect data from multiple sources, such as social media feeds, logs, sensor data, and more. The data can then be processed and analyzed based on the needs of the business, rather than being transformed at the point of ingestion.

For instance, a company might collect a variety of data types including JSON, XML, CSV, video files, images, and text data. In a traditional data warehouse, the data would need to be pre-processed and structured before it could be loaded. In contrast, a data lake allows this raw data to be ingested without needing to adhere to predefined schemas.

Code Example: In Python, you can use the boto3 library to store raw data in Amazon S3, a popular data lake storage solution:

```python
import boto3

# Initialize the S3 client
s3_client = boto3.client('s3')

# Define the data and bucket
data = 'This is an example of raw data'
bucket_name = 'my-data-lake-bucket'
object_key = 'raw_data.txt'

# Upload raw data to the S3 bucket
s3_client.put_object(Bucket=bucket_name, Key=object_key, Body=data)
```

In this example, raw data is stored as a text file in an Amazon S3 bucket, which serves as a fundamental component of the data lake.

Benefits and Challenges of Data Lakes

Benefits

The primary benefit of a data lake is flexibility. Since data can be stored in its raw form, it enables organizations to collect a wide variety of data types from different sources. This flexibility allows for the exploration of new analytics use cases and enables businesses to perform advanced machine learning, artificial intelligence, and big data analytics.

Another key benefit is scalability. Data lakes can handle massive amounts of data, scaling up as needed without requiring significant restructuring or redesigning of storage systems. This scalability makes them a good fit for organizations with large and growing datasets.

Challenges

However, the raw nature of data stored in a lake introduces complexity. Data quality, inconsistency, and lack of a predefined schema can make it difficult to analyze the data effectively. Without proper data governance, organizations may face challenges in managing and accessing the data, leading to inefficiencies.

Data Lake Technologies

Several technologies are used to implement data lakes, each offering unique features suited to different business needs.

Hadoop

Apache Hadoop is one of the most widely used open-source technologies for managing large data lakes. Hadoop uses the Hadoop Distributed File System (HDFS) to store data across distributed clusters, making it scalable and fault-tolerant.

Amazon S3

Amazon S3 is a highly scalable object storage service provided by AWS, often used as a data lake for storing vast amounts of raw data. It allows businesses to store, retrieve, and manage large volumes of data across various use cases.

Delta Lake

Delta Lake is an open-source storage layer built on top of Apache Spark and Parquet, providing features like ACID transactions and schema enforcement for data lakes. It ensures data quality and reliability while maintaining the flexibility of a data lake.

Integrating with Data Warehouses

While data lakes provide flexibility and scalability, integrating them with data warehouses can create a unified ecosystem that optimizes both data storage and analytics. Data warehouses typically store structured and refined data, making them ideal for reporting and business intelligence. By combining data lakes with data warehouses, businesses can create a system that handles both raw and processed data, enabling complex analytics and insights.

For instance, after raw data is ingested into the data lake, it can be processed and transformed into a structured format before being loaded into a data warehouse for further analysis. This integration ensures that the business can efficiently use both the unstructured data from the data lake and the structured data in the warehouse for comprehensive insights.

Data lakes provide a flexible, scalable solution for storing raw data that can support advanced analytics and machine learning. While they come with challenges like complexity and data quality issues, integrating data lakes with data warehouses can create a more effective, unified ecosystem for managing and analyzing data across an organization.

Benefits and Challenges of Data Lakes: Flexibility vs. Complexity

Data lakes have rapidly gained popularity due to their ability to store vast amounts of raw, unprocessed data from diverse sources. However, with their flexibility come both significant benefits and challenges that organizations must navigate to fully realize the potential of a data lake architecture. Understanding the trade-offs between flexibility and complexity is crucial to designing an efficient and scalable data management solution.

Benefits of Data Lakes

1. Flexibility in Data Storage

One of the key benefits of a data lake is its ability to store data in a flexible, schema-less format. Unlike data warehouses, which require predefined schemas before data can be stored, a data lake can handle structured, semi-structured, and unstructured data. This includes files such as text, images, audio, and video, along with structured data like databases or CSV files. This flexibility allows organizations to ingest a wide variety of data sources without worrying about format compatibility.

This advantage is particularly valuable in the age of big data, where information is often unstructured and constantly evolving. Whether it's social media posts, IoT sensor readings, or transactional data, a data lake can accommodate all types of information without the need for rigid structures or transformations upon ingestion.

2. Scalability and Cost Efficiency

Data lakes are built on distributed systems, which enables them to scale horizontally. As data volumes grow, additional storage and computing power can be easily added to accommodate the increased load. This scalability is especially important for organizations dealing with large datasets, such as those in industries like finance, healthcare, and e-commerce.

Moreover, data lakes can be more cost-effective compared to traditional data warehousing solutions. Technologies like Amazon S3 and Hadoop provide affordable, high-capacity storage that grows with the organization's needs. This makes them an attractive option for businesses looking to handle big data without incurring the significant costs associated with legacy data warehousing systems.

3. Support for Advanced Analytics and Machine Learning

The raw nature of data in a data lake makes it well-suited for machine learning (ML) and artificial intelligence (AI) applications. By storing data in its native format, organizations can use advanced data transformation techniques to clean and process the data for ML models. Additionally, because all types of data can be ingested, businesses can combine various datasets for deeper insights, such as blending customer data with sensor data for predictive analytics.

Challenges of Data Lakes

1. Data Quality and Governance Issues

One of the primary challenges of data lakes is ensuring data quality and governance. Since data is stored in raw form, it may be incomplete, inconsistent, or contain errors. Without proper data cleaning and validation processes, organizations may face significant difficulties when attempting to analyze the data effectively.

Moreover, because data lakes are flexible, they may suffer from a lack of consistency and structure. This can lead to what is often referred to as the "data swamp," where the data becomes disorganized and difficult to navigate. Implementing robust data governance practices, including metadata management, data cataloging, and data lineage tracking, is critical to maintaining data integrity and usability.

2. Performance Issues

As data lakes grow, performance can become a bottleneck, especially if data is not properly indexed or optimized for retrieval. While data lakes provide scalable storage, ensuring fast query performance and minimizing latency during data processing can become challenging as the volume and complexity of data increases. This requires businesses to implement efficient indexing and data processing techniques, which may necessitate additional computational resources and expertise.

3. Security and Compliance Concerns

Storing large volumes of sensitive data in a data lake raises security and compliance concerns. Ensuring that access to the data is appropriately controlled and that the data complies with regulatory standards is crucial. Security measures such as encryption, access control policies, and auditing must be in place to protect data from unauthorized access and misuse.

Organizations must also ensure compliance with regulations like GDPR, HIPAA, or other industry-specific standards, which may require additional data classification, auditing, and reporting mechanisms within the data lake.

Balancing Flexibility and Complexity

While the flexibility of data lakes provides numerous benefits, businesses must weigh this against the complexity introduced by managing large volumes of diverse data. To strike the right balance, organizations should implement best practices for data governance, security, and performance optimization. Additionally, integrating data lakes with other data management systems, such as data warehouses and data marts, can help address the complexity of managing raw data while maintaining a unified ecosystem for analytics.

By applying the appropriate strategies, companies can maximize the value of their data lake architecture, turning raw, unprocessed data into actionable insights for business growth and innovation.

The benefits of data lakes, such as flexibility, scalability, and support for advanced analytics, make them a powerful tool for managing modern big data. However, the challenges related to data quality, governance, and performance require careful consideration and proper management practices. By understanding the trade-offs between flexibility and complexity, organizations can design data lake architectures that support both their immediate needs and long-term goals.

Data Lake Technologies: Hadoop, Amazon S3, Delta Lake

Data lakes rely on specific technologies to manage and store large volumes of raw data. These technologies provide the infrastructure and scalability needed to handle data in diverse formats, while also supporting advanced analytics. Among the popular data lake technologies are Hadoop, Amazon S3, and Delta Lake. Each has unique characteristics and advantages depending on the use case.

1. Hadoop: The Foundational Data Lake Technology

Hadoop is an open-source framework designed to store and process large datasets in a distributed computing environment. It is often considered the foundation of data lake technology. Hadoop consists of two primary components: **Hadoop Distributed File System (HDFS)** for storage and **MapReduce** for processing data.

HDFS (Hadoop Distributed File System)

HDFS is designed to store large volumes of data across multiple nodes in a distributed cluster. Data is split into blocks and stored across the cluster, ensuring redundancy and fault tolerance. This makes Hadoop highly scalable, allowing organizations to increase storage capacity by adding more nodes.

MapReduce

MapReduce is the processing framework that handles the computation on data stored in HDFS. It divides tasks into smaller jobs and processes them in parallel across the cluster, which enables the handling of vast amounts of data efficiently. While powerful, MapReduce can be slow for certain types of processing, especially real-time data processing, which has led to the adoption of newer technologies like Apache Spark for faster processing.

Use Case:

Hadoop is suitable for organizations that need to store vast amounts of data and perform batch processing. It is particularly beneficial for traditional data warehousing solutions and batch-based analytics.

2. Amazon S3: Scalable Cloud-Based Storage for Data Lakes

Amazon Simple Storage Service (S3) is a cloud-based storage service that provides highly durable and scalable storage solutions. S3 is a popular choice for building data lakes due to its cost-effectiveness, ease of use, and integration with other AWS services.

Scalability and Durability

S3 allows organizations to store an unlimited amount of data with virtually no management overhead. It is designed for 99.999999999% durability, making it a reliable option for long-term data storage. As data volumes grow, S3 automatically scales, providing on-demand storage capacity.

Data Management Features

S3 includes features such as lifecycle management, data versioning, and access control policies, which are essential for managing large datasets in a data lake environment. Furthermore, it integrates with various analytics services in the AWS ecosystem, such as Amazon Athena, AWS Glue, and Amazon Redshift, allowing organizations to query and analyze data directly from S3 without needing to move it into a separate database system.

Use Case:

Amazon S3 is ideal for organizations seeking a cloud-native solution for data lake storage. It supports a wide range of use cases, from storing raw log files to supporting analytics for big data and machine learning applications.

3. Delta Lake: Reliable and High-Performance Data Lake Storage

Delta Lake, an open-source storage layer built on top of Apache Spark, provides ACID (Atomicity, Consistency, Isolation, Durability) transactional capabilities to data lakes. It addresses some of the key challenges faced by traditional data lakes, such as data consistency and performance.

ACID Transactions

Delta Lake introduces ACID transactions to data lakes, which ensures that data operations are reliable and consistent. This is particularly important in environments where multiple processes are writing to the same data simultaneously. Delta Lake's transactional capabilities allow for high data integrity and make it easier to handle complex data workflows.

Schema Enforcement and Evolution

Delta Lake provides schema enforcement, ensuring that incoming data adheres to the specified schema. It also supports schema evolution, allowing changes to the schema over time without causing disruptions to the data pipeline. This makes it easier to work with evolving datasets.

Time Travel and Data Versioning

One of the standout features of Delta Lake is its ability to support "time travel," which enables users to query historical versions of the data. This is valuable for auditing, debugging, or recovering from data issues, as it allows users to access previous states of the data.

Use Case:

Delta Lake is best suited for organizations that need reliable, scalable, and performant data lake storage with transactional guarantees. It is especially useful in industries that require high data integrity, such as finance and healthcare.

Each of these technologies—Hadoop, Amazon S3, and Delta Lake—offers unique strengths when it comes to building and managing data lakes. Hadoop is ideal for large-scale, batch-based analytics; Amazon S3 provides a highly scalable and cost-effective cloud storage solution; and Delta Lake adds transactional support and performance improvements to data lakes. Choosing the right technology depends on the organization's needs for scalability, data management, and analytics. In many modern data lake architectures, organizations combine these technologies to maximize the benefits of each.

Integrating with Data Warehouses: Creating a Unified Ecosystem

Integrating data lakes with data warehouses is crucial for creating a unified ecosystem where data from various sources can be accessed, processed, and analyzed efficiently. This integration ensures that organizations can leverage the benefits of both architectures, allowing for the storage of raw, unstructured data in data lakes and the structured, analytics-ready data in data warehouses. A well-designed integration provides a holistic view of data, improves accessibility, and enables advanced analytics and reporting.

1. Data Lakes vs. Data Warehouses: A Brief Overview

Before diving into integration, it's important to understand the distinction between data lakes and data warehouses.

- **Data Lakes**: These store raw, unprocessed data, often in its native format. They are flexible, scalable, and designed to accommodate structured, semi-structured, and unstructured data. Data lakes are ideal for storing large volumes of raw data from various sources, including logs, sensor data, or media files.

- **Data Warehouses**: These store structured data that has been processed, cleaned, and transformed for analysis. Data warehouses are optimized for querying and reporting and often use relational database management systems (RDBMS) for storage. They are suitable for business intelligence (BI) tasks and historical analysis.

While data lakes offer flexibility and scalability, they require transformation before analysis. Data warehouses, on the other hand, offer quick querying capabilities but may struggle with large volumes of raw data.

2. Integration Strategies

440

Several strategies are employed to integrate data lakes with data warehouses, ensuring seamless data flow between the two systems.

ETL Process (Extract, Transform, Load)

The ETL process is a common approach for moving data from the lake to the warehouse. Data is **extracted** from the data lake, **transformed** into a structured format suitable for analysis, and then **loaded** into the data warehouse.

- **Extract**: Raw data is extracted from the data lake, which can be in various formats (e.g., JSON, Parquet, CSV).

- **Transform**: During this step, the data is cleaned, enriched, and converted into a consistent format that aligns with the schema in the data warehouse.

- **Load**: The transformed data is loaded into the data warehouse, typically into a predefined schema, where it is available for querying.

ELT Process (Extract, Load, Transform)

In some scenarios, organizations choose the ELT process, where data is first extracted and loaded into the data warehouse before transformation. This is more suitable for data warehouses that have powerful processing capabilities, such as cloud-based platforms like Amazon Redshift or Google BigQuery. This approach ensures that the data is immediately available in the warehouse for analytics, and transformations are done as needed.

Real-time Data Integration

For real-time analytics, integrating data lakes and data warehouses can be done via stream processing. Real-time data, such as logs, sensor data, or user activity, is continuously processed and stored in the data lake. It can then be transferred to the data warehouse for structured querying using tools like **Apache Kafka**, **Apache Flink**, or **AWS Kinesis**. Real-time integration supports use cases such as fraud detection and live recommendation systems.

3. Benefits of Integration

The integration of data lakes with data warehouses provides several advantages:

Holistic Data View

By integrating these two systems, organizations can have a unified view of both raw and processed data. Data scientists and analysts can access the full spectrum of data and conduct advanced analytics, such as predictive modeling, trend analysis, and machine learning, while also leveraging structured data for business intelligence.

Optimized Performance

Data warehouses are optimized for fast query performance, while data lakes excel at handling large, unstructured data sets. Integrating the two systems allows organizations to take advantage of the performance of data warehouses for querying processed data while still having the scalability and flexibility of a data lake for storing unstructured or raw data.

Cost Efficiency

Data lakes are more cost-effective for storing large volumes of data, especially unstructured data. By offloading raw data storage to the data lake and using the data warehouse for analysis and reporting, organizations can optimize their storage costs while ensuring they have access to high-quality, clean data for analytics.

---

4. Tools and Technologies for Integration

Various tools and platforms can assist in the integration of data lakes and data warehouses. Some notable examples include:

- **Apache NiFi**: A powerful data integration tool that automates the movement of data between systems.

- **AWS Glue**: A managed ETL service that allows for the seamless transfer of data from Amazon S3 (a data lake) to Amazon Redshift (a data warehouse).

- **Google Cloud Dataflow**: A fully managed service for processing real-time data streams and batch data, facilitating data integration between lakes and warehouses.

- **Databricks**: A unified analytics platform built around Apache Spark that can integrate with both data lakes and data warehouses, enabling complex analytics workflows.

Integrating data lakes with data warehouses creates a powerful ecosystem for data storage and analysis. By using appropriate strategies such as ETL or ELT processes, real-time data processing, and leveraging the right tools, organizations can unlock the full potential of both architectures. This integration enables holistic data analysis, optimized performance, and cost efficiency, all while providing easy access to high-quality, structured data for analytics and decision-making.

Module 39:

Data Security and Governance

Data security and governance are critical for ensuring the protection and responsible management of data. This module covers the importance of securing sensitive data, implementing encryption and access control measures, complying with regulations, and ensuring accountability through auditing and logging practices. Organizations must prioritize these factors to maintain trust and legal compliance.

Importance of Data Security: Protecting Sensitive Data

Data security ensures that sensitive information, such as personal, financial, and health data, is protected from unauthorized access, breaches, and cyberattacks. A strong security framework is essential for preserving confidentiality, integrity, and availability. As data grows in volume and value, securing it from both internal and external threats becomes increasingly critical for organizations and individuals alike.

Data Encryption and Access Control: Techniques to Ensure Confidentiality

Encryption is a fundamental technique for protecting data by converting it into a format that can only be decrypted by authorized users. It ensures that even if data is intercepted, it remains unreadable. Access control mechanisms, such as role-based access controls (RBAC), limit access to sensitive data based on user roles, minimizing the risk of unauthorized exposure. Both encryption and access control are essential for maintaining confidentiality.

Governance and Compliance: GDPR, HIPAA, and Other Regulations

Governance involves managing data in a way that ensures its proper use, security, and compliance with relevant laws and regulations. GDPR (General Data Protection Regulation) and HIPAA (Health Insurance Portability and Accountability Act) are examples of regulations that impose strict requirements on how data should be handled. Compliance with such laws is mandatory to avoid penalties and to protect individuals' privacy rights while managing sensitive data securely.

Data Auditing and Logging: Ensuring Traceability and Accountability

Auditing and logging are crucial for ensuring data traceability and accountability. By keeping a detailed record of who accessed data, what changes were made, and when these actions occurred, organizations can maintain a transparent system for data management. This also helps in identifying and addressing potential security breaches, ensuring that any unauthorized access can be traced back to its source for accountability.

Importance of Data Security: Protecting Sensitive Data

In the age of big data, ensuring the security of sensitive data has become a paramount concern for organizations across various industries. Data security is the practice of safeguarding digital data from unauthorized access, corruption, theft, and other potential risks. It involves implementing policies, processes, and technologies that secure data throughout its lifecycle, from collection to storage and transmission.

Data breaches can have devastating consequences, including financial losses, damage to reputation, and legal penalties. As such, protecting sensitive data is crucial not only to maintain trust with customers but also to comply with various regulatory requirements. Sensitive data may include personally identifiable information (PII), financial details, intellectual property, or health records.

1. Types of Sensitive Data

Sensitive data comes in various forms, and organizations must identify which types are critical to secure. Some common categories of sensitive data include:

- **Personally Identifiable Information (PII)**: Information that can be used to identify an individual, such as names, social security numbers, and email addresses.

- **Protected Health Information (PHI)**: Data related to an individual's health, protected under regulations such as HIPAA in the United States.

- **Payment Card Information (PCI)**: Credit card and banking details that are highly sensitive and subject to strict regulations like PCI-DSS.

- **Intellectual Property**: Proprietary company data, including patents, formulas, and trade secrets, that need to be protected to maintain a competitive advantage.

By classifying sensitive data correctly, organizations can focus on securing the most valuable assets first, using encryption and other protective measures.

2. Risks to Data Security

Several threats can compromise the security of sensitive data, including:

- **Data Breaches**: Unauthorized access to data, often due to hacking, system vulnerabilities, or employee negligence.

- **Insider Threats**: Employees or trusted individuals misusing their access to steal or leak sensitive information.

- **Data Loss**: Unintentional deletion, corruption, or system failure can lead to the loss of critical data.

- **Malware and Ransomware**: Malicious software designed to steal or lock data until a ransom is paid.

The ability to identify and mitigate these risks requires proactive security measures, including robust encryption, firewalls, and intrusion detection systems.

3. Importance of Data Security in Various Sectors

Data security is especially critical in sectors that handle large volumes of sensitive information. For example:

- **Healthcare**: Protecting patient data is critical, as it falls under strict regulations like HIPAA. Breaching healthcare data can lead to severe legal and financial consequences.

- **Finance**: Financial institutions store sensitive personal and payment information, making them prime targets for cyberattacks. Ensuring data security is essential for maintaining client trust and meeting regulatory standards.

- **E-commerce**: E-commerce platforms collect sensitive data such as customer payment details and shipping addresses. Security is vital to prevent fraud and maintain customer confidence.

For organizations in these sectors, data security must be integrated into every part of the data lifecycle.

4. Implementing Data Security Measures

Organizations can implement various technical and procedural safeguards to protect sensitive data:

- **Encryption**: Encrypting data both at rest and in transit ensures that even if data is intercepted, it remains unreadable without the decryption key.

- **Access Control**: Limiting access to sensitive data to only authorized users through role-based access control (RBAC) or attribute-based access control (ABAC) ensures that only those who need to view or modify data can do so.

- **Data Masking and Tokenization**: Data masking replaces sensitive data with non-sensitive data to obscure it from unauthorized users, while tokenization converts sensitive data into tokens that can be used without revealing the original data.

5. Compliance with Regulations

In addition to securing data, organizations must also ensure that they comply with various regulations governing data privacy and security. Some of the key regulations include:

- **General Data Protection Regulation (GDPR)**: The GDPR enforces strict rules on the collection, processing, and storage of personal data for European Union citizens. It mandates practices like data minimization, obtaining consent, and allowing individuals to access, correct, and erase their data.

- **Health Insurance Portability and Accountability Act (HIPAA)**: In the U.S., HIPAA protects the privacy of health-related data, ensuring that health providers and insurers maintain the confidentiality of patient records.

- **Payment Card Industry Data Security Standard (PCI-DSS)**: This standard applies to organizations that handle credit card information, outlining security requirements to protect cardholder data.

Failure to comply with these regulations can result in significant penalties, legal action, and loss of business reputation.

Data security is an essential component of managing sensitive information in the modern digital world. Protecting data from unauthorized access and breaches is crucial to maintaining business continuity, customer trust, and regulatory compliance. By adopting best practices such as encryption, access control, and complying with relevant laws, organizations can ensure that their data remains secure and their operations continue to thrive without compromising sensitive information.

Data Encryption and Access Control: Techniques to Ensure Confidentiality

Data encryption and access control are fundamental techniques for ensuring the confidentiality of sensitive data. These practices are central to preventing unauthorized access, preserving the integrity of data, and complying with regulatory standards such as GDPR, HIPAA, and PCI-DSS. By implementing robust encryption methods and strict access control mechanisms, organizations can safeguard their data against breaches and mitigate security risks.

1. Data Encryption: Ensuring Confidentiality

Data encryption is the process of converting plaintext data into a secure format using cryptographic algorithms, making it unreadable without the appropriate decryption key. Encryption ensures that even if data is intercepted or accessed by unauthorized parties, it remains unreadable and protected. There are two primary types of encryption:

- **At-Rest Encryption**: Data is encrypted when stored on physical devices like servers, databases, and storage systems. This protects data in case of hardware theft or unauthorized access to storage.

- **In-Transit Encryption**: Data is encrypted during transmission over networks to prevent interception during communication. This is particularly important for securing sensitive data during web traffic, email communications, and file transfers.

For example, the AES (Advanced Encryption Standard) algorithm is commonly used for encrypting data both at rest and in transit, providing strong encryption security.

Python Example: AES Encryption

Here's a Python code snippet to demonstrate AES encryption using the pycryptodome library:

```python
from Crypto.Cipher import AES
from Crypto.Util.Padding import pad, unpad
from Crypto.Random import get_random_bytes

# Generate a random 256-bit key for AES
key = get_random_bytes(32)

# Encrypt a message
data = b"Sensitive data"
cipher = AES.new(key, AES.MODE_CBC)
ct_bytes = cipher.encrypt(pad(data, AES.block_size))

# Decrypt the message
cipher_dec = AES.new(key, AES.MODE_CBC, iv=cipher.iv)
pt = unpad(cipher_dec.decrypt(ct_bytes), AES.block_size)

print(f"Encrypted: {ct_bytes}")
print(f"Decrypted: {pt}")
```

In this example, data is encrypted using AES and can only be decrypted using the correct key, ensuring the data remains secure.

2. Access Control: Limiting Data Access

Access control ensures that only authorized users or systems can access sensitive data. It restricts access based on specific rules or policies, ensuring that the principle of least privilege is followed. Access control can be categorized into:

- **Role-Based Access Control (RBAC)**: Users are granted access based on their role within the organization. For example, an administrator may have full access to data, while a regular employee might only have read access.

- **Attribute-Based Access Control (ABAC)**: Access decisions are made based on user attributes (e.g., department, clearance level), allowing more granular control.

- **Mandatory Access Control (MAC)**: The system enforces strict rules where users can only access data based on predefined classifications, ensuring that sensitive data is highly restricted.

Python Example: Simple RBAC System

Here's a simple Python example demonstrating role-based access control:

```python
class User:
    def __init__(self, name, role):
        self.name = name
        self.role = role

class AccessControl:
    def __init__(self):
        self.permissions = {
            "admin": ["read", "write", "delete"],
            "employee": ["read"],
            "manager": ["read", "write"]
        }

    def check_access(self, user, action):
        if action in self.permissions.get(user.role, []):
            return f"Access granted to {user.name} for {action}."
        return f"Access denied to {user.name} for {action}."

# Example usage
admin_user = User("Alice", "admin")
emp_user = User("Bob", "employee")
access = AccessControl()

print(access.check_access(admin_user, "write"))
print(access.check_access(emp_user, "delete"))
```

In this example, users are granted different access levels based on their roles, with administrators having more privileges than employees.

3. Combining Encryption and Access Control

To maximize data security, encryption and access control should be used together. Data can be encrypted both at rest and in transit, while access control policies ensure that only authorized users can decrypt or access specific data.

For instance, if an employee has read-only access to certain files, they can view the encrypted data, but without the proper decryption key, they cannot read the actual content. Combining these techniques ensures that even if access to data is granted to an unauthorized user, the encrypted content remains secure.

4. Benefits of Encryption and Access Control

By implementing encryption and access control, organizations gain several key benefits:

- **Confidentiality**: Sensitive data remains confidential, even in the case of breaches.

- **Compliance**: Encryption and access control help organizations comply with industry regulations such as GDPR, HIPAA, and PCI-DSS.

- **Protection Against Insider Threats**: Even if an employee gains access to sensitive data, encryption ensures that they cannot access the underlying information unless authorized.

Data encryption and access control are essential techniques for ensuring the confidentiality of sensitive data. By using encryption to secure data both at rest and in transit and implementing strong access control mechanisms, organizations can protect against unauthorized access and data breaches. Together, these techniques form a comprehensive security strategy that safeguards data and helps maintain compliance with regulatory standards.

Governance and Compliance: GDPR, HIPAA, and Other Regulations

Data governance and compliance play a critical role in ensuring that data is handled responsibly, ethically, and in accordance with legal requirements. As organizations continue to leverage AI and machine learning models, they must adhere to various regulations that govern the collection, storage, and use of data. Compliance frameworks such as GDPR, HIPAA, and other industry standards ensure that data is managed in a way that respects user privacy, security, and rights.

1. Importance of Governance and Compliance

Data governance involves the overall management of data availability, usability, integrity, and security in an organization. It includes ensuring data is processed in a transparent and accountable manner, which is crucial for building trust among users and stakeholders. Compliance refers to adhering to the legal and regulatory frameworks governing data use.

For instance, the **General Data Protection Regulation (GDPR)** is a comprehensive regulation from the European Union that provides guidelines on how organizations should handle personal data, focusing on protecting individual privacy and ensuring data security. Similarly, **HIPAA** (Health Insurance Portability and Accountability Act) mandates standards for securing sensitive patient information in the healthcare sector.

Organizations must implement policies and procedures that promote ethical practices, manage data in accordance with regulations, and avoid the risks associated with non-compliance, such as penalties or reputational damage.

2. GDPR: A Comprehensive Privacy Regulation

GDPR, enforced in 2018, applies to any organization handling data of EU citizens, regardless of the organization's location. It sets strict guidelines for data collection, processing, storage, and deletion. Key aspects of GDPR include:

- **Data Subject Rights**: Individuals have the right to access, rectify, delete, and restrict the processing of their data.

- **Data Minimization**: Organizations should only collect data that is necessary for specific purposes.

- **Consent Management**: Organizations must obtain explicit consent from individuals for data processing activities.

- **Data Breach Notification**: Organizations must notify authorities and affected individuals within 72 hours of a data breach.

For example, a healthcare company must ensure that patient data is encrypted and stored securely while adhering to GDPR guidelines.

3. HIPAA: Ensuring the Protection of Health Data

HIPAA applies to healthcare organizations and their business associates who handle patient information. Its primary goal is to protect the privacy and security of medical records, ensuring that individuals' health data is not misused. Key components of HIPAA include:

- **Privacy Rule**: Ensures that healthcare providers and insurers protect patient information from unauthorized access.

- **Security Rule**: Establishes safeguards for electronic health records (EHRs), requiring organizations to implement appropriate security measures like encryption and access controls.

- **Breach Notification Rule**: Healthcare organizations must notify individuals in the event of a data breach.

4. Compliance in AI Development

AI models, especially those used for decision-making or customer-facing applications, must comply with these governance frameworks. A key concern is **bias in AI**— ensuring that models do not discriminate against individuals based on protected attributes like race, gender, or age.

To maintain compliance, AI developers should:

- **Monitor Data Use**: Ensure that training datasets are ethically sourced and represent diverse populations.

- **Explainability**: AI models should be interpretable, and organizations should be able to explain their decisions to users.

- **Audit Trails**: Implement auditing mechanisms to track how data is used and processed by AI systems, ensuring accountability and transparency.

5. Ethical Guidelines for Responsible AI

Several organizations and academic bodies have developed ethical guidelines for AI development. These guidelines focus on ensuring that AI systems are fair, transparent, accountable, and do not harm individuals. Prominent principles include:

- **Fairness**: Ensuring AI decisions are made without bias and that they are equitable for all individuals.

- **Transparency**: Providing users with clear insights into how AI models make decisions.

- **Accountability**: Holding organizations accountable for the outcomes of their AI systems.

For instance, using techniques like **LIME** (Local Interpretable Model-Agnostic Explanations) or **SHAP** (Shapley Additive Explanations) can help provide explanations for AI model decisions, making the AI process more transparent.

6. The Role of Auditing and Logging

To ensure ongoing compliance, organizations should establish robust data auditing and logging practices. This includes tracking data access, modifications, and processing, along with maintaining logs that capture any changes made to sensitive data.

Data auditing and logging are essential for regulatory compliance as they provide a traceable record of actions taken on data. This is particularly crucial in industries such as finance and healthcare, where maintaining a clear audit trail is required by law.

Data governance and compliance are essential components of responsible AI development. By adhering to frameworks like GDPR and HIPAA, and following ethical guidelines for AI, organizations can ensure they are processing data responsibly while protecting user privacy and maintaining security. Continuous monitoring, auditing, and a focus on transparency are key to maintaining compliance and fostering trust in AI systems.

Data Auditing and Logging: Ensuring Traceability and Accountability

Data auditing and logging are vital practices in ensuring the traceability, accountability, and compliance of data usage within an organization. These practices play a significant role in monitoring access to sensitive data, tracking data transformations, and maintaining a historical record of all data-related activities. In highly regulated industries such as finance, healthcare, and government, maintaining thorough audit trails is not only a best practice but also a legal requirement.

1. Importance of Data Auditing and Logging

Data auditing is the process of reviewing and recording the actions taken on data, such as who accessed it, what changes were made, and when they occurred. This practice ensures that organizations can trace the flow of data and verify that it is being handled according to established policies and regulations. Logging, on the other hand, involves capturing and storing detailed logs of all system events, which can include user actions, errors, and system-generated alerts.

The importance of data auditing and logging includes:

- **Regulatory Compliance**: Regulations like GDPR, HIPAA, and others require organizations to maintain logs of user interactions with data to ensure accountability.

- **Security Monitoring**: Auditing helps identify potential security breaches or unauthorized access, allowing organizations to take corrective actions.

- **Incident Investigation**: In the event of a data breach or incident, audit logs provide valuable insights into the origin and scope of the issue, facilitating a faster and more accurate response.

- **Operational Efficiency**: Regular audits can highlight inefficiencies or data misuse, offering opportunities for improvement.

2. Key Elements of Data Auditing

Effective data auditing involves several key elements that ensure the integrity and security of the data. These include:

- **Access Logs**: Record who accessed data, when, and from where. This helps track user behavior and prevent unauthorized access.

- **Data Modifications**: Log any changes made to the data, including updates, deletions, or additions. This ensures the integrity of the data and helps identify errors or inconsistencies.

- **Data Movement**: Track when data is moved between systems or locations, ensuring it is securely transferred and stored.

- **System Alerts**: Capture system-generated alerts, such as failed login attempts or suspicious activities, to monitor potential security threats.

- **Compliance Checks**: Record any compliance checks, such as data encryption or masking procedures, to ensure they are being followed.

3. Implementing Logging and Auditing in Python

To effectively implement auditing and logging, organizations can use programming tools to automate the process. In Python, libraries like logging and audit can be utilized to capture and manage logs.

Here's an example of how to set up basic logging in Python:

```python
import logging

# Set up logging configuration
logging.basicConfig(filename='data_audit.log', level=logging.INFO,
            format='%(asctime)s - %(message)s')

# Sample function to log actions
def log_action(action):
    logging.info(f"Action: {action}")

# Log some sample actions
log_action("Data accessed by user X")
log_action("Data modified: Field 'age' updated to 30")
```

This code snippet logs user actions to a file (data_audit.log), ensuring a historical record of activities. Each log entry includes the timestamp, the action taken, and any relevant details.

For more advanced auditing, a more robust logging setup can be created using databases or cloud-based logging systems like **AWS CloudWatch** or **Google Cloud Logging**. These tools allow for centralized management and real-time analysis of logs.

4. Benefits of Effective Auditing and Logging

Proper data auditing and logging practices offer several benefits to organizations:

- **Improved Accountability**: With logs capturing every action on the data, organizations can hold individuals or teams accountable for their actions.

- **Compliance with Regulations**: Detailed audit trails help meet legal requirements for data protection and privacy regulations, such as GDPR, HIPAA, and CCPA.

- **Enhanced Security**: By monitoring access and changes, organizations can identify potential threats, respond to security breaches, and mitigate risks proactively.

- **Increased Trust**: Transparent data management practices help build trust with clients and users, demonstrating that data is handled securely and responsibly.

5. Challenges in Auditing and Logging

While data auditing and logging offer significant benefits, they also come with challenges. Some common obstacles include:

- **Data Overload**: Storing extensive logs can lead to data overload, making it difficult to analyze and extract useful insights.

- **Cost and Storage**: The infrastructure required to store and manage audit logs can be costly, especially for large organizations dealing with massive volumes of data.

- **Privacy Concerns**: Logs may contain sensitive information, requiring careful management to ensure compliance with privacy regulations.

Data auditing and logging are crucial elements of responsible data management. They help organizations ensure data integrity, comply with regulations, and enhance security. By implementing robust logging mechanisms, organizations can create traceable, accountable systems that build trust with users and stakeholders. With the right tools and practices in place, auditing and logging become powerful assets in maintaining ethical and compliant data governance frameworks.

Module 40:

Scalable Data Systems

Scalable data systems are essential for managing and processing large volumes of data efficiently. This module focuses on the design principles for handling big data, leveraging distributed computing, ensuring reliability, and optimizing data storage and access. Scalable systems enable businesses to meet growing data demands while maintaining performance and reliability.

Designing Scalable Systems: Handling Large Volumes of Data

Designing scalable systems requires understanding how to manage large volumes of data efficiently. This involves selecting appropriate architectures that can expand as the data grows. Techniques such as horizontal scaling, partitioning data, and employing distributed systems are crucial for ensuring that data processing remains fast and reliable as data volumes increase.

Distributed Computing: Understanding MapReduce and Hadoop

Distributed computing enables the parallel processing of large datasets across multiple machines. MapReduce is a programming model that processes data in parallel, breaking tasks into smaller sub-tasks. Hadoop, a popular framework, uses MapReduce to distribute processing tasks over clusters, providing a scalable and fault-tolerant solution for big data processing. These technologies make it possible to process vast datasets effectively.

Load Balancing and Failover Mechanisms: Ensuring System Reliability

Load balancing ensures that computing resources are efficiently distributed across servers, preventing overload on any single node. Failover mechanisms automatically redirect traffic to backup servers in case of a failure, ensuring continuous service. These techniques are vital for maintaining the availability and reliability of systems, ensuring that data is accessible and operations continue smoothly, even during high traffic or system failures.

Optimizing Data Storage and Access: Sharding, Indexing, and Caching

Optimizing data storage and access is essential for ensuring fast performance in scalable systems. Sharding involves partitioning data across multiple databases to balance load and speed up query performance. Indexing allows for quick searching of data, while caching stores frequently accessed data in memory, reducing access time. Together, these methods improve overall system efficiency and user experience.

Designing Scalable Systems: Handling Large Volumes of Data

In the modern world of data science, handling large volumes of data is a critical challenge. As businesses and organizations generate vast amounts of data every day, it becomes essential to design scalable systems that can efficiently manage and process this data. A scalable system is one that can grow and handle increasing data loads without sacrificing performance. Effective scaling ensures that data storage, processing, and analysis are efficient, even as the data grows in volume and complexity.

1. Characteristics of Scalable Systems

A scalable system is defined by its ability to handle growing data demands without requiring a complete overhaul of the system architecture. Scalability can be approached in two primary ways:

- **Vertical Scaling (Scaling Up)**: This involves adding more power (CPU, memory, storage) to a single machine or server. Vertical scaling is typically easier to implement but has its limits, as hardware can only be upgraded so far.

- **Horizontal Scaling (Scaling Out)**: This approach involves adding more machines or servers to distribute the load. Horizontal scaling is the preferred method for handling large-scale systems because it allows the system to grow indefinitely by adding additional resources.

Scalable systems are designed to balance performance, cost, and resource utilization. By distributing data processing tasks across multiple nodes, they can improve throughput and reduce bottlenecks.

2. Key Considerations in Designing Scalable Systems

When designing scalable data systems, several key factors must be taken into account:

- **Data Distribution**: The system should be able to divide data into smaller chunks that can be processed in parallel. This ensures that large datasets can be processed efficiently across multiple machines.

- **Load Balancing**: To prevent certain nodes from becoming overwhelmed with requests, load balancing is used to evenly distribute incoming data requests across available servers.

- **Fault Tolerance**: In a scalable system, failures are inevitable. Therefore, systems should be designed with redundancy and failover mechanisms to ensure uninterrupted service in case of hardware or software failures.

- **Data Consistency**: In distributed systems, ensuring data consistency across all nodes can be a challenge. Techniques such as eventual consistency and distributed transactions help manage this issue.

3. Implementing Scalable Systems in Python

To build a basic scalable system in Python, we can utilize frameworks like **Apache Spark** or **Dask**, which are designed for distributed computing. Below is a simple example of how to use **Dask** to handle parallel data processing, an important aspect of scaling.

```
import dask.dataframe as dd

# Read a large CSV file in a distributed manner
df = dd.read_csv('large_data.csv')

# Perform data processing in parallel
result = df.groupby('column_name').sum()

# Compute the result
computed_result = result.compute()
print(computed_result)
```

This code snippet demonstrates how Dask can read a large CSV file and perform distributed operations like grouping and summing data across multiple cores or nodes. By leveraging parallel computing, it can handle datasets that are too large to fit into memory.

4. Distributed Computing with Hadoop and MapReduce

For systems that need to process massive datasets, frameworks like **Hadoop** and **MapReduce** are widely used. Hadoop allows for the distribution of data storage across a cluster, while MapReduce is a programming model that processes data in parallel across multiple nodes.

MapReduce works in two main phases:

- **Map Phase**: Data is divided into smaller chunks, and each chunk is processed by a mapper function to extract relevant information.

- **Reduce Phase**: The processed chunks are aggregated and reduced to a final result by the reducer function.

In Hadoop, the **HDFS (Hadoop Distributed File System)** ensures that data is stored across multiple machines, and MapReduce processes these data chunks in parallel to optimize performance.

Designing scalable systems is essential for handling large volumes of data efficiently. Horizontal scaling, data distribution, load balancing, and fault tolerance are key elements in creating systems that can handle growing data demands. Distributed computing frameworks like Hadoop and Dask play a crucial role in managing scalability in real-world applications. By building systems that scale seamlessly, organizations can ensure that they are ready for the future of big data processing.

Distributed Computing: Understanding MapReduce and Hadoop

Distributed computing is the backbone of modern scalable data systems. It involves dividing a task into smaller sub-tasks, which are then processed simultaneously across multiple nodes or machines. This parallel processing capability is crucial when handling large datasets, as it reduces the time required for computation and ensures that the system can scale to handle growing amounts of data. Two widely used technologies for distributed computing are **MapReduce** and **Hadoop**.

1. Overview of MapReduce

MapReduce is a programming model developed by Google to process vast amounts of data across a distributed system. The model is designed around two main phases:

- **Map Phase**: In this phase, the input data is split into smaller chunks, and each chunk is processed by a "mapper" function. The mapper performs a specific operation on the data, typically transforming or filtering it, and then outputs a set of key-value pairs. These key-value pairs form the basis for the next phase of the computation.

- **Reduce Phase**: The output from the mappers (the key-value pairs) is grouped by key, and a "reducer" function is applied to aggregate the data. This phase combines and processes the intermediate data from all mappers to produce the final output.

MapReduce allows for distributed data processing, enabling efficient parallel execution across clusters of machines, making it ideal for large-scale data analysis tasks.

2. Hadoop and the Hadoop Distributed File System (HDFS)

Hadoop is an open-source framework for storing and processing large datasets in a distributed environment. It includes several core components, including the **Hadoop Distributed File System (HDFS)** and the **MapReduce** processing model. HDFS is designed to store massive amounts of data across many machines, and it splits files into blocks for distributed storage.

- **HDFS**: It is a highly fault-tolerant system, designed to run on commodity hardware. Data in HDFS is split into fixed-size blocks (typically 128 MB or 256 MB) and distributed across different nodes in the cluster. Each block is replicated across multiple machines to ensure that data is not lost in the case of hardware failure.

- **MapReduce in Hadoop**: Hadoop uses the MapReduce programming model to process data stored in HDFS. Jobs are submitted to a **JobTracker**, which schedules tasks across the cluster's **TaskTrackers**. Each TaskTracker processes a portion of the data, performing the map and reduce operations.

3. Example of MapReduce in Hadoop

In Hadoop, the process of writing a MapReduce job involves defining the mapper and reducer functions. Here's a simplified example of how MapReduce might work in Python with a library such as **PySpark** (for distributed processing similar to Hadoop MapReduce).

```python
from pyspark import SparkContext

# Create a SparkContext
sc = SparkContext("local", "MapReduce Example")

# Load data
data = sc.textFile("input.txt")

# Define mapper function: split lines into words
words = data.flatMap(lambda line: line.split(" "))

# Define reducer function: count occurrences of each word
word_counts = words.map(lambda word: (word, 1)).reduceByKey(lambda x, y: x +
        y)

# Collect the result
result = word_counts.collect()

# Print the result
for word, count in result:
    print(f"{word}: {count}")
```

In this example:

- **flatMap()** splits each line into individual words.

- **map()** creates pairs of words and counts.

- **reduceByKey()** sums the counts for each word.

This approach processes data in parallel across multiple nodes, leveraging distributed resources to handle large datasets.

4. Benefits of MapReduce and Hadoop

The combination of MapReduce and Hadoop offers several key benefits for distributed data processing:

- **Scalability**: Both Hadoop and MapReduce are designed to scale horizontally. As data grows, you can add more nodes to the cluster to handle the increased load.

- **Fault Tolerance**: HDFS automatically replicates data blocks across multiple nodes, ensuring that the system can recover from failures. If a node goes down, the data is still available from other replicas.

- **Cost-Effective**: Hadoop is designed to run on commodity hardware, which makes it a cost-effective solution for processing large datasets without requiring expensive infrastructure.

MapReduce and Hadoop form the foundation of distributed computing in large-scale data systems. MapReduce enables efficient parallel data processing, while Hadoop's HDFS ensures reliable and scalable data storage. By utilizing these technologies, organizations can process vast amounts of data quickly and cost-effectively, making them essential tools in modern data science and big data applications.

Load Balancing and Failover Mechanisms: Ensuring System Reliability

In scalable data systems, **load balancing** and **failover mechanisms** are critical components for ensuring both the reliability and availability of services. As data volume grows and system demands fluctuate, maintaining system stability and uptime becomes increasingly important. These mechanisms ensure that a system can handle increased traffic, prevent service disruptions, and continue functioning even when parts of the system fail.

1. Load Balancing: Distributing Traffic Across Servers

Load balancing refers to the distribution of incoming network traffic across multiple servers or resources to ensure that no single server becomes overwhelmed. Load balancers sit between users and the servers, efficiently directing requests to the appropriate server based on various criteria, such as server health, resource usage, or proximity to the user.

- **Round Robin**: One of the simplest load-balancing algorithms, it routes requests to each server in a cyclic manner. For instance, if there are three servers, the first request goes to server one, the second to server two, and so on.

- **Least Connections**: This algorithm routes requests to the server with the fewest active connections, ensuring that the servers with lighter loads handle new requests.

- **IP Hashing**: Requests are directed based on a hash of the client's IP address. This can help maintain session persistence, ensuring a user is consistently routed to the same server for the duration of their session.

Load balancing not only prevents system overloads but also enhances performance by distributing traffic evenly, improving response times and scalability.

2. Failover Mechanisms: Ensuring Availability in Case of Failure

A **failover mechanism** is a process that automatically switches to a backup system, server, or network path in case of a failure. Failover is crucial for maintaining high availability and minimizing downtime.

- **Active-Passive Failover**: In this setup, one server (the primary) handles all requests, while a secondary (passive) server remains inactive, awaiting failure. If the primary server fails, the passive server takes over automatically.

- **Active-Active Failover**: Both servers are active and handle traffic. In the event of a failure, the load balancer automatically redistributes traffic to the remaining servers. This configuration offers better redundancy but can be more complex to manage.

Replication is commonly used alongside failover systems to ensure data consistency and availability. Data is mirrored across multiple servers, ensuring that if one server fails, the backup is always up to date.

3. Example of Load Balancing in Python with Nginx

One common approach for load balancing in web applications is using a reverse proxy like **Nginx** along with Python backends. Here's a simplified setup for load balancing Python web applications:

1. **Install Nginx** on the server.

2. **Configure the Nginx load balancer** to balance requests across multiple Python Flask applications:

```
http {
    upstream app_servers {
        server 127.0.0.1:5000;
        server 127.0.0.1:5001;
    }

    server {
        location / {
            proxy_pass http://app_servers;
        }
    }
}
```

In this example:

- Nginx will distribute incoming requests to two Python Flask applications running on ports 5000 and 5001, ensuring that neither becomes overloaded.

4. Monitoring and Alerting

For both load balancing and failover systems to be effective, they must be paired with monitoring tools that track the health of servers and services in real-time. Tools like **Prometheus**, **Grafana**, and **New Relic** can be used to monitor server performance, detect failures, and trigger alerts. When a failure occurs, monitoring systems can trigger automated recovery processes, such as redirecting traffic or activating backup servers.

Load balancing and failover mechanisms are essential for maintaining the reliability, scalability, and availability of scalable data systems. Load balancing helps evenly distribute traffic to prevent any single server from becoming overwhelmed, while failover mechanisms ensure continuity in case of failure. Combined with proper monitoring and alerting, these strategies ensure that large-scale systems can function efficiently and recover quickly from issues, providing a robust infrastructure for modern data applications.

Optimizing Data Storage and Access: Sharding, Indexing, and Caching

As data systems grow, optimizing **data storage** and **access** becomes essential to maintaining system performance and scalability. Large datasets can slow down query responses, increase load times, and create bottlenecks in real-time processing. To counter these challenges, techniques like **sharding**, **indexing**, and **caching** are implemented to improve data storage and access efficiency. These strategies ensure that large-scale systems can handle high data loads without compromising speed.

1. Sharding: Dividing Data for Scalability

Sharding is the practice of partitioning a database into smaller, more manageable pieces, called **shards**, each of which can be stored on a different server or cluster. This allows a system to scale horizontally by distributing the data across multiple machines, ensuring that no single server is overwhelmed.

- **Horizontal Sharding**: This method involves splitting data into smaller, equal-sized partitions based on specific criteria (e.g., user ID, region). For example, user data might be divided into different shards, with each shard containing users from a particular geographic region.

- **Vertical Sharding**: In this method, a database is divided into columns rather than rows. For example, a database might separate customer information into different shards, with one shard storing contact details and another storing purchase history.

The key advantage of sharding is that it allows a system to manage vast amounts of data by distributing the load across multiple servers. It also ensures faster access by keeping the data closer to where it's needed.

2. Indexing: Improving Query Performance

Indexing is a technique used to speed up the retrieval of data from a database by creating an index (a data structure) that provides a fast lookup for specific columns. Similar to an index in a book, a database index allows you to find records faster without scanning the entire database.

- **B-Tree Index**: This is the most common type of index used in relational databases. It organizes data in a tree structure, where each node points to multiple records, enabling fast lookups.

- **Hash Index**: Used in key-value stores, hash indexing allows for constant-time complexity when searching for a value. The index uses a hash function to convert the key into an address for fast access.

Here's a Python example of creating an index in **SQLite** for fast querying:

```python
import sqlite3

# Connect to the database
conn = sqlite3.connect('example.db')
cursor = conn.cursor()

# Create a table and index
cursor.execute('''CREATE TABLE users (id INTEGER PRIMARY KEY, name TEXT,
        email TEXT)''')
cursor.execute('''CREATE INDEX idx_email ON users (email)''')

# Query using the index
cursor.execute("SELECT * FROM users WHERE email = 'example@email.com'")
print(cursor.fetchall())

conn.close()
```

By using an index on the email column, the query performance is enhanced, especially with large datasets.

3. Caching: Reducing Latency with In-Memory Storage

Caching is the practice of storing frequently accessed data in memory to reduce retrieval time and improve system performance. Caching stores the results of expensive database queries, API calls, or computations, making it faster to retrieve the same data without needing to execute the operation again.

- **In-Memory Caching**: This type of caching stores data in the system's RAM for fast access. Popular caching solutions include **Redis** and **Memcached**.

- **Content Delivery Networks (CDNs)**: For web applications, CDNs cache static content like images, videos, and HTML pages on edge servers close to the user, reducing load times and server requests.

Here's a basic example of using **Redis** with Python for caching:

```python
import redis

# Connect to Redis server
r = redis.StrictRedis(host='localhost', port=6379, db=0)

# Cache a value
r.set('user:1000', 'John Doe')

# Retrieve from cache
name = r.get('user:1000')
print(name.decode('utf-8'))  # Output: John Doe
```

By caching frequently requested data, systems can reduce database load and speed up response times.

Sharding, indexing, and caching are powerful techniques for optimizing data storage and access in scalable data systems. Sharding improves system scalability by distributing data across multiple servers, while indexing speeds up data retrieval by creating efficient search structures. Caching enhances performance by storing frequently accessed data in memory, reducing latency. Together, these strategies ensure that large-scale systems can handle high volumes of data while maintaining high performance, reliability, and responsiveness.

Part 7:

Data Visualization and Storytelling

Principles of Data Storytelling

Data storytelling is a powerful tool for transforming raw data into compelling narratives that can engage audiences and drive decisions. In this module, learners are introduced to the art of data storytelling, which combines data analysis with storytelling techniques to convey insights in a meaningful way. The module covers how to structure a data story using a beginning, middle, and end approach to create a logical flow and keep the audience engaged. Learners will explore how to connect visuals to the context of the story, ensuring that data not only informs but also enhances the narrative. Finally, the module emphasizes how to present complex data to non-technical audiences, making it accessible without oversimplifying the key insights.

Advanced Visualization Techniques

In this module, learners delve into advanced visualization techniques that go beyond traditional charts and graphs. These techniques include heatmaps, violin plots, and radar charts, which can provide deeper insights into data patterns and relationships. The module also covers how to visualize geospatial data, using maps and GIS libraries to represent location-based information. Animation is explored as a dynamic way to add interactive elements to data visualizations, making them more engaging and easier to interpret. Learners will also discover how to create data visualizations that communicate insights effectively to business stakeholders, helping to inform decision-making processes.

Interactive Dashboards and Tools

Interactive dashboards are an essential tool for presenting real-time data and providing stakeholders with the ability to explore and analyze data dynamically. This module introduces popular dashboard development tools such as Tableau, Power BI, Dash, and Shiny, explaining how to use them to build interactive and user-friendly dashboards. Learners will explore how to create interactive elements like filters, sliders, and drill-down features to allow users to customize their view of the data. Best practices for dashboard design are covered to ensure clarity, usability, and a visually appealing layout. The module also discusses how to integrate live data feeds into dashboards, ensuring that the information presented is always up to date.

Communicating with Non-Technical Audiences

Effectively communicating data insights to non-technical audiences is a key skill for any data professional. This module focuses on how to tailor data presentations to suit the understanding level of the audience, ensuring that the message resonates with both technical and non-technical stakeholders. Learners will discover strategies for avoiding jargon and simplifying complex technical concepts without losing the essence of the data. The module also emphasizes the importance of using visuals like graphs and charts to clarify insights and make data more digestible. The art of storytelling with data is reinforced as a way to turn raw data into actionable insights that can drive decisions.

Data Art and Aesthetics

Data visualization isn't just about presenting data—it's also about making it aesthetically pleasing. This module explores the intersection of data and art, highlighting how design principles like color, size, shape, and layout can be used to enhance data visualizations. Learners will explore examples of stunning visualizations that are not only informative but also visually striking, showcasing how creativity can elevate the impact of data. The module also covers creative uses of data visualization beyond traditional business and analytics applications, such as in journalism, art, and activism, demonstrating the potential for data to tell unique and powerful stories.

Practical Case Studies in Visualization

The final module in this part brings the concepts learned throughout the section into real-world practice. Learners will explore case studies of successful data visualization applications from industries like healthcare, finance, and marketing. The module walks through the process of building a visualization pipeline—from collecting raw data to creating polished visuals that tell a compelling story. Learners will also gain insights into working with stakeholders to gather feedback and iterate on visualizations to ensure they meet the audience's needs. The module concludes with lessons from successful visualization projects, offering best practices and tips for creating effective and impactful data visualizations.

Module 41:
Principles of Data Storytelling

Data storytelling is a powerful technique for communicating complex insights through narrative. This module emphasizes the importance of crafting a compelling story using data. By following structured approaches and making data understandable, practitioners can engage audiences effectively and facilitate decision-making. Data storytelling combines analysis with creativity to captivate and inform.

The Art of Data Storytelling: Conveying Insights Through Compelling Narratives

Data storytelling blends data analysis with storytelling elements to create a persuasive narrative. Instead of just presenting raw numbers, it focuses on telling a story that resonates with the audience. By using clear structures and emotional hooks, data becomes a vehicle for connecting with people on a deeper level, making insights memorable and impactful.

Structuring a Data Story: Beginning, Middle, and End Approach

A well-structured data story follows a clear beginning, middle, and end framework. The beginning introduces the context and challenges. The middle presents data insights and analysis to support the narrative. The end concludes with recommendations, solutions, or actions. This structure helps maintain audience interest, provides clarity, and emphasizes key takeaways from the data.

Using Data to Tell a Story: Connecting Visuals to Context

Effective data storytelling leverages visuals like charts, graphs, and infographics to illustrate key points. Connecting these visuals to the broader context ensures they are not merely decorative but integral to the message. Contextualizing data with storytelling elements such as trends, comparisons, and milestones helps the audience understand how the data informs the narrative and decision-making.

Engaging Non-Technical Audiences: Making Complex Data Understandable

When presenting data to non-technical audiences, simplifying complex concepts is essential. Avoiding jargon and focusing on the core message ensures that the audience grasps the insights. Using analogies, relatable examples, and clear visuals makes the data accessible. The goal is to create a narrative that is both informative and engaging, empowering decision-makers regardless of their technical background.

The Art of Data Storytelling: Conveying Insights through Compelling Narratives

Data storytelling is the practice of transforming complex data and analytics into compelling narratives that resonate with audiences. Rather than simply presenting raw numbers and graphs, effective data storytelling allows data scientists, analysts, and business leaders to present insights in a way that makes them actionable and memorable. By merging the power of data with the art of storytelling, you can engage your audience, drive decisions, and inspire action.

1. The Power of Narrative in Data

The human brain is naturally drawn to stories. Narratives are easier to understand, remember, and relate to than abstract data or numbers. The power of **data storytelling** lies in its ability to connect the analytical world with the emotional world, making data accessible and meaningful. Instead of overwhelming audiences with raw statistics or technical jargon, data storytelling uses a structured narrative to provide context and insight.

A well-told story provides a **beginning**, **middle**, and **end**—beginning with a problem or question, continuing with the analysis and exploration of data, and culminating with a solution or decision. The journey through the story engages the audience, guiding them through the data to understand its implications and impact.

2. Structuring a Data Story: Beginning, Middle, and End

To craft an effective data story, it is essential to structure it clearly. Like any good story, it should have a **beginning**, **middle**, and **end**.

- **Beginning**: The story should begin by identifying the problem or question that the data addresses. This stage introduces the context and purpose of the analysis. For instance, "Our sales figures have been declining, and we need to understand why."

- **Middle**: In this phase, the data is explored to uncover patterns, trends, and insights. It's where the bulk of analysis happens and where data visualizations and exploration occur. Graphs, charts, and tables can be introduced to support the analysis, and data can be broken down into smaller parts for easier understanding.

- **End**: The story concludes with actionable insights or recommendations. It should tie back to the original problem and offer a solution or next steps. For example, "Based on the analysis, we found that our sales decline is primarily due to a drop in customer retention. We recommend implementing a loyalty program to address this issue."

3. Using Data to Tell a Story: Connecting Visuals to Context

The integration of **visuals** with the data is crucial in storytelling. A well-chosen graph, chart, or diagram can make complex data more digestible and give it the context needed for proper understanding.

- **Choosing the Right Visualization**: Different types of visualizations work best for different kinds of data. Bar charts may be useful for comparing quantities, line graphs can highlight trends over time, and scatter plots can show correlations between variables. Visuals should complement the narrative, not overwhelm it.

  Example using Python's **matplotlib** for a simple line graph:

  ```
  import matplotlib.pyplot as plt

  # Sample data: monthly sales
  months = ['Jan', 'Feb', 'Mar', 'Apr', 'May', 'Jun']
  sales = [120, 150, 180, 140, 130, 170]

  # Plotting the data
  plt.plot(months, sales, marker='o', color='b')
  plt.title('Monthly Sales Overview')
  plt.xlabel('Month')
  plt.ylabel('Sales (in thousands)')
  plt.show()
  ```

This graph illustrates trends, showing peaks and valleys in sales, which can be used to highlight specific periods in the story.

- **Contextualizing the Visuals**: Data visualizations should always be explained in context. What does the graph mean? How does it relate to the bigger picture? A good storyteller doesn't just present visuals—they explain what the audience is seeing and why it matters.

4. Engaging Non-Technical Audiences: Making Complex Data Understandable

One of the most important aspects of data storytelling is making complex information understandable to a non-technical audience. Not everyone is familiar with statistics, algorithms, or the intricacies of data models. Therefore, the story should be accessible, with a focus on key takeaways rather than technical details.

- **Simplifying Complex Concepts**: Avoid jargon and focus on simplifying complex concepts. For instance, instead of delving into the intricacies of a regression model, focus on what the model's results mean for the business or organization.

- **Relating to the Audience**: Use analogies or real-world examples to help the audience relate to the data. By connecting the data to experiences or concerns that are familiar to the audience, you can make the data feel more tangible.

Data storytelling is about weaving a narrative that makes data come alive. It allows audiences to see the "story" behind the numbers, making insights more actionable and memorable. By structuring the story effectively, using visuals to enhance understanding, and tailoring the message for a non-technical audience, data storytelling can be a powerful tool for driving decisions and inspiring action.

Structuring a Data Story: Beginning, Middle, and End Approach

When crafting a compelling data story, structuring it effectively is paramount. Like any engaging narrative, a data story needs to have a clear beginning, middle, and end. Each section should guide the audience through the data, providing context, analysis, and conclusions in a logical, digestible format. By following this structured approach, you ensure that your audience remains engaged and can fully grasp the insights that the data offers.

1. The Beginning: Setting the Stage

The beginning of a data story serves as the foundation for everything that follows. In this phase, you should introduce the context and purpose of the analysis, providing your audience with a clear understanding of why the data matters. This step sets the tone for the entire narrative, so it's important to make it relatable and intriguing.

- **Identifying the Problem**: Start by presenting the problem or question that you are trying to solve with data. For instance, "Our company has seen a decline in customer satisfaction, and we need to determine the reasons behind this shift."

- **Framing the Context**: It's crucial to provide some background to help the audience understand the relevance of the data. This could involve historical context, industry trends, or previous observations. For example, "Customer satisfaction has been a key metric for our success, and a drop in this metric could indicate underlying issues in our product or service."

In this opening section, the goal is to engage the audience by addressing something that matters to them. You're setting up the story so that they care about the outcome.

2. The Middle: Uncovering Insights with Data

The middle is the heart of the data story, where the bulk of the analysis takes place. In this section, you explore the data in depth, uncovering patterns, correlations, or anomalies that help to answer the problem or question introduced in the beginning. This is where the data takes center stage, and you present the evidence that will shape your conclusions.

- **Exploration and Analysis**: Present the data in an easy-to-understand format, using visuals to enhance comprehension. For example, when discussing trends, graphs and charts can clearly highlight patterns that might not be obvious in raw data.

Here is a Python example using **matplotlib** to show customer satisfaction trends over time:

```python
import matplotlib.pyplot as plt

# Sample data: customer satisfaction over months
months = ['Jan', 'Feb', 'Mar', 'Apr', 'May', 'Jun']
satisfaction_scores = [88, 82, 75, 80, 85, 77]

# Plotting the data
plt.plot(months, satisfaction_scores, marker='o', color='g')
plt.title('Customer Satisfaction Over Time')
plt.xlabel('Month')
plt.ylabel('Satisfaction Score')
plt.grid(True)
plt.show()
```

This simple line chart allows you to visualize fluctuations in customer satisfaction, helping to highlight trends that may need further investigation. In the middle of your story, you should emphasize these insights and explain their significance in the context of the problem.

- **Supporting the Narrative with Data**: Use clear, annotated visualizations to highlight key findings. For example, pointing out months with significant drops or improvements can guide the audience's focus.

3. The End: Drawing Conclusions and Offering Solutions

The end of a data story is where you summarize the insights and present actionable recommendations based on the analysis. This is the payoff for the audience, where the complex data is distilled into clear takeaways and next steps.

- **Drawing Conclusions**: Reflect on what the data reveals about the original problem. For instance, you might conclude, "Our analysis reveals that customer satisfaction dropped significantly in March due to delays in product delivery."

- **Offering Solutions or Recommendations**: This is where you offer actionable advice based on the findings. For example, "To improve satisfaction, we recommend investing in supply chain improvements and ensuring that delivery times are consistently met."

This section should feel like a resolution to the story's conflict, bringing everything together in a way that is both understandable and actionable.

4. Making the Data Story Memorable

To leave a lasting impact on your audience, end with a final thought that ties everything together. This could involve reiterating the key message or proposing an exciting opportunity based on the insights uncovered. In the case of our customer satisfaction story, a closing statement might be, "With the right actions, we can turn these insights into measurable improvements that will directly benefit our customers and our bottom line."

Structuring a data story with a clear beginning, middle, and end helps guide the audience through the data and makes the insights more compelling and easier to understand. By focusing on context, analysis, and actionable recommendations, you can create a narrative that resonates with your audience and drives meaningful decisions. A well-structured data story is not only about presenting data—it's about engaging the audience and helping them see the relevance and impact of the information in a way that inspires action.

Using Data to Tell a Story: Connecting Visuals to Context

Data storytelling goes beyond simply presenting raw numbers or charts. The key to making a compelling data story is to connect the data visuals with the context, ensuring that the audience understands the insights behind the data and its relevance to the problem at hand. This connection between visuals and context allows the audience to follow the narrative, grasp the key findings, and make informed decisions based on the data.

1. Contextualizing Data with Clear Visuals

One of the most important aspects of data storytelling is ensuring that the visuals you use support the message you're trying to convey. Visualizations like charts, graphs, and tables are essential tools to highlight trends, compare variables, and communicate complex insights in an easily digestible format. However, without proper context, these visuals can easily be misinterpreted.

For instance, if you're showing a bar chart of sales over several months, it's important to include labels, a title, and any relevant contextual information that can guide the audience's interpretation. A simple bar chart might look like this:

```python
import matplotlib.pyplot as plt

# Sample data: Sales data over months
months = ['Jan', 'Feb', 'Mar', 'Apr', 'May', 'Jun']
sales = [2500, 3000, 2800, 3500, 4200, 4500]

# Creating the bar chart
plt.bar(months, sales, color='blue')
plt.title('Sales Over Time')
plt.xlabel('Month')
plt.ylabel('Sales ($)')
plt.show()
```

While this chart clearly shows a positive sales trend, it lacks context. Adding information such as "the company launched a new marketing campaign in March" provides the audience with insight into why sales spiked that month. This ensures the audience can make informed conclusions based on the visualized data.

2. Telling the Story with a Narrative Flow

To effectively tell a story with your data, you need to guide the audience through the visuals in a logical and engaging way. Start by setting the stage with the background context, then move into the data analysis and present the key findings. As you present each visual, link it back to the overall narrative. This narrative flow ensures that the audience understands the journey the data takes, from the initial problem or question to the ultimate insights and conclusions.

For example, in a sales analysis story, you could begin by explaining that the company has been facing a decline in revenue and needs to identify the key factors contributing to the drop. Then, as you present visuals, you can show how sales numbers correlate with various events, such as new product launches, marketing campaigns, or seasonal trends. By explaining each step of the analysis as you go, you ensure that the audience stays engaged and understands the significance of the data.

3. Using Annotations to Clarify Key Insights

Annotations are another powerful tool in data storytelling. They allow you to highlight specific data points or trends within a visualization, providing additional context without overwhelming the audience. Annotations can help explain why certain data points are important or point out key trends that the audience should focus on.

For example, you could use annotations in a line graph to call attention to significant changes, such as a sudden drop or spike in sales. Here's how you can annotate a line chart in Python using matplotlib:

```
import matplotlib.pyplot as plt

# Sample data: Monthly sales
months = ['Jan', 'Feb', 'Mar', 'Apr', 'May', 'Jun']
sales = [2500, 3000, 2800, 3500, 4200, 4500]

# Creating the line plot
plt.plot(months, sales, marker='o', color='green')
plt.title('Sales Over Time')
plt.xlabel('Month')
plt.ylabel('Sales ($)')

# Adding annotation
plt.annotate('New Marketing Campaign', xy=('Mar', 3500), xytext=('Feb',
        3800),
            arrowprops=dict(facecolor='black', shrink=0.05))
plt.show()
```

In this example, the annotation highlights the effect of a new marketing campaign on sales, making it clear to the audience why March's sales spike occurred. Annotations are particularly helpful in data storytelling because they allow you to make your visuals even more informative.

4. Ensuring Simplicity and Clarity

While it's tempting to include as much information as possible, one of the cardinal rules of data storytelling is simplicity. Too many visuals or overly complicated charts can confuse the audience and detract from the core message. Stick to the most relevant visuals that directly support the story you're telling, and ensure that each chart is easy to understand at a glance.

A simple, clear design is more likely to capture the audience's attention and help them retain the key insights from the data. Avoid cluttered charts and focus on what matters most.

Using data to tell a story is about making the data relatable and understandable. By connecting visuals to the context, telling a cohesive narrative, and emphasizing key insights, you ensure that your audience is engaged and able to make informed decisions. The data should never speak for itself; rather, it should be guided by context, explanation, and visuals that help illuminate its meaning. When done well, data storytelling can transform raw numbers into a compelling narrative that drives action and insight.

Engaging Non-Technical Audiences: Making Complex Data Understandable

Data science can often seem intimidating to non-technical audiences, especially when it involves complex algorithms, intricate visualizations, or statistical jargon. However, the true power of data lies in its ability to inform decisions, and the challenge is ensuring that those without a technical background can access these insights. Engaging non-technical audiences requires simplifying the data story without losing its essence.

1. Simplifying the Language

The first step in making complex data understandable is to use simple language. Instead of discussing "multivariate regression models" or "machine learning algorithms," use relatable terms like "predictive models" or "data trends." Focus on the story behind the numbers rather than the technical details. For example, instead of saying, "Our model uses supervised learning to predict outcomes," you could say, "Our model helps predict future sales by learning from past data."

Additionally, avoid overwhelming your audience with technical jargon. Non-technical audiences benefit from clear, everyday language, which enables them to grasp the core concepts without becoming bogged down in specifics.

2. Visualizing Data Effectively

Visuals are one of the most effective tools for conveying complex data to non-technical audiences. Charts, graphs, and infographics can break down large amounts of information into digestible pieces. When selecting a visual, consider the type of data and the message you want to convey.

For example, when showing sales data over time, a simple line graph or bar chart can clearly illustrate trends. To ensure clarity, avoid overly complex charts with too many variables. Keep the visuals straightforward, with clear labels, titles, and legends, and use colors to highlight key data points.

Here's an example of a simple bar chart in Python using matplotlib:

```python
import matplotlib.pyplot as plt

# Example sales data for simplicity
months = ['Jan', 'Feb', 'Mar', 'Apr', 'May']
sales = [1000, 1500, 1800, 2200, 2500]

plt.bar(months, sales, color='skyblue')
plt.title('Sales Over Time')
plt.xlabel('Month')
plt.ylabel('Sales ($)')
plt.show()
```

This bar chart is simple and visually clear, making it easy for a non-technical audience to see that sales are consistently rising each month.

3. Storytelling with Context

To make data resonate with a non-technical audience, it's essential to connect the numbers to real-world contexts. Non-technical audiences are more likely to engage when they can relate the data to their own experiences or to broader, familiar concepts. Instead of just showing trends or results, explain why they matter.

For instance, rather than simply showing that "sales increased by 20%," explain the impact: "Our sales have increased by 20% since we introduced our new marketing campaign, which means more customers are engaging with our brand, resulting in higher revenue."

By framing the data within a story that reflects real-world scenarios, you make it more meaningful and easier to understand.

4. Focusing on Key Takeaways

Instead of overwhelming your audience with every detail of your analysis, focus on the key takeaways. Distill the message to the most important insights. For example, rather than diving into the technicalities of statistical significance or model performance, emphasize how the data can inform action. A non-technical audience is often more interested in what the data suggests and what steps to take next.

A good approach is to answer the following questions for your audience:

- What is the main finding?

- Why does it matter to the business or project?

- What are the next steps or recommendations based on the data?

For instance, instead of presenting complex results from an A/B test, you can summarize: "Based on our A/B testing, we found that version B of the webpage increased customer engagement by 15%. Therefore, we recommend implementing version B as the default."

5. Using Analogies and Metaphors

Analogies and metaphors can help demystify complex data concepts. For example, you could explain machine learning models by comparing them to how humans learn: "Just as a teacher helps students understand a subject through examples, our model learns by looking at past data to make predictions about the future."

Metaphors are powerful tools that connect the unfamiliar with the familiar, making complex ideas more accessible. By comparing technical concepts to everyday experiences, you make it easier for non-technical audiences to relate and understand.

6. Interactive Data Exploration

If possible, allow your audience to interact with the data. Interactive dashboards or visualizations give non-technical users the freedom to explore the data themselves. For instance, tools like Tableau, Power BI, or Python libraries like Dash and Streamlit enable the creation of interactive plots where users can filter, zoom, or drill down into the data.

Engaging non-technical audiences in data storytelling is about focusing on simplicity, clarity, and relevance. By using clear visuals, simplifying language, and providing relatable context, you ensure that the data resonates with everyone, regardless of their technical background. The goal is to make complex data accessible, empowering stakeholders to make informed decisions based on the insights presented.

Module 42:

Advanced Visualization Techniques

Advanced visualization techniques empower data scientists and analysts to communicate complex insights more effectively. This module delves into sophisticated charting methods, geospatial visualization, dynamic elements, and visualization strategies for business decision-making. By utilizing these advanced tools, users can engage their audience and convey insights that drive impactful decisions.

Advanced Charts and Graphs: Heatmaps, Violin Plots, and Radar Charts

Advanced charts such as heatmaps, violin plots, and radar charts provide more nuanced insights compared to traditional graphs. Heatmaps display data density and patterns, while violin plots combine aspects of boxplots and density plots to reveal distribution shapes. Radar charts allow for the visualization of multivariate data, helping in comparative analysis of several variables simultaneously.

Visualizing Geospatial Data: Maps, Geospatial Libraries, and GIS

Geospatial data visualization allows the representation of data points on maps, offering insights into location-based patterns. Using tools like geospatial libraries (e.g., Folium, Geopandas) and Geographic Information Systems (GIS), data scientists can create interactive maps to visualize data trends, regional distribution, and geographic relationships. This is crucial for industries like logistics, urban planning, and environmental monitoring.

Animation in Visualization: Dynamic, Interactive Elements

Animation enhances data visualizations by adding a dynamic, interactive layer. Animated visualizations can show temporal changes, helping to understand trends over time. Interactive elements, such as tooltips, clickable data points, and zoomable maps, allow users to engage with data in real-time, improving the overall user experience and providing more insightful analysis.

Data Visualizations for Business Decisions: Communicating Insights to Stakeholders

Data visualizations play a critical role in business decision-making by simplifying complex data and highlighting key insights. Effective visualizations communicate actionable insights to stakeholders, enabling informed decisions. Tailoring visuals to the audience—whether executives, marketers, or analysts—ensures that the right message is conveyed. Simplicity and clarity are key to ensuring stakeholders can easily interpret the data.

Advanced Charts and Graphs: Heatmaps, Violin Plots, and Radar Charts

Advanced visualizations are essential tools for extracting insights from complex datasets. These visualizations go beyond basic charts and graphs, enabling a deeper understanding of data through sophisticated patterns, distributions, and comparisons. In this section, we explore advanced charts such as heatmaps, violin plots, and radar charts, and their applications in data analysis.

1. Heatmaps: Visualizing Correlations and Data Density

Heatmaps are powerful tools for visualizing data density and relationships between variables. They represent data through a color-coded matrix, where each value is represented by a color. Heatmaps are particularly useful for showing correlations between different variables in a dataset.

In Python, heatmaps can be created using libraries like seaborn. For instance, a correlation matrix heatmap can be used to visualize the relationships between different features in a dataset:

```python
import seaborn as sns
import matplotlib.pyplot as plt
import pandas as pd

# Example dataframe
data = {
    'A': [1, 2, 3, 4],
    'B': [4, 3, 2, 1],
    'C': [5, 6, 7, 8]
}

df = pd.DataFrame(data)

# Compute correlation matrix
corr = df.corr()

# Generate a heatmap
sns.heatmap(corr, annot=True, cmap="coolwarm", fmt='.2f')
plt.title('Correlation Heatmap')
plt.show()
```

In the code above, the seaborn.heatmap() function is used to create a heatmap of the correlation matrix, helping identify how variables are related. The coolwarm color palette emphasizes high and low correlations.

2. Violin Plots: Understanding Distributions and Density

Violin plots combine aspects of box plots and density plots, providing a more detailed view of data distributions. They are particularly useful for comparing the distribution of multiple variables across different categories.

The key feature of a violin plot is its ability to show the distribution's shape, including its density, for each category. Here's how you can create a violin plot in Python using seaborn:

```python
import seaborn as sns
import matplotlib.pyplot as plt

# Example data
data = sns.load_dataset('tips')

# Create a violin plot
sns.violinplot(x='day', y='total_bill', data=data)
plt.title('Violin Plot of Total Bill by Day')
plt.show()
```

In this example, the violin plot displays the distribution of total bills across different days of the week. The wider sections of the violin represent areas where data points are concentrated, while the thin sections indicate fewer data points.

3. Radar Charts: Comparing Multiple Variables

Radar charts, also known as spider or web charts, are used to compare multiple variables in a multi-dimensional space. They are particularly useful for visualizing performance across different categories or comparing different entities.

To create a radar chart in Python, we can use matplotlib. Below is an example of how to visualize multiple features using a radar chart:

```python
import matplotlib.pyplot as plt
import numpy as np

# Example data
categories = ['A', 'B', 'C', 'D', 'E']
values = [4, 3, 2, 5, 4]

# Number of variables
num_vars = len(categories)

# Compute angle for each axis
angles = np.linspace(0, 2 * np.pi, num_vars, endpoint=False).tolist()

# Make the plot circular
values += values[:1]
angles += angles[:1]

# Plot the radar chart
fig, ax = plt.subplots(figsize=(6, 6), subplot_kw=dict(polar=True))
ax.fill(angles, values, color='blue', alpha=0.25)
ax.plot(angles, values, color='blue', linewidth=2)

# Set the labels
ax.set_yticklabels([])
ax.set_xticks(angles[:-1])
ax.set_xticklabels(categories)

plt.title('Radar Chart Example')
plt.show()
```

In the radar chart example, the fill() method creates a shaded area to represent the data, and the plot() method adds an outline. This visualization helps compare the performance or characteristics of multiple categories, making it easy to spot strengths and weaknesses across variables.

Heatmaps, violin plots, and radar charts are just a few examples of advanced visualization techniques that help uncover patterns and relationships within complex datasets. By incorporating these visualizations into your data analysis toolkit, you can provide deeper insights and make more informed decisions. Each of these charts serves a specific purpose, whether it's exploring correlations, distributions, or comparing multi-dimensional data. In data science, choosing the right visualization technique is key to effectively communicating findings and driving business decisions.

Visualizing Geospatial Data: Maps, Geospatial Libraries, and GIS

Geospatial data plays a crucial role in many areas, including urban planning, environmental monitoring, logistics, and even marketing. Visualizing geospatial data through maps enables data scientists to uncover spatial patterns and relationships that may otherwise go unnoticed. This section explores how to visualize geospatial data using Python libraries, such as geopandas, folium, and matplotlib, and also delves into the use of Geographic Information Systems (GIS) for more advanced analyses.

1. Understanding Geospatial Data

Geospatial data refers to information that is linked to geographic locations, often using coordinates like latitude and longitude. This data can represent anything from physical features like rivers and mountains to human activities like the locations of stores or distribution centers. The ability to visualize this data on a map can help uncover trends related to spatial distributions, accessibility, and proximity.

There are two main types of geospatial data:

- **Vector data**: Represents discrete features like points, lines, and polygons (e.g., cities, roads, or administrative boundaries).

- **Raster data**: Represents continuous data values, such as temperature, elevation, or satellite imagery.

Both data types can be visualized using specialized tools and libraries.

2. Visualizing Geospatial Data with GeoPandas

GeoPandas is an open-source Python library that extends the capabilities of pandas to handle geospatial data. It simplifies the process of working with shapefiles and other geospatial data formats. You can use it to visualize vector data, such as boundaries of countries, regions, or neighborhoods.

Here's an example of how to load and plot a shapefile (vector data) using GeoPandas:

```
import geopandas as gpd
import matplotlib.pyplot as plt

# Load a shapefile of world countries
world = gpd.read_file(gpd.datasets.get_path('naturalearth_lowres'))

# Plot the map
world.plot()
plt.title('World Map')
plt.show()
```

In this example, the GeoPandas library loads a built-in shapefile of world countries and then visualizes it. This map helps identify spatial patterns in the distribution of countries across the globe.

3. Interactive Maps with Folium

While static maps provide a good overview, interactive maps are increasingly popular for providing users with a more engaging and explorative experience. Folium is a Python library built on the popular JavaScript library Leaflet, which allows the creation of interactive maps. It supports a wide range of geospatial data types and can integrate with other Python tools like pandas and GeoPandas.

Here's how you can create an interactive map with Folium to visualize locations of cities:

```
import folium

# Create a map centered at a specific location (latitude, longitude)
m = folium.Map(location=[40.7128, -74.0060], zoom_start=10)  # New York City

# Add a marker for a specific location
folium.Marker([40.7128, -74.0060], popup='New York City').add_to(m)

# Display the map
m.save("map.html")
```

This code creates a map centered on New York City and adds a marker at the city's location. The map is interactive, allowing users to zoom in, zoom out, and click on markers for additional information.

4. Using GIS for Advanced Geospatial Analysis

Geographic Information Systems (GIS) are software tools designed for working with geospatial data. They provide advanced functionalities such as spatial analysis, distance calculations, and overlaying multiple data layers. GIS software like QGIS or

ArcGIS can be used in conjunction with Python libraries like PyQGIS or ArcPy for more sophisticated spatial analysis and visualization.

While Python libraries like GeoPandas and Folium are excellent for simpler tasks, a GIS tool provides a rich environment for data preparation, analysis, and visualization. These systems also allow users to perform spatial queries, such as determining proximity to certain locations or creating heatmaps based on geospatial data.

Visualizing geospatial data is essential for understanding spatial relationships and patterns that are crucial in fields like urban planning, logistics, and environmental monitoring. Libraries like GeoPandas, Folium, and GIS software offer powerful tools for transforming raw geospatial data into informative and interactive maps. By leveraging these tools, data scientists and analysts can gain deeper insights into the spatial dimensions of their datasets. Whether through static maps or interactive visualizations, geospatial data visualization enhances decision-making and helps in addressing spatial challenges.

Animation in Visualization: Dynamic, Interactive Elements

Data visualization is an effective way to communicate insights from complex datasets, and animation plays a crucial role in making those insights more dynamic and engaging. By adding movement to static visuals, animations can help highlight trends, transitions, or changes over time, making it easier to convey complex stories. In this section, we explore how to incorporate animation into data visualizations using Python libraries like matplotlib, Plotly, and Bokeh.

---

1. Why Use Animation in Data Visualization?

Animations are particularly useful when the dataset has temporal components or requires showing changes over time. For example, visualizing how a dataset evolves over months or years can bring clarity to trends that might be harder to detect in static plots. Animations allow viewers to track changes step by step, providing a clearer and more intuitive understanding of data transitions.

Some key benefits of animation in visualizations include:

- **Enhanced storytelling**: Allows users to follow a narrative or progression.

- **Focus on important changes**: Highlights how variables evolve over time.

- **Increased engagement**: Adds an interactive and dynamic element to the visualization.

2. Creating Animated Plots with matplotlib
482

matplotlib, a foundational Python plotting library, supports creating simple animations by updating the plot at regular intervals. The FuncAnimation class in matplotlib.animation provides an easy way to animate plots. Here's an example of animating a sine wave:

```python
import numpy as np
import matplotlib.pyplot as plt
from matplotlib.animation import FuncAnimation

# Set up the figure and axis
fig, ax = plt.subplots()
x = np.linspace(0, 2 * np.pi, 100)
line, = ax.plot(x, np.sin(x))

# Animation function to update the sine wave
def update(frame):
    line.set_ydata(np.sin(x + frame / 10))  # Update the y data
    return line,

# Create the animation
ani = FuncAnimation(fig, update, frames=100, interval=50, blit=True)

# Display the animation
plt.show()
```

In this example, the FuncAnimation object updates the sine wave, showing how the wave oscillates over time. The update function modifies the data points, and blit=True ensures that only the changed elements are redrawn, making the animation more efficient.

3. Interactive Animations with Plotly

Plotly is a powerful library for creating interactive plots, and it allows users to incorporate animations that respond to user input. Unlike static plots, Plotly animations enable zooming, hovering, and dynamic transitions.

Here's an example of an animated scatter plot that shows data points moving over time:

```python
import plotly.graph_objects as go
import numpy as np

# Create some sample data
t = np.linspace(0, 10, 100)
x = np.sin(t)
y = np.cos(t)

# Create the figure
fig = go.Figure(
    data=[go.Scatter(x=x, y=y, mode='markers')],
    layout=go.Layout(
        title='Animated Scatter Plot',
        updatemenus=[dict(
            type='buttons', showactive=False, buttons=[dict(label='Play',
                method='animate', args=[None, dict(frame=dict(duration=50,
            redraw=True), fromcurrent=True)])])],
        sliders=[dict(
```

```
            steps=[dict(label=str(i), method='animate', args=[[i],
                dict(frame=dict(duration=50, redraw=True), mode='immediate')])
                for i in range(len(t))]
        )]
    ),
    frames=[go.Frame(data=[go.Scatter(x=x[:i], y=y[:i], mode='markers')],
        name=str(i)) for i in range(1, len(t))]
)

fig.show()
```

In this example, Plotly animates a scatter plot showing data points following a sine and cosine curve. It includes interactive controls such as play buttons and sliders to control the animation speed and frame progression.

4. Dynamic Dashboards with Bokeh

Bokeh is another Python library that excels at creating interactive visualizations, especially for web-based dashboards. It offers features like dynamic updates, hover effects, and sliders. Bokeh is ideal for creating data visualizations that respond to real-time changes in the data or user input.

Here's an example of an animated line plot using Bokeh:

```
from bokeh.plotting import figure, show
from bokeh.io import output_notebook
from bokeh.models import ColumnDataSource
from bokeh.layouts import column
from bokeh.driving import count

output_notebook()

# Create a ColumnDataSource to hold the data
source = ColumnDataSource(data=dict(x=[], y=[]))

# Create the plot
p = figure(title="Animated Line Plot", x_axis_label='x', y_axis_label='y')
p.line('x', 'y', source=source, line_width=2)

# Define the update function
@count()
def update(i):
    new_data = dict(x=[i], y=[np.sin(i / 10)])
    source.stream(new_data, rollover=200)

show(p)
```

In this Bokeh example, the plot continuously updates as new points are added over time, simulating the behavior of an animated line plot. The @count() decorator ensures that each time the function is called, a new data point is appended to the plot.

Animations enhance the effectiveness of data visualization by making complex trends and changes more accessible to viewers. Whether it's a simple sine wave animation with matplotlib, an interactive plot with Plotly, or a real-time data update in Bokeh, adding movement to static charts helps viewers understand data over time. By

484

integrating animation into your visualizations, you create more engaging and insightful representations that are easier to grasp.

Data Visualizations for Business Decisions: Communicating Insights to Stakeholders

In the business world, data visualization is a powerful tool for communicating insights to stakeholders and decision-makers. By transforming complex data into visually appealing and easy-to-understand charts, graphs, and maps, data visualizations help businesses make informed decisions. This section explores how to use data visualizations effectively to communicate findings, drive business decisions, and engage non-technical stakeholders.

1. The Importance of Data Visualization in Business

Data visualization plays a crucial role in business decision-making because it helps distill vast amounts of data into actionable insights. For decision-makers, especially those without a technical background, visualizations offer a simple and direct way to interpret complex data. A well-crafted visualization can highlight key trends, potential risks, and opportunities, making it easier for stakeholders to align on critical decisions.

Effective visualizations allow for:

- **Quick insights**: Decision-makers can interpret data quickly through visuals.

- **Better engagement**: Visual formats are more engaging than tables or raw data, increasing attention and retention.

- **Improved understanding**: Complex patterns and relationships become clearer, enabling more informed decisions.

2. Choosing the Right Visualizations for Business Insights

The choice of visualization depends on the type of data being presented and the key message to be conveyed. Common types of visualizations used in business include:

- **Bar and Column Charts**: Used to compare categories, such as sales by region or product.

- **Line Graphs**: Ideal for showing trends over time, such as revenue growth or stock price movements.

- **Pie Charts**: Useful for illustrating proportions or percentages within a whole, such as market share distribution.

- **Heatmaps**: Effective for identifying patterns or concentrations in data, such as customer activity or performance metrics.

- **Dashboards**: Consolidated views of multiple visualizations that track business metrics, helping decision-makers keep track of performance at a glance.

3. Tailoring Visualizations for Different Audiences

Business data is often presented to a range of stakeholders with varying levels of technical expertise. When creating visualizations, it's important to tailor the design and complexity based on the audience. Here are a few guidelines:

- **For Executives and C-Suite**: Focus on high-level KPIs, trends, and strategic insights. Avoid technical jargon and use simple, clean visualizations that highlight business impact. Dashboards or executive summaries with key metrics and visualizations are ideal.

- **For Managers and Analysts**: Provide more detailed charts and graphs that offer deeper insights, allowing them to drill down into specific areas like operational performance, customer behavior, or market trends.

- **For Non-Technical Stakeholders**: Use clear and intuitive visuals with straightforward explanations. Avoid overly complex visualizations and focus on conveying insights that directly relate to business objectives.

4. Using Interactive Visualizations to Enhance Engagement

Interactive visualizations add an additional layer of engagement, enabling stakeholders to explore data on their own. Interactive charts allow users to filter, zoom, and drill down into specific data points, making the experience more dynamic and personalized. Tools like Plotly, Tableau, and Power BI support interactivity and can be used to create dashboards that stakeholders can interact with in real-time.

For example, an interactive sales dashboard might allow users to:

- Filter data by product category, region, or time period.

- Hover over charts to see detailed data points.

- Drill down into specific metrics to understand underlying drivers.

5. Communicating Insights Clearly

When using data visualizations to communicate insights, the goal is to tell a clear, concise, and compelling story. It's not just about displaying data but making it understandable and relevant to the business objectives. Key elements to include in your visualizations are:

- **Annotations**: Adding text or labels to highlight key insights, trends, or anomalies in the data.

- **Clear titles and labels**: Ensure that all axes, legends, and data points are labeled clearly.

- **Context**: Provide context around the data to explain what the numbers represent and how they tie to business goals.

For example, a bar chart showing sales by region could be annotated to show which region saw the highest growth and which has the potential for improvement.

6. Tools for Business Data Visualizations

There are various tools available for creating business-oriented data visualizations:

- **Tableau**: A powerful business intelligence tool that allows for easy drag-and-drop creation of dashboards and interactive visualizations.

- **Power BI**: A Microsoft product that integrates well with Excel and other Microsoft tools, making it easy for businesses to create dashboards and reports.

- **Plotly**: A Python library that provides interactive graphs and is suitable for creating web-based visualizations.

Data visualizations are essential in business for communicating insights and driving decision-making. The right choice of visualization can help stakeholders understand complex data, track performance, and identify opportunities for improvement. By tailoring visuals for specific audiences, using interactivity, and ensuring clarity and context, businesses can leverage data to make more informed and impactful decisions.

Module 43:

Interactive Dashboards and Tools

Interactive dashboards are powerful tools for presenting data insights in a dynamic, easily accessible way. This module explores various tools for dashboard development, creating interactive elements, best practices for dashboard design, and integrating dashboards with live data sources. Understanding these elements enables data scientists to create effective, user-friendly dashboards for decision-making.

Tools for Dashboard Development: Tableau, Power BI, Dash, and Shiny

There are several tools available for creating interactive dashboards, each with unique strengths. Tableau and Power BI are two widely-used platforms that allow users to build visually compelling, interactive dashboards without extensive programming knowledge. Dash, developed by Plotly, offers flexibility for Python users to create custom applications, while Shiny is an R-based framework for interactive web applications. Each tool offers specific functionalities, allowing users to select the one best suited for their data, audience, and technical skills.

Creating Interactive Elements: Filters, Sliders, and Drill-Down Features

Interactive elements enhance user experience by allowing the audience to explore data in depth. Filters enable users to narrow down data based on specific criteria, making dashboards more tailored. Sliders are useful for visualizing changes over a range, such as adjusting time periods. Drill-down features allow users to click on data points for more detailed information. These interactive tools empower users to customize their views and gain deeper insights from the data presented.

Best Practices for Dashboard Design: Ensuring Clarity and Usability

Effective dashboard design requires a balance between aesthetics and functionality. Clear, well-organized layouts ensure that data is presented in a digestible manner, avoiding overwhelming users with information. Consistency in color schemes, fonts, and graph types ensures that users can quickly interpret the visuals. It's essential to prioritize the most important metrics and avoid clutter. Keeping the dashboard intuitive and user-friendly enables stakeholders to engage with the data effectively and make timely decisions.

Integrating Dashboards with Data Sources: Connecting Live Data Feeds

A key feature of interactive dashboards is their ability to connect with live data sources. By linking dashboards to real-time data feeds, users can access up-to-date insights, which is crucial for dynamic business environments. Integration with databases, APIs, and cloud services enables seamless data updates. This integration ensures that dashboards reflect the most current trends and developments, offering stakeholders reliable information for decision-making.

Tools for Dashboard Development: Tableau, Power BI, Dash, and Shiny

Interactive dashboards are essential tools in modern data science for visualizing data and enabling decision-makers to engage with insights dynamically. This section explores popular tools for creating dashboards, focusing on their strengths, use cases, and how they empower data-driven decision-making.

---

1. Tableau: User-Friendly and Versatile

Overview: Tableau is a widely used business intelligence tool that offers a drag-and-drop interface, making it easy for non-technical users to create visualizations and dashboards. It excels in its ability to connect to multiple data sources and create visually appealing, interactive dashboards.

Features:

- **Ease of use**: No programming required; users can create dashboards with simple drag-and-drop actions.

- **Integration**: Supports connections with databases, cloud services, and flat files.

- **Interactivity**: Filters, tooltips, and drill-down options enhance the user experience.

Use Case: A sales team could use Tableau to track regional sales performance, applying filters to view data for specific timeframes or products.

2. Power BI: Seamless Integration with Microsoft Ecosystem

Overview: Power BI, developed by Microsoft, is an excellent tool for enterprises already using Microsoft products like Excel, Azure, or SharePoint. It allows users to create detailed dashboards with minimal coding and offers robust integration with other Microsoft tools.

Features:

- **Real-time analytics**: Enables live data updates from various sources, including SQL databases, Excel, and cloud services.

- **AI-driven insights**: Leverages machine learning to suggest trends or anomalies in data.

- **Cost-effective**: Offers free and affordable tiers for small teams and startups.

Use Case: A marketing team could create dashboards to monitor campaign performance, displaying metrics like impressions, clicks, and conversion rates in real time.

3. Dash: Python-Based Flexibility

Overview: Dash, a framework for building interactive web applications in Python, is ideal for developers who want full control over their dashboard design and functionality. It allows integration of custom Python scripts for complex data processing.

Features:

- **Customizability**: Leverage Python libraries like Pandas, NumPy, and Plotly for advanced analytics and visualizations.

- **Scalability**: Build dashboards for a wide range of applications, from small prototypes to enterprise-level systems.

- **Web integration**: Dash apps can be deployed as web applications accessible from any browser.

Example: Here's a Python snippet to create a simple Dash dashboard:

```
import dash
from dash import dcc, html
from dash.dependencies import Input, Output

app = dash.Dash(__name__)

# Layout with a slider and a graph
app.layout = html.Div([
    dcc.Slider(id='my-slider', min=0, max=10, step=1, value=5),
    dcc.Graph(id='my-graph')
])

@app.callback(
    Output('my-graph', 'figure'),
    [Input('my-slider', 'value')]
)
def update_graph(value):
    return {
        'data': [{'x': [1, 2, 3], 'y': [value * i for i in [1, 2, 3]],
            'type': 'line'}],
```

490

```
                'layout': {'title': f'Graph with Slider Value: {value}'}
    }
if __name__ == '__main__':
    app.run_server(debug=True)
```

Use Case: Data scientists could use Dash to create custom dashboards for predictive modeling results, including sliders to adjust parameters dynamically.

4. Shiny: R-Based Interactive Dashboards

Overview: Shiny is an R package that simplifies the creation of web-based dashboards. It is popular in academic and research environments due to its seamless integration with R.

Features:

- **Ease of use for R users**: R programmers can create dashboards without needing to learn a new programming language.

- **Integration**: Works well with R libraries for data visualization (e.g., ggplot2).

- **Deployment**: Dashboards can be shared online with minimal setup.

Use Case: A healthcare research team could build a Shiny app to visualize patient demographics and health outcomes based on clinical trial data.

---

5. Comparison and Tool Selection

Each tool has its strengths and is suited to different use cases:

- **Tableau** and **Power BI** are ideal for business users seeking ready-to-use solutions with minimal coding.

- **Dash** and **Shiny** cater to developers or researchers who prefer full control over their applications.

Selecting the right tool depends on the team's technical expertise, project requirements, and data ecosystem. By leveraging these tools effectively, organizations can transform raw data into actionable insights through interactive dashboards.

Creating Interactive Elements: Filters, Sliders, and Drill-Down Features

Interactive elements are the backbone of effective dashboards, enabling users to explore data dynamically and derive actionable insights. This section focuses on implementing key interactive components like filters, sliders, and drill-down features, essential for creating user-friendly dashboards.

1. Filters: Refining Data Views

Overview: Filters allow users to narrow down data based on specific criteria, such as dates, regions, or product categories. They help focus on relevant subsets of data, reducing clutter and improving decision-making.

Implementation in Tableau and Power BI:

- Tableau provides drop-down filters and range sliders that are easy to configure for any data field.

- Power BI offers slicers, visual elements that enable filtering directly from the dashboard.

Example in Dash: Using Python, we can implement a basic filter with Dash to display data for a selected category:

```python
import dash
from dash import dcc, html
from dash.dependencies import Input, Output

app = dash.Dash(__name__)

categories = ['Electronics', 'Clothing', 'Furniture']
data = {
    'Electronics': [100, 200, 150],
    'Clothing': [50, 80, 60],
    'Furniture': [300, 400, 250]
}

app.layout = html.Div([
    dcc.Dropdown(
        id='category-dropdown',
        options=[{'label': cat, 'value': cat} for cat in categories],
        value='Electronics'
    ),
    dcc.Graph(id='sales-graph')
])

@app.callback(
    Output('sales-graph', 'figure'),
    [Input('category-dropdown', 'value')]
)
def update_graph(selected_category):
    return {
        'data': [{'x': ['Q1', 'Q2', 'Q3'], 'y': data[selected_category],
            'type': 'bar'}],
        'layout': {'title': f'Sales Data for {selected_category}'}}
    }

if __name__ == '__main__':
    app.run_server(debug=True)
```

This example demonstrates how users can filter quarterly sales data by selecting a category from a drop-down menu.

2. Sliders: Dynamic Parameter Adjustment

Overview: Sliders provide a visual mechanism for users to adjust numerical values, such as price ranges or time intervals, in real time. They are particularly useful in exploratory analysis or forecasting scenarios.

Applications:

- Analyzing historical trends over a specified time range.

- Simulating scenarios by modifying input parameters dynamically.

Example in Power BI: Use a slider to adjust sales performance ranges and visualize data for different thresholds in real time.

Example in Dash:

```
@app.callback(
    Output('sales-graph', 'figure'),
    [Input('slider', 'value')]
)
def update_graph(slider_value):
    filtered_data = [x for x in original_data if x <= slider_value]
    return {
        'data': [{'x': categories, 'y': filtered_data}],
        'layout': {'title': f'Data Up to {slider_value}'}
    }
```

3. Drill-Down Features: Exploring Data Hierarchies

Overview: Drill-down features enable users to navigate from high-level summaries to detailed data layers, such as moving from total sales to sales by region or product. This functionality allows stakeholders to uncover insights at varying levels of granularity.

Implementation:

- **Tableau**: Offers hierarchical drill-down by grouping dimensions and allowing users to expand or collapse data levels.

- **Power BI**: Supports drill-down by configuring visuals to respond to clicks on grouped data.

Example in Tableau: A drill-down from "Yearly Sales" to "Monthly Sales" by double-clicking on a specific year.

Advanced Implementation in Dash:

493

```
@app.callback(
    Output('sub-category-graph', 'figure'),
    [Input('main-category-graph', 'clickData')]
)
def drill_down(click_data):
    main_category = click_data['points'][0]['x']
    sub_data = fetch_sub_category_data(main_category)  # Fetch data based on
            selection
    return {
        'data': [{'x': sub_data['subcategory'], 'y': sub_data['values'],
            'type': 'bar'}],
        'layout': {'title': f'Drill-Down for {main_category}'}
    }
```

4. Best Practices for Interactive Elements

- **User-Centric Design**: Ensure filters and sliders are intuitive and placed logically within the dashboard.

- **Responsiveness**: Interactive elements should update visuals seamlessly and without lag.

- **Data Context**: Provide contextual information, such as default selections or tooltips, to guide users.

Interactive elements like filters, sliders, and drill-downs elevate dashboards from static displays to dynamic tools, enabling users to engage deeply with data and uncover actionable insights. By leveraging these features effectively, data scientists can enhance the utility and appeal of their dashboards.

Best Practices for Dashboard Design: Ensuring Clarity and Usability

Effective dashboard design is critical for transforming complex data into actionable insights. A well-designed dashboard ensures clarity, usability, and engagement, empowering users to make informed decisions quickly. This section explores best practices for designing impactful dashboards, focusing on layout, visualization, interactivity, and performance.

1. Clear Objectives and Audience Awareness

Define the Purpose: Before designing a dashboard, clarify its primary objective. Is it for monitoring KPIs, exploring trends, or presenting detailed reports? Aligning the dashboard design with its purpose ensures relevance and focus.

Know Your Audience: Tailor dashboards to the intended users. Executives may need high-level summaries, while analysts may prefer detailed, exploratory tools. Understanding user needs helps strike the right balance between simplicity and depth.

2. Logical Layout and Minimalism

Structured Layout: Organize the dashboard in a logical flow. Place key metrics or visuals at the top (for quick insights) and detailed charts or tables below. Use white space strategically to reduce clutter and enhance readability.

Limit the Number of Visuals: Avoid overwhelming users with excessive charts or graphs. Focus on a few impactful visuals that convey the most critical information.

Example: A sales performance dashboard can display total revenue as a headline figure, followed by a bar chart of regional sales and a line graph for monthly trends. This hierarchy ensures clarity and accessibility.

3. Choosing the Right Visualizations

Match Visuals to Data: Use appropriate chart types for different data types and insights:

- **Bar Charts**: Comparing categorical data, such as sales by region.

- **Line Graphs**: Showing trends over time, such as monthly revenue growth.

- **Heatmaps**: Highlighting correlations or intensity, such as website traffic by time and day.

Avoid Misleading Visuals: Ensure visual integrity by maintaining consistent scales, avoiding 3D effects, and using clear labels.

Example in Python: Using Matplotlib or Plotly to create a visually appealing bar chart:

```
import matplotlib.pyplot as plt

regions = ['North', 'South', 'East', 'West']
sales = [300, 450, 400, 350]

plt.bar(regions, sales, color='skyblue')
plt.title('Regional Sales Performance')
plt.xlabel('Region')
plt.ylabel('Sales ($)')
plt.show()
```

4. Enhancing Usability with Interactivity

Intuitive Filters and Controls: Provide dropdowns, sliders, or date pickers to let users explore data dynamically. Ensure these controls are prominently displayed and easy to use.

Drill-Down Capabilities: Allow users to click on high-level data points to view detailed insights. For instance, clicking on a bar representing regional sales can reveal city-level performance.

5. Consistent Design and Branding

Standardize Fonts and Colors: Use consistent fonts, colors, and sizes across visuals to ensure uniformity. Choose a color palette that aligns with the organization's branding but also considers accessibility (e.g., colorblind-friendly schemes).

Legends and Annotations: Add legends and contextual notes to help users interpret visuals correctly.

6. Optimizing Performance

Efficient Queries: Design dashboards to handle large datasets efficiently. Use aggregated data where possible and optimize queries to reduce load times.

Test Responsiveness: Ensure the dashboard adapts to various devices and screen sizes, providing a seamless experience across platforms.

A well-designed dashboard is more than just a collection of charts—it is a tool that empowers users to derive insights efficiently. By adhering to best practices in clarity, usability, and performance, data scientists can create dashboards that drive meaningful decision-making and foster engagement.

Integrating Dashboards with Data Sources: Connecting Live Data Feeds

Interactive dashboards achieve their full potential when powered by live data feeds, enabling real-time updates and analysis. Integrating dashboards with data sources ensures a seamless connection between raw data and visual insights. This section explores techniques, tools, and best practices for establishing and maintaining robust connections to live data feeds.

1. The Importance of Real-Time Data Integration

Dynamic Insights: Real-time data integration enables dashboards to reflect the most current information, which is essential for time-sensitive applications like stock monitoring or anomaly detection.

Centralized View: By connecting multiple data sources, dashboards provide a unified platform where users can analyze diverse datasets without switching contexts.

Scalability: Live integration prepares dashboards to handle evolving data streams, ensuring adaptability as data needs grow.

2. Connecting Dashboards to Common Data Sources

Relational Databases: Databases such as MySQL, PostgreSQL, or SQL Server are common sources for structured data. They can be queried directly using tools like Tableau or Power BI to extract relevant information.

APIs: Many systems and platforms expose their data through APIs. For example, social media analytics dashboards often pull data from APIs like Twitter or Google Analytics.

Cloud Data Warehouses: Platforms such as Snowflake, Amazon Redshift, or Google BigQuery allow dashboards to access large-scale datasets stored in the cloud, facilitating fast queries on massive datasets.

Streaming Data Platforms: Dashboards can integrate with platforms like Apache Kafka to ingest and visualize live streams of data, such as real-time sensor readings.

3. Tools for Integration

ETL Tools: Extract, Transform, and Load (ETL) tools like Talend, Apache Nifi, or Fivetran can preprocess and feed data into dashboards.

BI Tools with Native Connectors: Software like Tableau and Power BI offers built-in connectors for various data sources, enabling quick integration.

Custom Scripts: Python, R, or JavaScript can be used to create custom pipelines for unique data integration requirements. For example, Python's pandas library and libraries like requests can process API data.

Example in Python: The following example connects to a MySQL database, fetches data, and processes it for dashboard display:

```python
import mysql.connector
import pandas as pd

# Connect to the database
connection = mysql.connector.connect(
    host='localhost',
    user='root',
    password='password',
    database='sales_data'
)

# Query the database
query = "SELECT region, SUM(sales) AS total_sales FROM orders GROUP BY
            region"
data = pd.read_sql(query, connection)

# Preview the data
print(data)

# Close the connection
connection.close()
```

4. Best Practices for Reliable Integration

Data Quality Assurance: Validate data at the source to ensure consistency and accuracy. Incorporate automated error-checking mechanisms to detect anomalies.

Secure Connections: Use encrypted protocols (e.g., HTTPS or SSL) and authentication methods like API keys or OAuth to protect data during transfer.

Monitoring and Logging: Continuously monitor data pipelines to identify bottlenecks or failures. Implement logging to track pipeline activities for debugging.

Caching: For dashboards accessing large datasets, implement caching to reduce load times and improve user experience.

5. Challenges and Solutions

Latency: Real-time integration may introduce latency if data sources are slow. Optimize queries and reduce unnecessary data transformations to minimize delays.

Complex Data Sources: Integrating unstructured or semi-structured data can be challenging. Tools like Apache Spark or specialized parsers can help handle such data formats.

Access Issues: Some data sources may have restricted access. Collaborate with IT teams to ensure permissions are correctly configured.

Integrating dashboards with live data sources transforms them into dynamic tools for decision-making. By leveraging the right tools, techniques, and best practices, data scientists can design dashboards that empower users with up-to-date insights, enhancing their ability to respond quickly to changing conditions.

Module 44:

Communicating with Non-Technical Audiences

Communicating data insights to non-technical audiences is an essential skill for data scientists. This module emphasizes how to effectively convey complex technical information in a way that is accessible and engaging. Key strategies include tailoring your message, avoiding jargon, using visuals, and leveraging storytelling to turn data into actionable insights.

Tailoring Your Message: Adapting Complexity for Your Audience

Understanding your audience is crucial when presenting data. Tailoring your message means adjusting the complexity of your explanations to suit the audience's knowledge level. For example, executives may need high-level overviews, while department heads might benefit from more detailed insights. By adjusting your message, you ensure that the data is relevant and understandable for everyone involved.

Avoiding Jargon: Simplifying Technical Concepts Without Losing Meaning

Data science is full of specialized terminology that may confuse non-technical audiences. To communicate effectively, avoid jargon and use simple, everyday language. Instead of discussing "logistic regression" or "p-value," explain the concepts in terms your audience can grasp. Simplifying complex terms helps maintain clarity without diluting the importance or meaning of the data insights.

Effective Use of Visuals: Using Graphs and Charts to Clarify Insights

Visuals are powerful tools for communicating data insights. Graphs, charts, and infographics simplify complex concepts and make patterns easier to spot. For example, a bar chart can highlight differences, while a line graph can show trends over time. Effective use of visuals helps ensure that non-technical audiences can quickly grasp the key points without getting bogged down in numbers.

Storytelling with Data: Turning Raw Data Into Actionable Insights

Storytelling is a powerful method for engaging non-technical audiences. By framing data in a narrative format, you create a compelling storyline that connects raw numbers to real-world impact. A well-structured data story, with a clear beginning, middle, and end, can help your audience understand the context and significance of your findings. Storytelling turns abstract data into actionable insights.

Tailoring Your Message: Adapting Complexity for Your Audience

Communicating data insights to non-technical audiences requires a strategic approach to make complex ideas comprehensible and actionable. Tailoring your message ensures that the content resonates with your audience's level of technical expertise and aligns with their needs. This section explores the principles and techniques for adapting complexity effectively.

1. Understanding Your Audience

Identify Stakeholders: Knowing the audience is the first step in communication. Stakeholders can range from executives and business managers to marketing teams or the general public. Each group has unique priorities and familiarity with data concepts.

Assess Their Knowledge Level: Gauge the audience's baseline understanding of data science. While business executives may prioritize actionable insights, technical teams may prefer detailed analysis.

Define Goals: Understand what the audience needs to learn or decide based on the data. For instance, executives might want a concise summary, while operational teams might seek detailed process insights.

2. Simplifying Complex Ideas

Focus on Key Takeaways: Avoid overwhelming your audience with intricate details. Instead, highlight essential insights and explain why they matter.

Use Analogies and Examples: Analogies can bridge the gap between technical concepts and everyday experiences. For instance, describing a machine learning model as a "digital detective" that identifies patterns can make the concept more relatable.

Break It Down: Deconstruct complex ideas into manageable pieces. Begin with the overarching concept, then dive into supporting details if necessary.

3. Structuring the Message

Use a Logical Flow: Structure your message to follow a clear narrative. A common framework is:

1. **Problem**: Define the issue being addressed.

2. **Analysis**: Summarize the data and methods used.

3. **Findings**: Present the results.

4. **Implications**: Highlight the relevance and actionable insights.

Example: Consider you are presenting the results of a marketing campaign analysis. Here's a structured summary:

- **Problem**: "We wanted to understand which marketing channels yield the highest return on investment."

- **Analysis**: "We analyzed data from social media, email campaigns, and paid ads over six months."

- **Findings**: "Paid ads generated 60% of total revenue, while email campaigns had the highest ROI."

- **Implications**: "Focusing on email campaigns can maximize cost-efficiency, while optimizing paid ads can drive higher revenue."

4. Tools to Tailor Complexity

Data Summarization: Use Python tools like pandas and numpy to summarize data. For example:

```
import pandas as pd

# Sample data
data = {'Channel': ['Social Media', 'Email', 'Paid Ads'],
        'Revenue': [50000, 70000, 150000],
        'Cost': [20000, 10000, 50000]}

df = pd.DataFrame(data)

# Calculate ROI
df['ROI'] = (df['Revenue'] - df['Cost']) / df['Cost']
print(df)
```

Output:

```
        Channel  Revenue   Cost   ROI
0  Social Media    50000  20000  1.50
1         Email    70000  10000  6.00
2      Paid Ads   150000  50000  2.00
```

This summary simplifies comparisons for the audience.

Visualization Tools: Use libraries like matplotlib or seaborn to create simple, digestible visuals.

5. Iterative Feedback

Engage the Audience: Encourage questions to clarify doubts. This engagement ensures that the audience follows the narrative and identifies areas for improvement.

Test the Message: Before a major presentation, test the content with a small sample of the target audience. This step can help refine the message further.

Tailoring your message is a critical skill for effective data communication. By understanding the audience, simplifying complex ideas, and structuring the message logically, data scientists can bridge the gap between technical analysis and actionable insights. Adaptation ensures that non-technical stakeholders grasp the value of data and use it effectively in decision-making.

Avoiding Jargon: Simplifying Technical Concepts without Losing Meaning

Communicating with non-technical audiences requires translating complex technical terms into accessible language while retaining the accuracy of insights. Avoiding jargon helps ensure your message is not lost in translation. This section discusses strategies for simplifying technical concepts effectively.

1. Recognizing Problematic Jargon

Understand What Constitutes Jargon: Jargon includes highly technical terms, acronyms, and specialized phrases that are not universally understood. For example, terms like "gradient descent," "hyperparameter tuning," or "ETL pipeline" may confuse non-technical stakeholders.

Identify Key Terms to Simplify: Review your presentation or communication materials to highlight terms that may require simplification or explanation. Ask yourself whether someone unfamiliar with the field could understand the term's meaning.

2. Simplification Techniques

Use Plain Language: Replace technical terms with plain, everyday words. For example:

- Instead of "data ingestion," say "collecting data."

- Instead of "classification model," say "a system that groups data into categories."

Provide Context: Explain technical concepts within the broader context of the audience's domain. For instance:

- When discussing a machine learning model, focus on how it solves a business problem rather than how it works internally.

Offer Visual Analogies: Analogies can demystify complex processes. For instance:

- Describe an algorithm as a "recipe" that tells a computer step-by-step how to solve a problem.

- Explain a neural network as a "web of interconnected decision points."

3. Examples of Simplified Explanations

Explaining Machine Learning Models
Original: "This logistic regression classifier uses sigmoid activation to determine probabilities."
Simplified: "This model predicts the likelihood of an event, such as whether a customer will make a purchase."

Explaining Data Pipelines
Original: "Our ETL pipeline extracts, transforms, and loads data into the warehouse."
Simplified: "We have a process that collects raw data, cleans it, and stores it so it's ready for analysis."

4. Practical Python Examples

Providing straightforward code examples can reinforce simplified explanations. For instance:

Concept: Calculating averages in a dataset
Jargon-Laden Explanation: "We compute the mean by aggregating values and dividing by the count."
Simplified Explanation: "We find the average by adding all the numbers and dividing by how many numbers there are."

Code Example:

```python
# Data: Sales figures in dollars
sales = [150, 200, 300, 250, 400]

# Calculate average sales
average_sales = sum(sales) / len(sales)
print(f"The average sales figure is ${average_sales:.2f}")
```

Output:

```
The average sales figure is $260.00
```

This practical example removes jargon while demonstrating a common data science task.

5. Best Practices for Maintaining Clarity

Limit the Use of Acronyms: Introduce acronyms sparingly, and always define them upfront. For example: "ETL stands for Extract, Transform, and Load, a process for preparing data."

Avoid Overloading with Details: Resist the temptation to dive into the mechanics of every concept. Instead, focus on what the audience needs to know to make informed decisions.

Use Visuals to Reinforce Clarity: Diagrams, charts, or flow visuals can replace dense text and make concepts more approachable. Tools like PowerPoint, Tableau, or Python libraries such as matplotlib can help illustrate key points.

6. Testing for Accessibility

Seek Feedback: Run your explanations by colleagues or stakeholders unfamiliar with the field to ensure clarity.
Iterate as Needed: Adjust your language based on feedback and questions received during presentations or discussions.

Avoiding jargon is essential for building trust and ensuring understanding among non-technical audiences. By simplifying terminology, providing relatable examples, and focusing on actionable insights, data professionals can create meaningful connections and empower stakeholders to leverage data effectively.

Effective Use of Visuals: Using Graphs and Charts to Clarify Insights

Visuals play a pivotal role in communicating data insights effectively, particularly to non-technical audiences. The appropriate use of graphs, charts, and visual elements can simplify complex data, highlight key trends, and ensure that your message is clear and memorable. This section explores best practices for selecting, designing, and presenting data visualizations.

1. Choosing the Right Type of Visualization

Understand the Data and the Story: The choice of visualization depends on the type of data and the story you want to tell:

- **Bar Charts**: Best for comparisons across categories.

- **Line Graphs**: Ideal for showing trends over time.

- **Pie Charts**: Useful for illustrating proportions or percentages (though they can be misleading if not used carefully).

- **Scatter Plots**: Effective for identifying correlations or patterns.

Example:
To demonstrate sales trends over months, a line graph is more appropriate than a pie chart. For a categorical comparison, such as regional sales, a bar chart would work better.

2. Simplifying Visuals for Clarity

Avoid Overcrowding: Limit the number of elements in a chart. Too many lines, bars, or data points can confuse the audience.

Highlight Key Insights: Use color, annotations, or bold lines to draw attention to the most important parts of the visualization.

Add Clear Labels and Titles: Ensure every chart has a descriptive title and labeled axes to eliminate ambiguity. Avoid technical jargon in labels, e.g., replace "X-axis" with "Time (in months)" or "Feature Importance" with "Factors Impacting Sales."

3. Tools and Libraries for Visualization

Creating effective visuals requires reliable tools. Python provides several libraries for data visualization:

- **Matplotlib**: A versatile library for basic plots.

- **Seaborn**: Ideal for creating aesthetically pleasing statistical graphics.

- **Plotly**: Great for interactive charts.

Code Example: A simple bar chart comparing sales across regions using Matplotlib and Seaborn.

```
import matplotlib.pyplot as plt
import seaborn as sns

# Sample sales data
regions = ['North', 'South', 'East', 'West']
sales = [20000, 15000, 30000, 25000]

# Plotting the bar chart
sns.barplot(x=regions, y=sales, palette='coolwarm')
plt.title('Sales by Region')
plt.xlabel('Region')
```

```
plt.ylabel('Sales ($)')
plt.show()
```

This visualization effectively compares sales across regions, ensuring clarity and relevance.

4. Designing Accessible Visuals

Consider Colorblind-Friendly Palettes: Use color schemes that are accessible to those with color vision deficiencies. Tools like ColorBrewer can help.

Ensure Text Legibility: Use large, readable fonts for titles, labels, and legends. Avoid small or overly stylized text.

Incorporate Visual Hierarchy: Arrange elements in a way that guides the viewer's attention naturally, from the most important insights to supporting details.

5. Connecting Visuals to the Narrative

Provide Context: A visual without explanation can confuse the audience. Always accompany charts and graphs with a brief description of what they show and why it matters.

Emphasize Actions or Insights: Instead of simply presenting data, use visuals to highlight what the audience should do or understand. For example:

- **Before**: "Here is the sales data by region."

- **After**: "Sales are strongest in the East, indicating where we should focus our marketing efforts."

6. Avoiding Common Pitfalls

Avoid Misleading Visualizations: Truncated axes or distorted proportions can lead to misinterpretations. Always ensure the visual accurately represents the data.

Limit Fancy Effects: 3D charts, excessive gradients, or animations can detract from clarity. Keep designs simple and professional.

Double-Check Accuracy: Verify that all values, labels, and legends in your visuals match the underlying data.

Effective use of visuals transforms raw data into actionable insights. By choosing the right type of visualization, simplifying design, and connecting visuals to your narrative, you can ensure clarity and impact. Well-crafted visuals not only make complex data understandable but also help engage non-technical audiences and guide them toward informed decision-making.

Storytelling with Data: Turning Raw Data into Actionable Insights

Data storytelling is an art that combines data, visuals, and narrative to convey insights compellingly. It bridges the gap between complex analytics and actionable decision-making by creating a clear, relatable context for stakeholders. This section explores how to craft an effective data story and emphasizes the importance of aligning it with audience needs.

1. Understanding the Structure of a Data Story

A strong data story has a clear structure, often modeled after the classic narrative arc:

- **Beginning**: Set the stage by describing the problem or opportunity. Present relevant background data to establish context.

- **Middle**: Dive into the analysis, highlighting trends, anomalies, or patterns. Use visuals to support your narrative.

- **End**: Conclude with actionable insights or recommendations based on the analysis. Connect the findings to organizational goals or strategies.

Example: When analyzing employee productivity:

- **Beginning**: "The company has observed a 10% drop in productivity this quarter."

- **Middle**: "Analysis reveals this trend correlates with increased remote work and inadequate access to resources."

- **End**: "Improving resource access could boost productivity by 15%."

2. Humanizing the Data

While raw numbers are essential, humanizing data makes it relatable:

- **Include Real-World Context**: Connect the data to tangible scenarios or impacts. For example, instead of stating "customer satisfaction dropped by 20%," say, "1 in 5 customers is now unhappy with our service."

- **Highlight Emotional Appeal**: Frame insights in ways that resonate emotionally. For example, explain how process inefficiencies are wasting team time rather than just listing inefficiency rates.

Example Code: Using Python to humanize a trend with relatable data.

```python
# Importing libraries
import pandas as pd

# Sample data
data = {'Month': ['Jan', 'Feb', 'Mar'], 'Revenue': [10000, 9000, 8000]}
df = pd.DataFrame(data)

# Highlighting the revenue drop
revenue_drop = df['Revenue'].iloc[0] - df['Revenue'].iloc[-1]
print(f"Over three months, revenue dropped by ${revenue_drop}, equivalent to
        a 20% decline.")
```

This approach links abstract figures to real impacts.

3. Using Visuals to Reinforce the Narrative

Visuals play a critical role in storytelling by making data more digestible:

- **Highlight Trends**: Use line graphs to show changes over time.

- **Compare and Contrast**: Bar charts are effective for side-by-side comparisons.

- **Show Relationships**: Scatter plots can illustrate correlations.

Pair visuals with descriptive titles and captions that explain their relevance to the narrative.

4. Tailoring Stories for Stakeholders

Different audiences have varying levels of technical expertise. Tailor your story accordingly:

- **Executives**: Focus on strategic implications and high-level insights.

- **Technical Teams**: Include detailed analyses, methodologies, and assumptions.

- **General Audiences**: Simplify jargon and focus on actionable outcomes.

For instance, when presenting revenue trends:

- **Executives**: "Revenue has decreased by 20% due to operational inefficiencies."

- **Technical Teams**: "Revenue dropped due to higher server latency and longer customer support response times."

5. Crafting Actionable Insights

A compelling data story doesn't end with findings—it concludes with clear recommendations:

- **Actionable Steps**: Suggest practical steps based on insights. For example, "Increase investment in marketing channels showing the highest ROI."

- **Impact Forecasting**: Estimate the potential outcomes of your recommendations, such as "Implementing this strategy could result in a 15% increase in customer retention."

6. Avoiding Common Pitfalls

Overloading with Data: Focus on key points. Too much information can overwhelm the audience.
Ignoring Context: Data alone isn't persuasive without context. Always connect insights to the bigger picture.
Unclear Recommendations: Ensure your story ends with actionable, well-supported recommendations.

Storytelling with data transforms raw figures into a powerful narrative, making insights accessible and actionable. By structuring the story, humanizing the data, leveraging visuals, and tailoring the message to the audience, you can create compelling presentations that inspire decision-making and drive meaningful change.

Module 45:

Data Art and Aesthetics

Data visualization is not only about conveying information but also about creating visual experiences that engage and captivate audiences. This module explores the intersection of data and art, highlighting the aesthetic principles in data visualization, the artistic potential of data, and creative uses beyond traditional business and analytics contexts.

The Intersection of Data and Art: Aesthetic Principles in Data Visualization

Data visualization blends technical precision with artistic expression. Aesthetic principles in data visualization, such as balance, harmony, and proportion, can significantly enhance the clarity and impact of visualized data. Using these principles thoughtfully allows data to tell a compelling story while also appealing to the viewer's sense of beauty and design.

Data as Art: Examples of Stunning Visualizations

Some visualizations transcend functionality and become true works of art. Examples include beautifully designed heatmaps, intricate network diagrams, and data-driven art installations. These visualizations not only communicate insights but also provoke emotional responses and challenge viewers to think about data in new and creative ways, blurring the lines between information and expression.

Design Principles for Effective Visuals: Color, Size, Shape, and Layout

Effective design plays a crucial role in data visualization. Color, size, shape, and layout must be chosen with care to enhance readability, emphasize important elements, and create an aesthetically pleasing design. Consistency in these elements ensures clarity, while contrast and visual hierarchy guide the viewer's attention to key insights, making the data both functional and beautiful.

Creative Uses of Data Visualization: Beyond Business and Analytics

Data visualization can extend far beyond business and analytics. Creative uses include visual storytelling, art exhibitions, and interactive experiences that allow people to engage with data in immersive ways. Artists and designers are increasingly using data to explore themes like identity, culture, and social issues, pushing the boundaries of how data can be experienced and interpreted.

The Intersection of Data and Art: Aesthetic Principles in Data Visualization

Data visualization has evolved from being a purely functional tool to an artistic expression, blending aesthetics with analytics. The intersection of data and art invites the use of visual design principles to enhance the presentation of data in ways that are not only informative but also visually captivating. Aesthetic principles such as harmony, balance, contrast, and simplicity are now key elements in creating compelling data visualizations. Data, when presented aesthetically, not only communicates insights but also evokes emotions, making it easier for audiences to engage with complex information.

Effective use of color, form, and layout can improve the legibility and interpretability of data. For instance, color gradients can signify progression or intensity, while shapes and sizes can emphasize importance or scale. By carefully choosing colors and layout configurations, designers can guide the viewer's focus, highlight trends, or create a visual hierarchy that aids in understanding.

Data as Art: Examples of Stunning Visualizations

Several visualizations have gained recognition for their artistic value, demonstrating how data can transcend its technical purpose and become an art form. One famous example is *The Flowing Data* by Nathan Yau, where he visualizes diverse datasets, turning them into elegant, interactive graphics that captivate audiences. Similarly, Hans Rosling's *Gapminder* visualizations combined complex global development data with dynamic, moving visuals that told stories in an engaging and insightful way.

Another excellent example is the *Wind Map* by Fernanda Viegas and Martin Wattenberg, which uses real-time data from wind patterns to create an ethereal, constantly changing digital artwork. Such examples show that data can be beautiful, inviting viewers to explore and reflect on patterns that might not otherwise be noticed in raw numbers.

These stunning visualizations demonstrate how data can serve as a medium for storytelling, providing a richer, more emotional connection with the viewer while maintaining the integrity of the information presented.

Design Principles for Effective Visuals: Color, Size, Shape, and Layout

Designing data visualizations with attention to color, size, shape, and layout is crucial in creating impactful visuals. Color helps set the tone and conveys emotions or meanings. For example, red can indicate urgency or danger, while blue can invoke calmness or trust. Size, on the other hand, communicates magnitude and importance. Larger elements tend to attract more attention, so they should represent the most important data points.

Shape plays a critical role in categorization and distinction. Circular shapes often represent continuous data, while squares or rectangles may denote discrete values. Layout, including grid systems and spacing, helps organize visual elements to make them easy to follow. A clean, structured layout ensures that viewers can quickly process and compare data points.

The best data visualizations rely on these design principles to create balance, clarity, and engagement, ensuring that viewers are both informed and inspired by the data.

Creative Uses of Data Visualization: Beyond Business and Analytics

While data visualization has been widely adopted in business and analytics, its creative uses extend far beyond these domains. Artists and designers are increasingly using data as a medium for personal and political expression. Creative data visualizations often challenge perceptions, provoke thought, or inspire action.

One notable example is *Data Humanism*, a movement that combines data with personal experiences to present complex social issues in an intimate, human-centered way. Visualizations like these create a dialogue between data and society, making statistics feel more relatable and meaningful.

In other creative applications, data is used in visual arts to create generative pieces that evolve over time. For instance, using real-time weather data to generate an abstract art piece that changes depending on current conditions or using social media activity to produce a constantly evolving artwork.

In essence, data visualization is no longer limited to business and analytics but has transformed into a multifaceted art form, expressing ideas, emotions, and societal changes through the lens of data.

Data as Art: Examples of Stunning Visualizations

In the world of data visualization, simplicity is often regarded as a key aesthetic. Minimalistic designs focus on removing unnecessary elements to ensure that the core message stands out clearly. This approach emphasizes clean lines, white space, and limited color palettes, creating visuals that are both easy to understand and visually appealing. Minimalism reduces cognitive overload and ensures that viewers can focus on the most important aspects of the data without being distracted by superfluous design elements.

In practice, this could mean avoiding excessive chart embellishments like 3D effects or complex borders. Instead, simple designs like bar charts, line graphs, and scatter plots allow the data to shine without distraction. The goal is to achieve a balance where the visualization is functional, aesthetically pleasing, and easily interpretable by the target audience.

Minimalistic data visualizations, while simple, often have a profound impact due to their clarity and straightforwardness. For example, the use of subtle gradients or monochromatic color schemes can convey deep insights without overwhelming the viewer. This approach aligns with the idea that "less is more," where the simplicity of the design enhances the overall effectiveness of the communication.

Interactive and Dynamic Visuals: Enhancing Engagement

While static visualizations are widely used, interactive and dynamic visuals have gained immense popularity due to their ability to enhance user engagement and provide a deeper understanding of the data. Interactive visualizations allow users to explore data by adjusting parameters, zooming in on specific sections, or filtering out irrelevant information. This interaction empowers users to discover insights on their own, turning passive viewers into active participants in the data exploration process.

Dynamic visualizations, on the other hand, include animations and real-time data updates. These types of visuals are particularly powerful when illustrating trends or changes over time. A great example of dynamic data visualization is animated choropleth maps, which display the movement of populations or the spread of diseases across different regions. Such animations not only make the data more engaging but also offer viewers an intuitive understanding of complex, time-dependent phenomena.

The creative use of interactivity and dynamic features can significantly increase the impact of data visualization by offering users a personalized experience that enhances their understanding and retention of the data.

Data Visualization for Storytelling: Crafting a Narrative

One of the most powerful uses of data visualization is in storytelling. By weaving data into a narrative, visualizations can communicate more than just numbers—they can evoke emotions, provoke thought, and inspire action. A well-crafted data story takes the viewer through a journey, from the introduction of a problem to the exploration of various solutions, ultimately guiding them toward insights that are meaningful and actionable.

To create an effective data story, the visualization should follow a clear structure. This could mean introducing the main concept first, then building upon it with supporting evidence and data points, before concluding with a call to action or summary. The design elements—such as color, layout, and transitions—should support this flow, helping guide the viewer's eye through the story.

One example of data storytelling is the *Data & Society* project, where data visualizations are used to tell stories about social issues like inequality, environmental change, and political movements. By combining compelling data visuals with narrative techniques, these projects turn complex datasets into stories that engage and inform the audience on a deeper level.

Storytelling with data helps transform raw numbers into a format that resonates with the audience, making complex ideas more understandable and actionable. It's about crafting a narrative that speaks to both the intellect and emotions of the viewer, making data more relatable and impactful.

Expanding the Creative Boundaries: Data Visualization in the Arts

Beyond its analytical applications, data visualization has increasingly found a place in the world of art. Artists have embraced data as a medium for creativity, using it to explore social, environmental, and personal narratives. In this context, data is not just a tool for analysis but an expression of culture, identity, and experience.

One striking example is the *Data Painting* project by artist Giorgia Lupi, where she visualizes her personal data—such as daily activities, moods, and habits—in the form of intricate hand-drawn artworks. These pieces are both personal and artistic, reflecting how data can be used to tell intimate stories.

Such creative uses of data visualization push the boundaries of traditional data presentation and explore the emotional and cultural implications of data. In this artistic context, data visualization becomes a medium for self-expression, allowing both artists and audiences to engage with data in a more profound and creative way.

The creative potential of data visualization extends far beyond business analytics. Through artistic, minimalist, interactive, and storytelling approaches, data can be transformed into a powerful form of visual communication that resonates with diverse audiences, making the complex more comprehensible and, at times, even beautiful.

Design Principles for Effective Visuals: Color, size, Shape, and Layout

The success of any data visualization lies not only in the data it represents but also in how it is designed. Effective design principles such as color, size, shape, and layout play a pivotal role in ensuring that the visualization is both aesthetically pleasing and functional. These elements help to create clarity, highlight important insights, and improve the overall user experience.

Color: Setting the Tone and Enhancing Clarity

Color is one of the most powerful tools in design and can be used to influence perception and interpretation. It helps to convey meaning, direct attention, and evoke emotions. When used appropriately, color can make a visualization more engaging and easier to understand. For example, using contrasting colors for different data series helps differentiate them clearly, making comparisons easier.

However, it's important to use color judiciously to avoid overwhelming the viewer. A common best practice is to limit the color palette to a few complementary colors, ensuring that the visualization does not become too busy. In addition, accessibility should be considered, particularly for individuals with color blindness. Tools like colorblind-friendly palettes ensure that the visualization remains effective for a broader audience.

```
import matplotlib.pyplot as plt
import seaborn as sns

# Sample data
categories = ['A', 'B', 'C', 'D']
values = [10, 20, 30, 40]

# Using color palette
sns.barplot(x=categories, y=values, palette='coolwarm')
plt.title("Example of Color in Visualization")
plt.show()
```

Size: Emphasizing Important Data

Size can be used to emphasize key points in a visualization. Larger elements naturally draw more attention, so size can highlight the most important data points, creating a visual hierarchy. For example, larger circles in a bubble chart can indicate higher values, while smaller circles represent lower values. Similarly, varying the size of bars in a bar chart can help highlight specific trends or patterns.

However, the use of size must be consistent and not exaggerated, as overuse can lead to a confusing or misleading visualization. Keeping the size variations proportional ensures clarity and prevents misinterpretation.

Shape: Adding Context and Clarity

Shapes are another key design element that can convey meaning. Different shapes can be used to represent various categories or types of data. For example, in a scatter plot, different markers (such as circles, squares, or triangles) can represent distinct data groups, making it easy to distinguish between them. When applied thoughtfully, shapes not only enhance aesthetics but also improve the readability and comprehension of the visualization.

When using shapes, it's important to ensure that they are easily distinguishable and not too complex, which could distract from the data itself. Simple shapes with clear distinctions can ensure that the audience focuses on the message rather than the design.

Layout: Structuring for Readability

Layout is critical in organizing the visual elements of a chart or graph. A well-structured layout guides the viewer's eye from one element to another in a logical and intuitive way. Good layout design ensures that the most important data is placed where it will be noticed first. This may involve strategically positioning titles, axes, legends, and other annotations to create a clean, organized visual flow.

A common guideline in layout design is to follow the natural reading pattern: left-to-right, top-to-bottom. This ensures that viewers interpret the data in the intended order. In addition, the use of whitespace (empty space around elements) helps to create a clean, uncluttered design, preventing the data from feeling crowded or overwhelming.

```python
# Example of a simple layout with clear positioning
plt.figure(figsize=(8, 6))
plt.bar(categories, values, color='blue')
plt.title("Simple Bar Chart Layout")
plt.xlabel('Categories')
plt.ylabel('Values')
plt.tight_layout()  # Ensures labels are not cut off
plt.show()
```

Balancing Aesthetics and Functionality

In data visualization, a balance between aesthetics and functionality is essential. While an appealing design is important, it should never overshadow the purpose of the visualization, which is to communicate data effectively. Aesthetic elements such as color, size, shape, and layout must be used to enhance understanding rather than to detract from the data's meaning.

A well-designed visualization makes the data accessible, interpretable, and engaging for the audience. By adhering to solid design principles, data visualizations can transform complex data into compelling stories that not only look great but also provide deep, actionable insights.

Creative Uses of Data Visualization: Beyond Business and Analytics

Data visualization has traditionally been used in business and analytics to convey insights in a clear, actionable manner. However, its potential extends far beyond these applications, enabling creative, artistic, and exploratory uses that bring data to life in new and exciting ways. By combining data and aesthetics, data visualization can transcend traditional roles and become a medium for storytelling, art, and even social commentary.

Data as Art: Artistic Expression with Data

The intersection of data and art is an exciting space where data is not just analyzed but also transformed into visually stunning representations. Data artists often use large datasets to create intricate, beautiful visuals that provoke thought and emotion. These pieces may not always serve a traditional analytical purpose but instead engage viewers with the aesthetic beauty of data, often revealing hidden patterns or emphasizing the inherent beauty of numbers and trends.

An example of this is the "Data as Art" project by Giorgia Lupi, a designer and data artist who creates visualizations that blend data with personal narratives. By representing daily activities such as eating, working, or commuting, Lupi's work brings attention to the rhythms and details of everyday life that often go unnoticed.

These types of visualizations can be exhibited in galleries or shared online as art pieces. The creative use of color, shapes, and layout transforms raw data into meaningful and captivating art, providing a powerful way to tell a story through visuals.

```python
# Example of an abstract artistic data visualization using random data
import numpy as np
import matplotlib.pyplot as plt

# Create random data points for an artistic effect
x = np.random.rand(500)
y = np.random.rand(500)
colors = np.random.rand(500)

plt.scatter(x, y, c=colors, cmap='viridis', alpha=0.5)
plt.title("Data as Art: Abstract Visualization")
plt.show()
```

Data for Social Change: Using Visualization for Advocacy

Beyond the traditional business use, data visualization has also become a powerful tool for social change. Activists and organizations use visualizations to raise awareness about critical issues such as climate change, social justice, or public health. By presenting complex issues in an easily understandable format, these visualizations can motivate action, provoke discussions, and influence public opinion.

For instance, visualizations depicting air pollution levels, deforestation, or income inequality can help highlight issues that might otherwise go unnoticed or seem too complex to comprehend. By transforming these datasets into clear, impactful graphics, organizations can make an emotional appeal to their audiences, driving action toward positive change.

Interactive Storytelling: Engaging Audiences with Data

One of the most powerful uses of data visualization in recent years is its ability to engage audiences interactively. Interactive dashboards, infographics, and charts allow users to explore data on their own terms, enabling them to uncover insights that are most relevant to their personal interests. This level of engagement creates an immersive experience that fosters deeper understanding and connection to the data.

For example, interactive visualizations that allow users to adjust variables or filter information make it easier to explore different scenarios, compare trends, and view data from various perspectives. This hands-on experience can also help demystify complex topics, making them more approachable and relatable to a wide range of audiences.

```
import plotly.express as px

# Example of an interactive scatter plot
df = px.data.iris()
fig = px.scatter(df, x='sepal_width', y='sepal_length', color='species',
          title="Interactive Scatter Plot of Iris Dataset")
fig.show()
```

Exploratory Data Visualization in Art and Science

In fields such as science, engineering, and the humanities, data visualization is often used for exploration rather than final reporting. Scientists and researchers use data visualizations to gain new insights, test hypotheses, and explore different facets of their data. For example, visualizations of genomic data or astronomical data allow researchers to spot patterns and correlations that might otherwise be invisible.

Moreover, data visualization techniques such as 3D modeling and simulation are increasingly used to create visual representations of abstract concepts like weather patterns, molecular structures, or the human brain. These visualizations serve not only as research tools but also as a way to communicate complex scientific concepts to the general public.

The Boundless Creativity of Data Visualization

Creative uses of data visualization show that the discipline goes far beyond traditional business and analytics. Data can be turned into art, serve as a tool for social change, create engaging interactive experiences, and help scientists explore complex concepts. By combining creativity with analytical insights, data visualization can transcend its functional roots, opening up exciting new possibilities for how we interact with and understand the world around us. Whether for artistic expression, social impact, or scientific exploration, data visualization offers a powerful way to communicate, inspire, and innovate.

Module 46:

Practical Case Studies in Visualization

This module explores real-world applications of data visualization across various industries, providing practical insights on building effective visualizations, collaborating with stakeholders, and learning from successful projects. By understanding the challenges and best practices in visualization, you can develop polished and impactful visual stories tailored to your audience.

Real-World Data Visualization Applications: Examples from Healthcare, Finance, etc.

Data visualization is widely used across industries to convey complex information. In healthcare, visualizations help track patient outcomes and identify trends in disease progression. In finance, dashboards allow for real-time monitoring of stock prices, market trends, and investment performance. These applications demonstrate how visualization transforms raw data into actionable insights, improving decision-making and outcomes.

Building a Visualization Pipeline: From Raw Data to Polished Visuals

Creating effective visualizations involves several stages. First, data must be cleaned and preprocessed to ensure accuracy. Next, appropriate charts, graphs, and visual elements are chosen based on the data type and insights being conveyed. The final stage involves refining the visuals for clarity, consistency, and aesthetic appeal, ensuring they communicate the intended message clearly to the audience.

Working with Stakeholders: Collecting Feedback and Iterating

Collaboration with stakeholders is key to developing relevant and effective visualizations. By collecting feedback from users—whether data analysts, business leaders, or designers—you can ensure the visualization meets their needs and expectations. Iterative refinement, based on user input, helps to optimize visuals for clarity, accessibility, and decision-making, ultimately ensuring the end product is both impactful and usable.

Lessons from Successful Visualization Projects: Best Practices and Tips

Successful visualization projects share key best practices, such as focusing on the message and not just the data, ensuring the visuals are accessible to all audiences, and maintaining simplicity while being informative. Clear labeling, using color effectively, and providing context for the data also contribute to the success of a visualization. These principles, honed through real-world examples, form the foundation for producing highly effective data visualizations.

Real-World Data Visualization Applications: Examples from Healthcare, Finance, etc

Data visualization plays a crucial role in translating complex data into actionable insights across various industries. Its application in sectors like healthcare and finance has proven invaluable for decision-making, communication, and process optimization.

Healthcare Data Visualization

In healthcare, data visualization allows professionals to track patient outcomes, monitor disease outbreaks, and manage resource allocation. One prominent example is the use of dashboards for monitoring COVID-19 cases. Interactive visualizations, such as heatmaps and time-series graphs, enabled public health officials to track the spread of the virus in real time. Visualizations highlighting the distribution of cases across different regions, age groups, or medical facilities provided actionable insights for resource planning and policy decisions.

```
# Example: Simple time-series visualization for tracking COVID-19 cases
import matplotlib.pyplot as plt
import pandas as pd

# Simulated COVID-19 case data (Date vs. Cases)
data = {'Date': pd.date_range(start='2021-01-01', periods=10, freq='D'),
        'Cases': [120, 150, 170, 200, 220, 250, 300, 350, 400, 450]}

df = pd.DataFrame(data)
plt.plot(df['Date'], df['Cases'], marker='o')
plt.title('COVID-19 Cases Over Time')
plt.xlabel('Date')
plt.ylabel('Number of Cases')
plt.xticks(rotation=45)
plt.grid(True)
plt.show()
```

Such visualizations are integral to disease prevention, helping governments allocate vaccines, staff, and other resources efficiently.

Finance and Business Visualization

In finance, data visualization is essential for tracking stock performance, market trends, and portfolio management. One of the most common visualizations used in the finance industry is the candlestick chart, which is used to show the opening, closing, high, and low prices of a stock over time. Such visualizations allow analysts and traders to identify market patterns, understand price fluctuations, and predict future trends.

```
import plotly.graph_objects as go

# Example: Candlestick chart for stock data visualization
```

```
fig = go.Figure(data=[go.Candlestick(x=['2024-01-01', '2024-01-02', '2024-
    01-03'],
                                open=[100, 105, 103],
                                high=[110, 107, 106],
                                low=[95, 100, 102],
                                close=[105, 103, 104])])

fig.update_layout(title='Stock Price Candlestick Chart', xaxis_title='Date',
    yaxis_title='Price')
fig.show()
```

These visualizations help businesses assess market conditions and make informed decisions regarding investments or adjustments in financial strategy.

Education and E-learning

In education, data visualization tools help institutions track student progress, optimize curriculums, and evaluate teaching methods. By visualizing student performance over time, educators can identify areas of improvement and intervene effectively. For instance, dashboards showing student grades, attendance, and behavior metrics provide insights for personalized learning plans.

Marketing Analytics

Data visualization is also crucial in marketing, helping businesses understand customer behavior, track engagement, and measure campaign success. Marketers often use pie charts, bar charts, and heatmaps to visualize customer demographics, website traffic, and conversion rates. Such insights are critical in developing targeted strategies for customer acquisition and retention.

In sectors such as healthcare, finance, education, and marketing, data visualization acts as a powerful tool for decision-making and strategic planning. By transforming raw data into visually accessible formats, organizations can gain deeper insights and make informed decisions, ultimately leading to improved outcomes and enhanced performance across industries.

Building a Visualization Pipeline: From Raw Data to Polished Visuals

Building a visualization pipeline involves several critical stages to ensure the creation of effective and polished visuals. Each stage requires careful consideration to ensure that the data is accurately processed and communicated in a visually compelling way. The process typically follows these steps: data acquisition, data cleaning, data transformation, and final visualization creation.

1. Data Acquisition

The first step in the visualization pipeline is collecting the data. Raw data can come from various sources such as databases, APIs, CSV files, and web scraping. The quality of the source data is crucial for building meaningful visualizations, as inaccuracies or incomplete data can lead to misleading conclusions.

For example, in a healthcare setting, data may be sourced from patient management systems, electronic health records (EHR), or public health datasets. In finance, stock prices or economic indicators can be collected via APIs like Alpha Vantage or Yahoo Finance.

```python
import yfinance as yf

# Fetch historical stock data for Apple
apple_data = yf.download('AAPL', start='2022-01-01', end='2023-01-01')
print(apple_data.head())
```

2. Data Cleaning and Preprocessing

Once the data is collected, it often needs cleaning and preprocessing. Raw data typically contains inconsistencies, such as missing values, duplicates, or incorrect formats. For effective visualization, this data must be cleaned to ensure accuracy and consistency.

Common preprocessing steps include:

- **Handling missing data**: This can be done using imputation methods or removing missing entries.

- **Outlier detection**: Identifying and managing extreme values that might skew the analysis.

- **Data normalization**: Scaling data to a uniform range for comparison.

```python
# Example: Handling missing values by filling them with the mean of the
         column
apple_data.fillna(apple_data.mean(), inplace=True)
```

3. Data Transformation

Once the data is cleaned, transformation steps are often required to format it into a structure suitable for visualization. Data transformations could include:

- Aggregating data (e.g., summing sales over a time period)

- Pivoting data to restructure it

- Creating derived columns based on business logic (e.g., calculating growth rates)

```python
# Example: Adding a new column for daily returns in stock price
apple_data['Daily Return'] = apple_data['Adj Close'].pct_change()
```

Data transformation ensures the data is in the right shape to support meaningful visual analysis.

4. Creating the Visualizations

The final step in the pipeline is the actual creation of visualizations. This step requires selecting the right chart types and ensuring the design effectively communicates the insights. Common chart types include:

- **Line charts** for trends over time

- **Bar charts** for categorical comparisons

- **Heatmaps** for correlation matrices

- **Scatter plots** for relationships between variables

For example, to visualize the stock price trends of Apple, a simple line chart could be created to show the adjusted closing prices over time.

```
import matplotlib.pyplot as plt

# Plotting stock price trends
plt.plot(apple_data.index, apple_data['Adj Close'], label='Apple Stock
        Price')
plt.title('Apple Stock Price Over Time')
plt.xlabel('Date')
plt.ylabel('Price (USD)')
plt.legend()
plt.show()
```

5. Refining and Polishing the Visuals

Finally, the visuals need to be refined for clarity and aesthetic appeal. This includes choosing appropriate colors, labels, and chart layouts. The goal is to make the visualization both visually engaging and easy to interpret. For instance, adding gridlines, adjusting axis labels, and providing a clear legend are small refinements that make a visualization more user-friendly.

Building an effective data visualization pipeline requires a structured approach to data acquisition, cleaning, transformation, and presentation. By following these steps, organizations can ensure that their visuals communicate insights clearly and effectively, driving better decision-making across industries.

Working with Stakeholders: Collecting Feedback and Iterating

Creating data visualizations that are not only accurate but also resonate with the target audience requires collaboration and feedback from stakeholders. Stakeholders, who may include business leaders, subject matter experts, or end users, provide valuable insights into the relevance and clarity of the visualizations. Their input helps ensure that the final product aligns with organizational goals and communicates the intended message effectively.

1. Initial Collaboration and Understanding the Stakeholder Needs

The first step in working with stakeholders is understanding their specific needs and the context of the data being visualized. Whether the visualization is for a business decision, operational monitoring, or strategic planning, identifying the purpose of the visualization is crucial. Engaging with stakeholders early on helps define the scope of the visualization and ensures that it addresses the most important questions.

For example, in a healthcare setting, stakeholders might include doctors or healthcare administrators who need to visualize patient trends or operational efficiency. In a finance context, stakeholders might be executives who need to track market trends, financial performance, or risk factors.

```
# Example: Surveying stakeholders to define key metrics of interest
stakeholder_needs = ['Trends in hospital admissions', 'Average length of
        stay', 'Mortality rates']
```

2. Prototyping and Early Feedback

Once a preliminary visualization is developed, it is crucial to present it to stakeholders for early feedback. At this stage, the visualization might not be polished, but it serves as a proof of concept. Feedback from stakeholders can highlight areas that require more clarity, adjustments in design, or the inclusion of additional data points.

Using prototyping tools or simple charts to showcase the data allows stakeholders to interact with the visualizations and express their thoughts. This feedback cycle is critical for refining the visualization before further investment in development.

```
# Example: Prototyping a simple line chart showing sales over time for
        feedback
import matplotlib.pyplot as plt

# Sample sales data (hypothetical)
sales_data = {'January': 1000, 'February': 1200, 'March': 1300, 'April':
        1500}

# Simple Line Chart for early feedback
plt.plot(sales_data.keys(), sales_data.values(), marker='o')
plt.title('Sales Over Time')
plt.xlabel('Month')
plt.ylabel('Sales')
plt.show()
```

3. Iterative Design and Refining Visualizations

After receiving initial feedback, it's important to iterate on the visualization, making necessary adjustments to improve clarity, usability, and overall effectiveness. Iteration might involve:

- Adjusting the color scheme for better contrast

- Simplifying labels or removing unnecessary data

- Modifying chart types to better represent the data

This iterative process ensures that the visualization not only conveys the message accurately but also resonates with the intended audience. Additionally, involving stakeholders in this process helps in making the final product more impactful.

```python
# Example: Refining the chart by adding annotations and adjusting the color
        scheme
plt.plot(sales_data.keys(), sales_data.values(), marker='o', color='purple')
plt.title('Sales Over Time', fontsize=14)
plt.xlabel('Month', fontsize=12)
plt.ylabel('Sales', fontsize=12)
plt.annotate('Highest Sales in April', xy=('April', 1500),
        xytext=('February', 1200),
            arrowprops=dict(arrowstyle='->'))
plt.show()
```

4. Collecting Final Feedback and Finalizing the Visualization

After several rounds of feedback and iteration, the visualization is ready for final presentation. Before concluding the process, it's important to collect one final round of feedback from stakeholders. This step ensures that no key elements have been overlooked and that the visualization is comprehensive and effective.

Stakeholder feedback can also help refine the context or provide insights into how the visualization might be better integrated into decision-making processes. Understanding how stakeholders will use the visualization in practice ensures it delivers its maximum value.

5. Documentation and Knowledge Transfer

Once the final visualization is completed, documenting the process, data sources, and any assumptions made is critical. Providing stakeholders with this documentation helps ensure that the visualization can be correctly interpreted and used in the future. Knowledge transfer also aids in maintaining the visualization, especially if it needs to be updated with new data.

Effective collaboration with stakeholders throughout the data visualization process ensures that the end product meets user needs and is both functional and informative.

By prototyping, iterating, and collecting feedback at multiple stages, data visualizations can be refined to deliver clear insights and guide decision-making.

Lessons from Successful Visualization Projects: Best Practices and Tips

Data visualization projects, when executed effectively, can transform raw data into meaningful insights. Studying successful visualization projects reveals essential lessons and best practices that can guide future endeavors. From understanding the audience to focusing on simplicity and adaptability, these insights form a roadmap to creating impactful visualizations.

1. Define Clear Objectives and Audience Needs

One of the first lessons is the importance of defining the project's goals and understanding the target audience. Successful projects often begin with a thorough analysis of the questions the visualization seeks to answer and the preferences of the end users. For example, a business executive may need concise dashboards with high-level metrics, while a data analyst may require more granular and interactive visualizations.

Defining these objectives early ensures that the project remains focused and aligns with the stakeholders' needs. Misaligned goals or a lack of understanding of the audience can lead to visualizations that are either too complex or overly simplistic.

```python
# Example: Define objectives for a sales dashboard
objectives = {
    "Goal": "Track monthly sales performance",
    "Key Metrics": ["Total Revenue", "Profit Margin", "Top-Selling
        Products"],
    "Target Audience": "Sales Executives"
}
print(objectives)
```

2. Simplicity Over Complexity

The best visualizations convey their message clearly and avoid unnecessary complexity. Overloading a chart with too much information can confuse users and detract from its purpose. Using minimalist designs with clean layouts ensures that the focus remains on the data.

For instance, instead of presenting a complex scatter plot with multiple dimensions, consider using simpler alternatives like bar charts or line graphs if they can communicate the same insight effectively.

```python
# Example: A simple bar chart to show product sales
import matplotlib.pyplot as plt

# Sample data
products = ["Product A", "Product B", "Product C"]
```

```
sales = [5000, 7000, 3000]

plt.bar(products, sales, color="skyblue")
plt.title("Sales by Product", fontsize=14)
plt.xlabel("Products", fontsize=12)
plt.ylabel("Sales", fontsize=12)
plt.show()
```

3. Leverage Automation and Interactivity

Modern data visualization projects often benefit from tools and technologies that support automation and interactivity. Interactive dashboards, for example, allow users to explore data dynamically, drill down into specific details, and filter results. Automation ensures that the visualizations remain up-to-date by seamlessly integrating live data feeds.

Successful projects utilize tools like Tableau, Power BI, or Python libraries such as Dash and Plotly to build interactive and automated systems that adapt to user needs in real time.

```
# Example: Interactive Plotly bar chart
import plotly.express as px

data = {"Products": products, "Sales": sales}
fig = px.bar(data, x="Products", y="Sales", title="Interactive Sales Chart")
fig.show()
```

4. Test and Iterate Continuously

Iteration is another key to success. Gathering feedback from stakeholders throughout the development process ensures that the visualization evolves to meet its intended purpose. By testing prototypes and analyzing user feedback, visualization projects can be refined for greater clarity and usability.

For instance, if users find it challenging to interpret certain visualizations, adjustments can be made to color schemes, labels, or even the type of chart used. Continuous testing and iteration lead to more polished and effective outcomes.

5. Storytelling: Weaving Data into Narratives

Successful visualizations tell a story. They not only present data but also guide users through insights in a logical and engaging manner. Integrating narrative techniques—like highlighting trends, outliers, or comparisons—helps create a memorable experience for the audience.

For example, annotating a line graph with key milestones or using contrasting colors to emphasize critical data points can make a significant difference in the visualization's impact.

```
# Example: Annotating a trendline
```

```
import matplotlib.pyplot as plt

months = ["Jan", "Feb", "Mar", "Apr"]
revenue = [20000, 25000, 30000, 40000]

plt.plot(months, revenue, marker="o", color="green")
plt.title("Monthly Revenue Growth", fontsize=14)
plt.xlabel("Months", fontsize=12)
plt.ylabel("Revenue", fontsize=12)
plt.annotate("Significant Increase", xy=("Apr", 40000), xytext=("Feb",
        35000),
            arrowprops=dict(arrowstyle="->", color="red"))
plt.show()
```

6. Document and Share Learnings

Finally, documenting the process and the lessons learned ensures that future projects benefit from the experience gained. Successful teams often create templates, style guides, and workflows that can be reused to maintain consistency and efficiency across multiple visualization initiatives.

By focusing on clear objectives, simplicity, interactivity, iteration, and storytelling, successful visualization projects deliver meaningful insights to their audiences. These best practices, combined with an openness to feedback and continuous improvement, create the foundation for impactful and enduring visualizations.

Review Request

Thank you for reading "Data Science: Unlocking Insights for Transforming Data into Knowledge"

I truly hope you found this book valuable and insightful. Your feedback is incredibly important in helping other readers discover the CompreQuest series. If you enjoyed this book, here are a few ways you can support its success:

1. **Leave a Review:** Sharing your thoughts in a review on Amazon is a great way to help others learn about this book. Your honest opinion can guide fellow readers in making informed decisions.

2. **Share with Friends:** If you think this book could benefit your friends or colleagues, consider recommending it to them. Word of mouth is a powerful tool in helping books reach a wider audience.

3. **Stay Connected:** If you'd like to stay updated with future releases and special offers in the CompreQuest series, please visit me at https://www.amazon.com/stores/Theophilus-Edet/author/B0859K3294 or follow me on social media facebook.com/theoedet, twitter.com/TheophilusEdet, or Instagram.com/edettheophilus. Besides, you can mail me at theoedet@yahoo.com

Thank you for your support and for being a part of our community. Your enthusiasm for learning and growing in the field of Data Sciense is greatly appreciated.

Wishing you continued success on your programming journey!

Theophilus Edet

Embark on a Journey of ICT Mastery with CompreQuest Books

Discover a realm where learning becomes specialization, and let CompreQuest Books guide you toward ICT mastery and expertise

- **CompreQuest's Commitment**: We're dedicated to breaking barriers in ICT education, empowering individuals and communities with quality courses.

- **Tailored Pathways**: Each book offers personalized journeys with tailored courses to ignite your passion for ICT knowledge.

- **Comprehensive Resources**: Seamlessly blending online and offline materials, CompreQuest Books provide a holistic approach to learning. Dive into a world of knowledge spanning various formats.

- **Goal-Oriented Quests**: Clear pathways help you confidently pursue your career goals. Our curated reading guides unlock your potential in the ICT field.

- **Expertise Unveiled**: CompreQuest Books isn't just content; it's a transformative experience. Elevate your understanding and stand out as an ICT expert.

- **Low Word Collateral**: Our unique approach ensures concise, focused learning. Say goodbye to lengthy texts and dive straight into mastering ICT concepts.

- **Our Vision**: We aspire to reach learners worldwide, fostering social progress and enabling glamorous career opportunities through education.

Join our community of ICT excellence and embark on your journey with CompreQuest Books.